THE

AWN FROM
THE LIBRARY

UNIVERSITY OF
WINCHESTER

KA 0399132 6

Cultural Responses to Occupation in Japan

War, Culture and Society

Series Editor: Stephen McVeigh, Associate Professor, Swansea University, UK

Editorial Board:
Paul Preston *LSE, UK*
Joanna Bourke *Birkbeck, University of London, UK*
Debra Kelly *University of Westminster, UK*
Patricia Rae *Queen's University, Ontario, Canada*
James J. Weingartner *Southern Illinois University, USA (Emeritus)*
Kurt Piehler *Florida State University, USA*
Ian Scott *University of Manchester, UK*

War, Culture and Society is a multi- and interdisciplinary series which encourages the parallel and complementary military historical and socio-cultural investigation of 20th- and 21st-century war and conflict.

Published:
The British Imperial Army in the Middle East, James Kitchen (2014)
The Testimonies of Indian Soldiers and the Two World Wars, Gajendra Singh (2014)
South Africa's 'Border War', Gary Baines (2014)
Cultural Responses to Occupation in Japan, Adam Broinowski (2016)

Forthcoming:
Jewish Volunteers, the International Brigades and the Spanish Civil War,
Gerben Zaagsma
The Japanese Comfort Women and Sexual Slavery During the China and Pacific Wars, Caroline Norma

Cultural Responses to Occupation in Japan

The Performing Body During and After the Cold War

Adam Broinowski

Bloomsbury Academic
An imprint of Bloomsbury Publishing Plc

B L O O M S B U R Y
LONDON • OXFORD • NEW YORK • NEW DELHI • SYDNEY

UNIVERSITY OF WINCHESTER
LIBRARY

Bloomsbury Academic

An imprint of Bloomsbury Publishing Plc

50 Bedford Square
London
WC1B 3DP
UK

1385 Broadway
New York
NY 10018
USA

www.bloomsbury.com

BLOOMSBURY and the Diana logo are trademarks of Bloomsbury
Publishing Plc

First published 2016

© Adam Broinowski, 2016

Adam Broinowski has asserted his right under the Copyright, Designs and Patents Act,
1988, to be identified as Author of this work.

All rights reserved. No part of this publication may be reproduced or transmitted
in any form or by any means, electronic or mechanical, including photocopying, recording,
or any information storage or retrieval system, without prior permission in writing
from the publishers.

No responsibility for loss caused to any individual or organization acting on
or refraining from action as a result of the material in this publication can
be accepted by Bloomsbury or the author.

British Library Cataloguing-in-Publication Data
A catalogue record for this book is available from the British Library.

ISBN: HB: 978-1-78093-596-6
ePDF: 978-1-78093-587-4
ePub: 978-1-78093-597-3

Library of Congress Cataloging-in-Publication Data
A catalog record for this book is available from the Library of Congress.

Series: War, Culture and Society

Typeset by Integra Software Services Pvt. Ltd.
Printed and bound in Great Britain

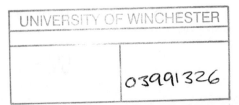

UNIVERSITY OF WINCHESTER

03991326

Contents

List of Illustrations

Preface

Grounded in periods of life spent immersed in society in Japan, in this book, I trace the 'performing body' in some key artistic works in prismatic relation to an environment conditioned by the reconfiguration of post-1945 Japan until the first decade of the twenty-first century.

From an overview of the foundational re-orientation of Japan during the US-led military occupation amid a geopolitical shift in world order, I outline the cultural responses to these conditions, primarily through the body, as identified in literature and film of 1945–1960. Working from the core tensions expressed during this period, I then provide an in-depth analysis of Hijikata Tatsumi's *Ankoku Butoh* from the post-war to the late 1970s. Through the physical practice of butoh in relation to socio-political conditions, I develop an understanding of its theoretical framework (*Butoh-sei*) informed by the artists' influences within broader confluences of thought. I follow the extension and re-thinking of this architecture into the work of Gekidan Kaitaisha (Theatre of Deconstruction) from the mid-1980s to the mid-2000s.

From research conducted on the *Bye Bye* series (1999–2006) and an intercultural collaboration series (*Dream Regime* 2004–2008), I analyse the transformation of the conception of the body with regard to historical memory, social identity and Japan's changing role in the world after the Cold War. Taking inspiration from Kaitaisha's workshops in Cardiff and Timor-Leste, in the final chapters I employ the theoretical frame of the 'occupied condition' developed over the previous chapters to analyse Timorese perspectives. This extends the discussion to the effects of colonization since European expansion, through Japanese invasion in the Second World War, to Indonesian neo-colonial occupation and Timorese independence. As an epilogue, I analyse a solo performance *Vivisection Vision: Animal Reflections* (2004–2008) made during the first five years of the 'War on Terror', to bring together the conceptual framework developed from this analysis of the post-1945 world order as it was implemented in post-war Japan.

Lived experience, particularly of those whose lives are not recorded in written accounts or by official registries and institutions, is always difficult to ascertain from solely archive-based accounts in a given historical period. This analysis of historical events through predominantly artistic responses is not to claim a definitive and totalizing account of the way things were. Similarly, rather than an exhaustive study on one particular artist, this is to introduce complexity from marginalized and neglected perspectives into pre-existing discursive formations concerning Cold War Japan, and after. This can be summarized as an in-depth engagement with the relational dynamic between occupier and occupied evident in post-war Japan, an organizing principle which has been reiterated on countless occasions in varied contexts until the present.

To do so, instead of adopting 'participant observer' status in which I am initiated in the 'native' practices of the other, this book engages in a form of cultural history that draws from a mutual language of performance, a relevant body of critical and cultural theory and readings of historical analysis. Building a genealogy of ideas as they are conceived and developed through embodied artistic approaches in this way yields insightful perspectives of historical change in the period of concern in Japan.

If the artistic works analysed here suggest concerns that are symptomatic of semi-colonial conditions, what are the implications for the existing historiography of post-war Japan? If Japan was a proponent of the dominant narratives of modernization theory, then how are such artistic works to be reconciled with those conditions in other decolonizing nations during the Cold War? How do concepts derived from these artistic perspectives sit within a framework for analysing the relationship between the human body and the nation-state more generally? Often concealed by the abstracted lexicon of treaties, borders, technologies, normativities and power relations that comprise much of international relations and security discourse, the inclusion of lived experiences at ground level in Japan introduces perspectives for consideration which have been both produced and ignored by dominant narratives.

Rather than a minority or obscure view of historical conditions per se, the potential of these perspectives lies in understanding translocal experiences of modernization beyond the limits of Japan studies in the Cold War period. While situated in and particular to geographical place and context in this period, this approach turns 'Japan' outward as a phenomenon produced within the broader systems of knowledge and power of modernity. In the current climate, the stakes have risen so as to demand more complex comprehension of regional experience within the dynamic flows of transnational human systems and planetary ecologies. While respectfully working from and building on the scholarship from Japanese historical and cultural studies within the humanities, my concern is to comprehend our contemporary present by re-thinking the past so as to contribute to shaping a better future.

In short, if anything is clear from this study it is that not only is Japan in many ways still an occupied nation but also the majority of societies continue to live with the very real and present effects of ongoing colonization, albeit in ever-changing forms. If the 'post-colony' of more vulnerable states (such as Timor-Leste) can be seen as a form of 'late modern colonial occupation' (Mbembé 2003: 25), then their 'failure' to obtain national sovereignty must be seen as part of the ongoing dynamics of neo-colonial interference alongside other forms of (semi-)occupation. In the myriad methods of enhancing capital accumulation, which includes the control of mediated discourse, concealing its cause and effect remains central. While resistance to occupation in its various guises is often dismissed as reactionary, whether in the form of communalism, provincialism, nationalism or essentialism, and read as a betrayal of liberal universalist ideals of the international community, the reality after the Cold War has proven to be far more cynical.

In the ongoing struggles for territorial and political independence from military interventions and occupations in Asia during and since the Cold War (Kamala 2012: 5), at times Japan (and South Korea) has been upheld as a model of successful transition to national independence and resumption of international status. It has been used to argue the positive effects of accommodating US foreign policy interests and hosting its military bases. The continuing political, economic and cultural influence from foreign military presence, primarily in Okinawan and also on mainland territories in the shared interests of the Japanese and US political elite, however, supports a more nuanced view of Japan's (and Okinawa's) actual independence. Post-colonial and decolonial frames of post-war Japan attest to more subtle forms of suppression and occupation within sectors and layers of Japan's population beyond the formal definition of national sovereignty.

The normalization of the occupier–occupied relationship in Japan over time is intrinsic to the use and resurgence of patriotic nationalism and perception of external threats in Japan's post-war political career. Negative accounts of the occupation and claims of Japan's subordinated status to the United States, often in conjunction with patriotic calls for national independence and greater military ambitions, once regarded as 'criminal' or 'terrorist', are increasingly supported by dominant political power. Yet ingenious counter-narratives that bear witness to loss and embody socio-political resistance to remilitarization and oppression through means other than violence are increasingly suppressed or ignored.

The unveiling of the nuclear age goes hand in glove with the reconfiguration of the post-1945 nation-state of Japan. Just as memories of 'Hiroshima' have proven to have a long tail, so too has the US-led Occupation programme left an indelible mark on post-war society in Japan. Despite the oft-obscured causality between health effects and radioactive materials deposited in the lived environment, the ongoing impact of the nuclear era has been filtered and recorded in an aesthetic archive. The nuclear disaster at the Tokyo Electric Fukushima Daiichi Nuclear Power Station on 11 March 2011 marked the return of this subterranean narrative to the surface of public consciousness. Just as an oeuvre of artistic mediations from the 1950s and 1960s in Japan, which in some cases have re-emerged in the present, sought to comprehend and dismantle the penetrating violence of 'Hiroshima' and its apparatuses, others have worked to re-write a dominant narrative that has underpinned 'new Japan'. The two are inextricably related as different parts of the same occupation within a broader geopolitical regime. In this praxis, we can find ways to re-think our lives in a (post-)'Fukushima' world.

Acknowledgements

This book has been made possible through both institutional and individual support. A Melbourne Research Scholarship during my PhD candidature and a Monbukagakusho research fellowship at the University of Tokyo, and a Japan Foundation artist research fellowship prior to my MA candidature contributed towards research and writing included in this book. The Centre for Ideas at the Victorian College of the Arts and Music provided the space and opportunities for practice-led research and additional teaching and lecturing, and the School of Historical and Philosophical Studies at the University of Melbourne offered assistance for conferences. The staff at the Lenton Parr and Baillieu libraries were highly responsive and great to work with. The research fellowship at the Alfred Deakin Research Institute, Deakin University, was a particularly timely and appreciated step. The Hijikata Tatsumi Archive, Keio University, was readily forthcoming in response to requests. The School of Culture, History and Language in the College of Asia and the Pacific, the Australian National University, has been a haven for completing this book.

For the impressive foresight in the Bloomsbury initiative on the War, Culture and Society series, my thanks go to commissioning editor Rhodri Mogford, series editor Steve McVeigh and assistant editor Emma Goode for their patience and positivity in the process, and the efficient and skilled work of the production team. In particular, I wish to convey my warmest gratitude to Elizabeth Presa, Vera Mackie, Tessa Morris-Suzuki and Gavan McCormack for their knowledge and encouragement as I developed my ideas, research and analysis. I extend my thanks also to the staff and scholars at the School of Culture, History and Language at the Australian National University.

The salutary generosity and commitment of Hino Hiruko and Shimizu Shinjin and the members of Gekidan Kaitaisha in their dedicated artistic work, the performance community in Tokyo and collaboration participants at various international workshops, venues and festivals have all had influence in the production of this work.

This work is dedicated to artists, scholars and others referred to in this book and the many who are not mentioned but nevertheless inform it. I respect and admire those who have shared their courage, integrity and commitment to explore and engage with political, social, cultural and historical phenomena beyond themselves and their territorialized zones. For their enduring love and support over this concentrated and extended period of practice, research and writing, I am deeply grateful – Emma and Myshka always, and Alison and Richard for introducing me to life and society in Japan.

Introduction

In Sophocles' version of *Antigone* in his Theban plays, Antigone's brothers Polyneices and Enteocles struggled over rights to the throne of Thebes, which was granted to them by their father Oedipus who had been banished from the kingdom by Creon. Polyneices, who was denied his share by Enteocles under the guidance of Creon, left the city and formed an army so as to lay siege to the city. In the battle of Seven Against Thebes, the brothers killed each other in mortal combat. Creon claimed the throne and honoured Enteocles with a formal burial, while he decreed that Polyneices' body, as the enemy of the state, was to be denied burial or mourning and was left to rot outside the city walls. Antigone, choosing to defy state law, dignified Polyneices' body with a proper burial. When she was caught, she claimed that her transgression of Creon's decree was legitimate as she was honouring both her brothers in death. For her disobedience, Creon had Antigone walled up in a sepulchre. Although Creon decided to relent upon receiving advice from Tiresias, Antigone had already chosen to hang herself rather than be buried alive.

Antigone's action ran counter to the official position of her time. Upon assuming the throne, Creon continued to define the enemy in death as in life. Antigone had challenged Creon's sovereign authority and the rule of law upon which it rested. Accordingly, Creon cemented his new position as the ultimate executor of the law through an act purported to protect the population in the name of state security.

While this can be read as a conflict between divine law (kinship) and civil law, *Antigone* is also a dramatic allegory for the way in which state wars are framed by the authorities in the collective memory. Even if legitimate war trials by an independent judiciary were not available in ancient Athens, kin burial and the performative narrative therein may have performed a similar function for polis society. Creon's sanction of such Antigone's act effectively prohibited reconciliation with the former enemy and preserved the conditions of the war as well as defining Creon's post-war sovereign authority in the public mind.

Instead of paying respects to the dead as a whole while examining causative relations so as to prevent war's recurrence in its aftermath, Creon reiterated and deepened the caesura between friend and foe in the minds of the living. Antigone's act, by contrast, was radical not only because she transgressed Creon's prohibition, but also for the respect she paid to an individual as friend and brother who was officially classified within the group of 'non-citizen enemy'.

This brief but pithy example from Sophocles' *Antigone* suggests the relationality of sovereignty and law and the status of citizen and non-citizen as determined through war and its memory. It shows how the important function of mourning and burial

UNIVERSITY OF WINCHESTER
LIBRARY

for the process of reconciliation between friend and enemy can be obstructed in the interests of maintaining authority through perpetual division and conflict. In this way, state violence, as the suppression of internal dissent, of relations with non-citizens and of the recognition and respectful remembrance of former enemies, continues in post-war orders. That is, thorough examination of and justice for past wrongs is denied through the righteous promotion of the authority of the new sovereign regime as victor over the enemy.

The example of *Antigone* is not to claim any direct correlation with the conditions in Japan under US-led Allied Occupation (1945–1952). But it permits a useful introduction to some of the key concerns I intend to engage as I navigate the shaping of the public mind in the formation of the post-war state of Japan and popular and alternative responses to it, by artists in particular.

Differentiating the universalized human subject: Grounding an approach

A fundamental division exists in Western epistemology with regard to the human body. For Plato (*Ion* and *The Republic*) the embodied and mimetic art of the actor symbolized distortion and disease. Aristotle (*Poetics*), by contrast, considered the actor as an active participant in the making of the human subject through imaginative configuration.[1] This conflict was grounded in differing conceptions of truth, absolute and poetic. Although well established that civilizations from Asia cross-fertilized with the west and influenced Greek tragedy,[2] it seems to have been driven by a desire to transcend older Eastern traditional wisdom with newer Western modern knowledge.

Nevertheless, the body continued to be central to human perception, symbolism and metaphor. Baruch de Spinoza was first in the canon of Western philosophy to base an ethical politics on the 'affective dimensions' of things. Spinoza emphasized 'pre-individual' essence, or the *conatus* of things in relation to the world, and so conceived of the body as pre-disposed to desiring empowerment through positive affective engagement with others (Negri and Murphy 2004: 70; Spinoza and Yessleman 2006; Montag 2009: 57).[3]

In the 1950s, appreciation for Spinoza was renewed both in former colonial and decolonizing countries. Similarly, the phenomenology of Maurice Merleau-Ponty articulated at the time a prevalent desire to re-establish a symbiotic connection with the world through the body's sensorium. Grounded in Husserl's notion of empathy, Merleau-Ponty formulated the world not as an object for possession via human-made law and knowledge, but as known through a body immersed within it (Husserl 1980: xi; Merleau-Ponty 2002: 474).

Based in the legacy of Nietzsche, Heidegger, Mauss and Bergson, Foucault traced a 'genealogy' of bodies to understand subject formation within disciplinary institutional formations in the application of sovereign power in eighteenth-century France (Foucault 1972: 53; Foucault 1977: 148). Critical of a reductionist tendency in Marxist thought, Foucault through extensive archival research traced an analysis of the body as an element that is disciplined within the larger formations of sovereign power. While interpretations of Foucault's position on power continue to be divided between his earlier analysis of power as dominating and all-pervasive to his later analysis of power as omnipresent 'because it is produced from one moment to the next... in every relation from one point to another', in the following chapters I explore both the formation of such disciplinary institutions in post-war Japan and the potential for greater 'ontological autonomy', as another use of power, in their comprehension and by dismantling their structures at the site of the body (Laclau et al. 2000: 164).

Foucault critiqued sovereign power in the seventeenth-century Hobbesian model civil state as vested by its subjects with the legal right to determine both the 'death and life' of human bodies ('kill and let live') (Foucault 1978: 135–36). In perceiving the human as an 'animal whose politics places its existence as a living being in question' (Foucault 1978: 140–43), he observed how the modern state had replaced divine rule with a 'set of mechanisms through which basic biological features became the object of a political strategy of power' (Foucault et al. 2007: 1–4).

This set of mechanisms is a *techné* of the self enmeshed within the bureaucratic instruments of population management. For example, based on prototypes for racial categorization along a spectrum of behavioural and biological characteristics developed during European 'new world' expansion, a biological indexing system established by Linnaeus (1735) was used to establish an 'order of knowledge and power and a sphere of political techniques'. While the 'control' was the measure of the rational white European male as an embodiment of Descartes' notion of *cogito ergo sum* (Descartes 1972), the opposite end of the spectrum was the exotic other in colonial peripheries.

Having shaped these techniques in the colonies, depictions of unproductive and shameless 'primitive' bodies in the 'wild' were effective in disciplining a discrete and efficient modern ontology in the steady privatization of the commons in Europe for capital accumulation. As Marx wrote in the first volume of *Capital* on the genesis of industrial capital:

> The discovery of gold and silver in America, the extirpation, enslavement and entombment in mines of the indigenous population of that continent, the beginnings of the conquest and plunder of India, and the conversion of Africa into a preserve for the commercial hunting of black skins, are all things which characterize the dawn of the era of capitalist production. These idyllic proceedings are the chief moments of primitive accumulation. Hard on their heels follows the commercial war of the European nations, which has the globe as its battlefield .... These different moments are systematically combined together at the end of the seventeenth century in England; the combination embraces the colonies, national debt, the modern tax system, and the system of protection .... (Marx 1976: 915–16)

Indeed, in the colonization of Patagonia in the fifteenth century too, Spanish and Portuguese missionaries spread the salvation of Christ by stigmatizing the 'pagan' cultures as 'evil' and exercised authority through corporal punishment and executions.

Aiming to sever the sensory ties of collective indigenous cultures and their land, techniques of caesura between human and animal, law/culture and land, spirit and body developed together with the violent processes of primitive accumulation. Their degree of conversion was commensurate with their separation from culture, land and property (Federici 2004: 61–132).

As Foucault found, by the eighteenth century the replacement of authoritarian rule with the biopolitical management of the population to discipline its subjects saw state institutions pathologize dirt and disease and provide hygiene programmes as the solution, within modernizing urban enclosures. With the steady disappearance of death and sewage under state waste control programmes, 'life' replaced death as the central focus of control. State 'biopower', framed as the capacity of the state to manage the health and vitality of its citizens, also registered racialized categorizations as determining national belonging (Foucault et al. 2003: 137, 256). In this system, the human body could be read as a 'material artefact' of the modernizing programme to construct the individual subject as the basic unit of the nation-state.

Disciplining the national subject also had a behavioural component. Using 'neutral' scientific method, pseudo-medical criteria for variations of 'madness' were measured so as to inculcate rational norms in the population. While not discounting clinical mental illness, 'insanity' was a usefully vague term for pathologizing certain behaviours and facilitating social compliance to codes defined under the perception of a universal same (Foucault 1973).

It was only in the catastrophic absurdity of the First World War and its industrialized warfare that the crisis of the 'human' ideal became unavoidable. A phenomenon of estrangement emerged in which the human body was de-coupled from its subjective encoding as a unit within a larger uniform body to be sacrificed for the nation and its associated values (Ienaga and Minear 2001: 128). In response to unspeakable experiences in this war, the European artistic avant-garde became more overtly politicized in their depictions of the human condition in the interwar period. In a poem attributed to Brecht entitled 'The political illiterate', for example:

> ... The political illiterate is so stupid that he is proud and swells his chest saying that he hates politics.
> The imbecile doesn't know that, from his political ignorance is born the prostitute, the abandoned child, and the worst thieves of all: the bad politician, corrupted and flunky of the national and multinational companies. (Brecht 2002)

Seeking alternatives to Hegel's dialectical thought in which 'nothing ever stayed still, everything was continuously turning into its opposite' (Tatlow 2001: 223), Brecht admired the clarity in the Chinese operatic approach that aided him in his development of his notion of critical distance (Brecht 1964: 192).[4]

At this time too, Antonin Artaud found inspiration for his project to bring forth 'the thing itself' through gestural metaphysics in ritual performances of Bali dance at the Paris Exposition and indigenous dances of the Tarahumara in Mexico (Artaud and Schumacher 1991: 89–90). Immediately following the Second World War, in his canonical radio performance *To Have Done with the Judgement of God* (1947), Artaud proposed that 'when you will have made him a body without organs, then you will have delivered him from all his automatic reactions and restored him to his true freedom' (Artaud 1974: 67–118). Later taken up by Jacques Derrida and Gilles Deleuze and Felix Guattari (Deleuze 1990: 101), Artaud's critique of the relationality of subjecthood and state militarism only came to be recognized well after his death.

As part of the post-war postcolonial movement to differentiate from the European-derived universal human subject, Derrida and Chakravorty Spivak also found potential in 'treating differently every language, by grafting languages onto each other, by playing on the multiplicity of languages' (Derrida 1982: 120). Alterity in the form of 'ghosts', or various aporia that function outside, below and alongside state apparatuses, held the potential to liberate from the colonizing principle of the modern state order (Derrida [1990] in Bennington 1993: 347). For example,

> ... the univocity of being, is paradoxically the principal condition which permits difference to escape the domination of identity, which frees itself from the law of the Same as a simple opposition within conceptual elements. Being is always said of difference; it is the recurrence of difference. (Güven 2005: 155–59)

Yet even as marginal and/or non-Western subaltern bodies in both Western and non-Western artistic representation began to receive comparable and unremarkable value in the early post-war years, the ideal of eternal renewal and its concomitant liberal doctrine of aesthetic autonomy and the rational human subject remained a pre-occupation of both non-Western and Western artists. For example, in post-war Japan the importance of being 'lively' and '*modaan* (modern)' rather than '*wabi-sabi*', as Ohno Kazuo's son Yoshito described it (Fraleigh and Nakamura 2006: 36), continued to be measured against Asian (often portrayed as Sinitic in this period) anachronism and atavism as central to the modernizing dynamics of society.

Just as photographs are indefinite but valuable windows through which to consider lived experience, artistic reflections with particular concern for embodiment can be read as having agency through their interpretations of individual and collective memories in context. As discussed in the context of *Antigone*, if the reconstitution of the social or national body against a vital if illusory threat of the 'non-human' is a critical tool in legitimating sovereign power and its control of a population (Lindqvist and Tate 1996; Agamben 2004: 37), then re-thinking dominant narratives from perspectives of the 'non-human' and their artistic reflections can provide active and alternative responses to the colonizing discourses of sovereign power.

In recognition of a war that continues to be waged in the guise of 'post-war' (currently termed 'humanitarian policing'), read within the dialectical frames of the body and nation-state, periphery and centre, marginal and dominant sketched out above, the interdisciplinary analysis I develop in the following formulates a perspective 'from below' that emerged from within concrete conditions in post-war society in Japan. Seeking to destabilize the monolithic and predictable discourse of nation-state rivalry in international relations that continues to produce a fissure between actuality and mediated reality in post-conflict and decolonizing societies, this analysis through the lenses of embodiment and representation aims to help overcome 'our failure of imagination, of empathy' (Sontag 2003: 7) in a friend and foe narrative that for far too long has stood in as rationale for sovereign violence.

Hibakusha in post-war Japan: Ongoing war at war's end

The development of the atomic bomb and its subsequent use, in the continuum of wars in the twentieth century, is perhaps one of the most important examples of sovereign violence.

In 1939, a well-planned and exorbitant military-industrial research and development programme named the Manhattan Project ($2.2 billion, Manhattan-Rochester Coalition) and directed by General Leslie Groves was launched. It achieved the world's first nuclear chain reaction led by Enrico Fermi at the University of Chicago on 2 December 1942.

From the outset, a few high-level US scientists and military officers in the Manhattan Project understood the objective of the atomic project to be the development of bio-chemical, environmental and/or psychological weapons. While secrecy and censorship of the press and the compartmentalization of research and expertise was integral to this strictly classified Project, some US officials knew that exposure to radiation, both internal and external, would cause health complications and would have mutagenic and heritable effects (Conant et al., 'Groves Memo', 1943; Langley 2009: 24–35).[5]

With the Allied West–Soviet East divide having opened up as early as 1943, in a climate of bitterly racialized enmity, the mass incendiary and atomic bombings carried out over most Japanese cities were planned by the US Strategic Bombing Survey (USSBS) and led by General Curtis LeMay in 1944–1945. Along with Japan, Italy, Great Britain and Germany, aerial bombing conducted by the US Air Force was in breach of the rules of international humanitarian law, given its lack of distinction, precaution and proportionality as per the Geneva Conventions 1925. In addition, although there was no distinct classification of atomic bombs at the time and their action and effects included but exceeded that of bio-chemical weapons due to their deleterious effects on the body and the environment, their use could be argued to have been in breach of the existing ban on chemical and biological weapons. There has never been an internationally recognized legal trial for this.

Contrary to the received understanding that the USSBS campaign was to destroy Japan's war-making potential by targeting munitions and ship-building factories, including in Hiroshima and Nagasaki, it ignored the human law rights of civilians in Japan. In the lead-up to the USSBS campaign, it was common to find in US popular discourse depictions of Japanese people as human-insect hybrids for whom 'pest control' was deemed to be the 'solution to the Japanese problem'. The image of a dehumanized enemy seemed to banalize the indiscriminate violence that was about to be committed upon entire populations living in urban spaces. Framed as an act of 'cleaning', this served to break the bonds of human empathy and create moral distance from the targeted victims – to animalize the enemy – so as to construct general acceptance for the idea that annihilation was logical and necessary (Russell 1996: 1505, 1513).[6]

Although a successful atomic weapon test code-named 'Trinity' had already been achieved in the Alamogordo, New Mexico on 16 July 1945, in which personnel and people living downwind were exposed to radiation, instead of terminating the project after having 'beaten Hitler to the bomb' and Germany's surrender, the United States was eager to continue to test these weapons in 'real live conditions'. It then sought to legitimize this choice of action after the fact, in the eyes of the US public and the international community. The United States turned to Japan as a target, and after the first detonation of a uranium bomb over Hiroshima, Truman promptly declared the atomic bomb to be 'the greatest achievement of organized science in history' (7 August 1945). Another plutonium bomb was detonated over Nagasaki on 9 August. Truman claimed that the decision to use the atomic bombs saved more lives than were taken and had halted the Soviet advance and influence in Asia (Hasegawa 2005: 127). It also introduced for the first time the prospect of self-inflicted human extinction. Truman maintained a steadfast refusal to 'have regrets' and often expressed willingness to 'do it again' under similar circumstances (Lifton and Mitchell 1995: 211–12).[7] This position has been consistently maintained in US foreign and strategic policy, receiving bipartisan consensus over the decades until the present.

Certainly, the atomic bombs served to project US power into Japan, limit Soviet gains in Asia and reconfigure the geopolitical coordinates of war strategy across multiple territories in anticipation of the confrontation with the Soviet Union in the quest for hegemonic supremacy. While claiming 50 per cent of the world's GDP at war's end compared to the immiserated countries of Europe and Asia, from 1946, the Manhattan Project only escalated under the US Atomic Energy Commission (AEC) to remobilize US public towards a permanent war economy. The United States established the Marshall Plan to subsidize primarily West Europe and Japan with US foreign aid, as well as to strategically significant secondary countries in smaller amounts. This included commercial-military products from General Electric, Westinghouse and Du Pont among other companies, that were also heavily involved in US nuclear and chemical weapons production.

In June 1946 the United States presented the Baruch plan to the United Nations Atomic Energy Commission (UNAEC) in which the latter would be the world's controller and to which the United States would be the sole supplier of nuclear materials and technologies. Baruch framed atomic weapons control as a high-stakes game 'between the quick and the dead' and 'world peace or world destruction' and as representing either 'new hope for salvation or slavery to fear'. Suspecting a monopoly, the Soviets rejected the plan as disingenuous.

On 1 July 1946, the Americans responded with Operation Crossroads, the first in a series of atomic and hydrogen tests on Bikini Atoll in the Marshall Islands chain in the Pacific Ocean. Broadcast to the world through televised images, as modern 'totems' these nuclear tests territorialized the globe and demonstrated US military-industrial prowess and its capacity to threaten any nation that refused US demands. In a bid for global leadership status in a still fluid international space, in a heliocentric narrative accompanying these images the United States promised that the 'power of the sun' had been harnessed 'for all mankind' (Burchett 1983; Leo 1985: 7–8)

Truman's portrayal of the bombing of Hiroshima and Nagasaki as the crowning achievement of modernity and proof of superior Western knowledge reflected an epistemological architecture informed by scientific racism, not unlike that which helped mobilize the Nazi death camps, and developed with twentieth-century micro-photography, atomic physics and weapons systems. Using visual prostheses powerful enough to make visible the core structures of the physical world, scientists penetrated and shattered atomic particles to unlock the basic source of universal energy, irreversibly releasing unstable anthropogenic radionuclides into the atmosphere for the first time.

When deployed in a military delivery system, this epistemological apparatus, which I call the atomic gaze, realized a method of industrial-scale killing hitherto unprecedented. What distinguished the atomic bombs from conventional aerial or other forms of bombing was that they 'cleared' the target area with a bright flash (*pika*), followed by intense heat, force and radiotoxicity that exposed and transformed every living and non-living thing in a telos of light and matter. Either instantly extinguished in the overwhelming radiant heat and scorching thermal wave from the initial detonation, or exposed to radiation whether in 'ground shine' (gamma) or in ingested radioactive particles (alpha, beta, gamma emitters), *hibakusha* (被爆者, people of the fire bomb; 被曝者, people of the light bomb), commonly known as atomic bomb survivors, were produced by and were integral to the atomic gaze.

As Mizuta-Lippit theorized, the atomic bomb was an instantaneous mega-photograph that altered the molecular bonds (or 'liquid') of the photographed as if they were in a chemical emulsion (Mizuta-Lippit 2005).[8] But the vehicle-target-bomb device also both physically flattened almost everything within the 'test' zone and colonized those exposed to its radiation through the near-permanent subatomic occupation of their bodies, weakening the pre-existing ties to their life-world.

As mentioned earlier, the atomic gaze shared with the Nazi death camps, an underlying episteme of scientific racism. The apartheid machinery of the German National Socialist state, which included a eugenics programme (*rassenhygiene*) to actively prevent miscegenation (*blutschande*), was driven by what Agamben terms an 'anthropological machine' derived from eighteenth-century zoology and biology (i.e. Blumenbach, Haeckel, de Gobineau).[9] Seeking to reconstitute the population according to its ultimate vision (*endlösung*) of 'purifying the realm', the Nazi state determined (national) belonging to the *vaterland*, through biopolitical norms based on distinguishing forms of life: human (*bios*) and overman (*übermensch*) life from animal (*zōē/zooei*) and underman (*üntermensch*) life, home life (*oikos*) from public life (*polis*) (Agamben 1998: 6; Agamben 2004: 26).

In his reading of Carl Schmitt's *Political Theology* (1922) and Walter Benjamin's *Critique of Violence* (1921), Agamben contends that the operative extraction and purging of the *homo sacer* in a 'criminogenic' space was predicated in law. First, citizens' 'inalienable rights' were suspended and re-written under a 'state of exception' in accord with this identification of the 'non-human within the human' (Agamben

1998: 104–5, 170; Foucault et al. 2003: 254–59; Agamben 2004: 37; Agamben 2005: 40, 52–64). Then those found to contain degrees of the 'non-human' were quarantined and removed to concentration camps (*Konzentratsionlager*) and were eliminated at varying rates. To complete the purge, virtual projections ('viralities') on the 'outside wall of the camp' (in the minds of the public) sought to banalize and conceal the crime while naturalizing and internalizing the desired image of the sovereign in the form of 'truth', 'self', 'people' and 'nation'. Rather than aberrant, the 'cleansing' crime was framed as healthy, logical, responsible and ironically, life-giving (Agamben 1999: 62–64, 133; Agamben 2004: 3).

Although the overall US objective was not the reconstitution of the national body through the removal of a population, *hibakusha* were exposed to pre-meditated, organized violence in a criminogenic space (i.e. a zone where violence is made legal) in which the fundamental principles of the 'human' were destabilized. Although a smaller group (of the total residing in Hiroshima and Nagasaki) were 'chosen' from the greater whole to be consumed in the blasts as surplus raw materials (Heidegger's concept of 'Ge-stell', or the enframing of things as *bestand*, 'standing reserve') (Heidegger and Krell 1993: 322–30), relatively more *hibakusha* continued to live for varying durations after the event as compared to inmates of the Nazi death camps from which there were few survivors.

Along with those killed instantly in the blast, whether over days, months or years after, the life options for atomic *hibakusha* with chronic and degenerating illness, disabilities, sterility and genetic mutation were often reduced to a tiny orbit of existence.[10] Of those who lived, some became experimental subjects of US and Japanese medical scientists in the 'shielded' laboratories of Hiroshima and Nagasaki. To keep as close to optimal experimental conditions as possible, a formal 'research with no-treatment' policy was adopted in the Adult Medical Survey for the study of radiation effects in 1950 at the Atomic Bomb Casualty Commission (ABCC) in Hiroshima. Although some staff went against orders to assist in treatment, on the whole, in the denial of proper treatment, scientific information on radiation effects or proper compensation, as well as a ban placed on the circulation of photographic images of *hibakusha* under Occupation press censorship laws, *hibakusha* were unwittingly quarantined as test subjects. Only those with privileged access to specialized information on radiation mobilization and its chronic effects would have an accurate understanding of the etiology of their illnesses. Unknown to *hibakusha* at the time, the impact of the atomic gaze would also project over successive generations.

For the same reason that Agamben stresses that the production of the '*Muselman*' ('Muslim') in the camps, or the point at which the former occupant had withdrawn from their still living body (Levi 1989: 65; Agamben 1999: 62), was not a sacrifice but was killing (Baker 2008: 474); *hibakusha* were not sacrificed in an exchange for Japan's post-war recovery and were simply harmed and killed.

As the bodies of the *hibakusha* were penetrated, occupied and transformed at different rates over time, they were inextricably bound to the voice/will of the US sovereign through the atomic gaze. As if in an exchange, the greater the depth and rate of disruption within the target subject the more convincing the proof of the 'photographers'' world-view. In an unprecedented manner, by altering the cellular

UNIVERSITY OF WINCHESTER
LIBRARY

structure of the *hibakusha* and other living things exposed to atomic radiation, the US occupier literally inscribed itself into the bio-physical memory of the exposed environment while creating an urban laboratory for the further accrual and concentration of knowledge and power for future deployment.

In a continuum since the colonial era then, the death camps were more technologically sophisticated than the concentration camps of the late nineteenth century and earlier. The atomic gaze only 'upgraded' the form of this technology in terms of industrial-scale killing, human experimentation, power projection and subject formation in the colonizer's image. The biopolitical driver in these technologies seemingly allowed sovereign power to interpellate human and non-human subjects who are 'made to live or allowed to die' via the consumption of a surplus population as determined by naturalized criteria (Agamben 1998: 157; Agamben 2004: 37).

While the mushroom cloud became the icon of hegemonic US potentiality, frail *hibakusha* were its negative reality. The bodies of *hibakusha*, as represented by themselves and others, were also central to a counter-narrative to national recovery and remilitarization under the new US–Japan alliance. Some criticized the vertical hierarchy established within the new order, while others took up against their social stigma as 'damaged goods' within broader discriminatory practices entrenched in Japanese society. Many *hibakusha* joined mass demonstrations for nuclear disarmament in 1955, but in most cases, having to contain their rage against injustice and contingency, these voices adopted an ontology of the weak by embracing strategies of resilience.

Aware of this counter-narrative potential, particularly following the communist victory in China and the successful atomic test by the Soviet Union in 1949, the United States changed strategy. Members of the political elite in Japan and the United States crafted a campaign to transform the dreaded mushroom cloud into a neutral and utopian form of energy production. In a nation where resource scarcity was considered as pivotal in its relations with foreign powers, nuclear power offered the potential to lift Japan from its pariah status, overcome the consciousness of a defeated nation, and equip it with a claim to techno-scientific mastery. In 1953, the Japanese government became one of the earliest and largest investors in nuclear technology for energy production.

With the formation of a transnational nuclear club (UK in 1952, France in 1960, China in 1964), many non-nuclear nations coveted the new technology as it was thought that no nation could secure its independence without it (and protect against nuclear blackmail). The nuclear trap had been set. 'Going nuclear' meant a significant long-term state-level commitment in policy, finance, industrial technology and maintenance, while not necessarily guaranteeing more security. The United States would seek to control and profit from selectively extending a limited supply of nuclear technology to states, so to multiply the threat to the socialist bloc, and the Soviet Union would reciprocate in kind, triggering the first Cold War arms race.

Instead of marking war's end and saving lives, the atomic gaze continued the warring fires burning in the post-war. The atomic gaze re-defined the human as an unwitting test-subject for constant monitoring and data collection, from whom it was considered pragmatic to conceal prior knowledge of the damaging effects of radiation exposure, given the technology's geostrategic and nuclear energy potential.

Chapter outline: Alternatives to the atomic gaze in post-war Japan

For the three million repatriates who returned from the colonies of the former Japanese Empire in the early post-war years, confronted with firebombed cities, starvation and disease, black markets and slums, altered family relations and confiscated properties, it was clear that Japan was no longer what it once was. Japanese national identity had contracted from multi-ethnicity to relatively hermetic homogeneity, and the presence of a foreign occupier calibrated new and distinct coordinates for being Japanese over the years to come.

As in the post-Second World War Europe, amid the austerity and urban ruins of post-war society in Japan, almost every artefact generated roughly between 1931 and 1970 could be regarded as testimony, in varying degrees of directness, to the violence of sovereign power. While some sought to recover a redemptive and triumphant ideal of 'humanity', others maintained that it was precisely the modern concept of humanity that had been both the primary target and central driver of the holocaustal conditions in the colonies, mines, factories, farms, battlefields, ghettos, camps and bombed cities.

In the rapid reconstruction of public identity in occupied Japan, as detailed in Chapter 1, the re-education and reorientation programme under the Supreme Command of Allied Powers (SCAP) can be broadly understood as organized under three core terms. The first was 'feudalism', a term used to identify former patriotic militarist ideology and economic and social structures that did not comply with the US capitalist model of society. The second was 'communism', used to justify the introduction of evangelical Christian missionaries and suppress the resurgent left movement of political parties and labour unions, education, resident (*zainichi*) Korean organizations and artistic and grassroots movements. The third element was *Nihonjinron* or Japanese uniqueness which was proactively encouraged as a way to perpetuate and deepen pre-existing divisions between Japan and the East Asian mainland.

On the whole the most astute local artists embraced these discursive conditions passed down through the Japanese government. A host of popular narratives emerged that responded to conditions created from the atomic bombs and occupation (*Black Rain, Barefoot Gen, Astro Boy, Ultraman,* early neo-realist films of Ozu, Kurosawa, Naruse, Kobayashi). But it was *Gojira* (1954) that was the most well-known. As an allegory for past incendiary bombings and present nuclear testing, it depicted a deep-sea monster with a calloused hide, pained scream and a body pinging with polluting radiation from hydrogen bomb tests in the Pacific Ocean, arisen to cause havoc in Japanese cities. With Japan as the new linchpin in US geostrategy in the Asian region (Pacific Command – USPACOM), the narrative in the Godzilla series tapped contemporaneous anxieties by reflecting humans deploying their techno-scientific skills to survive as powerful titans battled over Tokyo and other cities. With ensuing high economic growth (*kōdo keizai seichō*), like a trickster Godzilla steadily shifted from allegory of destructive force from incendiary and atomic bombing to a guardian deity for prosperity and security against *future* nuclear wars (Igarashi 2000: 121; Tsuitsui 2004: 13).

But there was also a subterranean stream among post-war artists who sought to re-think not only the bankruptcy of the wartime ideology but who were also less certain about the bright new future being proclaimed by Japan's leadership, many of whom had performed *tenkō* (renunciation) as former militarists. Despite the heady post-war rhetoric of democracy and the 'free world', in reality these artists found their hopes for real democratic society based on solid principles of equality and social justice betrayed.

In what I call the 'occupied condition', for artists of *yakeato-ha* (burnt ruins) and *nikutai-ha* (flesh) literature, neo-realist film, action art and avant-garde performance (Avant-Garde Theatre Guild) in particular, focusing on the body was a way to confront the memories of past war and the actualities of Occupation. Bodily materiality provided an anchor in existential emptiness, and could help many to find solace amid loss by sifting through experiential layers secreted in their own bodies. That is, for many it offered ways to think from the wounds themselves, and from a marginal position, contest and articulate alternatives to the new narrative of history and memory as it hardened around them.

One of the key forms to have emerged from this post-war avant-garde artistic movement was *Ankoku Butoh* (dance of darkness). Hijikata Tatsumi (1928–1986), co-founder of *Ankoku Butoh*, was among the most interesting proponents of the *yakeato* generation. His original and distinctive artistic practice, eventually recognized as one of the most important dance forms to emerge in the latter half of the twentieth century, developed during Japan's transition from imperial centre to defeated and occupied nation, to economic super power. *Butoh* can be read from a perspective grounded in the body (from below), in relation to the nation's modern industrialization, imperial expansion, the Asia-Pacific War, Occupation and post-war subject formation.

As proposed in Chapter 2, *Ankoku Butoh* formulated a practical process of cultivating 'being-flesh', to 'empty' the body of an occupied or semi-colonized condition. A contradictory alterity in *butoh* shares many aspects with the aesthetics of the 'grotesque' (Shabot 2007: 51–68). Bakhtin, for example, described the grotesque as '[B]lended with the world, with animals, with objects. It is cosmic, it represents the entire material bodily world in all its elements... not impenetrable but open' (Bakhtin 1984 [1965]: 26, 317, 339).

In contrast with the discrete and unified Cartesian subject within a fixed social hierarchy, the grotesque ontology is hybridized, chaotically fluid and in permanent flux. It undergoes disfigurations, contradictions, collective assemblages and transformations. Akin with the horizontalizing effect of the bawdy Rabelaisian carnival and associated with the Surrealist tradition, *butoh* also accommodates Taoist naturalism, and the imperfection and ephemerality of Zen Buddhism. While not a strict doctrine, in its practice *butoh* broke from the narrow confines of modern subjecthood informed by sovereign power and its *techné* of biopolitics, liberal rationalism and capital accumulation.

In a period of decolonization in the 1950s and 1960s, and akin to the post-First World War avant-garde, *butoh* took part in the politicization of aesthetics of the time by focusing on high-contrast binaries; white/light (blinding, pure, reflective, absolute, dominant) and black/dark (polluting, defiling, inflecting, passive). In Chapters 3 and 4, these are further explicated through Hijikata Tatsumi's practical methods and underlying principles as evident in his notations (*Butoh-fu*) furthering the development of the concept of an occupied condition in post-war society in Japan.

In the interregnum of the 1970s, in which Japan reinforced its presence on the world stage as a hi-tech industrial giant, a resurgent cultural nationalism supported a strong movement to identify and recover original Japanese identity. In Chapter 5, in response to this politics of memory, the practice of *Ankoku Butoh* is explored as a form of poetic witnessing. Both as material evidence and mediums for neglected histories, *butoh* bodies suggested an ontology of marginalized subaltern lives that shared similar experiences and perspectives across multiple domains and territories – an occupied condition.

Hijikata passed away in 1986 as an imminent end to the Cold War seemed plausible. *Butoh* had been taken up first in the Euro-American arts scene and was fast spreading elsewhere. A Tokyo-based experimental theatre company named Gekidan Kaitaisha (Theatre of Deconstruction), under the direction of Shimizu Shinjin, reconceived and reconfigured *butoh* principles (*Butoh-sei*) to reflect the rapid attrition of the organic human body confined increasingly in a reality of networked enclosures. Kaitaisha's re-politicization of the *butoh* body went against the trend to commodify and assimilate it by grounding its principles once more in contemporaneous socio-political conditions. After the Persian Gulf War of 1991 in particular, Shimizu, informed by post-structuralist and critical media theory, engaged in a critical rethinking of our bodies in relation to contemporary media, war and capitalism. As developed in Chapter 6, this covergence between the body and the military-media complex, as manifested in open-air militarized urban battlefields (Virilio 2005) as they developed in the post-Cold War conflicts in Yugoslavia, Africa and the Middle East, is explored in an analysis of the scenography of Kaitaisha's performances and its collaborative productions.

Kaitiasha's *Bye Bye* series were performed in West Europe and New York prior to and just after the 9/11 attacks while we witnessed the transition from the post-Cold War US unilateral dominance to the 'War on Terror' by a US-led coalition of forces. The emergence of *otaku* bodies within networked spatial domains signified a deeper and more rapid penetration of networked warfare into the commercial and private domain. In response, a transnational workshop/production of *Dream Regime* focused on localized memories in bodies otherwise ignored by global channels inundated with dominant mediated post-9/11 narratives as discussed in Chapter 7. From a visit to Dili, Timor-Leste, as part of this project, the analysis returns to the problem of the body as a material site of contestation between justice and sovereign power over the formation of post-war memory and subject/nationhood formation. Having begun with lived conditions in post-war Japan, in the quest for 'truth' through the recovery of the dead in Timor-Leste, in grasping the communal significance of the physical bodies and their burial, we arrive at the fundamental relationality of body and earth to historical conflict and post-war subject/nation formation from a subaltern perspective marginalized in the drive to modernization.

As an epilogue and conceptual summary of the terms developed throughout, Chapter 8 offers a poetic and political critique in the form of a self-devised solo performed during the War on Terror in the first decade of the twenty-first century. In the sovereign determination of 'enemy' and 'friend' to mobilize public consciousness in support of the US-led 'Coalition of the Willing', this performance critically frames a 'seeing system' that mediates (a largely unwilling) public in active denial of sovereign responsibility for an illegal war of aggression in their name.

Drawing together this analysis of concepts and strategies developed in an oeuvre of embodied artistic expression in response to conditions established in post-war Japan, the following seeks to present alternative experiences and perspectives to the dominant narrative which has driven the US alliance and division system and its atomic gaze since 1945.

1

An Outline of Japan's Modern
Nation-State Formation

During the Second World War in the United States, much was made of the 'brutal and idle samurai class' of Japanese males who practiced a Shintō-based spiritualizing of swords (Dower 1986: 228).[1] Given the spiritual connection of the samurai and the sword in the *bushidō* warrior code, this was not surprising. Yet it also drew from a bitter legacy of Japanese state–Christian relations since the sixteenth century, in which many Christians in Japan were persecuted, killed and, by 1626, outlawed by Toyotomi Hideyoshi, which continued under Tokugawa Ieyasu.

In the Pacific War (1941–1945), a barrage of mediated exhortations on both Japanese and Allied sides to core values – identity and religion – sought to frame the enemy as an existential threat. Japanese propaganda vilified the Anglo-Saxon race ('bestial American-British'/'*kichiku Bei-Ei*') and criticized Western civilization as decadent as a whole. This was to instil a sense of superior Japanese spiritual and cultural purity as part of a military code in public consciousness in order to build morale and to counter greater Allied military firepower.

The Empire of Japan did not extend its ambitions to the US mainland or to Europe, at least not in any practical or immediate sense. Delimited to the Chinese mainland ('Greater East Asia') and its colonial acquisitions (Taiwan, Korea, Karafuto, the Caroline, Marshall, Marianas and Palau Islands), due to stretched resources the Imperial reach only later expanded to South and South-East Asia and contested parts of Melanesia and Micronesia with an aim to create a broad economic zone, or 'Greater Co-Prosperity Sphere' (*Daitōakyōeiken*).

The ideological focus of Japanese militarists and some of the political elite in the 1930s and 1940s was to legitimize Japan's 'rightful inheritance' to at least a share of Asia's colonial assets under Euro-American rule. Simply put, their justification was that Japan's rapid modern industrialization compared to its Asian counterparts put it ahead of these other nations in the international pecking order. They also proclaimed that the nation's successes were due to its inherent characteristics which were unique in Asia, such as disciplined industriousness and self-sacrifice to a semi-divine monarch. In short, Japanese authorities justified their imperialist ambitions in developmentalist terms as grounded in a modern episteme of human hierarchy and evolution.

In contrast to the Allies' approach to the German national socialist state, the rhetorical focus in propaganda against Japan drew from a lexicon that had been refined since European expansion into the new world in the fifteenth century. Instead of a rival worthy of competition as equals in an international arena, Japan was 'degraded' to a despotic and feudal civilization that concealed its barbarity beneath a modern veneer (Dower 1986: 4–32). Japan was denied Western recognition (and inclusion) as a responsible imperial power with a legitimate stake in its region because it had not yet demonstrated its maturity as a modern nation-state.

Certainly, the Japanese modern nation continued (after Tokugawa) to promote an 'agrarian fundamentalist' ideology to its own population of the nation as predominantly comprising of self-sufficient agrarian settler-farmers (*hyakushō*) who had been administered by court nobles (samurai) and ruled by a continuous imperial line (*tennō-sei*) on the Yamato plains since the Ritsuryō order of the sixth century (Amino 2012: 24–25, 64).

Similarly, Japanese society was imbued with a legacy of structural discrimination. Until the end of the thirteenth century, as in medieval Europe, based on the organizing principles of purity (*aware*) and pollution (*kegare*), populations of 'dog-people' (*inujinin*) and even lower 'non-human' (*hinin*) were allocated tasks (related to death and animals) as mediums of the sacred and profane. With growing competition for land and resources and concentration of power in the samurai nobility by the 1400s, these populations were stigmatized as they maintained tasks related to death-birth, ingestion-excretion, animal-human.

From national unification under Oda Nobunaga's 'one sword' policy in 1582 through the reign of Toyotomi Hideyoshi and the Tokugawa shogunate, Japan did seek to challenge its subordinate position in the world (to imperial China) through failed attempts to invade Korea between 1592 and 1598 and in competition with Korean and European sea-faring powers in a selective protectionist (Sakoku Edict) trade policy (while trading as far as South America).

The forceful entry of Commodore Perry's Black Ships into Uraga harbour in 1853 and imposition of the 'unequal treaty system' (*fubyōdō jōyaku*) by American and British powers came at a time when the Tokugawa Bakumatsu was destabilized from below (*yōnaoshi*, particularly in the 1830s and 1860s). Such factors triggered the Bōshin civil war (1863–1869), which led to the toppling of the Bakufu and restoration of the *tennō* structure in 1868. As a 'revolution from above', seeking to prevent further 'unequal treaties' and delay the economic or direct European colonization underway in China (in the Opium Wars, 1839–1842 and 1856–1860), between 1868 and 1899 the Meiji *genrō* and political elite pragmatically shaped the national structure to reflect Japan's geopolitical position.

Contrary to the idea that Japan emerged from its chrysalis of self-imposed isolation to join the 'international community' of liberal democracies, Japan's modernization concentrated power through a centralized hierarchy, national polity and national boundaries. In both Confucian and European modes, it enshrined the principles of a patrilineal national family state (*kazoku kokka*) in the Imperial Rescript of Education: good wives/wise mothers (*ryōsai kenbo*); ethnic uniqueness (*minzoku*); wealth and strength (*fukoku kyōhei*); patriotic virtue (*chūkun aikoku*, or *aikokuteki tokugi*); xenophobia (*sonnō jōi*).

At the elementary level, Japanese children and military cadets were taught the national myth of an unbroken imperial line of semi-divine Emperors with a heavenly mandate to protect an exceptional national family/race. At the high-school level, the professional elite were taught rational pragmatism (Tsurumi 1987: 24). So as they idealized the nation as a homogeneous and timeless closed society (*mura*) of *hyakushō* led by a spiritual father (Weiner 1997: 1), the *genrō* also embraced the logic and implemented the modern legal, political, financial and industrial structures required to trade and compete with Euro-American nations and dominate its near neighbours. The rice paddy was replaced with the factory as the new engine of Nippon. With greater urbanization, modernization of its organizational model and civic liberalization including the right of return for Christian missionaries, in return, Japan gained international recognition as a modern nation-state.

Having annexed Ainu (1855) and Ryūkyū (1875) territories as a process of 'primitive accumulation' to industrialize and fortify the nation-state by the 1890s, Japan's colonial expansion extended to Taiwan with the first Sino-Japanese War (1894–1895) and Korean with the Russo-Japanese War (1904–1905), as well as the post-First World War transfer of Germany's colonial possessions in Micronesia (Caroline Islands, Yap, Palau, Marianas and later the Marshall Islands).

To justify its formal annexation of Korea in 1910, the Japanese government pointed to the Taft-Katsura Memorandum of 27 July 1905, in which it was agreed that Japan would not challenge the United States over its control of the Philippines in return for its recognition of Japan's suzerain control of Korea. This 'gentleman's agreement' while Japan was still at war with Russia established an informal alliance between Japan, the United States and Great Britain. In short, Japan was admitted into the Euro-American club as it projected the same imperialist practices (as Roosevelt and Wilson administrations) in East Asia. Where China was once the dominant imperial power in the region, it was now widely considered an anachronistic and disorderly order of corrupt oligarchs, religious elite, warlords and peasantry. For Meiji government intellectuals, as well as Japanese militarists in the early 1930s, Japan's position as the region's industrial powerhouse with significant skilled labour power made it the rational choice for accessing and managing China's massive agricultural resources in mutual benefit to their 'struggling Chinese brothers' on the mainland (Morton 1937: 309).

Even as late as the Pacific War, in spite of Japan's modern industrialized capacity, racialized caricatures by Allied nations of the Japanese enemy continued to emphasize the cruelty of a truly feudal civilization steeped in mysterious traditions and ruled by oppressive samurai nobility. The Allied intelligence officers and propagandists had chosen to ignore the fact that Japan was not just an island agrarian civilization but also comprised multi-lingual semi-nomadic peoples who traded across the archipelagic mountains and seas (Amino 2012: 38–40).[2] Ironically, their approach reflected that adopted in Meiji Japan wherein the 'Asiatic' was just as much a signifier against which to mark Japan's superiority as it was in the West.

By the 1880s, a circle of younger *Meirokusha* intellectuals (Katō Hiroyuki, Fukuzawa Yukichi, Nakamura Keiu, Toyama Shōichi, Noritake Kōtarō, Ariga Nagao) impressed by liberal entrepreneurialism (Samuel Smiles' *Self Help* and Swett Marden's *Pushing to the Front* were best-sellers in Meiji Japan) were seeking to implement modern laissez-faire economics, liberalism and biological determinism. The impact of social Darwinism was significant and can be found in clusters of social and political philosophers including Kant, Hegel, Marx and Comte (Marx later recognized indigenous land and ownership),[3] as well as in the sociology of diplomat Comte de Gobineau, anthropology of Cesare Lombroso and pedagogy of G. Stanley Hall.[4] But they were most impressed by the popular social evolution theory of Herbert Spencer in *The Social Organism* (1860), which attached political, social and economic characteristics to evolutionary science (and erroneously coined the term 'survival of the fittest' as derived from Charles Darwin, J. F. Blumenbach, Ernst Haeckel, Jean-Baptiste Lamarck). In short, Spencer, inspired by Thomas Malthus, argued that natural law determined the superiority of Western civilization, the proof of which was in its achievements, wealth, values and institutional systems. Spencerism rationalized 'human' development in proportion to the ability to harness 'nature' towards industrialization; the 'primitive scavenger' ('tribal') developed through cultural 'adolescence' of agricultural and semi-urbanized societies ('Asiatic') to the modern capitalist nation-states of full adulthood (Euro-American).

A visiting American zoologist Edward S. Morse to Japan in 1877 at the invitation of Katō Hiroyuki championed Spencerism at Tokyo Imperial University. In *The Evolution of Animals*, Morse argued that heredity was the root of inequality, and rather than allow humane impulses to interfere with 'selective action', he argued that 'reformers ... are unfit for their work if they are ignorant of the doctrines of natural selection and derivation' (Howland 2000: 67–86). Akin to Lombroso's theory of 'criminal atavism', this served to rationalize the criminalization and incarceration of 'labour agitators and the unemployed' to prevent the reproduction of inferiority.

Katō then published a new human rights treatise in 1882 in which he regarded the 'free market' competition *as* evolution and necessary for Japan's survival:

> The basic principle of all principles, the victory of the superior and the defeat of the inferior, applies not only to the world of animals and plants but also with the same compelling necessity to the world of human beings. (Katō in Watanabe and Ose 1968: 72–73, fn. 70; Cross 1996: 339)

Institutionalized discrimination was to ensure control and efficiency through the production of an ethno-national identity based on martial discipline (Roden 1980: 519). Under the Family Registration Law (*kosekihō*) of 1871, for example, subjects' family heritage was made visible to the state. When outcaste (*hisabetsu burakumin*) populations gained access to non-*burakumin* forms of employment as they were registered as 'new-commoners' (*shin-heimin*), *heimin* (formerly *hyakushō*) protested and the sanction was quickly reintroduced. In fact, Meiji society reflected similar problems to other modern liberal societies. Social mobility was restricted through unequal treatment of pauperized merchants, peasants and workers (*mujinkō* – anonymous public; *heimin* – commoners) to benefit an elite class of industrialists, financiers, large landowners, bureaucrats and intellectuals. In spite of the activism of groups like *Jiyū Minken Undō* (Hani 1946), the priority to compete with powerful nations meant that only disciplined self-sacrifice would be rewarded with civil rights (Balibar and Wallerstein 1991: 43, 79; Suzuki and Oiwa 1996: 96–98; Morris-Suzuki 1998: 97–101).[5]

So, although the Meiji reformer Yoshino Sakuzō defined the citizen (*shimin*) as the core unit of 'democracy' (*minposhugi*) in 'On the meaning of Constitutional Government' (1916), naturalized and individualized competition within an ethno-nationalist conception of blood, race and soil and fealty to the *minzoku no ōsa* (people's father) ensured that other horizontalist or collective ontologies were effaced. As the Meiji intellectuals (mis)understood, the 'neutral' rational epistemic claim to universal reality based on a world-historical value of 'human' was a powerful tool to justify colonial exploitation. Grounded in a Spencerian 'survivalist' contest and 'maturationist' colonial policies, newly colonized populations (*shin-heimin*) were regarded as 'childlike' and were stripped of their traditions, given Japanese names, language, education, practices and assimilated within state institutions. After all, as in the pedagogy of the respected American educator G. Stanley Hall, it was necessary to discipline children to selflessly love the nation, or alternatively, it was necessary to selectively breed out 'weakness' from the social body (Hall 1903: 4–13; Hall 1911: 152–59). Remaining outside and beneath the ruling and working classes in the metropolis or peripheral towns, the internally and externally colonized became surplus labour in their former homelands – soldiers, clothing, housing, food, agricultural and marine producers, cultural providers.

This Meiji hybrid 'internal combustion engine' of Prussian (Bismarckian) state monarchy, institutionalized Shintō ritual, Confucian moral order and laissez-faire capitalism (Gluck 1985: 91–93; Wiener 1997: 2) drove the Japanese Empire founded on an 'Asian Monroe Doctrine' based on 'co-existence and co-prosperity' (Oguma 2002a: 125–42; Saaler 2007: 21).

Yet it was the denial of the 'open door' to Japan by the United States, the United Kingdom and the League of Nations that helped largely to re-direct this engine away from the western alliance and split Japan's politics into ethno-nationalist (and militarist) and liberal internationalist camps. In 1918, Prince Konoe Fumimaro argued that Japan was condemned to 'remain forever subordinate to the advanced nations'. In 1919 at the Paris Peace Conference, the Australian delegation led by Billy Hughes rejected Japan's Racial Equality Proposal and appealed to Britain to defend its Dominions and protect the White Australia Policy (Shimazu 1998: 14–15, 117). This was tacitly endorsed by Britain, Canada, New Zealand and the United States (and formalized in the 1924 Immigration Act, Johnson-Reed Act Section 13c, or 'Japanese exclusion act'/*hi-nichi imin hō*) (Auer and Watanabe 2006: 289).

With the onset of the Great Depression and a civil war between nationalist and communist forces destabilizing China since 1927, the Japanese Kwantung Army seized the resource-rich region of Manchuria and installed the remaining

Qing Emperor Pu Yi as head of Manchukuo, a Japanese-run colony, in 1931. In response to demands that Japan withdraw its troops already operating in China, Japan withdrew from the League of Nations in 1933. Launching the Second Sino-Japanese War in July 1937, Japanese forces toppled the capital of Nanjing in December that year.

Instead of Japan's 'incomplete [transition to] democracy', it is more likely that the Anglo-American return to 'maturationist' civilizational discourse to deny Japan's 'entitlement' as an equal rival with competing imperialist claims over a region played a significant role in Japan's invasion of China and slide into total war. In mirror fashion, a similar discourse was deployed by Japanese Pan-Asianist ideologues to mobilize public support for Japan as an Asian 'family' in the formation of a non-Western 'new world order'. On both sides, the rhetoric obscured the underlying geopolitical drivers.

Following Japan's military occupation of French-Indochina on 24 July 1940, the United States placed an embargo on all Japanese assets in the United States followed by Britain and the Dutch East Indies. Japan lost access to three-quarters of its overseas trade and 88 per cent of its imported oil leaving it with oil reserves to last three years. Japan promptly occupied Saigon, with a view to gain control of Southeast Asia, including Singapore and Malaya, for its resources. It was forced to fight a war it could not win, or submit to United States hegemony in the Pacific. Although Navy Admiral Yamamoto had been a proponent of not engaging the Allied forces, he argued that if Japan must fight, it would be better to attack pre-emptively than wait to be attacked by the US navy stationed at Pearl Harbour. Japan signed the Tripartite Pact with the Axis powers of Germany and Italy on 27 September 1940. The then prime minister and Minister of the Imperial Army Tōjō Hideki chose this option with the support of the Cabinet. On 7 December 1941, Japanese war planes bombed Pearl Harbour, although they crucially missed the aircraft carriers and submarines, and 2,500 people were killed and 1,000 wounded. On 8 December, the 25th Army led by General Yamashita landed in Malaya and charged towards Singapore to claim it in February 1942, causing heavy civilian casualties. On 10 December, the 14th Army landed at Luzon and advanced to take Manila from General MacArthur, who withdrew his US forces to Bataan. The Japanese military and pro-independence armies steadily upturned the former European colonial order in Asia – French-Indochina, Dutch-Indonesia, American-Philippines and British-Burma-Malaya. Nevertheless, the battles of Coral Sea and Midway, the resistance of the Indian Raj armies, the Kuomindang nationalist forces and Chinese communist forces in China wore down the offensive. Cut off by the Allied Pacific operations led by General MacArthur, the Japanese Imperial Army was a spent force.

Over time, with the Imperial Army's exploitation of human and material resources to support its over-reach and of its practices of racial and cultural superiority, it became clear that the anti-colonial Japanese propaganda campaign had become a parody of itself. Yet this drive had ruptured the 'White Republic [in Asia]' and contributed to the subsequent permanent removal of the European colonizers (Williams in Stockwin et al. 2006: 152–53).

Enemy destruction and friendly re-construction

Not limited to immediate government policies, the racialized propaganda deployed during the Asia-Pacific War was grounded in a legacy of social Darwinism, imperialist conquest and inter-state and institutionalized discrimination in the world order.

Back in the United States, a cadre of social scientists, journalists and filmmakers were employed by the Office of War Information (OWI) to conduct information warfare to promote distrust in the American public for Japanese military leaders and the nation's people as a whole. The Japanese enemies were 'animalized' down to their 'pagan souls'. Frank Capra's 'Prelude to War' in the *Why We Fight* series showed Emperor Hirohito, consistent with the imagery used for Mussolini and Hitler, as a 'barbaric and grinning yellow face, a buck-toothed monkey with coke-bottle glasses about to steal your bride who was promised eternity for fanatical service to the God Emperor' (Capra 1971: 326–47).[6] Capra's *Know Your Enemy* (1944) used the samurai sword to symbolize Japanese treachery – more than any gun, plane or bomb.

In Japan, while 'the West' was certainly targeted, the Imperial film censorship programme was more concerned to protect the integrity of the Emperor and the Imperial institutions through prohibitions:

- profaning the dignity of the royal family
- questioning the Imperial Constitution
- harming the interests of the Empire
- hampering the exercise of national policies
- threatening national morality
- undermining Japanese language
- obstructing national culture (Hirano 1992: 15).

In the United States, denigrating the enemy through orientalist stereotypes (i.e. in the case of Japanese, 'Hashimura Togo', 'Fu Manchu') was common in government, military and journalistic war narratives. Aggravated by the humiliations at the hands of the Japanese Imperial Army in the Asia-Pacific, traits of a lower species were used to characterize the Japanese enemy: hollowness (immorality), mindless conformity (no subjective will), neuroticism, deviousness and fanaticism (unstable mentality). As was verified by US, Australian and other Allied soldiers who served in New Guinea, without supplies and with orders to never surrender, Japanese companies often kept their prisoners as a food source. Instead of perceiving these as human actions under harsh conditions, such atrocities were used to support racialized analyses of the Japanese – paradoxical refinement and brutality (Kelley and Ryan 1947: 19; Uzawa 2008).

The dehumanization campaign was so successful that high-level officials decided that Japanese-Americans posed a 'security threat'. The Secretary of War Henry Stimson put it most politely: 'their [Japanese] racial characteristics are such that we cannot understand or trust even the citizen Japanese' (Stimson, 10 February 1942). Others demanded their 'mass evacuation' (Texas Congressman and Chairman of the House Un-American Activities Committee Martin Dies), mass incarceration in a civilizational conflict (Democratic Congressman John Rankin (tenBroek et al. 1970: 87)) and extermination (Idaho Governor Chase A. Clark):

> [A] good solution to the Jap problem would be to send them all back to Japan, then sink the islands. They live like rats, breed like rats and act like rats. (Victoria in Selden et al. 2006: 105)

In an article in *Time* magazine on the Battle of Iwojima entitled 'Rodent Exterminators', Admiral William Halsey preferred a simian analogy. 'We are drowning and burning the bestial apes all over the Pacific, and it is just as much pleasure to burn them as to drown them' (Halsey 1945: 226; Dower J. 1999: 213). These perspectives mostly ignored the huge number of victims from countries in Asia.

As the tide turned in the Pacific War in May 1942, a notable shift in the US propaganda campaign split the Japanese enemy into two factions: the Emperor's civilian faction and Tōjō's militarist faction. Following the US intelligence trend of psycho-pathologizing the enemy (i.e. Erik Homburger Erikson's Hitler study), Tōjō was likened to a 'Hitler replete with Oriental mysticism', diagnosed as psychopathic and compared to notorious historical warlords – Nero, Attila, Caligula (Dower 1986: 87, 141, 153–56, 163; Friedman 1999: 164–65; Cavin 2007: fn. 9, unpag.).

In parallel, OWI sought to undermine public 'morale' and trust in the enemy population for their own leaders. In 1944–1945, the United States Army Airforce (USAAF) commander General Curtis LeMay carried out the US Strategic Bombing Survey (USSBS) area bombing campaign of Japanese cities. Following the Luftwaffe aerial bombing of London, the British fire-bombings of Dresden and the Japanese bombing of Chongqing a year earlier, LeMay's 'psychological warfare' campaign ('carpet' or 'terror-bombing') over Germany and Japan was informed by First World War 'strategic bombing' theory (Douhet 1942 [1921]; De Seversky 1942), which held that aerial bombing was justified as long as it motivated local resistance against enemy rulers, hastened surrender and softened civilian reception to occupation. Area bombing was developed in parallel with photography for aerial military devices (balloons and dirigibles) from the 1880s. This 'scopic regime' was based on the occupation of Cairo in the 'first total war' fought by Napoleon's forces in 1798–1801 (see Bell 2007). Aerial bombing was found to violate international legal conventions in a series of international conferences from 1899 to 1923, to protect non-combatants from indiscriminate bombardment (The Hague Report 1923: 250–51).

In the final campaign between August 1944 and August 1945, 205 Japanese cities were bombed repeatedly with incendiary and more 'conventional' explosives. The infamous *iki-jigoku* (living hell) 9–10 March raid on Tokyo by 279 B-29 bombers dropped 1,700 tonnes of explosives (including M69 napalm bombs) and left between 100,000 and 300,000 dead and 1 million homeless (Potter et al. 1981: 349).

Meanwhile, negotiations over the terms of surrender between the Allied forces and Japan were underway. The USAAF 393rd Bomb Squadron of the 509th Composite Group commanded by Colonel Paul W. Tibbets, dropped 'Pumpkin' bombs ('dummy runs') on the 20, 23, 26 and 29 July, and 8 and 14 August 1945

(Weller 2006: 27). Since September 1944, Tibbets had been trained as part of the Manhattan Project to use 'inert' and then live bombs (49 'Composite B' slurry bombs) with ballistics identical to the 'Fat Man' plutonium bomb dropped on fourteen cities near to Hiroshima and Nagasaki (Campbell 2005: 27–29, 72–75, 90).

From 17 July to 2 August, opening the day after the Trinity test in the Nevada desert, the United States, Great Britain and the Soviet Union (and ROC by telegraph) met at Potsdam to decide Germany's fate and plan the end game for Japan. On 26 July 1945, Truman, Attlee and Chiang Kai-Shek presented the Allied demands for Japan's surrender, while Stalin abstained as the submission of the Soviet delegation was denied inclusion by the Americans. The day before, Tibbets and his team were put on standby on Saipan with an order to drop the bomb from General Carl Spaatz given to him by General Handy should Japan not comply with the terms. Handy had received the order drafted by Groves and approved by Marshall and Stimson in Potsdam. The Potsdam Proclamation demands included the unconditional surrender of all Japanese armed forces; relinquishing Japanese Pacific territories acquired since 1914; the Allied occupation of Japan; disarmament and abolition of the Japanese military; elimination of the political influence of the military; justice for war criminals; continuation of non-military industries; freedom of speech, religion and thought based on the legal recognition of human rights. The bombing runs had already underlined these demands with credible force. But it remained ambiguous as to whether or not the Emperor system would remain, and why the Soviets had not signed the Proclamation.

Without going into all the details here, ultimately the Japanese cabinet response via Prime Minister Suzuki Kantarō was reported by the press as '*mokusatsu*' (黙殺) and was interpreted by the Allies as defiant rejection. Actually, Prince Konoe had already issued several proposals of peace to Stalin and Molotov who were assumed to be mediating between Japan and the Allies in April 1945. Even if ministers and commanders debated the terms from 26 July on, the term '*mokusatsu*' suggested demurral as they awaited a peace party (Kawai 1950: 409–14). Their concern was not whether or not to surrender, but on what terms. Namely, how to negotiate the inherent ambiguity to the demands and preserve the Emperor as sovereign ruler and ensure some autonomy in demilitarization, military trials and rebuilding their nation.

Since 1944, it was estimated by US intelligence that Japanese surrender would come earlier than November 1945. In April 1945, it was clear to Psychological Warfare planners that all the elements essential for surrender already existed. Japanese cities and its navy, airforce, military and industrial capacities were largely destroyed, there was no strategic capacity to pose a threat and civilian populations were almost completely exposed to air attacks (USSBS July 1946: 16, 52–56). Generals Eisenhower, MacArthur and Leahy among others concurred that the atomic bombs were not necessary to end the war. In fact, the timing of the bombs, the Potsdam conference and the anticipated entry of the Soviets into the war was finely tuned. The Trinity test, proceeded by the Conference, enabled the Americans a superior position from which to bargain with the Soviets over the future conditions in Europe. The atomic bombs used on Japan were unnecessary to force Japan's surrender but were used to accelerate it unilaterally without acceding too much power to the Soviets in depending on their entry into the war against Japan (8 May) and allowing them to gain too much territory. The Americans had calculated that the demands would be either impossible for the Japanese to accept as it would mean national suicide or they would produce sufficient delay as the Cabinet worked out the true meaning of the terms and the possibility to negotiate. The Potsdam Proclamations broadcast through the US Office of War Information (a propaganda arm) would appear to produce an at least inferrable decision to fight on therefore justifying the use of the new super weapons which the Americans were clearly keen to brandish and use (Hasegawa 2005: 151–73).

The overall aerial bombing campaign was only possible due to a dehumanization campaign and psychological warfare theory. But aerial bombing only engrained more deeply the spirit of resistance (Young 2010). Among six target options, Hiroshima was chosen as an 'AA' site for its urban and industrial density, and its surrounding hills which would reflect the thermal wave (Murthy et al. 2000: 20–21). At 2.45 am on a cloudless 6 August 1945, a Silverplate B-29 Superfortress nicknamed the 'Enola Gay' flew from the Tinian Islands to Honshu. As the streets of Hiroshima were filled with people going to work, at 8.15 am an 8,900-pound (4,036.97 kg) Uranium 235 weapon named 'Little Boy' was dropped and detonated over the city. Ninety per cent of the target area was levelled, 70,000 to 80,000 people were instantly eviscerated and 140,000 people died over the following weeks.

Sixteen hours after, in a snap broadcast, Truman declared a US capability that exceeded the British 'Grand Slam' bomb (20,000 tonnes of TNT) by two thousand times. He warned that Japanese defiance would lead to 'a rain of ruin from the air the likes of which has never been seen on this earth' (Truman, 'Presidential statement', 6 August 1945). After changing course due to overcast skies, at 10.58 am on 9 August, the Plutonium 239 'Fat Man' bomb was detonated above Nagasaki destroying one-third of the city and instantly killing 42,000 people, followed by 75,000 more deaths soon after.

Early on 10 August, the Japanese Cabinet and the Supreme Council agreed to the Postdam Declaration but requested that the emperor remain as sovereign ruler. US Secretary of State James Byrnes relented from the original unconditional terms of surrender to grant this request but reinforced that Japanese authorities would be subordinate to the Supreme Commander of the Allied Powers (SCAP). As OWI in Saipan broadcasted the Japanese surrender and prepared leaflet drops, on 14 August another 'pumpkin' was dropped.

By the end of 1945, roughly 230,000 people had perished from the effects of the atomic bombs, including 70,000 Koreans. Half a million people had died from the aerial bombing campaign, and there were roughly 1 million casualties and 10 million homeless. As was distinct in the Second World War on the whole, the majority of victims were civilians (Young 2010). While radiation dose effects remained contested, it has been estimated that 690,000 people were exposed to various types of radiation (Lee 2009), and a physical and psychological legacy has persisted over several generations due to lack of official recognition.

After General MacArthur arrived at Atsugi airforce base on 30 August 1945, Japan was placed under direct control by a foreign power for the first time. The Occupation was secured under SCAP led by the United States (1947–1952) and the Far Eastern Commission and Allied Council for Japan (China, Great Britain, Soviet Union, United States) and was to carry out Truman's directive to (further) eliminate Japan's war potential and reorientate the nation in a pro-American direction.

According to his mandate, MacArthur ordered the immediate arrest of over 100 Japanese military commanders and high-ranked officials who were suspected of crimes of aggression. This included Tōjō, who was derided when found by American GIs and journalists on 11 September 1945 following a botched suicide (Shibusawa 2006: 128).[7]

At the International Military Tribunal for the Far East (1946–1948), the prosecution led by Joseph B. Keenan had two aims: to try individuals for conspiracy to wage aggressive war in East Asia and the Asia-Pacific between 1928 and 1945; to indict those who were guilty of waging aggressive war against the British Commonwealth of Nations, France, the Mongolian People's Republic, the Netherlands, the Republic of China, the Soviet Union and the United States (including the Philippines). All but one defendant were convicted of conspiracy or crimes against peace.

Although war crimes and crimes against humanity were included as violations against rules and customs of war, the two were not distinguished. Individual criminal acts, criminal negligence or systemic forms of slavery were neglected (treatment of prisoners, forced labour, sexual slavery) and the principal victims were Allied nationals (Totani 2008: 154). While the defence (Takayanagi Kenzō) raised cultural specificity as mitigating the universality of war crimes – 'crimes no less than masterpieces of art may reflect the mores of a race' (Totani 2008: 158) – and sought to exempt Cabinet ministers who despite prior knowledge had no authority over military decisions, these arguments were not persuasive.

Certainly, the Tribunal had a clear Euro-American bias. The lack of translation for the defendants for half the proceedings, for example, did not ensure balanced proceedings. Western Allies lost roughly 5 per cent of the 36 million Asian lives lost in the Asia-Pacific War (roughly 27 million were Chinese). Only later did Justices Radhabinod Pal and Delfin Jaranilla (who was in the Bataan Death March) join Justice Mei as the Asian representation on the bench led by Australian Justice Webb. As some observed: 'The US [and Allies] was not to be accused; guilt was only for Japan' (Braw 1991: 142; Koshiro 1999: 127). In fact, while critical of Japanese imperialism and war crimes, Pal did compare 'the decision to use the atomic bomb as the only near approach to the directives of the German Emperor during the First World War and of Nazi leaders during the Second World War' (Pal 1999: 621). Telford Taylor, the chief counsel for war crimes prosecution at Nuremberg, also recognized the overall crime of aerial bombing campaigns.

> Aerial bombardment had been used so extensively and ruthlessly on the Allied side as well as the Axis side that neither at Nuremberg nor Tokyo was the issue made a part of the trials. (Chomsky 2006: 83; Selden 2007)

Had a Japanese court been mandated to try their own nation's wartime leaders, perhaps with some international guidance, then greater juridical agency and a more just perspective could have been founded. Alternately, had an international trial of all sides for war crimes and crimes against humanity taken place, international law would have had a stronger precedent. Yet unresolved problems continued in the post-war, aggravated no less by the fact that the Koreas, PRC, ROC and South-East Asian and Pacific island nations received far less post-war aid than Japan from the United States. This prolonged their pain and resentment alongside difficulties in economic, social and political recovery while helping to facilitate the United States to establish its particular vision of a post-1945 world order.

The atomic gaze as US geostrategic policy

The use of the area bombing (including atomic) on the Japanese mainland extended beyond precipitating Japan's surrender, 'saving American lives' or 'softening up' Japanese society. Rather, it was a strategic display of the centrepiece of US warfare and the 'first shots' in the United States's coming wars (Edwards 2005; Selden 2007).

The atomic bombs were not the product of the misplaced genius of a few amoral mostly émigré scientists vying for recognition. The Roosevelt administration understood the geostrategic significance of atomic weapons and provided near-unlimited investment for the top-secret Manhattan Project led by Brigadier General Leslie R. Groves beginning in 1942. Initially based at the National Laboratories at Oak Ridge ('Site X'), Tennessee and Los Alamos, New Mexico ('Site Y'), the Project was re-named the US Atomic Energy Commission (US AEC) in 1946. This suggested one reason for the tensions between the United States and the Soviet Union at the conferences of Tehran (November 1943) and Yalta (February 1945).

In the first atomic test named 'Trinity' at Los Alamos on 16 July 1945, the awesome light produced from 'harnessing the basic energy of the universe' seemed to demonstrate literal 'proof' of legitimacy of the US claim to the apex of the international order. Where once Japanese bodies (i.e. *kamikaze* pilots and soldiers) had mediated the 'crystallizing divinity' of the Emperor as 'the Sun' to invest them with the spiritual power of the gods (Morris 1980: 314), the atomic bombs now served as symbolic capital for an eschatological vision of American destiny. Both powers utilized radiant signifiers to bind racialized and religiously inspired concepts to concentrate and magnify the power of the Empire as the pivotal centre of the universe.

In the spectacular and totalizing capture of all elemental material in the targeted area, however, the atomic gaze seemed to manifest the ambition to temporarily halt the inexorable movement of time and even nature itself. As a product of the world-historical episteme of civilizational hierarchy and scientific rationalism, nevertheless, the bomb appeared inextricably entwined with religiously inspired violence and heliocentric delusions of universality. This was recognized by General Omar Nelson Bradley, one of the few US officials to resist the sublimation of the atomic bomb, who observed on Armistice Day in 1948:

We live in a world of nuclear giants and ethical infants, of brilliance without wisdom, power without conscience. We solved the mystery of the atom and forgot the lessons from the Sermon on the Mount. We know much about war and little about peace. (Fleming 2009)

Yet this was not solely an ethical problem of US leaders to agonize over; as discussed earlier the use of the atomic bombs was a crime, and along with the dead, many *hibakusha* remained as living testament to this crime. As explored in the following chapter, the illnesses and inherited effects from internal and external radiation exposures, and lack of sufficient treatment despite existing scientific knowledge at the time, can be included in claims against this act of indiscriminate killing and injuring non-combatants.

Indeed, as Japanese authorities understood, *hibakusha* were a useful symbol of transcendent human suffering that served to replace Japan's militarist image with a post-war pacific image. Through 'victimology and phantasms of innocence' *hibakusha* were transformed into 'perverse national treasures' (Dower 1995: 281; Yoneyama 1999: 13–15), which ignored the complicating presence of Korean, Chinese, Ainu and Okinawan *hibakusha* (Minear 1990: 7; Yoshibumi 2010).

Instead, SCAP suppressed public understanding of the effects of the atomic bombs so as to quickly pacify and return Japanese society to 'normal', contain a budding anti-nuclear movement, promote its nuclear industry and its possible export to Japan and promote the use of nuclear power technology. Without official US public apology and restitution paid directly to all *hibakusha* and their descendants, the Japanese government could also escape scrutiny, public apology and restitution to individual victims and their relatives for war crimes (forced labour, sexual slavery, mass murder, aerial bombing, human experimentation, cannibalism, etc.) committed by the Imperial Japanese regime (Tatara in Danieli 1998: 143).

In any case, the final campaign over Japan became the US blueprint for 'collateral damage' to 'end wars and save lives'. Informed by a strong and growing belief in the intrinsic naturalness of American values, lack of apology or culpability supported the US strategic military plans for the Cold War, and after. As indicated in the US area bombing of North Korea and later Vietnam, the demonstrated capability and use of force seemed to be driven by a concept of American exceptionalism. As Cumings writes, however, 'a people that thinks its goals are self-evident and universal has trouble grasping that it is bound by its own history and particularity' (Cumings 2002a: 63).

The re-orientation of forbidden subjects

The US-led military Occupation of Japan saw the defeated power subdued and subordinated to the supreme authority of the new ruler (Braw 1991: 151). From the outset, the objective of the US Occupation Army and SCAP was to restructure the military order in Japan to serve US interests. Simultaneously, the dimensions of a looming Cold War took priority, in which the United States would seek hegemony by engaging and seeking to contain the Soviet Union and PRC to the Eurasian 'world island' (Mackinder 1969: 89). As a result, Occupation reforms were aimed to demonstrate the success of United States's brand of capitalist democracy in Asia, which ultimately undermined the putative mission to democratize Japan (Cumings 2002a: 261; Dobbins 2003: xiii).

Arriving from the Philippines 'unarmed' in his signature cap, aviator glasses and corn cob pipe, MacArthur assumed the role of 'great Western liberator'. Ensconced in the Tokyo Dai-ichi Seimei Building (GHQ) from 2 September, on 7 September, as Commander of United States Armed Forces Pacific MacArthur then declared Korea south of the 38th parallel to be under US military control (General Order No. 1) which lasted until 1948 (under local command of Lieutenant General Hodge). On 3 November, MacArthur received the Basic Directive from Truman and the Joint Chiefs of Staff permitting him whatever was required to eradicate the 'vicious and cruel savages' who were responsible.

MacArthur was born on 26 January 1880 and was the son of Arthur S. MacArthur, Governor-General of the Philippines, who had also helped suppress nationalist insurgencies against the United States (Vera Cruz, Mexico 1914). MacArthur instilled in his son a typically colonialist ethos. As an Episcopalian drilled in social Darwinist logic (i.e. the pedagogy of G. Stanley Hall and others), MacArthur considered the Japanese to be in an 'elastic' stage of human development and still suggestible to Western ideas. As the parent–teacher colonizer, MacArthur treated his new charges as ambivalent children who vacillated between 'petulant innocence and vindictive brutality'. As if to chide Tōjō for his expressed fear of Japan becoming a 'third-class nation', on 11 September 1945, Douglas MacArthur described Japan as a 'fourth-class nation [*yontōkoku*]'.

> If the Anglo-Saxon was say 45 years of age in development in the sciences, the arts, divinity, culture, the Germans were quite as mature. The Japanese, however, in spite of their antiquity measured by time, were in a very tuitionary condition. Measured by the standards of modern civilization, they would be like a boy of 12... They were still close enough to origin to be elastic and acceptable to new concepts. (MacArthur 1951: 1: 312–13)

MacArthur's '4th class' became instantly infamous and fodder for satire. Japan's largest advertising firm Dentsū even launched a 'We are not 12 years old!' campaign to promote Japanese material inventions (Koshiro 1999: 246, fn. 88).[8] Yet MacArthur's comment was consistent with US social science at the time. Geoffrey Gorer's diagnosis of a special Japanese sensitivity, based on insecure, contingent, compulsive, resentful and ritually aggressive tendencies (Gorer 1943: 106–24), for example, informed 'Japan hand' George Atcheson's urging of 'Occupation authorities to stimulate Japan's racial pride and its inferiority complex regarding the Anglo-Saxon race' (Koshiro 1999: 32). MacArthur's comment was also consistent with the US Morale Analysis Division (June 1945) from manuals developed from assessments of prisoners in detention camps (Japanese, Italian, German Americans) by anthropologists Ruth Benedict, Margaret Mead and Gregory Bateson among others, who served on the 'Committee for National Morale' (CNM) for the Office of Strategic Services (OSS) under the direction of General ('Wild Bill') Donovan and Robert Sherwood (OWI). In short, these recommended that the Occupiers make it publicly known that the militarists were their targets of punishment for harming the Japanese people, who were their objects of aid.

> [T]he militarists may effectively be used as a scapegoat, ... leading other people to
> feel there is something to hope for in surrender. (Orr 2001: 17)

The 'ink had scarcely dried' on the 1946 Constitution (promulgated 3 November 1946, enforced May 1947) when SCAP intelligence resumed the debate over the Emperor. Put simply, the 'New Dealers' such as Earnest Hooton argued that Japan could not be a democracy with an Emperor system (*Tennōsei*) and Owen Lattimore, Atcheson and Elmer Davis held Hirohito, as Commander in Chief of the Japanese Imperial Army, ultimately responsible for the war of aggression. Conservatives such as Joseph Grew, Eugene Dooman, Ruth Benedict and Joseph Ballantine, on the other hand, maintained that the integrity of the imperial system would serve to contain the 'extremists' (communists and nationalists) (Price 2008: 188–92). Brigadier General Bonner Fellers, chief of psychological warfare operations in Japan, said the effect of punishing the Emperor would be like martyring Christ, provoking violent 'ant-like' reactions (Shibusawa 2006: 104).

The retention of the Emperor was less culturally sensitive than it may have seemed, however. In December 1943, going against the grain of the wartime press, Ambassador Grew and Mormon Senator Elbert Thomas argued that retaining the Emperor in the post-war would avail to the US administrators a bureaucratic machine of roughly 2.5 million people (Ball 1948: 212–13). Further, MacArthur was wary of the Soviet invasion of Manchuria and the possibility of a 'People's Republic of Japan' in Hokkaido. He wanted to nurture public antipathy for Soviet and Chinese 'aetheistic totalitarian materialism' (MacArthur to Gordon Lang 1947). With the Emperor as a spiritual totem, MacArthur could sustain popular focus on the familiar national and religious figurehead while utilizing its managerial structure. In the end, the consensus prevailed that Hirohito had been unfairly bullied and deceived by conspiratorial militarists.

The sentencing of seven war criminals served to erase the Shōwa Emperor's military identity and provide the Emperor's dowry to the Americans (Tsurumi 1987: 15–16). MacArthur also staged the Emperor's innocence by declaring that he had personally received Hirohito's 'manly' confession of responsibility for the crimes of his people, and even claimed to have discussed his possible conversion to Christianity (Schaller 1995: 69; Shibusawa 2006: 100–5).[9] This was reinforced with Gaetano Faillace's famous 'wedding photos' of Hirohito in a morning-suit and Douglas in ribbonless fatigues on 27 September 1945. It seemed Japan now had two Emperors. As one journalist put it, the 'Son of Heaven ... had come face to face with the man giving orders to the Son of Heaven' (La Cerda 1946: 95–102).

Re-branded as 'the people's Emperor', the Shōwa Emperor was demoted from a military monarch on a white horse, to a frumpy absent-minded amateur marine biologist in the attire of an American suburban family man. In this sanitized version of Japan's 'gentle father', this re-scripting as the 'little man who wasn't there' was to symbolize the newly pacified Japan. As Crown Prince Akihito was taught by Elizabeth Vining to elocute in American English, the American public referred to Hirohito as 'Charlie', after Edgar Bergan's 'Charlie McCarthy' ventriloquy act and 'Charlie Chan' who was popular in the American cultural imaginary (Morris 1945: 3). This too had been recommended during the war, wherein the Emperor would become 'a puppet who not only could be won over to our side but who would carry with him a tremendous weight of authority' (Reischauer 1942; Fujitani 2001; Hook and McCormack 2001: 7).

But MacArthur also envisioned Japan to be (the next) crucible upon which to forge an Asian Christian democracy in the purported fight against communism. As per the Potsdam Declaration, in the first few weeks of Occupation, officers of the Religious and Cultural Division of the Civil Information and Education Section (CI&E) were mobilized to force compliance with 'freedom of religion' directives (later enshrined as Article 20). MacArthur ordered the immediate dispatch of 1,000 missionaries, the first delegation arriving with translated Bibles in November 1945 and followed by 1,500 American missionaries every year until 1950 (Wittner 1971: 77–97). Many were escaping conflict in China and the Koreas, while others came from American denominations (The Far Eastern Gospel Crusade, The Navigators, The New Tribes Mission). At MacArthur's request, the Pocket Testament League organized delivery of 10 million translated Bibles, and the new missionaries toured the archipelago in American cars emblazoned with images of Jesus and the American flag.

Coinciding with a resurgence in Puritanism in the United States, MacArthur was convinced that 'true democracy resting on the Christian conception of the individual and society' would lead to a 'spiritual revolution' in Japanese society (Gunther 1950: 76). Treating Japan as a testing ground for new methods of indigenizing Christianity, MacArthur believed that replacing Shintō and Buddhism was the only towards 'spiritual recrudescence and improvement of human character [in Japan] that will synchronize with our almost matchless advance in science, art, literature and all material and cultural development of the past two thousand years' (Horton 1946: 26; Van Kirk 1946: 169; Hutchinson 1947: 39–41). By 1946, Buddhist and Shintō sects were protesting SCAP bias for Christianity over other religions.

Just three weeks after the Occupation began CI&E and Civil Censorship Detachment (CCD) units implemented a ten-point Press Code to enforce two main prohibitions: criticism of SCAP and promoting Japanese militarism. Initially, Occupation censorship policy targeted Japanese militarist and feudal traits: right-wing nationalists, politicians and officials from the old regime, military uniforms, patriotic slogans and songs (Ball 1948: 188). Films and plays, which celebrated samurai warrior ethics, or which showed American violence to Japanese civilians, excessive Japanese ruins, or revolutionary aesthetics, were banned or burned (Editors, Asahi 1972: 135; Buruma 2007). Over time, any negative representation of the atomic bombs and its victims, the Emperor system, the new government, the Occupation, crimes of Occupiers, American historic racism, Jim Crow segregation policies or racialized discrimination towards Japanese or others became the object of the censors' interest

(Coughlin 1952: 47; Children of the Atomic Bomb Publishing Committee 1980: viii; Nishimura 1989: 1–21; Molasky 1999: 150).

Despite the legal recognition of indigenous values, freedom of expression and equality before the law (Article 14), this programme covered all means of communications and was vaguely worded to permit maximum discretion to the censors. Just as MacArthur had assumed a studied invisibility in public, even the censorship programme itself was censored to reduce visibility of the censors' imprint (Braw 1991: 47). Censors adopted a 'neither confirm nor deny' approach with impunity. Even foreign journalists who pointed out contradictions in Occupation policies and practices were not spared (i.e. Gordon Walker, *Christian Science Monitor*; Frank Hawley, *New York Times*; David Conde, *Reuters*).

Although it seemed that MacArthur's vision of spearheading Christianity in Asia by leading the Japanese people from 'legendary ritualism to the maturity of enlightened knowledge and truth' might come to fruition as Christian Socialist Katayama Tetsu became Prime Minister on 24 May 1947, joining the pro-Christian Rhee government (ROK), Chiang Kai-shek's Christian leadership (ROC), Christian President Manuel Roxas (Philippines) and the resumption of French rule in Vietnam, the first three would be deposed shortly and the last would be overturned in 1954 (MacArthur 1947: 763–64; Schaller 1985: 69). MacArthur's vision was not to be.

Occupied landscapes

From old Japan to 'Japan', the post-war order seemed to have had an aporetic short-circuit built into it. Unlike occupied Germany, which was divided into four zones by a coalition of Allied powers and which had fewer cultural differences with Americans, Japan was essentially a US-led SCAP-administered satrap. Hirohito remained 'the only head of state in modern times who stayed in office after his country's defeat' and he formally opened the first post-war session of parliament (Shillony 2005: 217–18). This democratic revolution from above was clearly contradictory. The occupiers lectured on democracy and equality while they ruled by fiat through a religious monarch and were immune to sanction. The legal code was founded upon discrimination, censorship and religious bias. The people were 'pacified' with bribes, their independence was incumbent upon being host to foreign military bases, and post-war peace rested in the cross-hairs of an escalating cold war. This outcome betrayed the 'republican and egalitarian' ideals that had mobilized the American people in a war against Japan. It also prevented the necessary conditions for a secular juridically sound democracy to take root in the new nation-state. At root lay the colonial perception of Japanese society requiring civilizing as 'human' and hence its re-making in the image of an exceptional American culture (Mears 1948: 6; Dower 1999: 211–12).

Occupation was a process of re-defining spatial interaction. People were purged of old values, structures and positions and were re-mobilized with new ones. Following the initial landing of 430,000 US troops from Hokkaido to Kyushu, communities were dispossessed of their lands, sometimes at gunpoint, to make way for 600 US bases and military installations. These included four of the five largest US bases on foreign soil (Yokosuka, Kadena, Misawa, Yokota), with several bases clustered around Tokyo (Zama, Yokota, Yokohama, Atsugi, Tachikawa) and many independent garrison towns throughout. In the cities and towns occupied by foreign forces, exclusive zones in trains, stations, utilities, buildings and theatres were arrogated to Allied personnel only, signed in English; 'Allied Personnel Only', 'Japanese Keep Out' (Koshiro 1999: 70–73; Takemae 2002: 75).

Yet, in the first months, despite initial prohibitions on inter-marriage it was less easy to control promiscuity. No sooner had the troops landed than brothels and clubs, and the associated sexual violence sprung up. The requisite 'six-inch' distance between Japanese women and American men was not strictly enforced. Miscegenated offspring were scorned on both sides, which was aggravated by the ban on Japanese immigration to the United States until 1948. For many of the 5 million repatriates from the former-colonies over the following years, the country was altered beyond recognition.

For all the preparation by OWI and OSS intelligence units, the occupiers seemed most ill-prepared for the sub-standard living conditions and infectious diseases, undernutrition or malnutrition in cities. Stringent wartime food rationing, a bad harvest from a harsh winter, a trade embargo and lack of fertilizer and labour, made hunger the most effective Pavlovian tool for instilling obedience to the new order (Aldous 2010: 236). Bedraggled people were quickly overwhelmed with desire for all things American as they watched healthy American GIs walk by, often with Japanese women.

It was not until 15 December 1945 that MacArthur took action to support agrarian farmers' food production. SCAP had continued nationwide rice rationing from 1942, and farmers were forced to hand over back taxes and rice crops and were prohibited travel to the city to prevent the spread of diseases. In response they hoarded supplies to sell on the black market (*yami-ichi*) to city dwellers. As the health of children diminished (and vulnerable groups), officials warned of 'disease and unrest' and its negative image for America (as a hegemonic power) (Harrison in Aldous 2010: 241–42).[10] By spring of 1946, food stocks had fallen below even wartime levels and brought public protests to the gates of the Imperial Palace (Food May Day, 19 May 1946).

SCAP could not compete with the socialistic appeal for millions of homeless and destitute people, who sought the right to strike for food and work and to oppose renewed militarism and the Emperor system. The liberation of political prisoners and introduction of civil rights brought a sharp rise in union membership in the industrial combines (3.7 million by early 1946). And the Labour Union Law of 1945, which permitted the right to organize, bargain and strike, was quickly changed in the Labour Relations Adjustment Law (1946) to bar the right of government workers to strike. A US Famine Emergency Committee (including ex-President Herbert Hoover) visited Japan in May 1946 and identified maldistribution, and agricultural products, fish and fertilizer as key issues. Despite the Great Vietnam Famine, world food shortages, and the needs of other Allied nations (i.e. Vietnam, South Korea, Okinawa, Taiwan, the Philippines, Burma), Japan became Washington's privileged beneficiary of US aid. Healthier Japanese bodies would undermine 'leftist' claims of a crisis and would equate with a successful US democratization programme.

While SCAP and the government blamed conditions in 1945–1946 on the former regime, from December 1946, MacArthur authorized stop-gap rationing and launched an emergency food distribution programme (Government's Appropriation for Relief in Occupied Areas – GARIOA) of rice, food products and commodities through the US Army PX stores and LARA (Licensed Agencies for Relief in Asia) (SCAP 1951: 136). Farmers (self-suppliers) were subsidized to stimulate food production and distribution, rations were given to Japanese workers and Japan was permitted to double its fishing zone and resume whaling. The US food aid plan was mediated as recovering 'the dignity of man from the economic bondage of centuries of feudal oppression by removing economic obstacles so as to strengthen democratic tendencies' (Gilmartin and Ladejinsky 1948: 315).

Together with purging 'political undesirables' in 4 January 1946, on 31 January 1947 MacArthur issued a threat to use military force on a 1 February general strike planned by communist and union organizers. MacArthur declared that he would not tolerate 'so deadly a social weapon in the present impoverished and emaciated condition of Japan' (MacArthur 1946: 756–57; Ball 1948: 187; Schaller 1985: 50).

In what was regarded as the cornerstone of the Occupation reform programme, SCAP issued directives for the Land Reform Law and the Agricultural Readjustment Law (1946–1947) (Ladejinsky and Berrigan 1949: 29; Ladejinsky 1959: 95–109). Touted an 'agrarian revolution', land that was redistributed (sold or leased at fixed prices) from 2.43 million to 4.3 million farming families should have effectively weakened the control of the political elite (Dore 1966 [1959]: 147). Tenant farmland was reduced to roughly 10 per cent (Hane 1982: 247). The reforms re-created an American small family-farm model of the 1930s in which rental profits were capped, inflated re-sale prices controlled and contractual relations established. But in the Council of Allied Powers, while Australian MacMahon Ball re-asserted that land reform was central to liberating peasants from 'agricultural feudalism' (Hewes 1955: 47), the Soviet representative General Derevyanko regarded the creation of a petit bourgeois class of private property owners as inhibiting significant re-distribution of wealth. Yoshida Shigeru claimed that any land reform programme interfered with private property rights.

In its confusion of egalitarianism and elitism, SCAP missed the chance to tap radical potential for democratic reform present in Japan since the 1880s (and further back to the sixteenth century (Bix 1986)) and ended up reproducing the contradictions already present in American capitalist liberalism. Initially, Occupation reforms were welcomed by progressive intellectuals and workers. Yet gains for tenant families over slightly larger land-owning families only placed greater control in large land-owners (top 3 per cent) and maintained structural poverty overall. Even Yoshida came to endorse the reforms as they had effectively quietened rural areas compared to the cities (Ward 1990: 86–112), especially after the land reforms were re-adjusted to abolish newly acquired tenant land rights for corporate expansion (as 'efficient producers') (Moore 1990: 103–4, 293–306).

The reverse course: Purges and nuclear escalation

The division of the Korean peninsula at the 38th parallel between US (UN) and Soviet occupations in August 1945, division of Germany, ongoing civil war in China, Viet Minh resistance to French rule in 1946, and frozen Soviet–West European relations, US relations with the socialist bloc had already become bitterly antagonistic.

At this point, the United States was still the sole possessor of atomic weapons. Nevertheless, Allied strategists perhaps exaggerated the potential for vastly superior conventional Soviet and Chinese forces to flood West Europe, Eurasia and East Asia. Truman called on Acheson, Lilienthal and Baruch to draw up the Baruch Plan for an international ban on the 'aggressive' use of atomic weapons. On 14 June 1946, Baruch presented what was the first step in nuclear arms control to the United Nations (UNAEC). It proposed to share with all nations the necessary technical information for the peaceful use of nuclear power, the elimination of all atomic weapons from national arsenals, and an effective safeguards system to protect states against breaches (US State Department, 14 July 1946). The Soviets rejected this plan as disingenuous, as the United States had cast itself as the sole supplier (and controller) of nuclear material and technology to the UNAEC, which the former contended was not a neutral body. Instead the Soviets proposed that the United States eliminate its own atomic weapons, before implementing controls and inspections. The Americans responded with Operation Crossroads (1 July 1946), as part of a series of hydrogen and atomic bomb tests on the Bikini Atoll in the Marshall Islands, which were now under American administrative control.

The 'Truman Doctrine' formulated in early February 1946 and announced on 12 March 1947 formalized the US confrontation with the 'global forces of communism'. Its public launch was forestalled until after MacArthur's failed bid for President in mid-1948. Dubbed the 'Reverse Course', the US–Japan relationship was re-set to 'sovereign equals, as difficult as it may be' (Dulles, San Francisco Peace Conference speech, 5 September 1951). In a mix of pragmatism and ideology by architects such as George Kennan, William Draper and James Forrestal, this course was neatly described as 'no longer covering our eyes with our left hand while our right is extending an imperialist paw' (Mailer 1998 [1948]: 321–22). Its justification seemed only to be reinforced with the 'loss of China' to Mao Zedong's Communist victory and formation of the PRC on 1 October 1949, and further underlined with the Soviet Union's first atomic bomb test (29 August 1949). In answer, Truman vowed that if the United States could not be the only atomic power it would be the strongest (US State Department 1976: 481–82).

In Occupied Japan, emergency measures may have averted mass starvation, but US SCAP personnel lived in a bubble surrounded by desperation and subterfuge. When Kennan visited Tokyo in 1947, he observed that 'everything of luxury had been monopolized and abused by the Americans' (Schaller 1985: 123). In 1948, bans on duty-free imports were lifted, and hyper-inflation rose between 50 and 365 per cent a year. Industrial materials were recycled and excess labour was laid off, leading to stoppages and strikes. The targeting of internal 'communist' or 'red' agents in Japan reached new heights.

In fact, widespread dissatisfaction with the betrayal of Constitutional rights and poor living and working conditions was demonstrated in union demands for collective bargaining, salary increases, political participation, fair treatment and free emigration for all Japanese people (including non-Japanese residents). Unionized producers at Yomiuri and Tōhō demonstrated against censorship and dismissals. The mass sit-ins at the Tōhō film studios (Free Film Workers Group, Zen-Ei) in August 1948 protested against the rehabilitation of the remaining unindicted war criminals at Sugamo Prison (Hirano 1992: 239). The Hanshin Dispute protested suppression of the curriculum at ethnic Korean schools ('red textbooks') for their critical portrayal of the Japanese colonial period in Korea and the Asia-Pacific War (Ikegami 2011). In December, twenty cabinet ministers including Kishi Nobusuke, mafia boss Kodama Yoshio, Kenpeitai (wartime police intelligence) officer and Yomiuri Shimbun boss Shōriki Matsutarō and chief biological and nuclear weapons scientist Ishii Shirō were released.

It is no secret that the CIA, US Information Service (USIS) and US Embassy (post 1952) collaborated with rehabilitated war criminals in Japan for their experience with 'communist' activists and labour unionists (Korean, Japanese). These collaborations played an important part in undermining the political left to ensure Japan did not choose neutralism or develop stronger ties with China or the Soviet Union, and helped to re-shape Japanese society's 'nuclear allergy'. Reminiscent of Kenpeitai tactics, it was again deemed necessary to monitor 'aka dani' (communists) in Japan. SCAP units compiled a blacklist of 'communist elements' for a massive 'red purge' (the Second Red Purge) in 1948–1949. Hundreds of labour leaders, Universities staff and workers in the public service suspected of communist sympathies were sacked or forced to resign. Communist newspapers were suspended or banned. MacArthur issued directives to lay-off more than 100,000 workers from the Japanese Government Railway (JGR). The JGR Union led by Shimoyama Sadanori representing the most vital transport link and most powerful union in the country strongly opposed such lay-offs. The SCAP G-2 (Counter Intelligence Corps) director General Charles Willoughby (aka Adolph Charles Weidenbach) and the Canon Agency (Jack Canon) contracted Kodama Yoshio to carry out 'wet work' with his yakuza affiliates. As 'communists', JGR Union members were framed for acts of sabotage such as train derailments in the Shimoyama, Mitaka and Matsukawa incidents of 1949 (Ōmori in Johnson 1972).[11] The Japanese Communist Party (JCP) leaders Nosaka Sanzō, Tokuda Kyuichi and Shiga Yoshio were accused of misusing citizen liberties and barred from their seats in the Diet. Moscow criticized the JCP's 'peaceful revolution' approach and in 1950 a less moderate course was adopted (Oguma 2002b: 281).

In 1949 and 1950, in a renewed sense of public anxiety 'many believed a revolution in Japan was inevitable' (Oguma 2002b: 342; Hajimu 2012: 555). Alongside the

McCarthyist push to stop the 'spread of [Communist] doctrine through cells in schools and colleges' in the United States (Waln 1950: 120) which escalated into Truman's 'Campaign for Truth' and 'charm offensive' (Congress-of-Cultural-Freedom operations) in 1950, with the departure of many US tactical troops to Korea, the US Army built up the Japanese National Peace Reserve as a paramilitary riot control and internal security force (JNPR – initially 75,000 in 1947, expanded to 360,000 as the National Safety Force and Ground Self Defense Force by 1954). This was paid for with MacArthur's 'M-Fund' of unofficial or unrecorded non-convertible sums of money and property gained from US aid surplus, confiscated property, the black market and Japanese military stockpiles (Johnson 1995).

Economic centralization

Together with the purge of 'anti-democratic' elements, several wartime economic structures were re-introduced. After completing economic reconstruction plans in Germany, in 1949, the US economic advisor Joseph Dodge moved to Tokyo and introduced the Dodge Line austerity measures. The Americans sought a stable, pro-American government in Japan to facilitate its rapid re-build (*fukkō*) as an industrial and economic powerhouse in Asia, along with those in West Germany and in West Europe, as bulwarks to communism. The 'Japan hands' and 'insiders' on the American Council on Japan (ACJ) recruited Kishi Nobusuke, who had served in Manchukuo as Minister of Munitions under the then Commander of the Kwantung Army General Tōjō Hideki, and served as Minister of Commerce and Economy in Tōjō's war cabinet. Kishi's experience would prove useful in concentrating power in the Ministry of International Trade and Finance (MITI) integrated with re-formed corporations. Top-level US officials also authorized financial and logistical support to Kishi and others to stymie the popular Japan Socialist Party in the early 1950s and 'control the government' (Schaller 1995; Weiner 2007: 116).

Following skirmishes along the border, when North Korean troops crossed the 38th parallel into South Korea on 25 June 1950, US forces as part of a multi-national UN 'policing' effort launched a counter-action from bases in Japan to begin the Korean War (1950–1953). Massive GHQ procurement contracts for military equipment, uniforms, ammunition, kit and vehicles, repairs and refitting and weapons, saw Japanese steel, automobile, munitions and manufacturing industries 'miraculously' bloom in 1950. Mitsubishi, for example, produced four-wheel drives for the JNPR modelled on the Willy's jeep with US technology and machine imports (French 2013: 11).

Described by Yoshida as 'heaven sent', the Korean War was a steroidal booster for the economy with a 40 per cent boost in Japanese exports in 1950, and roughly $2–4 billion in profits between 1950 and 1953 (Schaller 2004). This marked Japan's first post-war contribution to US military operations, as a launching platform for Curtis LeMay's area bombing campaign of North Korean cities (as Japan experienced five years earlier). It also started Japan's rapid economic growth era (*kōdo keizai seichōki*).

The Treaty of Peace between the United States and Japan was signed at the San Francisco Peace Conference on 8 September 1951. The 1951 San Francisco Treaty sustained existing tensions in the region as it did not consult the Soviet Union, PRC, ROC or North Korea while binding Japan, ROK, Okinawa and other Asia-Pacific nations to US strategic objectives (Ball 1952: 31–32). ROC was rendered 'neutral' territory.

In the *ANPO* Security Treaty (*Nichi-Bei Anzen Hoshō Jōyaku*), which came into effect on 28 April 1952,[12] Yoshida insisted that Japan be allowed to subsequently re-arm if it had the capacity or if peaceful international conditions transpired. But Dulles and Yoshida agreed that the 'objective conditions and prospects for Japan's defense and defense of the free world' necessitated continuing dependency on US protection (as a 'client state') in which Japan 'desired US presence and the US [was] willing to grant the request' (Igarashi 2000: 76).

The Truman Doctrine, confirmed in the San Francisco Treaty made Japan and Okinawa a keystone in a 'great crescent' island chain from Alaska to the Aleutians to Okinawa and the Philippines lining the Soviet and PRC coastlines. As a forward deployment platform and storehouse (or 'aircraft carrier'), the United States could operate its military base network and rotate troops and weapons (including nuclear) in its command of the Pacific Ocean (and its islands) as an 'American lake' (Schaller 1985; Dower 1986). As early as 1953, however, Vice President Richard Nixon declared that Article 9 was a mistake and should be repealed (Morris 1969: 292).

Yet there was significant business left unfinished by the Treaty that posed problems in the following decades. The Ryūkyūs and Ogasawara (Bonin) islands became a US garrison colony, for example, 'for as long as communism was a threat' (Nixon 1960; Cheng 2010). The Treaty secretly confirmed to place the M-Fund under bilateral control (Yoshida already had access) (Terashima 2010b). Article 19 released the United States from obligations to compensate *hibakusha*. *Zainichi* Koreans (residents of Korean origin who had been used in forced labour, conscription, or POWs in the colonial period) were rendered stateless in Japan, and lost military pensions or compensation. A lump sum payment by Japan to the South Korean government in 1952 failed to resolve these issues for these populations and both governments denied responsibility. Further, the Treaty lifted the ban on Japan's research and development of nuclear technology, albeit for 'peaceful purposes'.

Desite post-war rhetoric, a new type of war was being waged under the Pax Americana in the region. With stalemate on the Korean peninsula by late 1950, the United States triggered a chain of reciprocal nuclear 'tests' with its first thermonuclear explosion on 1 November 1952 ('Mike' as part of the 'Ivy' test series) on Eniwetok Atoll, on the Marshall Islands 'Pacific Proving Grounds' comprising five islands and twenty-nine atolls. The UK followed on Monte Bello Island in 1952.

In Eisenhower's inaugural address on 20 January 1953, he reiterated the Cold War binary by cathecting religion and atomic capacity in a prayer: 'forces of good and evil are massed and armed and opposed as rarely before in history. Freedom is pitted against slavery, lightness against dark'. In his 'New Look' doctrine, Eisenhower escalated Truman's nuclear first-strike doctrine from 1,000 strategic and tactical nuclear weapons to 20,000. These weapons were normalized at least in the minds of the US military strategists so that it was conceivable for MacArthur to threaten dropping roughly thirty atomic bombs and creating a cordon of radioactive cobalt in the Sea of Japan as the United States withdrew after the 27 July armistice (Cumings 1964). The Soviet Union responded in August 1953 ('Joe 4'), which the United States countered with a volley of 'shots' on Bikini Atoll from 1 March 1954.

On 8 December 1953, President Eisenhower had launched the 'Atoms for Peace' programme. Conditions were conducive for the 'hot sell' of nuclear technology and the 'Atoms for Peace' programme to promote peaceful nuclear energy generation provided the perfect alibi to conceal its 'dual-use' nature (Chernus 2002: 51). The US AEC, with a near monopoly, received contracts with thirty-seven nations and expressions of interest from fourteen others (Tanaka and Kuznick 2011). It also promised value-added atomic powered ships and aeroplanes.

In Japan by this point, atomic power was heralded as the 'third fire' for a 'second industrial revolution' to progress from post-war austerity (Takekawa 2012). While blaming Japan's defeat on over-reliance on foreign energy imports and superior American technology, a campaign led by Yomiuri boss Shōriki Matsutarō (who with Shibata Hidetoshi launched Nippon Television which broadcast the first professional all-Japan baseball game in 1953), de-coupled the 'bad' atom to sell the good, safe, clean, cost-effective and peaceful atom to the populace. Behind the scenes, Kishi and Shōriki gained Japanese government approval to secretly store atomic warheads in Okinawa and at the Atsugi airbase in return for US nuclear technology blueprints. Kishi's and Kissinger's protégé Nakasone Yasuhiro, freshly returned from Harvard and elected to the Diet, championed a sizeable nuclear research and development budget (235 million yen in March 1954). In December 1954, John Jay Hopkins, president of General Dynamics, suggested an 'Atomic Marshall Plan' for Japan (Zwigenburg 2012). Japan became one of the first and largest investors in US nuclear technology (General Electric). The first US commercial nuclear reactor came on-line in July 1955.

The US Basic War Plan was announced in March 1954. As a precursor to the Single Integrated Operational Plan (SIOP), this would deliver 'massive retaliation' on all 'industrial' targets ('Totality', 'Broiler', 'Halfmoon', 'Offtackle') in or near densely populated Soviet cities. The 'ancillary nuclear effects' of delayed radiation beyond the 'blast damage frame' were already known to planners, some of who called them 'bonus' kills. To prove that thermonuclear bombs could be credibly deployed on bombers, from 1 March 1954, the US AEC and Department of Defense (DoD) conducted the nuclear fission shot series called 'Operation Castle' on Bikini Atoll. This included a 15 megaton 'Castle Bravo shot' thermonuclear bomb (1,000 Hiroshima bombs) which produced a much larger yield than was apparently anticipated. In fact, there were adequate warnings of such a yield and sufficient information to indicate the fallout would blow over inhabited areas (Kunkle and Ristvet 2013: 58–80).

Along with 856 Japanese trawlers, indigenous Marshall islanders and surrounding marine-life, twenty-three fishermen of the *Daigo-Fukuryū maru* were showered with irradiated white ash from the exploded coral reef (Gusterson 1998: 63–72). After the ship returned to Yaizu port in Shizuoka prefecture in mid-March the entire crew were hospitalized with symptoms of acute radiation exposure including itching, swelling, alopecia, nausea, diarrhoea, and serious pigmentation and skin anomalies (Ōi and Kawamoto 1954; Lapp 1957: 38–56; Homei 2012). The radioman, Kuboyama Aikichi, died six months later, followed by thirteen others in months and years after.

Although the United States provided 'hush money' to the crew (roughly 300 million yen, or 2 million yen each), the visible effects of radiation exposure together with the distribution of the contaminated catch nationwide were enough to lift the decade-old veil of misinformation of radiation effects in Japan. To offset the public 'allergic' reaction, the US Operations Coordinating Board (OCB) and Japanese government organized the *Shinkotsu Maru* inspection tour by sixty-seven scientists and associated journalists of the affected areas around Bikini between April and July 1954. Radioactive contamination in the environment was found up to 500 km from the warning area, and radiation bioaccumulated in fish was found for months after. The levels were recognized as 'fairly high' but health danger was downplayed due to low levels of Strontium 90 (Leonard 2011: 112–14; Jacobs 2015: 77–96).

Petitions for the abolition of nuclear weapons by citizens of Tokyo and local governments led to the collection of 32 million signatures nationwide and 600 million worldwide by August 1954. Stout resistance from a nascent anti-nuclear movement, including leading anti-nuclear groups Gensuikin and Gensuikyō, converged in the first World Conference against Atomic and Hydrogen bombs in Hiroshima in August 1955.

In May 1954, the US National Security Council (NSC, Admiral Radford) also proposed to use nuclear weapons, alongside US naval, air and ground forces on the Viet Minh, who were routing the French at Dien Bien Phu (Gravel ed., 1: 465–72). With the Korean War armistice, Eisenhower had lifted Truman's 7th Fleet blockade in the Taiwan Straits to protect the ROC from PRC invasion (1953) and ratified the US-ROC mutual security treaty (1954). The United States then intervened in the first Offshore Islands dispute between late 1954 and early 1955 and promised 'massive retaliation' should the USSR or the non-nuclear PRC intervene (Huntington 1961: 79; Clarke 2008). The US government continued testing on the Marshall Islands until 1958 completing sixty-seven atmospheric nuclear weapons tests, forcing hundreds of Marshallese into exile and causing health damage to many more who were not evacuated. In 1963, a global campaign compelled the United States, the Soviet Union, and the United Kingdom to ratify the Limited Test Ban Treaty.

Food for weapons

By this time, Japan was already a 'tacit' participant in these US-led military operations, but in 1954 it entangled itself further. In the 'PL480 sales' legislated for in the Mutual Security Act, Japan received bulk US agricultural surplus in return for technical assistance to rebuild its 'war potential' (Borton 1957: 147; Tsurumi 1988: 85; Moen 1999). Using a counterparts' fund formula, officials from the US state department and Federation of Economic Organizations (*Keidanren*) used yen payments for US wheat imports ($50 million) for land acquisitions for extra US military installations. Japanese corporations such as Mitsubishi Heavy Industries (1.5 billion yen) were 'loaned' the remainder to manufacture weapons (F-86 fighter) that were then deployed by the United States and ROC (Bix 1972: 25).

It did not seem to matter whether Japanese rural households had ovens or not. Initiated in Mrs Douglas MacArthur's 'Food for Peace' programme, in nation-wide

UNIVERSITY OF WINCHESTER
LIBRARY

primary and secondary school lunches staple rice and soybean was replaced with powdered milk, white bread and meat-based stew (Ohno 1988: 18; Moore 1990: 256; Sams 1998: 67). The US Wheat Association even dispatched a fleet of kitchen buses to show how to use bleached, white flour to bake (Hammond and Ruyak 2008 [1990]: 46–48). Whether to 'stamp out' social revolution or undermine Japan's food sovereignty, US food surplus was an early means to boost Japan's economy and its remilitarization.

The Liberal Democratic Party (LDP) was founded on 15 November 1955. This was in the same month the Atomic Energy Basic Law was passed and the Yomiuri co-sponsored Atoms for Peace exhibit opened. In this '1955 system', the US–Japan Atomic Energy Agreement of December 1955 committed to the Japanese Atomic Energy Commission (JAEC) opening on 1 January 1956 and Agency for Industrial Science and Technology (AIST). Shōriki was appointed Japan's first nuclear patriarch, assuming Minister of Atomic Energy, chair of the JAEC and head of AIST.

Japan also made its first significant gesture in international politics since defeat with a delegation to the Bandung Conference, Indonesia (17–24 April 1955), attended by twenty-nine newly independent Asian and African nations. As US proxy, they sought to recover some former colonial markets as economic markets (Koshiro 2003: 197). On the side of the 'free nations', Japan assumed its role as mediator ('bridge') between the West and Asia, arguing against an Afro-Asian bloc and for a broader global view. Some Japan Socialist Party (JSP) members dissented by indicating their support for PRC inclusion.

It was Kishi's LDP victory in 1957, however, that consolidated Japan's future as a pro-nuclear, pro-American bulwark in Asia. Kishi and Ambassador Douglas MacArthur II negotiated significant revisions to the 1951 Security Treaty to include air, naval, repair, and logistic facilities, 'defensive' weapons upgrades and the conveyance of nuclear weapons through Japanese territory to Okinawa. In the Diet, Kishi also argued that it was not unconstitutional ('not expressly prohibited') for Japan to acquire tactical nuclear weapons if they were deemed necessary for self-defence (i.e. communist 'human sea' tactics) (Office of Intelligence Research 1957: 2).

Coinciding with the foundation of the UN International Atomic Energy Association (IAEA) in 1957, Japan announced the completion of its first experimental research reactor (British Magnox). The IAEA, as a technopolitical instrument, enabled the United States greater control over the flow of uranium processing and nuclear technologies. Following the Soviet's pioneering Sputnik launch in October, the United States sought to intensify its nuclear deterrence capacity and share the costs of military basing across a US–Japan–ROK tripartite treaty in East Asia (Lee 2009; Lee 2013: 183–92). The United States reduced its troop numbers in ROK in January 1958, but in August, the Second Offshore Crisis between the PRC and ROC (and the United States) erupted over the ROC installations on the Matsu and Kinmen Island groups (Tachen, Yijiangshan, Quemoy, Hainan). Again, the United States threatened the PRC with 20–30 nuclear weapons (Lee 2009).

This conflict only galvanized Kishi and Nixon in concluding the Treaty of Mutual Cooperation and Security of 1960. The Status of Forces Agreement (SOFA, 1960) permitted roughly 40,000 US military personnel (with 50,000 civilians and dependents) to occupy bases and installations anywhere in Japan without Diet approval. This continued the policy built into the San Francisco Security Treaty that that the United States could maintain as much force as it wanted, anywhere it wanted for as long as it wanted (Dulles to Johnson based on MacArthur's memo in June 1950) (Sugita 2004: 76). Article 5 stipulated that each party 'would act to meet the common danger in accordance with its constitutional provisions and processes'. Nixon also agreed to relinquish control of the M-Fund to Kishi, in return for continuing Japanese contributions to it (Schlei 1995), and promised to return Okinawa to Japan by 1972, possibly in return for Japan's support for his presidential bid. This led to further agreement, as per a private discussion between Secretary of State Dean Rusk and Foreign Minister Kosaka Zentarō 4 November 1961, to the conveyance and storage of Mace nuclear missiles at Yomitan Missile Launch Control Centre, Okinawa (Schlei 1995; Wampler 2009; Niihara in Mitchell 2012; Ota 2015). Okinawa's strategic importance in deterring the PRC from invading Taiwan and in projecting power into PRC and Soviet territory (or, into Japan) meant that Okinawans remained hostages to the shifting greater game.

UNIVERSITY OF WINCHESTER
LIBRARY

Occupied Bodies: Aesthetic
Responses in New Japan

The defeat of Japan ensured that Japanese wartime atrocities were opened to a degree of opprobrium that Allied atrocities committed during the Second World War were not. This created a notable difference in post-war discourse. Japanese 'thinking from the wounds' was conspicuously absent in the victors' narratives. As discussed so far, political conditions made it difficult to air critiques of the systemic causes of Japan's colonial occupation of East Asia and its war with Western powers in the Asia-Pacific. The SCAP censorship and re-education programmes implemented with the assistance of the Japanese government were intended to re-orient public consciousness through behavioural modelling, active proscription and controlled dissemination of information. It sought to internalize taboos (self-censorship) on particular facts, issues and perspectives to facilitate consensus for liberal democratic ideology (see Orwell 2000). By the Reverse Course of mid-1948, an already punitive vetting programme became even sharper and more widespread.

The CI&E Educational Film Unit (EFU) of the Motion Pictures and Theatrical Branch (MPTB) clearly understood the utility of film as a seminary mode of indoctrination. As Edward Bernays had identified in the motion picture in 1928:

> The greatest unconscious carrier of propaganda in the world to-day ... The motion picture can standardize the ideas and, habits of a nation ... made to meet market demands, they reflect, emphasize and even exaggerate broad popular tendencies rather than stimulate new ideas and opinions ... As the newspaper seeks to purvey news, it seeks to purvey entertainment. (Bernays and Miller 2005 [1928]: 166)

The CI&E EFU imported and commissioned over 300 re-education films to promote science and productivity; utopian visions of American society free of class, racial and gender inequalities; the United States as the leader of Western civilization and unifier of the free world (against Communism) (Maier 1977: 607–32; Tsuchiya 2002: 196, 204, 208). Films such as *The National Police Reserve* and *How to Hold a Meeting* were instructional manuals for democratic behaviour and moral conduct (Tsuchiya 2002: 202). Embedded in these films were the Occupier's desired encodings intended for mainstream consumption. For example, as consistent with OWI and OSS manuals, war-fatigued audiences were shown scenes of comfortable affluence and civilized decency in American middle-class multi-racial society, implanting material envy, desire and respect for such lifestyles. A consistent pattern showed white male authority figures assisted by white professional women instructing or helping non-white people in need. The message: material affluence will come to a de-politicized and harmonious non-white nation that follows the US liberal democratic model.

Neo-realist post-war Japanese films, by contrast, produced and released during the Occupation by directors such as Kobayashi Masaki, Taniguchi Senkichi, Imai Tadashi, Sekigawa Hideo, Shindō Kaneto and Kurosawa Akira were more self-conscious. Yoshida Kijū, one of Japan's leading new wave directors wrote,

> [t]he snow white walls, the thick garden lawns, chandeliers, electric refrigerators, and the abundance of food and canned goods – all of these things that engendered a comfortable daily life, it was the ultimate dream and as such I was happy. I did not just watch these films; inevitably, I envied the world the films reflected. (Yoshida 1971: 21)

Kamei Fumio, a documentary filmmaker, was critical of Japanese nationalism and the false democracy of the Occupation. Kamei's perspective, honed through experiences of the war in China, focused on common vernaculars of haiku, folk stories, and soldiers' war stories. After the 1937 invasion, the Tōhō Culture Ministry sent Kamei to make official propaganda documentaries for military and domestic audiences in Japan. With a local Chinese cinematographer, Kamei produced *Shanghai – Record of Incidents in China* (77 min, 1938) in which he subverted the propaganda format. In minimizing the number of battle scenes, focusing on slower life in the barracks, and juxtaposing officers proudly talking strategy over operational maps in the sheltered International Settlement with Shanghai's ruins, Kamei complicated the triumphant narrative. He showed maudlin battlefields, war refugees, a bullet-punctured helmet rolling in a ditch, rows of fresh graves with Japanese names, and long close-ups of hostile Chinese people and confused Chinese children being offered candy and donkeyrides by Japanese soldiers. Some military officers were offended by *Shanghai* and Kamei was placed under surveillance. In his next film *Kobayashi Issa*, Kamei satirized the drudgery of peasant farmer emigration to settle in the frontier colonies of Manchukuo. Kamei was finally imprisoned in October 1941 for his film *Fighting Soldiers* (*Tatakau Heishi*), which was banned under the Peace Preservation Law.

After defeat, when Makino Masahiro's *Sophisticated Wanderer* (1946) was censored for its nationalist symbology (Mt. Fuji), Kamei saw the chance to directly critique the wartime system. Commissioned by the CI&E chief David Conde, Kamei's newsreel montage *Japan's Tragedy* (Iwasaki Akira (prod.), 1946), initially titled *The Dark Period*, called for the trial of those responsible for driving the Japanese people into Imperial wars of aggression. The film named Baron Tanaka Giichi for the Japanese decision to invade China, the Emperor for starting the war with the United States and the war cabinet for bringing suffering to ordinary Japanese people (political prisoners, villagers, urban workers, children), POWs, slave labour (labourers, 'comfort women') and the victims of mass slaughter. Referring to the Potsdam Declaration, the film urged its audience not to be deceived again by the 'nice words' of the militarists and ruling class who 'changed their fronts' (*tenkō*) in support of the new government policies (Hirano 1992: 130). Kamei placed responsibility for the Asia-Pacific War squarely on the shoulders of the emperor and the capitalist Imperial system.

When the Civil Censorship Detachment (CCD) censors brought *Japan's Tragedy* to the attention of Yoshida Shigeru, it became one of the only known films to have been banned outright during the Occupation. Its permission for release was withdrawn and copies and negatives were confiscated. Having been political prisoners both Kamei and Iwasaki Akira expressed their surprise at the ban (Hirano 1992: 102).

The ban set an example for how the war and war responsibility was to be publicly remembered in new Japan. It also exposed the Occupiers' agenda: no Marxist analysis; no critique of the Emperor; no incitement of political dissent (Hirano 1992: 125–36). In Kamei's *Between War and Peace* (1947, (co-dir.) Yamamoto Satsuo), a Japanese POW who is treated favourably by Chinese captors recognizes the wrongs of Japanese militarism. Although this was released and despite a national audience of 10 million SCAP censors listed it as 'communist-leaning' and in the 1948 purge, Conde's support for Kamei and Iwasaki led to his replacement by Lt. Col. Donald R. Nugent, also a former OWI officer and a former historian and teacher in Japan.

SCAP censors filtered many commercial film imports into Japan with a binarized lens of 'communist' or 'democratic' alignment. Films considered 'communist' leaning included the *Enemy of the People, Those Who Create Tomorrow, As Long as I Live, Eleven High School Girls, The Day Our Lives Shine, The Morning of the Osone Family, Amerikan shakutori* (American caterpillar), *Citizen Kane* and *The Grapes of Wrath.* 'Democratic' films included *The Big Lie, Open City, The Bicycle Thief, Gone with the Wind, Bitter Rice, Germany Year Zero* and *Can-Can Girls of Ginza* (Hirano 1992: 244–46). Films with individualist, anti-unionist and/or spiritual messages were rewarded. Ichikawa Kon's 'anti-war' film *The Burmese Harp* (1956), for example, was highly acclaimed and Ichikawa was later awarded the film rights to the 1964 Tokyo Olympics (Quandt 2001: 133).

Even as a general anti-war message was encouraged, the CI&E censors showed particular sensitivity for references to the atomic bomb and the US atomic research programme. The Hiroshima Peace Memorial cenotaph, for example, carries the epitaph '*Anraka ni nemutte kudasai ayamachi ha kurikae shimasenu kara*' ('Please rest in peace, for the error shall not be repeated'). This was translated as 'Let all the souls here rest in peace for we shall not repeat the evil'.[1] An additional plaque added on 3 November 1983 clarified that 'we' referred to 'all humanity' and the 'error' was the 'evil of war'. In Nagasaki, a stone statue of a child holding an atomic bomb was altered to include an engraving of '$E = MC^2$' at its base. In the universal scientific humanism of these statues, lies the unresolved politics of responsibility left over from Occupation.

The CI&E also required that in Shindō Kaneto's *Children of Hiroshima* (*Genbaku no Ko*, 1952) and Sekigawa Hideo's *Hiroshima* (1953) the atomic bombs be shown as precipitating Japan's defeat; the denunciation of Japan's role in the war; and that Hiroshima symbolize peace. Shindō's directorial note reflected these conditions:

> The atomic bomb was given as a revelation of science to the Japanese, who had preferred savageness, fanaticism and an intolerant Japanese spirit to freedom, culture and science. (Hirano 1992: 61–62)

Children of Hiroshima was an adaptation of essays by 100 children who ranged between five and fifteen in 1945. The story tells of Takako who encounters victims on her visit to her hometown (*furusato*) in the aftermath. The opening montage established the iconographic language that came to signify 'Hiroshima': a busy urban-scape, a ticking clock nearing 8.15 am, the shadow of a 'vapourized' body on outdoor steps, an empty playground. Takako discovers her father's work colleague Iwakichi, who is blind and begging near a well-known bridge at Kokutaiji (near Hiroshima). She learns that Tarō, Iwakichi's grandson and sole surviving relative, has been sent to an orphanage she then visits. There Takako discovers several other orphans and becomes a compassionate witness to the absence and loss, and to a surviving remainder as a symbol of hope after the cataclysm.

This pattern can also be found in *Kimi no Na ha* (NHK, 1952), an enormously popular radio drama. Set around Sukiya Bridge in Tokyo where 'war remainder' gathered – prostitutes, orphans, hawkers, former soldiers, labourers, gangsters, salvationist preachers – the female protagonist refuses to remove her shelter-hood (a civilian item distributed for use in air-raids to protect against fire) after losing her relatives who died in the Great Tokyo Air Raid of 9–10 March 1945. She is 'saved' by a wholesome romance with a young man she met in a shelter. The romance blossoms together with the demolition of the bridge. In the transition from ruin and loss to an optimistic future the protagonists' traumatic fixations are literally buried beneath reconstruction as her prospects flourish. And yet, the erasure of mnemonic triggers only made such memories more spectral, creating the conditions for their re-visitation.

Lt. Col. Daniel A. McGovern of the USSBS, who studied the British aerial bombing effects in Germany, was ordered by the USAF to shoot 35 mm colour film of 20 Japanese cities in 1945–1946. In September 1945, USAF and Japanese film units shot several hours of film of the atomic aftermath in Hiroshima and Nagasaki. In the USAF unit of eleven were Kurosawa's cinematographer Harry Mimura and Herbert Sussan (Mitchell 1983; Sussan 1983: 10–15; Nornes 2003: 244, fn. 47; Mitchell 2005). A Japanese unit (Nippon Eigasha, Itō Sueo (dir.), Iwasaki Akira (prod.)) also produced nineteen black-and-white reels with notes and photos. It was then ordered to relinquish it to US officers for 'scientific research' and desist from further filming (24 October 1945). The footage was classified 'Secret' and stored in the United States for twenty years.

McGovern's colour footage revealed life on the ground in Hiroshima, including shadows of vapourized civilians and structures inscribed in walls, steps and bridges and bewildered people in the flattened landscape. Survivors were shown lying on the floors of a hospital. They dutifully displayed their lesions, skin-grafts and hair loss to the camera. A Japanese doctor traced the red scars covering several patients' bodies, then removed his shirt to reveal his own wounds (Mitchell 2005). This methodical documentation was not only for scientific research. Its objectifying gaze also issued 'a warning to the world' of American power.

McGovern's unit also staged scenes. In 'Hiroshima Way of Life' for example (Roll 219, USAF: 22 March–8 April 1946), a young white Catholic priest steps out from beneath the balcony of a ruined church (likely to be Our Lady of the Assumption) holding the hands of several small Japanese children (possibly orphans). As he removes his hat and kneels, he looks to the sky. The camera pans from the remaining walls of the church to a close-up on a little boy hiding in the priest's habit, followed by a mid-shot of perplexed children and the priest. Scenes follow of new temporary wooden houses, people cleaning graves and praying at a shrine filled with cremation boxes, children picking over rubble, women and men preparing soil, planting rice, hanging seaweed and washing pots in the river and soldiers collecting scrap.

Such scenography was consistent with SCAP policy and its Christian paternalism in 1946. Yet underlying this scientific theatre was the fact that US military command was already cognizant of the damaging health effects of radiation exposure. On 30 October 1943 (declassified 5 June 1974), three scientists in a subgroup of the S-1 Committee on 'Use of radioactive materials as military weapons' (Drs James Conant, A. H. Compton, H. C. Urey) wrote to Brigadier General Groves about the weaponization of uranium products collected from nuclear pile rods. They stated:

> As a gas warfare instrument the [radioactive] material would be ground into particles of microscopic size to form dust and smoke and distributed by a ground-fired projectile, land vehicles, or aerial bombs. In this form it would be inhaled by personnel. The amount necessary to cause death to a person inhaling the material is extremely small. It has been estimated that one millionth of a gram accumulating in a person's body would be fatal. There are no known methods of treatment for such a casualty. (Conant et al. 'Groves memo', 1943)

It was known by the 1930s from physicians' reports on radium exposure, dust particles and radon gases in miners that powderized coal laced with uranium produced pulmonary diseases. Dr Herman Müller's 1927–1928 studies on the mutagenic and generational effects of X-rays (Drosophila fly) also led to the formation of the International Commission for Radiological Protection (ICRP) in 1928 to establish limits for occupational exposure (for physicists and radiologists).

Between 1939 and 1941, Manhattan Project scientists knew that 'fission products' emit photon and particulate radiation and that when ingested had carcinogenic effects (they used the calcium analogue of radio-strontium – Sr 89, Sr 90). Prior to the concept of an atomic bomb, this material was 'weaponized' for dispersal as a 'poison gas' and contamination of enemy food and water supplies. The idea was to make areas (airports, railroad yards, etc.) uninhabitable and cause casualties in enemy military and civilian populations. US troops and civilians would be radio-protected with potassium, iodine, vitamin D and calcium concentrates.

The US-led studies of *hibakusha* by the Atomic Bomb Casualty Commission (ABCC) (1946–1956) provided the basis for the international formula for radiation exposure and safety standards. Based on acute and short-lived external gamma exposure to a thirty-year-old male ('radiation man') from a Hiroshima-type bomb within a 2 km blast radius, the US AEC calculated the risk of fatality from cancer in proportion to the dose received (linear no threshold model). Their aim was to calculate exposure effects on military personnel, with particular concern for genetic mutation as opposed to disease. The dose exposure limit was set at 100 mSv/year.[2] Anything below was deemed negligible to human health. The ICRP adopted this model as the international standard for radiation exposure and safety (Hecht 2012: 185).

This calculation did not allow distinctions in gender, age, physiological differences, diet, period of exposure and ecological particularities in distribution. It also disregarded all non-cancerous, non-genetic or non-fatal illnesses as radiation-induced (i.e. auto-immune disease, fertility impairment or birth defects or combination with other carcinogens) (Satō and Kodaira 1996: 226; Nakamura 2006: 47).

As early as two weeks after the Hiroshima bomb, civilians and medical scientists already knew that people were sickened from radiation poisoning beyond its heat and light effects (Burchett 1945). As the health of Allied servicemen, Japanese workers and residents living in and near the bombed areas including beyond the city limits declined (i.e. low white and red blood corpuscles), General Groves' expressed concern was for the potential damage to the US public image in its war with communism (Groves to Lt. Col. Rea, 'Memo of telephone conversation', 25 August 1945).

The suppression of the Nichi-Ei and USAF film, the SCAP prohibition on the circulation of atomic bomb-related images and information on effects (*kōka*) and the secrecy around the ABCC studies was to protect the ABCC *in situ* 'research without treatment' programme on the effects of bomb-induced injuries and chronic and acute radiation sickness.

One reason was to take advantage of the optimal conditions for the collection of reliable A-bomb data in 'real live' (human) conditions (Lindee 1994: 117–18). This included studies of 77,000 newborns between 1948 and 1954 (almost 100 per cent of newborns in Hiroshima) and thousands of tissue samples and medical records including 850 preserved body organs and parts from newborns and babies sent to the US Armed Forces Institute of Pathology (AFIP) (Takahashi 23 April 2012). Further, if prior knowledge of the etiology of radiation exposure was exposed, it would destabilize the strategic use-value of Japan as a host for US bases and an economic powerhouse for US ambitions. Finally, as introduced earlier, the criminalization of the use of atomic bombs as in breach of the Geneva Conventions for bio-chemical and indiscriminate and disproportional aerial bombing (aka atomic or nuclear) (Spaight 1924: 276) would challenge the legitimacy of the US claim to hegemony in the Asia-Pacific and its ongoing nuclear weapons programme in its contest with 'global communism'.

American and Japanese popular atomic representations

During the cognitive transformation of suffering into optimism through CI&E and CCD proscriptive censorship, the US government also re-narrated 'the bomb' for the American population. In the weeks following August 1945, although no other country had an atomic bomb, American commentators for the *New York Times*, *Life* and the *Chicago Tribune* depicted vivid scenarios in which US cities were instantly incinerated and reduced to rubble by atomic detonations. In 'Japan's fate' they grasped not the threat the US government posed to others but the potential of Americans becoming such victims (Easlea 1983: 120; Boyer 1985: 14).

As the quintessential American bomb testimonial, John Hersey's best-selling studiously objective account in the *New Yorker* in August 1946 derived lived experiences of the atomic bombs from six interviews with *hibakusha*. Hersey's unimposing and sparse style in describing the horrific destruction attracted many letters and reviews. Hersey wrote, for example,

> a great number sat and lay on the pavement, vomited, waited for death, and died... on some undressed bodies, the burns had made patterns... the shapes of flowers they had had on their kimonos ... some tried to [take her by the hands but] her skin slipped off in huge, glove-like pieces... Their faces were wholly burned, their eye sockets were hollow, the fluid from their melted eyes had run down their cheeks (they must have had their faces upturned when the bomb went off; perhaps they were anti-aircraft personnel). (Hersey 2009 [1946]: 3, 68)

Critics Dwight MacDonald called Hersey's style 'antiseptic' and Mary McCarthy called it 'insipid falsification of the truth of atomic warfare', while Ruth Benedict praised its 'calm restraint' as a reflection of the bomb's 'destructive power'. Benedict essentialized Japanese 'patient fortitude' as passivity 'inculcated over centuries' that she likened to being 'shepherd-less sheep' (Boyer 1985: 209). The focus on style and Japanese-ness in response to Hersey's essay allowed the readers to focus on something other than the confusing guilt such an event inspired.

Another response was to universalize the bomb as a phenomenon confronting 'mankind'. One particular film entitled *The Beginning or the End* (1947), for example, made in collaboration with the 'War Department and the White House', followed a movie star and an atomic scientist who once were childhood sweethearts and who were employed on the Manhattan Project. They propose to make a movie on Hiroshima and Nagasaki to 'impress upon the public, the horrors of atomic warfare and the vulnerability of civilization to attack by other countries [that] could produce atomic bombs' (Hershberg 1995: 289). In the film notes the editor wrote that this was 'the timeless moment that gives all of us a chance to prove that human beings are made in the image and likeness of God' (Editor, *The Beginning or the End*, 1947).

Inculcating the American public with images of an atomic sublime seemed to remove any responsibility and transform the bomb into a *force majeure*. As a paranoid inversion of repressed guilt fuelled by a fear of revenge, this timely narrative designed for popular consumption appeared to invoke an eschatological 'end time'. 'Moral pathology' and limited self-introspection combined with aggravated nationalism conditioned this American reception of the bomb so as to preserve the nation's self-image of a humane, pragmatic and just people. Recognition of the crime of Hiroshima and Nagasaki seemed to be beyond most US filmmakers at the time.

In 1945 RCA, Westinghouse, GE, Motorola and others introduced mass-produced television sets onto the American market (Hilgartner et al. 1983: 72). For Operation Crossroads (1 July 1946), four television transmitters and 750 cameras were set up by Joint Task Force One to stage the event for international public consumption. This broadcast spectacle integrated mass communication with US military-scientific capacity to deliver devastation on hundreds of warships and planes and show its effects (or lack thereof, on goats, pigs, rats and humans many of whom were without protective clothing) at various stages from zero point (Saffer and Kelly 1983: 205–10).

In 1948–1951, 250,000 to 500,000 servicemen were exposed in one hundred atomic tests in the Nevada desert. Due to ongoing public concern, the first live coverage on 22 April 1952 of the AEC Tumbler Snapper test series was to 'prove' a 'safe threshold' for radioactive fallout while demonstrating AEC procedures in home bomb shelters and Ground-observer Corps security against the communist menace (Barnouw 1978: 162). With live tests shown in *Yucca Flat* following daytime shows like *I love Lucy*, the bomb was banalized while showing methods to survive a nuclear war. With accelerated testing under Eisenhower, to keep the public confused about 'fission and fusion' the AEC publicity omitted terms like 'thermonuclear', 'fusion' and 'hydrogen' (Freeman 1981: 294). Public anxieties were mocked in films like *The Atomic Kid* (1954) and sci-fi films like *Them!* (1954) (Evans 1998: 64). The underlying mission objective was to demonstrate that a nuclear war could be won.

While normalizing the bomb, attempts to re-gain moral superiority over the American use of the atomic bombs continued. In the Hiroshima Maidens project a short home-stay charity tour of twenty-five young *hibakusha* women to middle-class American homes in 1955–1956 was organized by Norman Cousins (New York Quaker) and Reverend Tanimoto from Hiroshima. The Maidens received reconstructive surgery in New York City hospitals. While ordinary Americans could demonstrate moral superiority in their kind treatment of the stigmatized *hibakusha* from Japan and contribute revenue for orphans in Japan (Barker 1986), the majority of *hibakusha* were not privy to such generosity (Von Eschen 1997: 125–28) and compassion and surgery could not erase an act of indiscriminate killing and maiming that would last for generations.

As portions of the American middle-class negotiated the US use of the atomic bombs through literary accounts, televised spectacles and moral salves, *Gojira* (Honda Ishirō (dir.), 3 November 1954), allegorized in the figure of a prehistoric monster (or, *kaijū* as a combination of 'gorilla' and 'whale') the mass pain experienced in aerial and atomic bombings of Japan (Honda was a repatriated POW from China who witnessed the damage to Hiroshima). It also followed after the *Daigo Fukuryū-maru* incident and was released amid mass anti-nuclear protests in Japan. On board a fishing boat in the daily routine of fishermen at sea, the boat suddenly bursts into flame, killing the sailors, followed by an H-bomb detonation. A reptile emerges from the sea pinging with radiation. It terrorizes small towns before moving to Tokyo, engulfing the streets in flames. Just before they are burnt alive, a tearful woman repeats to her two children that they will see their father soon. A doctor takes Geiger counter readings of small children who are mortally irradiated. In the context of nuclear weapons proliferation, the authority figures in the film are preoccupied with what to do about Gojira – whether to destroy, restrain, or simply endure it.

As a figurative atomic bomb, Gojira (re-)visited mnemonic sites of destruction. Gojira's thickened scaly hide invokes the disfigurement of *hibakusha* and burnt-out cities (*yakeato*) of the war, and provides the melancholic subject with the option to sublimate loss into a proliferation of signs (Kristeva 1989: 202). Morphing from an alien enemy to be feared, Gojira becomes a metonymic warning to humans of nuclear apocalypse (Igarashi 2000: 121; Kerner in Franko 2007: 102–24).

Yet, Gojira's demented cries and stomping feet were not indiscriminate. The Imperial palace or Yasukuni Shrine, for example, remained preserved thus avoiding severance between sovereign and the Imperial nation's sacrificial sons (*eirei*). While in sync with the anti-nuclear weapons movement of 1954–1955 and consistent with the brutal wartime realities in Japan's destroyed cities (Merchant 2013), this popular monster movie performed regeneration through purgative healing.

Over roughly thirty films produced in Japan since 1954, Gojira's anti-nuclear and *hibakusha* perspectives would be hollowed out. Instead, like a trickster, Gojira, in the high-stakes of international relations of the time, shifted to a guardian deity of prosperity and even power. A re-edited US version of *Godzilla: King of the Monsters!* (Terry Morse and Honda Ishirō (dir.), 1956) gave Godzilla a science-fiction gloss in which an American reporter in Tokyo followed Japanese technocrats during a Cold War stand-off. This between-nuclear-titans theme continued in eight more Godzilla films throughout the 1960s and continued until the end of the century. This theme was repeated in other films such as Matsubayashi Shūei's *The Great World War* (1961) which concluded that human flaws amid increasing techno-scientific development would be the source of nuclear cataclysm (Dixon 2003: 107).

Kurosawa's *A Record of a Living Being* (1955) depicted the social pressures involved in Japan's position. Nakajima Kiichi, an ageing Japanese industrialist grows obsessed with the dangers of nuclear war between the superpowers. He decides to sell his foundry and move his family to Brazil. Nakajima's sons do not share his concerns and file an injunction to have their father committed. When Nakajima realizes that not even Brazil would be spared from radioactive fallout he becomes erratic and is institutionalized. Dr. Harada, a judge on the panel for Nakajima's trial, having read 'The Ash of Death' (*shi no hai*), wonders whether Nakajima might be sane after all. *Record* was first shown in Berlin (1961) and New York (1963) and only received a theatrical release in the United States in 1967. The slow take-up in the United States suggested the level of concern for public anxiety concerning nuclear tensions, which came to a head in the Cuban Missile Crisis (October 1962). In Japan, in 1961, Donald Richie, the US soldier turned cultural commentator, adopted Benedict's line that 'polemic-filled' social-realist response in film to nuclear weapons was 'essentially alien' to the 'authentic Japanese attitude toward death and disaster'. He claimed that the Japanese response to 'Hiroshima' was better explained in the concept of impermanence (*mujō*) and *mono no aware*; the 'awareness of evanescence and the resulting lamentation' in recognition of life's eternal flux (Richie in Broderick 1996: 22–23, 28; Richie 2009).

By 1998, in *Godzilla: Size Does Matter* (Roland Emmerich (dir./co-scr.)), any trace of social protest, collective memorialization or accurate radiation effects was evacuated from the 'Godzilla'-brand. Trumpeting 'new' geopolitical dimensions, powerful special-effects and US military prowess, the indestructible mutant reptile emerges in New York harbour after French nuclear testing only to be dispatched by a team of radiation scientists and US military personnel.

The works of artists such as Iri and Toshi Maruki and writers such as Ōta Yōko (*City of Corpses*) and Hara Tamiki (*Summer Flowers*) remained, however, as testament. Committed to mediating the actual suffering of wartime violence to avoid their repetition, these independent thinkers overcame censorship to reach wide audiences. Maruki Toshi's description is worth quoting at length.

> People lost their feet or their hands. Their skin was burned and coming off. So they covered themselves with Mercurochrome and were red. When that ran out, they put on a white salve. Their eyelids and lips were like raw meat. Their eyes were all swollen and they couldn't see. They were called ghosts ... They couldn't lower their hands because it hurt too much, so they held them out from the body. They walked in a line for two or three kilometres to where twisted houses were still standing. In the outskirts, people were afraid of the victims ... So the victims walked farther and farther until they lost strength and collapsed. After the bomb, winds swept dust and ash into the sky. Then black rain fell. If we were wearing white shirts, they turned black. (Suzuki and Ōiwa 1996: 14)

This moment marked the induction of a new human taxonomy that was structurally bound to an atomic mode of production. Humans instantly vapourized at the bomb's epicentre, and barely upright 'semi-humans' further away destabilized the meaning of 'human' (Treat 1996: 30; Braw in Hein and Selden 1997: 155–72). Ōe Kenzaburō recognized that '[t]he most terrifying monster lurking in the darkness of Hiroshima is precisely the possibility that man might become no longer human' (Ōe 1996: 182), while others like Ōta Yōko, ironically, perceived in *hibakusha* a sort of evolutionary order: 'perhaps those who survived were like some kind of insect, were not human' (Minear 1990: 252).

As the chronicler of *hibakusha* Hayashi Kyōko also described in her short story about 'Takako', a co-worker in a wartime arms factory in Urakami, Nagasaki, many *hibakusha* suffering from acute radiation poisoning adopted self-help remedies as they lacked sufficient information. As those with no apparent wounds began to die suddenly, these *hibakusha* were forced to use self-help remedies against 'the light'. Takako dressed her burns with a mixture of newspaper ash and sesame oil while she lived under a room-size mosquito net to prevent flies from laying eggs in her wounds. They construed the A-bomb as a malicious demon that would return relentlessly over months and years. This uncertainty around morbidity and mortality from radiation exposure in the slow erosion of the *hibakusha's* physical condition created a liminal suspension in which the familiar boundaries between life and death became unstable.

As Ōta described, 'now subject, now object, we victims could not help feeling that death was forever tugging at us' (Ōta Yōko in Minear 1990: 176–77). This only ended when death finally arrived.

As 'Takako' experienced the slow rot of her own body, which Hayashi described as 'bursting [her skin] like warm ripe fruit', she had a mastectomy that led to complicating infections. Takako eventually died at forty-five from cancer of the liver and pancreas in 1974. She is consecrated at the A-bomb memorial tower of the Nagasaki Peace Park, together with many others who also died from radiation-related illnesses and complications (Hayashi 2005).

Indeed, anxiety, isolation and fatalistic resignation were symptoms of being *hibakusha*, particularly for women. Young women in particular hid their status to increase their marriage prospects and avoid discrimination. Aborting their own pregnancies was common practice. Takako was one of the minority who resisted the stigma ('guinea-pig', 'flawed merchandise') and tacit denial of rights to choose as a *hibakusha* to give birth to her own son.

To avoid prenatal influence, Takako hid the photos of her dead family. Her son was born mentally disabled. When he accosted her in adolescence, she had him sterilized. He soon died from intense convulsions. Takako also kept special 'figurines/*objet*' by a young handicapped male artist which she called the 'masks of *nanjamonja*'. As if in resistance to the radically distant and vertical relationship between bombed civilians and governments of the United States and Japan, Takako saw her dolls as 'screaming against the sky'. She admonished them not to 'stand on your feet and look upward. Crawl like me and set a red eye on the ground' (Hayashi 2005).

This suggested two things. One was an assumption of 'animality' in subordination to the punitive force that came from the sky. More hopefully, another was a pragmatic approximation of 'animal' in greater intimacy with the earth so as to endure not only physical deterioration but also moral injustice. This human 'animality' could be seen as the resilient ontology of the weak. By transferring her deep sense of moral injustice to her dolls, Takako taught herself to focus on basic living as she ground away her final term while remaining fully aware that she was entangled in the occupier's atomic gaze and its concomitant logic that had violated her. Reduced to a tiny orbit by the voice/will of the US sovereign, Takako's body was inextricably tied to the apparatus of the A-bomb. Just before she died she burned and crushed her dolls underfoot.

Just as keloid scars grow back after surgical removal, re-education could not erase the act of indiscriminate killing and poisoning (Lifton 1987: 180–84). Whether choosing to speak out or remain silent, *hibakusha* are living evidence of the crime and expose its profoundly and precisely irrational yet rationalized violence. Due to their 'contagious' qualities, they attracted degrees of prohibition, through local ostracism, official censorship and ongoing scientific control. In their uncertain limbo from the slow-acting poison, *hibakusha* exist as revenant who unsettle proper 'divisions between death and life' (Lifton 1987: 194), neither wholly forgotten nor adequately remembered.

Hibakusha populations have grown as these poisonous nuclear rituals have extended around the world. In the reflection of military and political interests of responsible actors, techno-scientific and media protocols have reinforced the structural order of the supranational security state, its political and economic clientele, and internally colonized and precarious surplus populations.

Cultural negotiations of occupation reforms

Alongside tenant farmers, women were the main beneficiaries of the SCAP Civil Rights Committee's revision of the old Meiji triumvirate of family, *minzoku* (people) and nation. Released from traditional duties of marriage and reproduction (Ueno in Gelb and Palley 1994: 38), in their award of equal individual, electoral, property and wage rights, the new middle-class Japanese woman became the occupiers' symbol of choice for the 'reborn' nation (Hirano 1992: 195). Twenty-two-year-old Beate Sirota Gordon, who was mainly responsible for Article 24, took inspiration from the Soviet constitutional model in making social welfare inseparable from women's rights. Overall, however, the Committee's anti-communist elite Japanese female majority (led by Baroness Katō Shizue) assumed that the 'instructions for democratic procedures' imparted to the grassroots level was a tutelary exercise in civilizing Japanese society. With occupied Japan as a test site for applying a gender egalitarian Western model to an Asian nation, it was unlikely that liberal professional American women and their elite Japanese counterparts would consider that they had much to learn from let alone be empowered by Japanese grassroots traditions or culture (Koikari 2002: 25–27).

As the SCAP campaign still pivoted on the idea of reforming Asiatic despotism and feudal chauvinism through precepts of freedom over oppression, love over duty, modernity over feudalism, women in Japan and other Asian nations had to be in need of saving, by liberal, mostly white, American men and women. This was the 'softer' side of the 'harder' hegemonic drive to re-make Japan in the image of America under the pretext of defending the free world against communism.

In Kurosawa's first post-war film, *No Regrets for Our Youth* (1946),[3] Yagihara Yukie embodied the desired formulation of the 'new post-war woman'. In the revolutionary spirit of the early occupation years, *No Regrets* opened with the words, '(m)ilitarists, zaibatsu and bureaucrats condemned as "red" anyone opposing the [Manchurian and Chinese] invasion, thus trying to create a national consensus' (Hirano 1992: 187). Loosely based on the dismissal of the Kyoto University law professor Takigawa Yukitoki by Education Minister Hatoyama Ichiro in 1933, Yukie is a budding pianist and daughter of a law professor who prefers a kimono-clad, proletarian anti-war student activist (Noge) to a privileged law student wearing a suit (Itokawa). When Noge is imprisoned for his activities, Yukie renounces her comfortable city life to 'get her hands dirty' in the country, but is rejected by the villagers. At war's end, Yukie attempts to return to village life.

Following an arc from urban Japan embroiled in total war, to national defeat and the collapse of empire, to the simplicity of village life, Kurosawa frames the urban middle-class re-discovery of the Japanese 'heart' in Yayoi culture in the return to physical labour in the rural soil.

While recovery of 'feminine and proto-feminist libidinal qualities in the return to the soil' (Chow 2007: 72) is qualified by an aggressive 'agrarian fundamentalism' that informed the Imperial colonial period, it is worth noting that *No Regrets* reflected broad concern for the food crisis between 1945 and 1949 as much as it re-examined identity (and ideology) under foreign occupation.

Where Kamei would have focused on Noge's activism during the food crisis, however, *No Regrets* elicited sympathy for a petit-bourgeois female protagonist who valiantly took up village life. While not a CI&E script *per se* (Hutchinson 2007: 369–89), among a host of 'democratization/problematization films' that neatly aligned to SCAP directives (Hirano 1992: 148), *No Regrets* anticipated the movement of capital into rural areas for factories and monoculture farming and the urban migration of peasant farmers as seasonal (*dekasegi*) or permanent surplus labour. Jameson's observation – 'third world texts project a political dimension in the form of national allegory in the global context through the private destiny of the struggling individual' (Jameson 1986: 65–88) – applies to *No Regrets* as urban industrial Japan (Yukie) cannibalizing agrarian rural populations (villagers, in Asia) under the sign of Americanized democracy (post-war Japan). The mission to create self-interested competitive individuals for a dynamic industrial capitalist nation was no less problematic than in the laissez-faire capitalism of the Meiji *genrokusha*. The difference was that now women were increasingly included in the labour market and differently inflected in the national imagination.

In Kurosawa's *To Live* (1952), in a subtle allusion to Hirohito's famed imperial hunch (Igarashi 2000: 103), a cowed and stagnant middle-aged bureaucrat (Watanabe Kanji) learns he only has a few months to live due to a cancerous growth in his stomach. To live it up, he takes a young female employee to a nightclub and learns that children give her joy to live. To champion her dream he cuts through bureaucratic obstacles to obtain a permit for a children's playground on municipal grounds, after which he slowly freezes to death on a playground swing, blanketed in cold white snow as he sings Nakazawa Keiji's 'The Gondolier's Song'. The Gondolier's Song is well known as a message to 'young maidens' (*otome*) to find love as life (and youth) is short and is related to young *hibakusha* women ('maidens') and even wartime ideology. Kurosawa's opaque metaphor and middle-class characters in *To Live* alluded to, subconsciously or otherwise, the quiet passing of the Shōwa militarist period. As Iwabuchi noted, the 'conception of the post-war that negates continuity with the past, made it possible for Japan not to face seriously the aftermath of its own imperialist violence in the former colonies and occupied territories' (Iwabuchi 1994: 10).

Guided by CI&E prescriptions, Kurosawa as 'the Emperor' of post-war film cultivated an 'apolitical' narrative of an optimistic people living in a brand new day of opportunity. He depicted individuals who were given democracy rather than those who 'fought for [it] and won' (Hirano 1992: 200–1). He was 'not [concerned with] what "forces" had made of people but what people make from what the "forces" have made of them' (Richie 1998: 36), and publicly scorned those (Tōhō 'unionist and communist' demonstrators) who 'swallowed the concepts of freedom and democracy whole, waving slogans around without really knowing what they meant' (Kurosawa

1983: 145). Kurosawa even reported the Teacher's Union to the CI&E for its pressure to portray Yukie in *No Regrets* as less politically naïve.

Kurosawa's wholesome pictures were in stark contrast to the 'animalistic' ambivalence of malnourished urban shack-dwellers who eked vegetables and food tins from relief agencies and peripheral villages and struggled with disease while being harassed by military police.

The avalanche of daily rapes and other crimes by Allied troops during Occupation that began upon arrival (1300 rapes in Kanagawa prefecture between 30 August and 10 September 1945; Tanaka 2002: 117) saw rape placed at the top of the agenda of the first meeting between MacArthur and Commander R. Eichelberger (US 8th Army). To contain the rapes and sexually transmitted diseases, which one in four American soldiers had contracted by December 1945 (gonorrhoea, venereal disease), the non-fraternization policy for Occupation soldiers was overridden to permit consort with 'new women' (20,000 hostesses, prostitutes, 'criminals') in a chain of zoned military 'comfort stations' (*gaikoku chūton gun ian*) coordinated by the Recreation Amusement Association (RAA) set up by GHQ and the Japanese Ministry of Home Affairs.

Considered a national 'shock absorber' for the protection of elite blood-lines and Japanese virtue (Tanaka 2002: 147), many young and poor women of Japanese, Korean, Okinawan and other Asian ethnicities were 'volunteered' (duped or abducted and/or raped by private organized gangs – *gurentai*) to such 'stations' for sexual services to the Occupiers. Such women were stigmatized and often turned to relationships with Allied soldiers, casual solicitation as *panpan* (lit. 'bang bang') or suicide when they were abandoned when foreign troops were repatriated (Koshiro 2003: 198). In May 1956 prostitution and brothels were outlawed (taking effect in April 1957). Soliciting did not stop (particularly by non-Japanese), however, near US military bases in Japan or elsewhere in Asia.

Even as filing complaints against Occupation forces was prohibited, high-level (i.e. G-2) authorities collaborated with criminal and mafia organizations (Takemae 2002: 67). SCAP secretly conducted trials of its own troops in the gallows of the 8th Army stockade, but they were over-represented by African-American ordinary soldiers for capital crimes (Svoboda 2009), reflecting the US Army's segregation policy.

While the censors tried to control it, it was a *sine qua non* that the contradictions of 'democratization' in the gritty realities of profligate black-marketeering, prostitution and organized crime featured in novels, plays and films. As sung by *enka* star Ishida Ichimatsu, '[e]verybody is talking about democracy, but how can we have democracy with two Emperors?/ Women are not equal to men./ If you are a real Japanese, you know who is the real boss in a Japanese home./ Seducing Japanese women is easy, with chocolate and chewing gum' (Hirano 1992: 72).

Tamura Taijirō, a member of the *nikutai-ha* group ('literature of the flesh') who had served as an ordinary soldier of the Imperial Japanese Army in mainland China, was also not blind to the internal contradictions of the Occupation. Amid post-war austerity he reflected on the recent wartime regime:

> I saw Japanese people with plausible intellectual credentials and respectable ideologies transformed into animals. I was one of these animals at the front ... I

was forced to realise that such intellectual thinking has nothing to do with our bodies and will never be able to control them. (Hirano 1992: 92)

Between 1946 and 1947, Tamura was prolific. In 1946 he published *Nikutai no Akuma* (Devil of the Flesh), a serialized novel depicting a brief sexual encounter between an ordinary soldier and a Chinese Communist female prisoner. In January 1947, the CCD approved a censored version of *Shunpuden* ('Diary of a Prostitute') as lead story in a collection of short stories whose protagonist was Harumi, a young 'comfort woman' (Japanese) living in Japanese barracks on the frontlines in mainland China. In March 1947 his best-seller *Nikutai no Mon* ('Gateway to the Flesh') was published in which teenage *panpan* girls 'hunted' clients to survive in post-war Tokyo slums. This received several theatrical productions and tours (one saw 780 performances in city theatres in 1947) and a film production (Suzuki Seijun (dir.), 1964). Cultural producers like Tamura exploited the existential hunger in urban areas by providing solace in the form of cheap scenes of nudity and salaciousness, as evident in many other live performances ('Ice Cream Girl', 'Free Market for Passion', '49 Virgins', 'Home Run Show', etc.). The CCD censors kept close watch, recording the duration and amount of female nudity exposed.

Tamura's unexpurgated version of *Shunpuden* submitted to the May 1947 edition of *Nihon Shōsetsu* was banned for its 'incitement to unrest'. Similarly, *Akatsuki no Dassō* (Taniguchi Senkichi (dir.), 1950), a film version of *Shunpuden*, was subjected to repeat revisions before being released and screened widely. The censors' concern was that Harumi was originally written as Korean, and reflected the experiences of many poor young Korean farming women taken from villages, mostly tricked or against their will, and kept in military brothels to supply sexual services to the troops in frontline camps (conservatively estimated at 80,000) (Kerkham in Mayo et al. 2001: 315).

Tamura shows Harumi defiantly resist harsh treatment from one particularly torturous Japanese officer, which he contrasts with her love for and eventual suicide with a common Japanese soldier. The authoritarian structure is reflected in the abusive Japanese officers and Japanese comfort women as compared to the earthy passions of Harumi and the soldier. Tamura's 'gratitude' for the help received from Chinese and Korean women to sustain the courage of Japanese troops to live or face death at the fronts seemed form, at least in the story, a transnational and inter-ethnic commonality of farmers and workers living under oppression.

Tamura's *nikutai-ron* approach pointed to the contradiction in the 'emancipated' lives of middle-class Japanese woman and the proletarianized sex workers living in post-war rubble. He may have evoked 'raw, erotic energies' in libidinal spaces in the Occupation (McLelland 2005: 167–71), but the bodies of '*panpan*' boys, girls and transvestites working in brothels and gay and straight cabarets were those of hungry people seeking to 'fatten themselves' (Koshiro 1999: 168).

Tsurumi observed that in this primary loss of faith in a value system to which Japanese people had committed to *en masse*, many privileged 'the lowest common denominator of human existence … emphasizing the flesh rather than spirit' (Tsurumi 1992; Koschmann 1996: 57). As in the informal RAA centres, however, immediate gratification was tacitly encouraged by the CCD as a way to redirect potentially large-scale volatile (young male) energies unlocked from wartime demands away from political organization.

As 'safety valves' in 'comfort zones' to absorb the structural violence inherent to both regimes, Tamura's *nikutai* characters exposed how bodies, particularly of the less privileged, were the mutable materials upon which sovereign authority was inscribed and re-inscribed. As witnesses to the subordination of people's *seishin* (spirit) to the ethereal delirium of Japan's Imperial ideology (Slaymaker 2004: 25) and the elite's contortions under the legally duplicitous post-war 'democracy', Tamura, Kamei and others sought out material testimonies to reclaim reality. As Tamura wrote,

> [T]he fundamental element forming the human must be freed. We must undo the various restrictions that squeeze the flesh to let it breathe naturally like a baby. We must strive for this and in doing so we will no doubt learn what a real human is.... (Tamura 1947: 47)

They shared the aim to liberate independent thought through the body from a world-view perceived as false. As Sakaguchi wrote, 'I am certain that the future of literature rests upon the discovery of the language of the thinking body' (Sakaguchi 1975: 576–78). Even Maruyama Masao recognized this objective in 1947 in his support for indigenous democracy:

> [T]he bearer of freedom is no longer the citizen as conceived by liberals since the time of Locke; but must rather be the broad working masses with workers and farmers (*rōdōsha nōmin*) at the core. Even then the issue is not merely the sensual liberation (*kankakuteki kaihō*) of the masses, but rather how and how thoroughly the masses are to acquire a new normative consciousness. (Barshay 1992: 391)

Occupation and the role of the medium in cultural imagination

Undeterred, the authorities persisted to find ways to control the public imagination and undermine political movements for self-determination. They turned to baseball (sport and entertainment in general) as a useful tool. Its team ritual of uniformed young men ordered in a disciplinary lexicon of 'foul, play ball, strike, out' had proven useful to Meiji reformers who had it taught at Tokyo Imperial University in 1873 (by Americans Horace Wilson and G. H. Mudgett). It was then indigenized as a national ritual (*yakyūdō*) so that by the early 1900s it was imbued with nativist spirituality and martial principles (*bugei*), as a game of self-sacrifice with bats symbolizing a sword or Shintō *shaku* on a sacralized pitch for a chanting crowd (*ōendan*) (Whiting 1977: 37; Kelly in Linhart and Frühstück 1998: 95–111; Whiting 2004: 50–72).

Baseball had also been useful in Japan–US cultural diplomacy between 1900 and the 1930s (i.e. Lefty O'Doul and Shōriki Matsutarō) (Shimizu-Guthrie 2012: 92). It was used to convey a multi-ethnic united Asian brotherhood in films such as Ide

Kinnosuke's *The Baseball Period* (1929) and Kawate Jirō's *Bridal Champion* (1933). MacArthur approved the resumption of the Kōshien (national high school) tournament in January 1946 who declared its 'great moral power' of competitive individual and team spirit as a 'prerequisite for free development politically, economically and socially' (16 June 1946, Blackwood 2008: 236). Similarly, *The Babe Ruth Story* was promoted to turn 'confused young minds' away from harsh realities to 'concentrate their energy and spirit ... to shoulder the future of reborn Japan' (Shimizu 2012: 2422). True to form, Kurosawa also featured baseball in *Stray Dog* (1949). Kōshien unified the nation in the dreams of its youth, including Okinawa, and when it was broadcast for the first time in 1953 on Shōriki's Nippon TV, it became the summer pastime. It was also a mechanism of forgetting.

In Ōshima Nagisa's *Gishiki* ('Ceremony', 1971), which sums up twenty-five years of the post-war, baseball functions as a mnemonic. Masuo (lit. man from Manchukuo), a repatriate from Manchuria and sole remaining heir of the powerful Sakadura clan, plays imaginary baseball with a lost brother Kanichiro (Korea), who was killed while fleeing from Soviet troops at the end of the war. Similarly, when Masuo's pre-arranged bride does not show up he must carry out the wedding ritual with an imaginary one. In both instances the obsessive ritual takes primacy in support of the patriarch who fails to relinquish control (Iwasaki 1971: 10; Burch 1979: 342; Satō 1982: 346–47; Standish 2011: 72).

Ōshima's central concern in *Gishiki* is the family-nation (*kazoku kokka*) system and its continuation in hollowed out post-war form. This typifies the post-war concern for the emperor as an empty or hybridized signifier in the new order. Yet Okinawa (and base towns on the mainland) is the most visible medium of exchange between the dominant actors of the United States and Japan, as reflected in the Okinawan literature of the time.

In Ōe Kenzaburō's *Human Sheep* (1958), for example, a male student is entangled in an argument between a local sex worker and a GI on a bus. The sex worker refuses to mediate and a fight ensues. Eventually, the group of GIs line up some passengers on their knees including a teacher and spank their bare bottoms. After the soldiers get off, the onlookers demand that those spanked seek justice, but when the teacher goes to the police he is ignored. In Kojima's *The American School* (1954), as another case in point, the newly occupied local community splits over the decision to learn English. For some refusing to speak the foreigner's idiom was a way of resisting dilution and self-erasure, while for others English represented opportunity under the new American order.

In *Human Sheep*, as over-empowered immature GIs humiliate the local passengers they reflect the greater wrong to a sovereign people. While *Human Sheep* is resonant with the contemporaneous and building civil rights movement as symbolized by the Rosa Parks bus incident in the United States (1943, 1955), in both stories power relations are exposed in the refusal by the occupied to mediate in the language of the occupier.

Ōe's 'Unexpected Muteness' (1958) is set during the 'bulldozer and bayonet' period of forcible dispossession and land appropriation for USCAR military installations ('all island struggle', 1952–1958) (Johnson 1999: 5). A US Army unit stays overnight in a village on a rural scouting-mission. When the interpreter loses his shoes and threatens the village headman, the latter runs away and is promptly shot in the back by the soldiers. The headman's son murders the interpreter in the night and the soldiers are ignored the next day. Similarly, in this case, when the mediator (translator) reneges on his role, the conflict between occupiers and occupied is exposed.

In Ōe's *Shiiku* ('Prize Stock' [1958] 1977), echoing Ishikawa Jun's 'Golden Age' (*Ōgon Jidai*, 1946) and adapted as *The Catch* by Ōshima Nagisa (1961), villagers take an African-American pilot prisoner during the war. In a mixture of repulsion and awe the bawdy villagers perceive the caged and muted black soldier as 'an animal of genius'. Not necessarily derogatory, Ōe used animal appellations for villagers (weasels, wild dogs, hunting beasts) in recognition of the intimacy between animal and human in animist village culture. As the children assume medium-ship by inviting the soldier into their utopian space in nature, the adults permit the pilot entry to village life. When the pilot learns he is to be taken away (into custody), however, he takes a child hostage. With mediation by the children denied, the former roles determined by nationality are resumed and the villagers kill the soldier.

In Kishiba Jun's *Dark Flowers* (1955), an African-American soldier who is married to a local young Okinawan woman despairs at his discrimination on a US base. The young woman also is alienated for having married outside the community. As mediums, the couple occupy their own minor independent space beyond physical and racial boundaries of the village and base. At the same time, they signify the hegemonic Japan–US conjunction that is to come.

Roughly 200,000 children were reared from mixed couples by 1952, and many of them were put in orphanages. The Truman administration refused the demands by local communities that US immigration restrictions be lifted to allow for the orphans' adoption, effectively isolating children and sometimes their mothers without financial assistance. This was evident in *Konketsu-ji* ('Mixed-blood children', Sekigawa Hideo (dir.) 1953) in the pariah-status of Henry and Tommy born from an African-American GI and Japanese mother who live in an orphanage near a US base. Yet while these children were denied the role of mediums by the communities, the United States and Japan, the orphans issue became central to a national civil rights campaign, championed by *burakumin* leader Matsumoto Jiichirō in 1954.

On the other hand, Arakawa Akira, in his poem 'The Colored Race' (1956), rejected censorship codes by declaring the occupation of Okinawa as consistent with Euro-American imperialism (Arakawa 1956: 39–43; Molasky 1999: 90). He called for a unity of 'yellow' forces in East Asia as part of a broader 'yellow and black' experience of the 'welts' of white violence. In his strategic ethno-nationalism he condemned the mediums (local interpreters) who collaborated with the Occupiers as 'treacherous'.

As a counter-point, the failure of racialized solidarity can be seen in Ōshiro Tatsuhirō's *The Cocktail Party* (1958) which begins with the rape of a young Japanese-Okinawan woman by an American officer on a beach during a Chinese language party on a US base. The woman's father seeks justice for what the Americans call 'a personal matter', only to find his alliances gradually slip from Japanese-Chinese-Okinawan, to Chinese-Okinawan, to Japanese, to Okinawan. Powerless but freed from his illusions, the father recognizes the reality of Okinawa's occupied condition. As the occupier and occupied are not equal before the law, in this case it is the law that fails in its role as the ultimate medium.

The impact on youth in satellite towns of US bases (Kōza) is further explored in Higashi Mineo's short story *An Okinawan Boy* (1971). Young Tsuneyoshi grows up in a brothel run by his father. Surrounded by 'trees which stink of semen, underwear in branches, condoms floating like maggots in the slush' (Molasky 1999: 61), Higashi shows the life of a child in a system that mediates mainly Okinawan bodies as sexualized currency.

In Imamura Shōhei's film *Pigs and Battleships* (1961), a young local couple in Kanagawa scrounge for scraps of work as US aircraft carriers are unloaded at the Yokosuka naval base. The female lead is raped by three GIs as they sing 'I been working on the railroad'. When her boyfriend is betrayed by local *yakuza* sub-contractors, he takes revenge with a machine-gun and is killed. The efforts of the naïve couple are dwarfed by the organized 'traffic' of troops, goods and weapons through Japanese ports by a consortium of mafia, US military and Japanese private and state contractors. In this case, the mediums are *yakuza* who profit from working with both sides, while their sub-contractor protagonists are consumed as disposable surplus in the stream of goods and services exchanged between the main agents. Imamura eschews heavy moral judgement, false optimism and sentimentality as he depicts life in a violent 'food chain', from local rape to labour exploitation to the larger US protection racket in collaboration with the Japanese state.

Takechi Tetsuji's *Black Snow* (1965) similarly constellates US military bases, racialized and sexualized relations, nationalism, student protests, the anti-nuclear movement and the American War in Vietnam. In the film's opening sequence, nineteen-year-old Jiro spies on his pale naked mother and a semi-naked black US sergeant in post-coital daze. His mother runs a brothel next to the Yokota air base in Tama. When the African-American sergeant murders his aunt with whom he profiteered from stolen stocks from the PX store and steals a large sum of money, Jiro takes violent revenge. *Black Snow* was censored for obscenity (nudity) (Standish 2011: 95). Yet, in the absence of the father as a 'corrective' to destabilizing corruption in the community, the resolution in the son's 'purifying' violence as an initiation into manhood would seem to appeal to masculinist nationalism. It was perhaps the film's incitement to this brand of nationalist (as opposed to leftist) violence against the corrupting influence of the US bases that most concerned the censors. In this sense, while the bodies in the brothel as sexualized currency remained the core mediums between the US base and local society in Japan, this breaks down in the corruption of the representatives of each group (the aunt and the sergeant). When the film itself was banned it demonstrated the priority to protect the US–Japan basing system from the corrupting influences exposed in the film.

As indicated in these cultural reflections, the 'peace' is kept through mediators as local bodies are re-organized under the new order of the (ongoing) occupation. Most of the various efforts to negotiate and/or resist these conditions have failed to achieve their goal due to the asymmetry of power relations and exploitative conditions of the regime. Yet these explorations helped to at least distance viewers and readers from such impoverished conditions so to imagine life outside the narrow baseball diamond of occupation. In the red purge of the 1950s, Ōshiro, Higashi and other writers in the Ryūkyū University Literature (*Ryūdai Bungaku*) movement (i.e. Matayoshi Eiki, Merodoruma Shun, Nagadō Eikichi, Yamanoguchi Baku) were pressured by management to resign or go silent (Stewart and Yamazato 2011: xi). As they have on the mainland, the bases remained after Okinawa's 'reversion' to Japan in 1972. In response, Okinawans focused on ways (i.e. indigenous Inaihō and other ethnic traditions) to unify and distinguish the entire population from all occupiers, whether Japan, the United States or China.

Occupied responses: Activists and artists in the protest decades

Despite the impression of an all-powerful dominant order, from the first post-war May Day protest in 1949, waves of political demonstrations by a mixture of *Zengakuren* (all-Japan league of student organizations), *Sōhyō* (General Council of Trade Unions), *Nihon Shakaitō* (JSP), *Nihon Kyōsantō* (JCP), ordinary workers and even right-wing nationalists continued to assemble. First, they were against the harsh conditions of increased unemployment, poverty and surplus labour created by the 'Dodge Line' revival of the *zaibatsu* and undermining of small business and agriculture. Second, as they continued over the following two decades, they were against continuing US military presence after the end of Occupation.

Two of the main intellectual proponents were Maruyama Masao and Tsurumi Shunsuke who called for the preservation of the 1947 Constitution under threat of revision and who criticized the lingering *Tennōsei* ideology and morality. Maruyama's challenge was to develop *shutaisei* (subjectivity, interiority, autonomy) by overcoming 'Imperial subjecthood' (*shinmin*) as fixed within the family state (*kokutai*) through the democratic praxis of public debate. To become real citizens (*shimin*), Murayama proposed that anti-authoritarian 'volunteers' exercise the 'active, doing' clauses (Articles 12 and 97) to indigenize a more horizontal democracy by re-making themselves through collective debates and organized, spontaneous protest.

Maruyama regarded the critique of Japanese ultra-nationalism as more important than decrying American interference or occupier's 'sham' or 'hollow' democracy housed in the residual *Tennōsei* structure (Articles 1–8) (Murayama in Morris 1969: 135–56, 290–320; Ienaga and Minear 2001: 127). Others, such as Matsushita Keiichi, pointed to the Subversive Activities Prevention Law (1952) and Police Duties Law (1958), variations of the Peace Preservation Laws (*Hakai Katsudō Bōshihō*) of 1925 and 1929, as ensuring the interests of monopoly capital at the expense of a proletariat population (Matsushita 1956: 32).

The Soviet invasion of Hungary in 1956 and the fissures in Soviet Union–PRC relations splintered the Left alliance of the Zengakuren, JCP and JSP (Koschmann 1996: 404). In 1957, the JCP intervened to call off the railway workers' strike against mass lay-offs, causing many members to leave. The Zengakuren focused on *zaibatsu* profiteering from the Korean War, worker exploitation and cut-backs to tertiary education. In 1958 in response to a JCP march to deliver a petition to the Diet against 'USA imperialism', the *Zengakuren* (with the Japanese Revolutionary Communist League (JRCL)) rejected reformism and militated for industrial action (mass linked-arm sit-downs) (Onada and Kurokawa in Rosemont and Radcliffe 2005: 149–53).

A nationwide formation led by *Zengakuren*, including JCP, JSP and trade unions, citizens' groups, and comprising roughly 16 million people, resumed the *Anpo* struggle (*Anpo tōsō*) between 1959 and 1960 through strikes, boycotts and occupations of official buildings in the lead-up to the US–Japan security pact renewal (Mutō and Inoue 1985: 25; Avenell 2008: 711–42). JCP and JSP officials collaborated with police during the demonstrations to separate Zengakuren activists from workers. At the time, these Parties sought the middle ground of 'responsible, civic-minded oppositional' politics in working for the independence of Japan (Desser 1988: 34).

On 27 November 1959, students fought the police in the grounds of the Diet. On 19 April 1960, in Seoul, tens of thousands of South Koreans led by students and workers also demonstrated against twelve years of dictatorship under the US-backed President Syngman Rhee. Days later, Rhee stepped down and was evacuated courtesy of the CIA. The protests were blamed on small groups of 'communists'. In May 1960 in Tokyo, massive demonstrations rose against the suppression of dissent and political due process. Socialist Party members had been forcibly removed from the Diet so as to promptly ram the treaty through the Lower House in the middle of the night. On 15 June 1960, 12,000 student protesters entered and occupied the grounds of the Diet for three hours. In a clash with police, one Zengakuren leader, Kanba Michiko became the movement's first martyr (Kelman 2001: 9; Mackie 2011: 1). The Treaty was automatically ratified on 19 June. On 15 July 1960, while having achieved his objective, Prime Minister Kishi was forced to resign over the mishandling of the treaty renewal. The US–Japan political collusion and failure of parliamentary democracy had been exposed.

Kuno Osamu, one of the key organizers in the 1960 protests, conceived of the political 'citizen' (*seijiteki shimin*) as an autonomous auto-didact who practiced political responsibility through informed activism (Kuno 1960: 9). In the journal *Tayori* ('news', 'story'), launched in June 1960 by Kobayashi Tomi and Takabatake Michitoshi and which marked the inception of the Voiceless Voices association (*Koe naki no koe*) (Ueno 1960), Kuno and Maruyama called for broader participation on an anti-war, disarmament platform.

The Korean War boom in construction in the shipyards and urban construction sites had absorbed some of the farmers, war veterans and coal miners who had been laid off in the Dodge rationalization programme. But the 'National Income-Doubling Plan' under Ikeda Hayao, a ten-year rapid economic growth and trade liberalization package, only increased US surplus imports and deregulation for corporate investment. This form of high-speed economic growth decimated the remaining small farmer population as farmland was diverted to industrial use. In the shrinking supply of labour from rural areas, a pool of unskilled urban surplus labour grew. As urban consumption grew, this semi-itinerant labour force was fed into gargantuan construction projects, such as the Shinkansen railways, Tokyo Olympics and Osaka Expo.

While Zengakuren continued to support labour organizations against false union leadership (railway, post office, coal mines), their main focus was on international solidarity against US and Soviet militarization (Onada and Kurokawa in Rosemont and Radcliffe 2005: 150). As the window for supporting the South Korean student movement was closing, however, and against the calls for reunification with North Korea, the Japanese Imperial Army-trained Park Chung-hee led a successful military coup d'etat in May 1961 to 'stabilize' South Korea as a capitalist dictatorship. He remained in power until his assassination in 1979.

In response to two decades of protest, Ōshima Nagisa's *Night and Fog in Japan* (1960) depicted a wedding between a former activist and a present activist. Through the window of a wooden hut in a forest, the camera spies a groom and bride standing behind a table in a formal tableau, as students report on recent clashes with police. This is spliced with documentary footage of *Zen Gakusei Jijikai Sō Rengō* (All-Japan Federation of Student Self-Government Associations, 1948) protests. A fugitive is discovered and arrested, and the film ends with a long speech by the new party spokesman. The camera pulls back and is enveloped in fog.

Ōshima's background as a law student and activist leader in Kyoto informed his formalist tone, which he adopted as a parody of the male-dominated centrist Left. While the stiff wedding ritual satirized the 'Stalinist' tendencies in the movement (Turim 1998: 51–60), it also reflected the factionalism and shattered ideals that had undermined the movement. In the punishment of the fugitive and resumption of stiffened leadership, the group ultimately exposed its underlying conservatism.

The assassination of the JSP chairman Asanuma Inejiro on 12 October 1960 and withdrawal of *Night and Fog in Japan* from circulation reinforced the need to resist organized intimidation from the right as a lever of sovereign power. As the Zengakuren and JCP formalized the split in 1962, under pressure from the violent tactics deployed by state riot squads, some student factions adopted *geba-bō* (long sticks), Molotov cocktails and helmets in 1963–1964 (Box and McCormack 2004).

As Japan celebrated its 'miraculous' return to the world stage with the 1964 Tokyo Olympics (opened by a *hibakusha*), poorly paid rural émigré workers (Moore 1990: 13), many of whom were unprotected by sub-subcontractors, were expected to work with a 'do or die' (*gyokusai*) spirit in a daily 'holy war' (*seisen*) on urban construction sites. Ultimately, it was these legions of cheap, disposable labour that supplied the false economy of US preferential markets for Japan's manufactured products (and the PL480 sales). At this point, in 1965 a second wave of activists and graduates emerged to form a new constellation of multiple interest groups (roughly 400) to reflect the views of ordinary workers, farmers, students, feminists and anti-Vietnam War activists.

Against the de-politicized *taiyōzoku* ('sun tribe') generation, sharing the office of *Beheiren* (Peace to Vietnam! People's Committee) and the Anti-war Youth Association, a stream of rhizomatically connected members and friends formed in 'anti-authoritarian, anti-bureaucratic, egalitarian camaraderie'. They sought to resist Japan's support for US military presence in Japan and Okinawa and its 'surges' in Vietnam. While castigated for a lack of political discipline, voluntary participation and debate between heterogeneous, decentralized, collective assemblages seemed a viable alternative to centralized party hierarchy (Dowsey 1970; McCormack 1971; Sasaki-Uemura 2001: 189). Ōda Makoto, a central *Beheiren* activist, called on Japanese people to re-orient themselves towards Asia and sought affinities between 'coloured races' (*yūshoku jinshu*), including US GIs in the black power movement and deserters (Ōda and Tsurumi 1968: 14). They expressed commonality with the people of Indochina exposed to the USAF bombing campaign of Indochina between 1961 and 1972 (and after). Characterized by Nixon as 'anything that flies on anything that moves', more payload was delivered on South and North Vietnam (roughly 5 million tonnes), Laos (roughly 2 million tonnes) and Cambodia (roughly 500,000 tonnes) than the total dropped by the Allies in the Second World War (Kiernan and Taylor 2007 and 2015).

By this time, the United States had stored nuclear missiles on Okinawa and replaced some conventional forces with 1,000 nuclear warheads in ROK and conducted regional joint-force military drills. In 1967, to prevent Kishi's brother Prime Minister Satō from departing to South Vietnam, activists from a prolonged blockade in Sunagawa adjacent to Tachikawa Air Base (1952–1957) turned their support to farmers in a lock-down at Bentenbashi near Haneda airport. One activist was killed. In December 1967, Prime Minister Satō received the Nobel Peace Prize for his 'three non-nuclear principles': not to possess, produce or convey atomic weapons through Japanese territory.[4]

In *Diary of a Shinjuku Thief* (1968), Ōshima took up Sartre's theory of self-negation (*jiko hitei no ronri*) to argue that 'self-negating movement – a law of the movement of all things' – led to human flourishing (Ōshima and Michelson 1992: 48). This postulated that to detach the self from the ego so as to scrutinize its socially constructed nature one could actively change it. In his trilogy on Japan's colonization of Korea, *Death by Hanging* (1968) addressed the case of Ri Chin-u, a poor 22-year-old Zainichi Korean who was arrested and executed in 1962 for the murder and molestation of two Japanese female high school students. Ri committed the crime, but Ōshima's film portrayed Ri's lack of opportunity for social advancement as a zainichi Korean with limited civic rights. He pointed to the institutionalized discrimination of sentencing a member of an oppressed minority by the same measure as an accepted member of society.

At this point, Imamura Shōhei, in his concern for systemic oppression, continued Tamura's focus on the eroticism of ordinary people across different periods in Japanese history. Also seeking to dismantle the fixed ontology of the modern subject, Imamura embraced ambiguity, non-linearity, fragmentation and contradiction (Ogawa 1970: 6; Standish 2011: 77). His combination of phenomenology and permanent flux reflected a contemporaneous desire to undermine the official discourse mediated in the national citizen.

Demonstrations in Tokyo at Shinjuku Station in October 1968 interrupted rail transports of fuel to supply US forces. These were followed by student demonstrations at Tokyo University in December against censored curriculum and staff retrenchment. The *Zenkyōtō* (All-Campus Joint Struggle Committee) occupied Yoshida Hall and other campus buildings, to hold political debates and collective bargaining between student leaders and campus administrators. Faced with circumlocution and dissimulation and plagued with internal stalemates, students bunkered down in the lead-up to the Treaty renewal in October 1969. They were 'kettled' (*kessein*) by police and infiltrators, which stifled their outward trajectory, turning the students upon themselves (*uchigeba*) in a *quid pro quo* violence. When classes were resumed in 1969 exhausted students faced long court battles as the 1970 Security Treaty became effective (McCormack 1971: 48).

Yoshida Kijū's *Eros + Massacre* (1969) captured these political conditions in his rendering of the execution of Ōsugi Sakae and Itō Noe after the 1923 Great Kanto Earthquake. Yoshida perceived Ōsugi's execution as based not on a particular crime but on the disruptive potential of his ideas. In the debates concerning the 'emancipation of the peasant' during the 1910s and 1920s, Ōsugi's concept of 'free love' challenged the patriarchal family axis upon which private property and primogeniture pivoted. Without private possession (*sokubaku*), institutional power through marriage, primogeniture and inheritance could not continue (Yoshida 1971: 32).

Although the *Zenkyōtō* closed down in 1971 (Desser 1988: 30–31), activists migrated to Okinawa and South Korea or across to environmental issues, such as the mercury leaked from the Shin Nihon Chisso chemical plant into Minamata bay since the 1930s (Hane 2003: 313–14). In 1969, anti-*Anpo* activists also moved to support local farmers in long sit-ins and clashes with police at Sanrizuka, Chiba to obstruct the seizure of their land for the future Narita airport construction and protest the Security Treaty renewal in 1969. The Okinawa Reversion Agreement between Nixon and Satō Eisaku of 22 November 1969 (*Okinawa Henkan Kyōtei*) committed Japan to $20 million for new US base facilities in Okiwawa (75 per cent of all US bases in Japan) and storage of chemical and nuclear weapons (Matsumoto 2009; Mitchell 2015).

In Prime Minister Tanaka Kakuei's 'Remodelling of the Archipelago' plan in 1972, which he set up as finance minister in the Ikeda administration by selling M-Fund assets (Hayes 2005: 262), heavy industry was outsourced to rural areas (and overseas). This helped to soothe urban anti-pollution groups, while it lured corporations with the promise of low-wage, non-unionized labour in politically vulnerable rural communities for public works projects. Farmers were compensated for enforced 'fallowing' of paddy land (*gentan taisaku*) (Yamamoto 1972; Tanaka 1973; Moen 1999).

This period saw the removal of *Beheiren*'s major sources of opposition: US–PRC rapprochement (President Nixon's 1971 China visit), the Okinawa reversion (15 May 1972), the US armistice in Vietnam (1973) and an agreement with PRC over Vietnam. Yet, it was unknown to activists at the time that, as the United States prepared for final withdrawal, Nixon used a 'madman' strategy to make 'the other side think that we might be crazy and might really go much further'. Between 13 and 30 October 1969, this took the form of a massive joint forces coordinated military operation of strategic bombers, tactical air and various naval operations around the world, as well as subsequent threats to mine Haiphong harbour and use tactical nuclear weapons on passages through Vietnam and across its borders. The objective was to coerce Moscow to encourage North Vietnam to accede to diplomatic negotiations with the United States (Burr and Kimball 2015). Further, in 1972 Nixon and Henry Kissinger seriously discussed such a final exit strategy.

President: See, the attack in the north that we have in mind, power plants, whatever's left – POL [petroleum], the docks. And, I still think we ought to take the dikes out now. Will that drown people?

Kissinger: About two hundred thousand people.

President: No, no, no, I'd rather use the nuclear bomb. Have you got that Henry?

Kissinger: That, I think, would just be too much.

President: The nuclear bomb, does that bother you? … I just want you to think big, Henry, for Chrissakes (Operation Linebacker II 1972, Ellsberg 2002: 418).

Beheiren disbanded in 1974 as the United States partially withdrew from Indochina, leaving Vietnam, Cambodia and Laos as the most bombed places on earth.

Art and activism in reaction

It is a truism that in post-1945 Japan, the suppression of political dissent and decay of democratic institutions left unfinished business.

Certainly, after failing to incite a *coup d'état* to replace the Satō administration with direct Imperial rule, Mishima Yukio's choreographed suicide on 25 November 1970 was symptomatic of this unsettled history. Mishima's exhortation of 1,000 hastily assembled servicemen from the balcony of the Ichigaya headquarters of the Self-Defense Forces (*Ji-ei tai*) to reclaim 'real Japan, real Japanese, and real *bushi* spirit' (Starrs 1994: 74) by returning the emperor as head of state failed to move his audience. Mishima returned to the offices of the Eastern Defense Force Commander who four Tatenokai (Shield Society) officers had taken hostage and committed *seppuku*. His faithful retainer Morita Masakatsu beheaded Mishima's body and followed suit (Oka 1970).

As a spectacularly narcissistic and ironic 'opening without closure', Mishima enacted his rejection of Americanization and 'purified' himself in dedication to the emperor. Widespread speculation, particularly in Western media, considered the return of Japan's martial cult.

Japan's modern weaponized sacrifice (*nikudan*, *kamikaze*) had been inscribed in its Imperial Rescript for Soldiers (Sakaki 1999: 63), and was useful to Allied propaganda to mobilize popular fear of the enemy. While it has been argued that *kamikaze* missions were not suicide but were divine sacrifice in a 'holy war' (Ohnuki-Tierney 2006: 17), it is undeniable that *bunbu ryōdō* (martial arts) and thought of neo-Confucian samurai moralists, *kokutai* scholars and *Nippon Roman-ha* writers underpinned Mishima's masculinity, sexuality, religious beliefs and cultural identity (Nathan 1974; Scott-Stokes 1974; Starrs 1994; Piven 2004).

Mishima's thought also aligned with European chivalry and knighthood traditions and the aesthetics of the aristocratic baroque. This was reflected in a collaboration with photographer Hosoe Eikoh on a photographic publication entitled *Barakei* (*Ordeal by Roses*, or *Killed by Roses*, 1963), in which classical renaissance images (Botticelli's *The Birth of Venus*, Boltraffio's *Madonna and Child*, Perugino's *Apollo and Marysas*) were overlaid with images of samurai and sadomasochism (Hosoe 1985). While somewhat kitsch, this reflected a syncretic hybrid of ultra-nationalism (Washburn 2007: 221; Yayoi 2009: 11).

Mishima's trajectory, through wartime, defeat and post-war occupation, was a series of 'dress rehearsals' for his ultimate literal act through his fiction and film projects (i.e. *Runaway Horses, On Hagakure, Yūkoku* – Mishima and Dōmoto (dirs.), 1966). This act authenticated his ideal of a masculinist sovereign order based on fealty (Mishima 1976). Despite his anachronistic and stiff martial values and faux elitism (Iijima Kōichi, 'Streams and Rivers', Ōoka et al. 1987: 115–21), Mishima was also a product of the Occupation and the US–Japan corporate-state order.

On the other side of the political spectrum, some activists went underground with cellular units (*kageki-ha*) to conduct guerrilla actions such as bombing police stations and other authority symbols coinciding with the 1967 blockade at Haneda airport (McCormack and Box 2004: 91–112). Formed in 1969, the Japan Red Army Faction (JRAF, *Sekigun-ha*) aimed to publicize their cause, destablize the existing order and trigger simultaneous actions in other cities (known as the 'Tokyo, Osaka, Kobe wars') (Ōsawa 1999: 228). Under surveillance, the JRAF splintered into three cells – the 'Yodo' Group that hijacked a plane to North Korea; the Japanese Red Army (JRA) that collaborated with the Popular Front for the Liberation of Palestine (PFLP) in Lebanon; the United Red Army in Japan (URA). The 'Yodo' Group were instrumentalized in Kim Il Sung's 'Juche' (autonomy) programme to re-educate kidnapped Japanese civilians towards insurrection. JRAF members (Shiomi Takaya) who remained in Japan formed the Rengō Sekigun (URA) with the Maoist-oriented Keihin Ampo Kyōtō (led by Nagata Hiroko).

While Ōshima produced *Tokyo Wars: The Man Who Left His Will on Film* (1970), other new-wave filmmakers Adachi Masao, Wakamatsu Kōji, Suzuki Seijun and photographer Takuma Nakahira embraced the 'eros plus massacre' formula. Inspired by Bataille and Marcuse and theories of eroticism and chthonic power (Bataille 1962 [1957]: 402–12), as shared by Andrej Wajda, Paolo Pasolini, Werner Fassbinder and Dusin Makavejev, Adachi's *Fūkeiron* (landscape theory) proposed a horizontal ontology that could reflect the factional anarchist tendency of 1967–1968 and post-1968 guerrilla exile (Adachi 2003: 232, 289).

These filmmakers combined political activity and erotic animality to release libidinal energy from the 'organism as an instrument of work' in an alienating system based on private ownership (Marcuse (1955) 1972: 50; Bataille 1987: 31; Alexander 2003). They were also plagued with legal battles over obscenity charges.

For example, in Wakamatsu's *Sex Jack* (1970) a charismatic cell leader warns of a factory-enclosed proletariat on the other side of the river seeking revenge on society for bitter hardship, while his revolutionary acolytes engage in orgiastic bliss (Yomota and Hirasawa 2007: 23). In Adachi's *Gushing Prayer* (1971), youth who despair of their lives in prostitution turn to suicide. In Wakamatsu's *Ecstasy of Angels* (1972), based on the formation of the URA, two political cells led by a woman and a man, which are named by year (faction), season (cell), days of the week (members), vie for control over a cache of appropriated weapons and cash.

In reality, the URA, exposed to the pre-emptive techniques of state control (surveillance, harassment, infiltration), retreated with a cache of US military weapons and funds from bank robberies to Mt. Asama in 1971–1972. In paranoid self-recrimination, eight people were 'purged' (killed) as the group imploded (*uchi geba*). JRA members who evacuated to Lebanon received PFLP training in preparation for a series of attacks (including the Lod Airport massacre and Hague hostage incident). Adachi, after making *Red Army/PFLP: Declaration of World War* (1971) with Wakamatsu, followed the JRA to Lebanon in 1974.

The affiliated East Asia Anti-Japan Armed Front (*Higashi Ajia Hannichi Busō Sensen*, EAAAJF), active between 1971 and 1975 in Japan, self-funded and with no centralized leadership or blueprint for revolution, bombed imperial wartime symbols: Buddhist and Shintō sites (Koa Kannon temple, 12 December 1971; Sōji-ji Ossuary, 6 April 1972), a historic statue of Ainu and Wajin (*Fusetsu no Gunzō*) and Institute of Northern Cultures (23 October 1972) in Hokkaido, and the Mitsubishi Heavy Industries headquarters among others (1974–1975). When seven EAAJAF members were arrested in mid-1975, the JRA successfully obtained their release by taking hostages from the US consulate in Kuala Lumpur. Most EAAJAF members were re-captured and sentenced to death or life imprisonment. Some joined the JRA. Imprisoned since 1982, Nagata Hiroko (URA) died in 2011. Shigenobu Fusako (JRA) was arrested in 2000 and remains in prison.

Certainly, self-denunciation by some imprisoned cell members of acts that killed and maimed innocent people (Nagata 1982: 102) is a positive outcome. Yet, as with Mishima's suicide, with little serious consideration of the conditions that produced and to which these acts responded, such as the exploitative, corrupt and violent large-scale Japan–US operations discussed so far, the reproduction of related resentment and violence by non-state actors is more difficult to comprehend. The analysis of cellular politicized violence is remiss if it ignores the state-authorized terror in support of sovereign power. In the context of the US-led and coordinated covert and proxy wars in Asia, the Middle East and Latin and South America in this Cold War period (Stockwell 1978; Blum 1986), it is evident where greater culpability lies.

As in Teshigahara Hiroshi's film *The Face of Another* (1966), based on Abe Kōbō's novel (1964) and inspired by Georg Franju's *Face without Wyes* (1959),[5] a man (Okuyama) who has keloid scars from a nuclear accident and must conceal his criminal identity, has his face surgically removed and transplanted with the face of another. When Dr Hira fits the mask (based on a paid model) he warns Okuyama of the dissociative effects that can be morally destabilizing. Having told his wife he is away on business, Okuyama rents an apartment near his house and seduces his wife. When he confronts her she is disgusted by his deception and denies him entry to their house. Okuyama wanders the streets, assaults a woman and is arrested. Dr Hira and Okuyama then wander in a crowd of faceless people before Okuyama stabs Hira.

This is interspersed with a second story in which a woman with a disfigured face who works at a hospice for Second World War veterans. Tormented with solitude and anxious about imminent war, she repeatedly asks her brother if he remembers the sea at Nagasaki (of their childhood). She leaves her brother a suicide note and walks into the ocean.

The voided and reconstructed identity that conceals a traumatic history of violence in *The Face of Another* is a key allegory for Japan's post-war condition. Un-grounded in reality and caught in obsessive patterns, the conditions reproduce nihilism and self-destruction. As the film's opening captions suggest:

> A man without a face/ Civilization demands light, even at night, but a man without a face is free only when darkness rules the world./ Liberation! Adultery! Knife! What is freedom? (Teshigahara Hiroshi (dir.), *The Face of Another* 2008)

While the Emperor had changed into a cardigan and slacks, the rehabilitation and renewal of wartime sovereign power in the *tennō-sei* family state, *zaibatsu* corporations integrated with centralized institutions and re-education programme to designed to protect the interests of trans-Pacific monopoly capital and a single-party elite bloc in close collaboration with American 'Japan handlers'. The 'prosperous peacetime' consensus stunted autonomous indigenized democracy and stymied the renewal of independent regional relations. Counter-narratives offered by activist organizations (guilds/groups/unions), individual artists and progressive intellectuals, stimulated the nerves and fibres of society in mass demonstration, but were largely suppressed. More broadly, Japan's continued support through base-hosting, servicing, manufacturing, and investment in the US foreign policy of political interference and military intervention in the Asia-Pacific since 1946 produced the 'terroristic effects' at the end of two decades of mass political struggle. Yet the post-Cold War tendency to focus on scapegoats misrecognizes and reproduces the source of violence.

Given the US–Japan conjugation in lieu of the lack of direct apology and restitution to the victims and their families of their collective past aggression and indiscriminate violence in Asia-Pacific nations, the reconstructive surgery to reconfigure Japan as a proxy and instrument in US geopolitical interests produced an 'occupied condition' of amnesia, inverted moral pathology, victimology and reactionary national pride.

In the following chapter I turn to examine *Ankoku Butoh*, the most significant new dance form to have emerged from post-war Japan, and how the performing body can be thought in relation to this occupied condition.

3

The Performing Body in a Bicephalous State:
Ankoku Butoh in Context

The 1950s saw a host of popular narratives that promote science and technology as the way not only to achieve 'recovery' (*fukkō*) but also to overcome the nation's past weaknesses to grow even stronger. Despite this dominant focus, less convinced by the optimistic consumer modalities being taken up in society, the most politically astute artists critiqued not just the former regime but also negotiated the new 'master illusions' of the 'free world' order. As with the work of Tamura, Sakaguchi, Nosaka, Ōta, Hayashi and Ōe, in the more experimental or avant-garde performance art, theatre and performance of the 1950s, bodily materiality was the locus of power, memory and identity upon which to contest values and ideals as well as for grounding after significant loss and destruction.

A primary example of an embodied aesthetics was *Ankoku Butoh* (lit. 'dance of darkness'). Founded by Ohno Kazuo (1906–2010) and Hijikata Tatsumi (1928–1986), the evolving stages of butoh paralleled the development of post-war identity formation. Ohno was a former physical education instructor and soldier of the Japanese Imperial Army repatriated from a prisoner of war camp in New Guinea. Hijikata was in his early twenties when he emigrated from Akita in a wave of rural migration from Tōhoku to the major cities at the end of military occupation in 1952.

Hijikata's idiosyncratic originality derived from a broad range of life experiences and exposure to an eclectic palette of aesthetic forms and ideas. Working menial jobs and boarding in cheap rooming houses, Hijikata likened his life to 'a dog of an inferior breed sniffing out criminal-like fellows' (Hijikata and Kurihara 2000 [1961]: 45–49). Gravitating to Ueno, he discovered a seedy bar called 'Rimbaud' where he met and subsequently collaborated with individuals at the epicentre of Tokyo's avant-garde: Okamoto Tarō, On Kawara, Shinohara Ushio, Ikeda Tatsuo and Kanamori Kaoru, among others.

Trained in ballet, jazz, modern dance by Masumura Katsuko, as well as flamenco and pantomime in his hometown, Hijikata experimented with 'neo-Dada' art performances (which included members of Hi-Red Centre, Gutai and Fluxus) and performed for several years in Ando Mitsuko's modern dance group. Hijikata formed a strong collaboration with Ohno Kazuo after witnessing 'Jellyfish Dance', Ohno's first solo performance in Tokyo in 1949, which was a meditation on the sea-burials Ohno had observed while being repatriated as a Japanese POW (Ohno and Ohno

2004: 85). Hijikata first collaborated with Ohno in *Crow* (1954, a play on *kuro*/black) in an ensemble dance piece choreographed by Yoneyama Mamako.

The antecedent influences of butoh can be traced to modern dance teachers Eguchi Takaya, Ishii Baku and Itō Michio, and the German expressionism of Mary Wigman and Harold Kreutzberg in the early decades of the twentieth century.[1] Other important inspirations included vaudevillian performers such as Antonia Mercé ('Queen of the Castanets'), an Argentinian flamenco and cabaret dancer who toured Japanese clubs in the 1950s. There were also convergences with the contemporaneous European avant-garde, such as the Vienna actionists (Otto Muehl, Hermann Nitsch, Gunter Brus, Rudolf Schwartzkogler), as well as the local 'Action' artists such as Murakami Saburō, Shiraga Kazuo, Yoshihara Jirō and Gutai, Shinohara Ushio, Akasegawa Genpei and Hi-Red Centre, and Jikken Kōbō. These contemporaries shared an expressive and embodied anger, whose heterodox values deviated from normative modes and had affinities with minority identities in Japanese society (Havens 2006: 148).[2]

In anticipation of the American 'Happenings' and the flowering of politicized aesthetic movements in the coming decade of revolt, and ahead of the turn from neo-realism and *shingeki* (modern realist drama) by avant-garde filmmakers, photographers and theatre artists of the new wave (*nouvelle vague*) such as the ATG (Avant-Garde Theatre Guild),[3] Hijikata spawned a miscegenated collage of neo-Dada, Surrealist and rural agrarian heresies under the prismatic sign of *ankoku* or 'darkness' (Broinowski 2011). While his influences can be traced to nineteenth- and twentieth-century French literature (Isadore Ducasse, de Sade, Breton, Genet, Bataille), to the post-First World War European Dada and Surrealism, and to the neo-realist cinema of his youth, the meaning of 'darkness' or 'blackness' (*ankoku*), as I will explore further, is symbiotically entangled within broader socio-political conditions.

Under the prismatic sign of *ankoku*, Ohno Kazuo likened the *butoh* condition to an 'animal' scuttling across the barren, poisoned desert of Tokyo's (firebombed) aftermath. '[In the] stark ecology of the desert there is an absolute relatedness of the rodent to the landscape. The rodent feeds on the dying landscape much like the foetus consumes the nourishment of the mother's body' (McGee 1986: 49). For Hijikata, darkness was a sense of crisis that 'runs away from the light' – an ambiguous state of acquiescence and coercion, disobedience and rebellion – a criminalized condition (Hijikata 1987a: 84).

Ankoku Butoh valued decay, death and regeneration, and took inspiration from the pitch black nights of rural Tōhoku; the local black volcanic soil and its scorched aftermath in the bombed out cities; the weathered agrarian farmer and the grimy urban worker; the collective histories of all-night rituals and folkloric arts (*mingei, kōgei, taishū engeki*) and those of mass political demonstration. It extended to the informal economy of illicit crime as an essential element in post-war austerity. Through a dense poetic language, Hijikata created gradated contrasts in response to the dominant telos of light (*hikari*), and valued decay and regeneration as part of a worldly orientation towards death.[4]

Butoh's darkened sphere carved out from a vitalist and techno-nationalist regime that created space for those who had become targets in the new biopolitical order. Darkness, or a crepuscular light, offered optimal conditions for subterraneous collective existence of the stigmatized, pauperized and internally colonized in a landscape of accelerated production, individuated competition and selective amnesia. *Ankoku* suggested a habitus for the abject, which offered the site for a paradoxical dynamic of empowerment via self-cancellation.

As a life philosophy, *Ankoku Butoh* emerged organically as an inverse reflection of the normative values and taboos installed as part of the new cultural narrative. In this ambivalent condition of retreat and resistance, masking the ugliness of social shame, darkness accommodated and animated the profane. Where organized political action helped defined citizenship in the 1950s and 1960s, artists like Hijikata and Ohno configured a new language to represent otherwise ignored subaltern identities. Crucial in this process was the recovery of a capacity to feel and desire with a body otherwise mediated and socialized towards production and commodification.

In 1959, Hijikata made *Kinjiki* (*Forbidden Colours 1*). Using the title of Mishima Yukio's novel initially without his consent (Mishima 1951), it was performed with Ohno Kazuo's son Yoshito in a recital of dances. The 'dark and unspoken' world evoked in the performance scandalized and drove a young mostly female audience from the theatre. As a result, Hijikata was 'hounded out of the contemporary dance world' (Gōda in Hanaga 1983). Whether voluntary or forced, the impact of *Kinjiki* could have been attributable to the shock of an implied (homo)eroticism.

Consistent with Mishima's novel (312–13), in a silent and dimly lit space, the *Kinjiki* performances showed an older, darker skinned man with a shaven head in bell-bottomed pants (Hijikata covered in oil) chase a younger man with longer hair in lemon-yellow shorts and a black scarf (Ohno). The young man is handed a chicken by the older man, which he suffocates by sitting on it. After laying the chicken down on the stage, the men roll on the floor accompanied by recorded heavy breathing. A blues harmonica was played as the lights went up (Baird 2012: 20).

As Baird's forensic study indicates, plotting the narrative sequence of the dance is important to clarify ambiguities as it is remembered many years later. Due to a noted tendency to exaggerate the shocking qualities of butoh, for example, Ohno Yoshito downplayed the suffocation of the chicken in *Kinjiki* (Gōda in Klein 1988: 81; Kuniyoshi 2006: 154).[5] It is unlikely, however, that the killing of the chicken was the only object of shock in *Kinjiki*. Arguably, it had exposed something unrecognized or consciously forgotten.

From corroborating accounts, it is plausible that *Kinjiki* was concerned with some form of violent exchange, whether rape and/or lynching, that may have been but was not necessarily male to male (Baird 2012: 21). What did the exchange of the chicken between Ohno's feminized and Hijikata's masculinized roles allegorize within the socio-temporal context? Considered within the occupied–occupier dyad as outlined in earlier chapters, the violence of *Kinjiki* reflects a sadomasochistic dynamic. More concretely, a rape of an innocent local man or woman (Ohno) by a foreign soldier-sailor man (Hijikata) is framed in the binary of white (innocence, lawful, moral) and black (guilty, criminal, immoral).

As discussed with regard to sexualized violence inherent to the power relations established under SCAP during occupation, 'the forbidden' exposed in this performance was the collective memory of criminal abuse in Japan and other territories occupied by the US military. Another element of the forbidden was rural animist traditions the modern Japanese subject had learned to be ashamed of and bury in their subconscious.

Whether literal or metaphorical, in a sacrificial exchange, the chicken becomes a gift of love. In doing so, it inscribes significance beyond its representation. That is, when considered as a rite of passage, Ohno Yoshito decides to accept the chicken from his 'older brother' that he 'gifts' (kills) to mark the dedication of his life to dance. Hijikata is the guide in Ohno's initiation as witnessed by a community.

These layers of significance overlap. As cognitive shock is integral to the psychic recognition of suppressed reality, when it occurs, a dominant structure is destabilized and its natural permanence is relativized. In this sense, and much like other artistic works discussed earlier, *Kinjiki* offered a medium through which the tension between conflicting visible and less visible realities could be recognized. Since the early post-war eroticism of *Nikutai no Mon*, a notable desire to express the body's ontology through sexual relations indicated the neutering effect of Fordist cybernetic production amid frenzied industrialization (Ōoka 1987: 11). Sexual expression seemed to provide a more direct route to capture the broader problem of finding agency in an occupied society.

Hijikata's original contribution to the post-war avant-garde was to combine ritualistic *and* modernist approaches, 'secret ceremony' *and* street performance, in re-poeticizing the narrow moral and material values of the new capitalist society. Unlike Mishima's romantic formalism, Hijikata's modern paganism combined *nōmin* (peasant–farmer) culture and Surrealism. As an urbanized artist who grew up in a rural village, his appreciation of vernacular culture was neither forced nor was it essentialist. As Genet described it, this was a 'talent for courtesy towards matter, for giving [poetic] song to the dumb' (Hijikata and Kurihara 2000 [1961]: 47; Genet 2004: 86).

Hijikata's movement was animated by memories of practices and figures from an agrarian and artisanal economy in a harsh northern climate. The village communalism of farmer–fisher people common to most indigenous cultures (or 'First Nations'), also at the heart of *butoh*, prioritized collective over individual interests. Grounded in folk animist 'truth in land and nature' and ancestral cosmology (*sosen sūhai*) (also in Pure Land Buddhism, Taoism, Shintō), natural elements are animated with ancestral spirits and gods (*kamigami*) (Ohnuki-Teirney 1993: 97–98, 131–33).

The regional and generational history in these rural communities of suppression by centralized government in Kyoto and Edo can also be read in his work. In the post-war techno-managerialism driven by the United States, indigenous regional folk cultures were scorned as feudal or backward. While this tendency also explained the middle-class rejection and marginalization of butoh, the critique of an atavistic return to primordial origins in butoh was misplaced. Certainly, the obscurantism and essentialism as part of wartime or post-war neo-Nihonjinron should be critiqued; however, as discussed earlier, the meme of feudalism used as a signifier of evil by US intelligence units in the transformation of the post-war state ironically perpetuated the rural exploitation as practiced by the Meiji elite and Tokugawa bakufu that sought to 'infuse a heterogeneous population with a sense of homogeneity and community'

(Weiner 1997: 1). Understanding this aspect of *Ankoku Butoh* was no more predicated on special insight into Japanese culture than evil was unique to any particular class or culture. As Brecht anticipated, 'On my wall hangs a Japanese carving, the mask of an evil demon, decorated with gold lacquer, sympathetically I observe the swollen veins of the forehead, indicating what a strain it is to be evil' (Brecht et al. 2003: 115). The following examines in a little more detail why this sort of misrecognition of *Ankoku Butoh* may have occurred.

'Tōhoku' as signifier in modern Japanese colonialism

Although local animist beliefs were initially tolerated as long as peasant–farmers could deliver their quotas of labour and produce, as productivity demands increased in the inter-war period as the mobilization towards war intensified, conversion to Shintō became a patriotic obligation. The ideology of *Nōhonshugi* (pure agrarianism), subscribed to by farmers who sought greater wealth re-distribution from the metropolis to regional areas, was nuanced. Rightists, or ultra-nationalists, subscribed to the State Shintō cult of the semi-divine Emperor and its sacralising of Japanese identity in the soil (such as the *Ketsumei-dan*). Leftists (such as Shibuya Teisuke and Nagano Akira), by contrast, sought to represent and improve the conditions of tenant–farmers through collectivist organization and to sustain their ritual folk traditions, which were integral to their seasonal farming practices (Hane 1982: 62–66, 119). State ideologues suppressed those *Nōhonshugi* supporters whose values opposed rallying to the imperial cause by the 1930s, whether on the political right or left. If not conscripted, many *hyakushō* from Tōhoku were lured to the new colonies of Manchukuo so as to improve their prospects in a fabled multicultural utopia and to produce more food, resources and wealth for the Empire.

Prior to the Russo–Japanese war and the formal annexation of the Korean peninsula, a nostalgic sentimentality for peasant or 'Asiatic' life was already being cultivated in Japanese society. As found in the *Mingei* art movement founded by Yanagi (Sōetsu) Muneyoshi (1889–1961), the chronicles of folktales and ethnic research by Yanagita Kunio (1865–1962), the poetry of Miyazawa Kenji and sensibilities in Yasuda Yōjirō's Japan Romantic (*Nippon Roman-ha*) literature, proponents of *jōmin* (ordinary folk) were significant in the formation of Japan's 'cultural diplomacy' in its internal and external colonies.

Typical of the Meiji trend, Yanagi assimilated foreign ideas to reform national discourse, which was disseminated as 'transnational and translational' ideology across the colonies with the explicit intention to compete with Western interests (Kikuchi 2004: 6, 243). As a member of the Taishō literary group *Shirakaba-ha*, Yanagi focused on the concept of self-negation, developing it through an eclectic group of modern European and Japanese philosophers: Zen Buddhism and aesthetics (Dōgen, Suzuki Daisetz, Nishida Kitarō), Christian mysticism (Erigena, Eckhart, Tolstoy, Blake), theosophy (Blavatsky, Steiner, Metchnikoff) and modernist aesthetics (Fry, Read, the Vorticists, Bergson). Ingeniously digesting this composite, Yanagi tailored *Mingei* to support a national, oriental(ist) platform.

Inspired by the *fin de siècle* orientalism of Lafcadio Hearn, Okakura Kakuzō,[6] Bruno Taut, Charlotte Perriand and Itō Chūta, Yanagi selectively fetishized anonymous village craftspeople (*hyakushō, mujinkō*) to craft a modern aesthetic for an idealized Asian nation-state. Okakura's 'Asia is one' policy, in particular, self-appointed Japan as curatorial manager of the flow of rustic Asian artefacts between East and West.

> The Chinese person who does not appreciate sophisticated beauty... [is] uncouth ... They need the eyes of the Japanese to appreciate its beauty ... Japanese recognize the value and promote Chinese innate beauty, childlike innocence and purity of uneducated craftsmen who produced miraculous [Oriental] beauty [from] sad and humble objects. (Okakura in Kikuchi 2004: 175)

In general, the aesthetic criteria of these professional impresarios were formed from their excursions to the west and to Asia and based on exploiting the oriental/occidental divide. Through their work in the 1920s, Yanagi and Yanagita both assisted in the formation of cultural policy (*bunka seiji*) to shape colonial subjects into imperial subjects (*kōminka*). In journals like *Minzoku Taiwan*, they praised local folk traditions as the antithesis of Anglo–American culture. Yanagi assumed pastoral care for the 'gentle collective natures' in the peripheries, to protect them from the dominating influences of 'superior' external European civilization, while reinforcing their hierarchical inferiority (Robertson in Vlastos 1998: 14). Okinawa, Japan's colony from 1875, was considered to contain the seeds of Japanese ancestral origins that had vanished from the mainland in the process of modernization. Seizing upon Ryūkyūan cultural practices as the opportunity to revitalize 'Japanese spirits' led to the design of a model for 'respectful' preservation and protection of the 'degenerating' indigenous cultures in Formosa (Taiwan, 1895–1945) and Korea (1910–1945) from pragmatic development. These indigenous traditions were folded within Japanese aesthetic concepts of *wabi sabi*, asymmetrical imperfection, process over ends, contentment within limits and ascetic wealth (*hin no tomi*). *Mingei*, as a Japanese orientalist aesthetic, was instrumentalized to encourage pride in indigenous Asian traditions as an antidote to Japan's inferiority complex 'caught' from its 'shameful' admiration of the Occident. Rather than the concepts, which are worthy in themselves, it was their instrumentalization in an ideological package re-exported to the imperial realm for strategic modern state interests that is doubtful.

The benevolent paternalism was selective. The material and strategic value of Ainu territories of Ezo (Hokkaido, Sakhalin) to the central government as hunting grounds and a buffer zone against possible invasion from the north meant that the Ainu, who upheld sustained resistance, were not afforded such respectful condescension and were exposed to harsh policies of displacement, assimilation and erasure as a 'dying race' (Siddle in Weiner 1997: 19–40).

In the modern formation of strong homogeneous (cosanguineous) identity, the timeless topos of the rural village offered a core administrative unit for centralizing control over multiple and distinct cultures in the realm. Based on the idea that 'love of nation [Japan] could transpire from loving (your) *furusato*' (Yanagi 1981: 418), disseminated over the empire, this idealized emotional heartland would ripple from the locus of the Emperor to the peripheries and back (Kang in Calichman 2005: 93). Applied by state administrators in the colonies, this ideological construct helped to 'authorize' ideas and practices of 'family' coexistence and co-prosperity (*kyōzon kyōfuku*) in a greater Asian *furusato* with the Emperor at its apex. It also mirrored the Occidental exoticization of the Oriental other as a recognizable method of colonial rule (Iwabuchi 1994: 49–82).

Even so, in a similar way to other colonial empires,[7] naturalization criteria were measured in fractional degrees of biological origin; Okinawans were 'half'-Japanese, Ainu were quarter-Japanese. Imperial subjects were dignified with Japanese identity to the degree they were prepared to sacrifice their identities for the greater family. To avoid very real ostracism, many subordinated or rejected their former identities, with little choice but to inter-marry and hide their birth-origins behind Japanese names (Siddle 1996: 157).

By the mid to late 1930s, as wartime austerities began to pinch and household metals were requisitioned by the government for the production of munitions, a rustic renaissance was embraced by sophisticated mainlanders (Brandt 2007: 125–39). *Mingei* crafts made of bamboo and ceramic materials provided sturdy, simple, pure and cheap replacements. The *mingei* aesthetic was marketed not only as healthier and thriftier, but also more spiritually sound than imported Western products. For example, one advertisement read,

> [the e]xistence of a nation has significance in its original identity… A Japanese spiritual movement in terms of objects [*mono no aware*] (ordinary household things and architecture) is the very thing that keeps the flag high. (Kikuchi 2004: 16)

'Empty' spirituality, collective, self-sacrificial labour and frugal resilience welded together as essential components of Japanese 'Zen nationalism' ('no-mind'/*tariki*) in the 1930s (Sharf 1993: 1–43) formed a hardened ideological bulwark to resist the seductions of Western materialism (ego-mind/*jiriki*). Fraught with contradictions, this ideology was designed to consolidate the peripheries under the oppressive daily reality of Japanese colonialism.

Positioning *Ankoku Butoh*

Given half a century of laissez-faire individualism, *Nōhonshugi*, Asian orientalism, Zen nationalism and Imperial colonialism and militarism, it is possible to understand how Hijikata's inclusion of Tōhoku folk aesthetics combined with his association with Mishima in butoh could have suggested essentialist and ultra-nationalist tendencies.

This suggestion only seemed to become more ingrained with the fact that Ohno Kazuo was a professed Baptist. A division opened up where Ohno came to be regarded by some critics as the improvisatory 'soul' of *butoh*, while Hijikata was cast as its dark, non-Christian 'architect'. Ohno, whose mother among other female figures was central to his poetic reflections, was considered the feminine 'yin' of *butoh*. Even though

UNIVERSITY OF WINCHESTER
LIBRARY

Hijikata also focused on female figures, he became its masculine 'yang' (Fraleigh and Nakamura 2006: 24) as discussed further in the next chapter. Given the feminization of Japan in the orientalized relations of the Occupation, however, it is more likely that Ohno's and Hijikata's subversive black-and-white clowns in their incomprehensible dances parodied both themselves and the Japan–US conjugation.

While Hijikata and Ohno sought to define their own laws through original practice amid the ideological moulding in transitional Japan, this did not prevent them from drawing inspiration from a past and contemporaneous European avant-garde – Genet's scandalous eroticism, Alberto Giacometti's totemic and mournful human sculptures, Antonin Artaud's embodied disassemblages, Jean Dubuffet's irrational outsider art, Jean-Paul Sartre's critical literary eroticism.

The influence of Antonin Artaud, Andre Bréton and Takiguchi Shūzō did not confine Hijikata to Surrealism, although it was undoubtedly pivotal in the making of *butoh*. Hijikata's poetic eroticism also aligned with the *nikutai-ha* in that its street-level eroticism grounded in material need, far from the romantic wartime self-sacrifice, aimed to liberate desire and its embodiment from normative restraints.

Hijikata's expression of the ontology of rural and urban *mujinkō* – outcastes and vagabonds (Genet), *burakumin* (Shimazaki Tōson, Takiguchi), rural collectivist practices, disease (smallpox, Hansen's disease, *hibakusha*), animals and plant-life (folk culture) – inverted the exclusive post-war values of capitalist techno-pragmatism and its materialist domestication.

For their next performance, Hijikata and Ohno Kazuo chose the title of *Divine* (*Divīnu*) based on Genet's main character (Louis Culafroy) from *Our Lady of the Flowers* (1943). Ohno's signature *onna-gata* (female style) role, or a 'non-bio fem' *chūsei*/transvestite character, was also inspired by nightclub acts and cabaret tours in Tokyo and the peripheries of US bases (Yokohama, Yokosuka, Tachikawa). At the time, both Josephine Baker (1954) and Katherine Dunham (1957) had conducted tours to Tokyo, and could have inspired Hijikata and Ohno in their desire to transgress dominant mores. Ohno's *onna-gata* was a mode widely deployed by many avant-garde choreographers to destabilize gendered (and national) identities, and its mutability intrinsic to a performer's consciousness was a process of defining self.

> There is no being behind doing, effecting, becoming, the doer is merely a fiction added to the deed – the deed is everything. One's attitude is one's posture is one's psychology is one's identity. Drag is a performance of gender identities. Desire causes bodies to merge and become one another. (Butler 1990: iii)

Hijikata choreographed Ohno in a series of short studio-based pieces which celebrated the feminine, as well as a certain masochism: '*Ōjune-sho*', '*Banzai Onna*', '*Hanayomeneko*', '*Hanatachi*', '*Shōrijō*', '*Shōshi*', '*Divīnu*', '*Kirisuto*'. Fragments of these pieces were also included in larger productions directed by Hijikata: *DANCE EXPERIENCE 650* (1960), *Blind Masseurs: A Theatre That Supports Passion/Anma: aiyoku o sasaeru gekijo no hanashi* (1963), *Rose Coloured Dance/Barairo dansu* (1965).

While possible to frame *butoh* as a 'coming out' post-war dance of newly liberated sexuality, or an homage to great female divas as was Ohno's preoccupation, in these early days, Hijikata seemed drawn to the subversive potential of *Divīnu* and Genet's texts. In 'To Prison', for example, Hijikata described how severe hardship and abuse in imprisonment becomes a way to instil discipline towards 'revolutionary struggle for the human solidarity of the naked body' (Hijikata 1961: 45).

> I wager reality on a nonsensical vitality purged of the echo of logic from my body and I dream of the day when I am sent to prison ... sitting smack in the middle of a mistake. (Hijikata and Kurihara 2000 [1961]: 45)

As with *Kinjiki*, Genet's eroticization of transgression and criminality can also be considered a major theme in *butoh*. The onanistic dances in the film 'Un chant d'amour' (1950) based on *The Thief's Journal* (1946), and Abdullah Bentaga's dance 'like a narcissist with an erection' in 'The Tightrope Walker' (1958) reflected Genet's sexualized celebration of incarcerated and marginal bodies (Plunka 1992: 53; Finburgh et al. 2006: 107–16). As Genet wrote,

> The convict's outfit is pink and white striped ... there is a close relationship between flowers and convicts. The fragility and delicacy of the former are of the same nature as the brutal insensitivity of the latter. Should I have to portray a convict – or criminal – I shall so bedeck him with flowers that, as he disappears beneath them, he will himself become a flower ... Towards what is known as evil, I lovingly pursued an adventure which led me to prison ... Erotic play discloses a nameless world which is revealed by the nocturnal language of lovers. Such language is not written down. It is whispered in the ear at night in a hoarse voice. (Genet 2004 [1946]: 4)

It is interesting to note that in spite of physical or social incarceration, the wordless language of the moving body offered solace in the pain of suppressed desire and forbidden contact. As Ohno Kazuo recognized, dancing a 'flower' was a way to live in a 'dead body'.

> [I]f you wish to dance a flower, mime it and it will be everyone's flower but if you place the beauty of the flower into your dead body, then the flower you create will be true and unique and the audience will be moved. (Masson Sekine and Viala 1988: 23)

For Ohno, as for Genet and Hijikata, 'becoming a flower' was not apolitical. In adulation of the diva, Ohno unravelled the homosocial conditioning of his military past. Ohno's modern Taishō aesthetic also cultivated a post-war audience of mostly young middle class women. As symbolized by *Divīnu*, *butoh* beatified a set of qualities that were sanctioned as ugly, wrong or socially repugnant. Genet's primary identification with 'glory in abjection' (Genet 1964: 48) was shared by Hijikata and Ohno who held a vagabond (*fūraibō*) affinity for 'moss, lichen, dog-roses' in the cracks of the concrete jungle (Genet 2003: 88). Their social grotesque valourized debasement in juxtaposition with the modes of efficient materialism in the new capitalist family-state structure. With intense empathy expressed for the crippling effects of enclosure, they proposed to grow flowers in those who experienced social death – transvestite, prostitute, vagrant, criminal – who belonged to their local *mizu-shōbai* (bar trade) sub-culture in Tokyo. As Genet recognized, 'nothing must be protected so much as a little heap of rubbish' (Genet 1973: 168).

Ankoku Butoh celebrated 'forbidden nocturnal society' in the rationalized light of post-war conformity through 'undesirables' whose marginalization serviced the normative inscription of the new and shiny social order. In addition to the usual complement of marginal figures in industrialized environments, Hijikata included displaced and itinerant farmer–labourers. His admiration for these lumpen bodies caste out and pauperized in rapid economic growth that carried their 'pre-modern' rural traditions with them was only surpassed by his love of non-human beings, such as an emaciated orphan dog as I will explain later.

In a critique of the quotidian habits of modern society in the 1950s and 1960s as also reflected in the 'clockwork' repertoire of ballet, Hijikata regarded society's construction of the body of the everyday worker as a corpse. It was a violation and source of great suffering to Hijikata that people should be robbed and numbed to their own bodies through the enervating 'my home' urban density in the 1960s. Arguing that profound and far-reaching revolution lay in re-possessing the human body itself (Hijikata and Kurihara 2000 [1961]: 43), Hijikata proposed the recovery of memory, lived connection to people and place and a more mutable sense of identity.

Around the same moment, identifying the denial of death at the core of the Western capitalist system, Genet volunteered to be the gravedigger who opened wounds through his theatre. He called for a multitude of calendars 'to put the Christian era out of business, for example, as it names and counts time 'from an event that is of interest only in the West' (Savona 1984: 103–5, 110).

In this early period, Hijikata collaborated with many other artists, including featuring in seventeen experimental film shorts, documentaries, and narrative fiction. Some of these included Donald Richie's *Gisei* (Sacrifice, 1959), Hosoe Eikoh's short experimental film *Navel and A-Bomb* (1960), the B-movie director Ishii Teruo's feature-length fiction trilogy,[8] and Ishii's and Iimura Takahiko's film-poem *Ai* (Love, 1962).[9]

In *Anma* (Masseurs, 1963), which Iimura Takahiko filmed onstage (Kerner, Iimura 2009),[10] Hijikata re-created a village festival (*matsuri*) atmosphere in a theatre. According to Iimura, Hijikata created on-stage the 'closed' village mentality, which delineated between insider and outsider. As the audience entered, a number of informal events were already underway: boys doing warm-up exercises and playing catch-baseball, dancers being daubed in thick white body mask, old women in kimono sitting on tatami playing popular shamisen folk songs. As outsiders (*murahachibu*), Ohno enters in Western clothing carrying a pachinko ball and dancing *butoh* and Hijikata rudely interrupts on a bicycle.

In creating the distinct temporality of urban back alleys (*rōji*) or rural villages, modern and local mixtures of dress, music, dance and materials merge pagan folklore with modern consumerism. In this intimate space, daytime street baseball as a motif of youthful hope sat alongside the accumulated collective wisdom mediated by old village women, which also converged with the nocturnal urban *rōji* economies of the brothel and nightclub.

As Genet observed of the mutuality of the palace and the shanty-town (and its red-light district), betrayal is born from poverty in the shanty-town and from anomie in the palace (Genet 2003: 70–72). Desiring to subvert the slum-palace structure, the inverted morality cultivated by Genet (and Hijikata) developed a praxis of treason that emanated from both.

This quotidian preoccupation continued in *Bara iro dansu* (*Rose Coloured Dance* 1965), only in a longer historical sweep. Filmed by Iimura in short takes on a wind-up 8-mm camera, the production was staged on an all-white set designed by Akasegawa Genpei. It included large images of acupuncture diagrams, a vagina and Hijikata's back painted with a flayed spine, live barbers cutting men's hair, Ohno and Hijikata in elegant white ballroom gowns, and a *jinrikisha* pulled by a barefoot Hijikata in long black underwear with Yoshito as a passenger in a white mask and white dress with a fancy hat on a white floor (see Figure 3.1). Signifying the Western origins of anatomy, holistic (Chinese) medicine, militarization through army crew-cuts and cross-dressing colonial/class legacies from Meiji through Occupation, the iconographic images in these scenes and bodies encoded the historicity of modern industrialized Japan.

Iimura distinguished between Ohno Kazuo's 'Westernized' and 'feminine Christian' appearance, which he associated with a more ballet-oriented Taishō modernity, and Hijikata 'as ... not [necessarily] macho, ... [but] more direct than Ohno' (Kerner and Iimura 2009). Despite the cliché of ballet as ascending and *butoh* as descending,

Figure 3.1 Hijikata Tatsumi, Ohno Yoshito. *Rose Coloured Dance.* Photo: Nakatani Tadao, 1965. Courtesy of Butoh Laboratory Japan, Keio University Art Center

this perception delivered purchase. Just as Genet's plays (*The Maids, The Blacks, The Screens*) urged French audiences to confront the state's illusory superiority as its rule over its colonies in north Africa and Indochina was collapsing (Lavery in Finburgh et al. 2006: 95–105), this could be regarded as a repudiation of the paternalistic order in the cosy US protectorate of Japan.

As Genet eroticized prisoners of the State, Hijikata identified the rural villager body as already guilty by the standards of urbanized technocratic 1950s culture. In the anti-collectivist privatized land reform and economic adoption of wheat and dairy in the Japanese diet, rural villagers had been forced to 'to stand' for the 'Good', as Hijikata put it. While Ohno transcended gender norms, Hijikata urged his dancers to 'spurt blood for audiences who come to experience evil' (Hijikata and Kurihara 2000: 38).[11] The 'evil' dance he sought would inspire his dancers to transcend the conforming machines of productivity and growth: to 'pour a secret ritual into the flesh and blood of young people that finishes them as lethal weapons that dream' (Hijikata and Kurihara 2000 [1961]: 44, 47).

Like a cockfight in a farm shed, Hijikata's embodiments of 'small evil' contained the residue of alcohol-fuelled domestic tyrannies that reproduced larger regimes of structural violence and discrimination. As depicted by writers such as self-professed *burakumin* Nakajima Kenji, who migrated from a rural hamlet (*buraku*) to Tokyo in 1965, and in the base-towns of Ōe, Kojima, Ōshiro, Kishiba, Imamura and Takechi previously discussed, these marginalized and impoverished communities were fuelled by the informal economies of gambling (*Go*, backgammon, mahjong, horse racing, pachinko), blood sports, prostitution and male initiation rites in the *rōji* of small *buraku*. In the 1960s, Nakagami described a scene in a *buraku*:

> [T]he razors tied to their right legs caused the cocks to move with a slight limp … as they pecked and kicked each other, the razors dug deep into their flesh, instantly drenching them in blood … This was a world of men in which the older initiated the younger via cruel violence to animals, sake and gambling, using money that could otherwise be better spent on the family. (Nakagami 1999: 134–36)

In 1965, Hijikata toured with Hosoe Eikoh through Tōhoku villages to record Hosoe's childhood memories of rural life for a photographic black and white series entitled *Kamaitachi*.[12] Like many other children who lived through the war, Hosoe was evacuated during the fire-bombings of Tokyo. In an attempt to explore these memories in high-contrast images, Hijikata was shown with his thumb prodding at the sky, with a clumped fist on top of his head standing amid stalks of wild grass playing the fool for rural villagers on a break (see Figure 3.2); watching a rural bride with a bottle of *sake* and gold-filled teeth from a thatched roof; running through a rice paddy with a squawling baby; sitting on a wooden drying fence looking at a stormy horizon; with three dark male forearms supported on their fists (like a horse) below a pale, reclining female buttocks (Holborn and Hosoe 1999: 18–19, 26–29).[13] This was complemented by Moriyama Daidō's grainy images of people in relatively depressed, semi-industrialized towns in Tōhoku in *Nippon Gekijō* ('Japanese Theatre', 1966).

Figure 3.2 Hijikata Tatsumi and villagers. *Kamaitachi*. Photo: Hosoe Eikoh, 1965. Courtesy of Butoh Laboratory Japan, Keio University Art Center

An important function of this work so far is to bring heterogeneity of regional and urban identities and practices to homogenized and amnesiac urban audiences. As part of this broader movement, in *Kinjiki*, *Anma* and *Bara iro dansu*, an ethnographic choreography of a rural and urban subaltern – prostitutes and pimps, rickshaw pullers, barbers, repatriated soldiers, rural brides, farmers, shamisen players, blind masseurs, shamans, children, animals – clearly delineates between privileged 'whiteness' and criminalized 'blackness'. In the broader social movement to reject the 'security' promised by the state in its renewed treaty with the United States, this work indicates the social perspective of a group of rural émigrés living in the polluted density of rapidly industrializing Tokyo.

As a praxis of decolonization, in which the internally colonized (rural émigré, proletarianized worker) seek to express and represent their specific ontology, Hijikata and Ohno re-shaped the (dancer's) body into a weapon of resistance against normative modalities. As I will extrapolate further, their process can be introduced here in two steps:

1. empty the body of 'self';
   so as to,
2. become receptive to otherwise neglected, abandoned or silenced selves
   (Broinowski 2004).

Schismatic frames in *Ankoku Butoh*

'Blackness', as perceived by DuBois in early twentieth-century United States, was negatively configured within a gestural, semiotic space of whiteness (Du Bois and Edwards 2007). Far from a Cartesian thing that thinks (*res cogitans*) as the basis for the modern individual subject, the 'black' body in the dominant Euro-American colonial narrative was perceived as incomplete and in need of development through an internalized mirror of 'whiteness'.

> The Negro is a sort of seventh son, born with a veil, and gifted with second-sight in this American world – a world which yields him no true self-consciousness, but only lets him see himself through the revelation of the other world. It is a peculiar sensation, this double-consciousness, this sense of always looking at one's self through the eyes of others, of measuring one's soul by the tape of a world that looks on in amused contempt and pity. One ever feels this two-ness – an American, a Negro; two souls, two thoughts, two unreconciled strivings; two warring ideals in one dark body, whose dogged strength alone keeps it from being torn asunder. (Dubois and Edwards 2007 (1903): 8)

Locked within 'natural' givens (authenticity, particularity) and subjected to internal surveillance, the colonized body either reacts or settles into resentful, semi-existence (Johnson 1993: 595–614). Becoming estranged, Dubois' 'black' corporeal schema of exclusionary gestures experienced evacuation and return to itself as *past*. Narrow biological parameters reinforced social enclosure and internal 'reform' of the black body, while the indignities of poverty, sickness and inequality stemming from systematic discrimination constituted the negative or collateral effects of 'whiteness'.

In the anti-colonial struggles in decolonizing territories in the 1940s and 1950s, theorists such as Leopold Senghor in Senegal and Aimè Césaire in French-Martinique and Frantz Fanon in French-Algiers, who championed the 'Negritude' movement for an independent, if idealized, Africa, confronted the quandary of a divided polity of the colony that may never be whole. In Fanon's, 'The so-called dependency complex of Colonised Peoples' (1952) and Césaire's 'Discourse on Colonialism' (1955), 'doubled consciousness' could only be overcome through national self-determination (Fanon 1967: 29–44; Césaire 1972). Even Japan was upheld by some as a model of non-Western resistance to Euro-American colonialism (Miyoshi 1991: 41). Despite criticism for naturalizing mythic origins and a noted imperviousness to self-scrutiny (as critiqued by Wole Soyinka and Kwame Appiah), the subaltern could not wait for permission from the European proletariat to act. '[T]his anti-racist racism is the only road that can lead to the abolition of racial differences' (Sartre 1988: 296).

Fanon's own proposition in French-Algiers was to re-define racialized space, so as to reverse the colonizer's monopolistic claim on rationality. Amid competing visions of belonging and selfhood between colonial and decolonial movements, there is an undeniable distinction between a bio-determinist hierarchy enforced by an occupying power through a comprador elite, and horizontally organized resistance who seek independence and agency, re-claiming what they perceive to be a prior-owned habitus. The comprador elite tutored by 'former' colonizers used the modern *techné* of 'nationalism' to suppress their own indigenous formations (Guha 1982: 1; Chatterjee 1986: 100). To counteract an internalized inferiority, identity helped mobilize pride in authenticity in those below and establish common ground, albeit irrational, among ordinary (semi-literate) Africans to assemble resistance to the divisive colonial dispensation. As Fanon pointed out, this phenomenon was similar in French-Algiers.

> Every colonized people – every people in whose soul an inferiority complex has been created by the death and burial of its local cultural originality – finds itself face to face with the language of the civilizing nation ... the colonized is elevated above his jungle status in proportion to his adoption of the mother country's cultural standards. He becomes whiter as he renounces his blackness, his jungle. (Fanon 1967: 18)

Instead of romanticizing 'the jungle' or mythic origins *per se*, this 'nativist' thinking or 'blackness' was a mythic construction to resist the effects of social death from colonial dominance, and is arguably transversally applicable across localized temporalities and territories. Having already applied a Pan-Asianist orientalized form of doubled consciousness to its colonial populations, a semi-colonized Japan perpetuated this form of discrimination as intrinsic to the political economic programme primarily directed by the US hegemon. Just as Fanon perceived 'the black man's soul as the white man's artefact', white, once a colour used for funeral rites in Japan (Ohnuki-Tierney 1990: 203–5), had become the colour of ubiquitous domestic appliances.

The aesthetic signature in butoh of the 'naked body in white paint' suggests more than a refined cosmetic foundation derived from modern *Kabuki*, *Nihon Buyō* (Japanese traditional dance) or geisha performers. While later generations of *butoh-ka* (*butoh* dancers) aestheticized the whitened body, adding shaved heads or semi-closed eyes to convey a sense of detached equanimity, the crumbling lumpy body masks of early *Ankoku Butoh* suggested a different political ontology.

Resembling botched reconstructive surgery, Hijikata's epidermal metaphor alluded to a normative layer concealing otherwise inhumed layers akin to other forms of 'double consciousness'. This 'schismogenesis' or 'duality schism' (Bateson 1979: 116–17) reflected the ontology of an urban subaltern community. As Hijikata wrote:

> This cast-off skin is totally different from that other skin that our body has lost. They are divided in two. One skin is that of the body approved by society. The other skin is that which has lost its identity. (Holborn 1986: 121)

This view was not dissimilar from the broader civil rights movement emerging in Japan in the late 1950s. In the desire to give voice to minority cultures in Japan, several focus groups engaged the distinction between privileged 'whiteness' and pauperized 'blackness'. The journal *Buraku*, for example, published a special edition on racism against black people and the *burakumin* in 1963 (Reid 1963: 44–48), and the *Asahi*

UNIVERSITY OF WINCHESTER
LIBRARY

Journal featured a round-table discussion with Nōma Hiroshi, Asada Zennosuke and Yukiyama Yoshimasa in 1968 (Nōma and Yukiyama 1968: 82–89).

Celebrating the so-called dark, abject or inferior – the less visible or totally invisible – through the deformé bodies of *Ankoku Butoh* was to conduct a struggle with a mediated social diet of commodity fetishism and exoticized tradition, or 'whiteness'. Challenging the internalized image in this way was to repossess a body that had been stolen.

More than competition with other artists for a niche audience as the modus operandi for *butoh* artists, Ohno's chthonic eroticism imbued in his improvised clownish children and his modern charismatic women and Hijikata's criminalized subalternality reflected their dedication to re-sensitizing the social underlayers from within the dominant 'luminous analysis'. As the *butoh* critic Mikami Kayō observed, Hijikata's discontentment was rooted in a Cartesian subject that determined universal rational truth within a vertical order (Fraleigh and Nakamura 2006: 18, 40). Hijikata's perspective from an urban ghetto in semi-colonized post-war Japan and from an internal colony in Tōhoku since the Meiji period, informed a dance imbued with the tension of competing layers of meaning ordered in an imposed hierarchy of value. As Fanon writes,

> It is one thing to displace a people as Other within a dominant discourse. It is another to subject them to that 'knowledge', by the power of inner compulsion and subjective con-formation to the (white) norm. (Fanon 1967: 395)

The primary struggle intrinsic to Hijikata's butoh was over lived reality. The feeling of not being real or not existing in society that fuelled the desire for self-expression, recognition and status in society was a powerful driver for Hijikata in creating *Ankoku Butoh*. In this regard, the *butoh* body employed irrationality, sensation, myth and memory to re-claim a sense of reality that was otherwise not availed to it. As Fanon wrote,

> [T]he native's challenge to the colonial world is not a rational confrontation … it is not a treatise on the universal, but the untidy affirmation of an original idea propounded as an absolute. The colonial world is a Manichean world. (Fanon 1963: 41)

Rebellion of the flesh

As waves of revolt were engulfing the streets of major cities across the world over the 1960s, 'blackness' had already been a primary site of mobilization for self-determination for nearly two decades (Sartre 1988: 296). For Hijikata's contemporary Terayama Shūji, an experimental poet and theatre and filmmaker, 'blackness' was mutable, a set of behaviours that are 'performative' in relation to context. Recognizing commonalities with the contemporaneous struggles of African-Americans, Terayama appropriated Norman Mailer's notion of the 'white negro' (Mailer 1957).

Just as in America, where there has been the emergence of a type called white Negroes, I feel as though we were raised very much like yellow Negroes in the upheaval of all values during the immediate postwar era in Japan. I think there is a resemblance in so to speak, being 'under domination'. (Terayama 1978: 260–62; Yamashita et al. 1986: 26–31; Cornyetz 1999: 159)[14]

From the perspective of the internally colonized, Nakagami Kenji identified with black jazz and its reflection of a legacy of slavery on American plantations. As the late poet-activist Amiri Baraka (LeRoi Jones) observed, on the plantations 'the drum was banned, which should draw attention to its political nature, because it could fuel and communicate rebellion ... black music is about feeling ...' (Bermel 1996 [1973]: 247).[15] In contrast to the commercial jazz exported in the 'charm offensive' organized by the CIA-sponsored Congress of Cultural Freedom (CCF) in the 1950s (rarely benefitting the musicians), Nakagami referred to the jazz of Albert Ayler, Cecil Taylor and Sun Ra. These artists preserved the early Sorrow Songs while engaging the polemical tone of the Black Liberation Movement. Un-recuperable to the easy melodies of American capital, the experiences of the historically oppressed as intrinsic to 'free jazz' were observed by Nakagami and others as reverberating in '[neo] ghettos throughout the world'.

As leftist jazz enthusiasts nothing gave us more pleasure than participating in a violent anti-war day, rock-throwing in Shinjuku and overturning cars near Shinjuku station, setting things on fire, rioting ... no one dissented when someone intoned 'this is free jazz'. (Nakagami 1990)

Certainly, the 'black' body was a socio-historic site of violence and trauma not just in the United States (Thompson 2008: 16) but in other colonies and territories of the 'new world' as well. Indeed, Third World solidarity with the anti-colonial revolutions in Asia, Africa and Latin America inside the United States peaked while the American war in Vietnam raged in the late 1960s to early 1970s. Some in the Black Arts Movement such as African-American playwright Sonia Sanchez in *Sister Son/ji* (1968) attempted to connect this with the contemporaneous movement in Japan but seemed to fall short. Sanchez paired a Hiroshima Maiden with an African-American man against two white businessmen in a card game, in which the former pair fail to collaborate (Wood in Kolin 2007: 53).

While their concerns overlapped, rather than essentialized as 'Being', however, blackness was a useful signifier to cohere a fragmented identity due to oppression, express solidarity with other liberation struggles and invert the bio-politicized production of social strata in a political and economic system of 'whiteness'.

In sync with this energy, in October 1968, Hijikata made a seminal solo-work *Hijikata Tatsumi and the Japanese: Rebellion of the Flesh* (*Hijikata Tatsumi to Nihonjin: Nikutai no Hanran*).[16] As indicated by the titular 'Hijikata and the Japanese people', this performance was a series of iconographic sartorial changes that arguably evoked the radical social transformations undergone in Japan's late and rapid modernization in the twentieth century.

From an animist shamaness surrounded by her 'animals' who is stripped and caged like a demonic barbarian, who becomes an elite sophisticate and is re-educated as an innocent girl, we can see Japanese people purged of 'evil' and re-created in an image preferable to the Occupier and comprador elite.

> A stuttering post-war country bride enters trailing an animist dowry of rural backwardness and a live pig in a bassinet; stripped to reveal a golden phallus strapped to the convulsing hips of his bare body, in the 'wild flame of immediacy', slams itself into brass plates in front of which hang dead roosters; dancing passionately in a waltzing and flamenco-dancing in a red and white satin ball gown and black rubber gloves; skipping innocently like a young girl with his hair in pigtails; after which his body in a white loincloth is bound by ropes and drawn up and suspended in the air. (author's observation of 'Nikutai no Hanran' CD ROM, 2004)

If a narrative is to be derived from this performance, the strange and reclusive shamaness surrounded by animals emerging from rural Tōhoku village life on a palanquin switches to 'wild' masculinity of muscle, sweat and death (hung roosters), a golden prosthesis interpreted by some as Artaud's anarchic hermaphrodite emperor 'Heliogabalus' (Artaud 1958: 154; Barber 1993: 5; Barber 2005). Although compelling, I posit that this is less likely a Greco–Roman reference (as in Dionysus, 'Heliogabalus', Adonis) and more likely a visitation of a *tengu* deity replete with a crashing storm in a local Shintō fertility ritual.

In the Lacanian view, this 'evil', erotic, passionate, vital and emasculated figure would suggest a transcendent Japanese 'lack' (*manqué*) (Lacan and Fink 2006: 575–84). In actuality, the prosthetic device was likely inspired by a show by the 'Matriarch of black dance', the American choreographer and activist Katherine Dunham, whose troupe toured Tokyo dance-halls and clubs in 1957 (Elam and Krasner 2001: 193).[17]

As *Nikutai no Hanran* was held in the centenary year of the formation of the modern nation-state of Japan under the Emperor Meiji, in a slightly longer *durée* the rural bride with her animist dowry transforms into a warring demon who is eventually contained and 'civilized' in modern elegant behaviour and eventually re-born in youthful innocence. The memento mori of the palanquin, animals and dead roosters offers stark contrast to the aristocratic ballroom gowns of modern national elite, which Hijikata then satirizes in his lascivious flashes of his underwear. The dyad of a joyful innocent school girl and doubtful teacher in a loincloth suggests the pedagogical and future oriented dynamic during Japan's post-war re-birth. The bound and suspended body of Hijikata in the penultimate scene suggests an overall condition of sacrifice (of the past) to preserve the power elite and institutions of the reconstructed nation-state. When Hijikata re-appears with a fish in his mouth for the curtain call, it appears that he has crossed the river to the other world. We can read a century of subordination and enculturation of rural fisher–farmer and proletarianized people to the modern centralized capitalist state, first under the Japanese sovereign and then under bicephalous Japan–US authority.

Akin to Ohno Yoshito's killing of the chicken in *Kinjiki*, 'gifting' is again central in this performance. Baird usefully finds that Hijikata's initial idea of using a live pig was denied and so he hoisted himself instead (Baird 2012: 115–30). Whether human or pig, in the auspicious centenary of the modern Meiji state, we can see an offering made from the lowest (animalized) in the social strata in subordination to and preservation of the existing order in its (new) Japan–US iteration.

This transition from older rural animist cosmology through industrial modernization to late capitalist society evokes, to this author, a process in which power is concentrated in sovereign authority through the dispossession, devaluation and sacrifice of sensuous bodies (surplus) of their accumulated pasts. Rather than a celebration of or devotion to this process, *Nikutai no Hanran*, I contend, contained an irreverent eroticism that undermined the binding of 'inferiorized others' in the logic of centralized authority. As Ohno Kazuo described it, it was the 'eroticism [of his performances] ...', as that 'which people feared' (Slater 1986: 8). Eroticism, in Bataille's formulation, disrupts self-containment through a generous act of losing the self 'in another to the point of death' (Bataille 1962: 15; Bataille 1991: 76–78). This eroticism in Hijikata's oeuvre, 'the disorder of lost beings' as Bataille puts it (Bataille 1962: 113–14), is what was antithetical to the disciplinary and unifying telos in the conical order of sovereign power.

The synchronicity of *Nikutai no Hanran* with the civil rights and black power movements in the United States and international revulsion for the slaughter of rural agrarian peasants in Vietnam televised for the first time was part of the struggle for decolonization of the Third World. The internally colonized and those poor and primarily agrarian peoples in decolonizing nations already shared commonality in their exposure to the visitation of state terror through aerial bombardment in the US intervention in Asia between 1945 and the mid-1970s. Consistent with colonization by earlier imperialist powers, the Cold War saw a slightly different process of 'regime-change' that included covert operations such as the non-democratic installations of Syngman Rhee (Yi Seung-man) and Park Chung-hee (ROK), Ramon Magsaysay (Phillippines 1953), Shah Reza Pahlavi (Iran 1953), Ngo Dinh Diem (South Vietnam 1955) and his attempted removal (1963), the 'Gulf of Tonkin Incident' (Vietnam 1964) and General Soeharto (Indonesia 1965–1966), among others.

The fear of the emergence of a global power from Eurasia that could challenge its geostrategic primacy (Mackinder 1969: 89) was shared across the upper echelon of the Western political and military establishment. President Kennedy declared to General De Gaulle in 1963 that 'the Chinese would be perfectly prepared [to enter a nuclear war] because of the lower value they attach to human life to sacrifice hundreds of millions of their own lives' (Chang 1988, 1293). This was echoed by US Armed Forces commander General Westmoreland (1966–1968) who observed that the 'Oriental doesn't put the same value on human life as the Westerner' when interviewed about the My Lai massacre (*Hearts and Minds*, Peter Davis (dir.), 1974).

As the public mythology of American altruism began to fall away during this war, articulations of renaissant theories of 'blackness' articulated by political activists and authors James Baldwin, Richard Wright, Malcolm X, Angela Davis and Martin Luther King were gaining broader acceptance. In reclaiming 'blackness' from an otherwise axiomatically devaluing narrative, these activists extended their own experiences of conflict between a hegemonic other as self and minority self as other to those diverse groups exposed to the state terror of the American war in Vietnam.[18] 'No Vietnamese ever called me nigger', as Mohammad Ali put it in 1967 after his conviction for draft evasion and five-year prison sentence, was part of an eloquent statement that is worth quoting at length.

> Why should they ask me to put on a uniform and go 10,000 miles from home and drop bombs and bullets on Brown people in Vietnam while so-called Negro people in Louisville are treated like dogs and denied simple human rights?... I will not disgrace my religion, my people or myself by becoming a tool to enslave those who are fighting for their own justice, freedom and equality. If I thought the war was going to bring freedom and equality to 22 million of my people they wouldn't have to draft me, I'd join tomorrow... So I'll go to jail, so what? We've been in jail for 400 years. (Marqusee 1999: 219–20; Allen 2008: 94)

On 4 April 1967, in his Riverside Church speech 'Beyond Vietnam: Time to Break the Silence' in Chicago, Martin Luther King considered the leviathan US military industry to be 'the greatest purveyor of violence in the world today', which abstracted the deaths it produced through its interventions and its skewed body counts and which lacked moral equivalence. King asked,

> [h]ow can they trust us when now we... charge them with violence while we pour every new weapon of death into their land?... Surely we must see that our own computerized plans of destruction simply dwarf their greatest acts. (Marable and Mullings 2009: 442–43)

Indeed, from the 'pacification' tactics – indiscriminate incendiary and chemical aerial bombings and scorched earth actions, concentration camps, torture – they knew that Vietnamese self-determination was never the primary US concern. In a war to prevent the 'first domino' from falling (Eisenhower, 7 April 1954), the US military conducted a war both for the geostrategic importance and for the resources Vietnam represented. In what General Westmoreland called a 'war of attrition', a conservative estimate finds 4 million Vietnamese killed in total, and 3 million casualties in 1965–1975 (Hirschman et al. 1995: 807; Ngo Vinh Long in Kutler 1996). In the continuing use of chemical weapons in contravention of the Geneva Conventions, 3 million Vietnamese are estimated to have been victims of Agent Orange (Neilands et al. 1972: 30–32; Cecil 1986: 179). Together with punitive embargoes, using chemical 'defoliant' and dropping more explosives than the total used by the Allies in the Second World War was the reality of 'containing' the PRC and 'opening up' the 'under-developed' lands of South-East Asia for industrialization by the centres of global capital (Smith 2005: 163–64; Nelson 2008). Further secret operations in 1964–1973 to combat the Pathet Lao support for the North Vietnamese Army saw the USAF drop more than 2 million tonnes of ordinance over Laos on 580,000 bombing missions (1 plane load of bombs every 8 minutes, 24 hours a day for 9 years). Roughly 30 per cent of the 260 million cluster bombs dropped in Laos failed to detonate, and continue to cause injury (Legacies of War, April 2010).

The war crystallized people's feelings against the United States and Japan's complicity with it, particularly in Okinawa which served as the war's 'launch pad' and through which US troops rotated and military armaments were repaired. In 1965, with Prime Minister Satō Eisaku's 'moral support', Japanese construction corporations provided base-building materials and supplies for US troops and received roughly $1 billion a year from the conflict (Havens 1987: 96). When negotiations began for Okinawa's reversion to Japanese control, Okinawans were promised that US bases would be reduced to the mainland level (*hondō nami*). This was betrayed following reversion as US troops and bases remained in use, only now they were paid for by the Japanese people (Mitchell 2015). As discussed earlier, the effects of this betrayal is seen reiterated in Nakagami's collage of the degrading reality of the informal economy sprung up around the bases:

> Of the ocean of the thirty thousandth embrace, of the condom in the brown dog's mouth, of the bed-wetting urine of someone stoned, of self-deception, of the giddiness of cheap whiskey, of the assholes of men who love men, of the ejaculations of prep-school students, of falling soldiers sent to Vietnam, of the penis soaring above and undulating in the clouds, of a revolution betrayed, of comic tragedy. (Nakagami 2000: 223)

So, 'whiteness', encapsulated in the neo-Hayekian post-war US–Japan state-corporate formation, extended through US-led operations and proxy wars in Asian 'pieces' of greatest geopolitical purchase for the United States. It can be understood as a normative set of 'free world' principles and practices to support a world-historical system of capital accumulation and military dominance. 'Blackness', by contrast, held the counter-hegemonic potential to bridge divisions and alliances of nation-states, institutions and corporations to identify commonalities of oppression. Although biopolitics was one tool of division, race was not the ultimate raison d'etre.

Discrimination and the village narrative

As outlined in Chapter 2, the hierarchy of values inculcated in the dominant techno-scientific narrative of national renewal (*fukkō*) supported the large-scale re-privatization of land and rural industrialization by renewed *zaibatsu* monopolies in Japan in close cooperation with the US corporate-state. Reminiscent of the movement of settler–farmers into the 'vacant' lands of Manchukuo under the Japanese Empire in the 1930s (Lee 1967; Tamanoi 2009: 49), and as demonstrated by the US-led wars in Korea and Indochina, the real target of US state policy was to liberate land from local village subsistence economies (Honda 1972) and transform them into export processing zones (EPZs) and economic engines to boost economic growth in the centres of capital. Japan's middle-class urban affluence in the 1970s was not discrete from this aim.

As planned by the Kishi and Ikeda administrations, cheaper and less-protected labour and less-organized environmental opposition in rural lands in the early 1970s, not to mention geostrategic value, saw heavy industry move from Japan's urban centres to establish industrial precincts in rural areas in Japan, South Korea, Taiwan, Thailand, Malaysia, Indonesia and the Philippines. This period, aided by the oil shock of 1973, also saw the intensive startups of Japan's commercial nuclear power plants, the first of which was the Mihama No. 1 reactor in Fukui-ken used to power the Osaka Expo '70. Politically vulnerable communities were selected and then plied with financial incentives and public works projects in return for the installation of large-scale nuclear reactors and other energy related facilities on their land (Tanaka 1973; Kōta in Hindmarsh 2013: 41–56).

In the giddy rush of financial buoyancy in the increasingly deregulated, networked financial systems of the mid-1970s, Japanese society returned to issues of identity, mythic origins, new-age spiritualism, futurist escapism and *Nihonjinron* nationalism. Perceived as a compensatory 'obsessive return' for social dissolution (Harootunian 1988: 66), in the literary world, theorist Etō Jun proposed Tokugawa epic poetry as the vessel for essential Japanese identity (Sherif in Jager and Mitter 2007: 145). Yanagita Kunio's post-war archaeology of *jōmin* identities also received greater attention. This trend seemed to reflect a yearning for peasant agrarian culture, though only vaguely related to a Third World politics of a global South.

Rather, it reflected the 'whiteness' dynamic in which collective fantasies (*kyōdō gensō*) were commodified to supplement for the generational memories and knowledge erased in the land's reconfiguration as industrial site. Production as perceived through an object and its industrial means was transformed into productive labour in the buying, selling and exchange of parts of space (Lefebvre 2003: 155).

Marxian theorists such as Yoshimoto Takaaki, a leader of the New Left, defended the collective ethos of 'sociality preceding individuality' and its indivisible connection with the land that had motivated the farmer presence at various protests since 1945 (Yoshimoto and Miyazawa 1989: 227–28). Validated by global financial institutions as economic 'maturation', the erasure of the subaltern farmer's capacity for collective agrarian self-sufficiency and their transformation into mobilized individuated labour was proportionate to the deep penetration of centralized capital into most areas of organized life in Japan and in East and South-East Asia more broadly. For Yoshimoto, temporary autonomy could be found in subaltern 'emotionality' that was 'coolly indifferent' to the 'evil animal/angelic human' binary that underpinned modernity (Simmel and Wolff 1950: 409–24; Yoshimoto 1968b).[19] This was consistent with Spivak's insistence that elite intellectuals 'de-hegemonize their position in learning how to be the Other' (Spivak 1988: 251–68; Murakami 2005: 110).

While commodified, some attempts to recover childhood memories of the rural village in this period were part of a genuine attempt to find alternative social meaning amid increasing environmental degradation. The village as a remnant of (mythic) 'original time' and a model of horizontal embodied relations became a repository of utopian yearning. This appealed to those who perceived the prevailing system as having lost social trust, as homogenizing or as unsustainable. For many artists, village collectivity offered sites wherein the reinvigorated senses could recover open, spontaneous, active, mutable sociality. They suggested a form of existence beyond the structures of 'whiteness'.

In this way, beyond binarized ontology, Hijikata's butoh 'horizontalized' knowledge by re-valuing a human ability to feel and articulate as opposed to its capacity to acquire and consume. In its exploration of wild, grotesque, erotic and ambiguous zones, *Ankoku Butoh* dilated the body towards a somatic intimacy with the non-human environment. Not a quest for origins, this villager ontology smuggled into de-realized urban density facilitated resilience through the body's fibrous ties to the world. In response to the urban body ossified in 'whiteness', the darkness of *butoh* offered a portal to feel the presence of others, both within and outside itself.

In short, darkness created space for collective emotions, senses, memories and imagination that existed beyond the 'polis walls' of rationalized capitalism. The impossibility and in many cases undesirable return to a completely pre-modernized actuality notwithstanding, darkness offered fertile conceptual ground to succour memory, or what Hijikata called 'the dead'.

> To make gestures of the dead, to die again, to make the dead re-enact once more their deaths in their entirety – these are what I want to experience within me. A person who has died once can die over and over again within me. (Hijikata in Holborn 1986: 127)

Just as a material ontology of whiteness filters out obstacles to the capitalist imperative, often with biopolitical tools, darkness extends beyond superficial cutaneous or racialized, alienating, amnesic and isolating logic.

As in Shindō Kaneto's silent black-and-white near-ethnographic feature film *Hadaka no Shima* (1962), a farming family comprising of a father (Taiji Tonoyama), mother (Nobuko Otowa) and older son (Shinji Tanaka) toils to eke a meagre existence in the sun, sea, wind and dirt on an isolated mountain island. Neither romantic nor nostalgic and not only drudgery sometimes attributed to the film (Acquarello 2003), *Hadaka no Shima* focuses solely on rhythmic labour and its temporary interruptions by seasonal village celebrations. This evokes memories of simpler self-sufficiency and resilience in the harsher climes of the archipelago. The family's isolation suggests social stigmatization and neglect. It also can be associated with Hijikata's stated aim to recover the simplicity of a 'naked culture', and by this I don't mean an immiserated one stripped of human rights.

Less poetic than *Hadaka no Shima*, Imamura's *The Insect Woman* (*Nippon Konchūki*, 1963) follows the social rise of a Tōhoku émigré from subaltern to proletarian to middle class status. 'Tome', a young woman living with her family in rural poverty moves to a factory during the war, where she falls pregnant to the foreman. Keeping the child but losing the father and her job, like many others, Tome turns to sex work in the city, eventually becoming a brothel 'mama-san'. Interspersed with newsreel footage of historical events – Fall of Singapore of 1942;

Figure 3.3 Hijikata Tatsumi. *Gibasan*. Photo: Yamazaki Hiroshi, 1972. Courtesy of Butoh Laboratory Japan, Keio University Art Center

1949 Matsukawa Incident; 1952 'Bloody' May Day riot; 1956 Sunagawa struggle; May 1960 *Anpo* struggle – in a time of silkworm farms and modern appliances, Tome learns to exploit herself and others as she transforms from anonymity to an aspiring individual within a liberal capitalist order.

Tome's transition typifies a rural émigré's options in post-war conditions. In contrast to the self-abnegating 'Mizoguchi woman', Tome demonstrates an 'insect adaptability' to not just survive but to prosper (Mihalopoulos in Saaler and Schwentker 2008: 278). Becoming a partial historical subject as she gains relative financial independence within a broader system of whiteness, Tome adopts the behavioural code of a cynical petit-criminal who accumulates wealth and status by repeating what had been done to her. Tome's daughter Nobuko, by contrast, having narrowly escaped the sexual attentions of Tome's 'keeper', returns to work on the land where Tome eventually joins her. Unlike Kurosawa's *No Regrets*, Nobuko returns from the city to reclaim her land and possible self-sufficiency.

Akin to both Hijikata and Shindō, Imamura's admiration for the tenacity of rural and urban working class women to survive in the post-war economy complemented his broader concerns for those who are written out of history.[20]

> If women had to use their bodies as weapons in order to obtain rice then that was fine. After all there was no other way. (Imamura 2000: 234; Standish 2011: 91)

In *History of Post-War Japan as Told by a Bar Hostess* (1970), Imamura converses with Madame Onboro, a bar hostess, in front of a screen projected with newsreel footage. Onboro's father was a black-market butcher, suggesting her *burakumin* status and also in loose association with the contemporaneous slaughter-house of the United States's war in Vietnam. Onboro describes her life from the bombing of Hiroshima to the present, detailing her affairs and children with US GIs on Yokosuka naval base. With no family, Onboro's story constellates the lives of *hibakusha*, *burakumin*, *mizu shōbai* workers, US soldiers and peasants in Indochina.

Both Tome and Madame Onboro occupy the informal grey zones prescribed and sanctioned by the state. As they embody the hypocrisy of 'civilized' society, these subaltern characters undermine the moral respectability of national projections in their daily sacrifices to insulate the dominant classes from the violence of transnational capital accumulation.

In *The Profound Desire of the Gods* (Hasebe Keiji (scr.), 1968), made as the anti-*Anpo* demonstrations were cresting, indigenous superstitions of the village community in Kurage-jima (Ishigaki, Okinawa) clash with the interests of mainland capital as represented by a visiting engineer (Kariya). The village headman (Ryūgen) and community regard a bad drought on the island as punishment for incest, which is held to be the gods' domain, and for which they blame on Yamamori the Futori family patriarch and task them with community service. Yamamori's granddaughter Toriko (lit. prisoner, or slave) is both a willing concubine and a *noro* (Okinawan shamaness). His son Nekichi, a cuckolder and a dynamite fisherman, is assigned to move a great rock to allow fresh water to flow to the rice paddies. Nekichi's sister Uma is Ryūgen's mistress and head priestess of the main shrine. Yet the source of the drought is more likely the city's use of water for sugar cane, for which Ryūgen has received funds. Kariya is to oversee a new well construction but is seduced by Toriko and Uma.

As his major preoccupation, Imamura presents three interwoven organizing structures in the village: matrilineal spirituality, extended patriarchy and modern state capitalism. An 'eros'-based matrilineal cosmology operates both in service to and conjunction with a patriarchal order based on collective village ownership on a fecund island. The matrilineal modes of affection misrecognized and regulated under the patrilineal law of bloodlines (family registration) attract taboo due to exogamous infidelity and incest.

Present also are entangled historical periods of modern contemporary, the pre-industrialized period of the Tokugawa (and earlier) and the modern Meiji state. We see the disruptive potential of eroticism re-directed by a patriarchal order into ritual, sexual service and manual labour. The modern capitalist state built around the nuclear family unit exploits this politically powerless community for wealth extraction (as development). Again, as with Ōshima's *Gishiki*, the United States is the state's silent partner.

As also suggested in Hijikata's *Anma*, to ameliorate the alienating sterility in the monochromatic urban corridors of single *danchi* estates from the 1950s to the 1970s, rural émigré workers brought local traditions to re-create a sense of collectivism (Imamura 2000: 59; Standish 2011: 86). Imamura's tales of eroticized collectivism in various periods, celebrated horizontal ties, generous affections and social fluidity that bind socially marginalized groups (*kiso shakai*).

The distinction between Imamura's village and feudalism can be seen in Shindō Kaneto's *Onibaba* (1964). Set in the Muromachi warring period tells of two peasant–farmer women who make a living from killing errant warriors and selling their armour,[21] this is typically framed in feudal terms: 'soul-corrupting', 'pre-Shintō', 'empty darkness'. The old woman's human cry at the film's end is sometimes regarded as the film's only redemptive moment (Acquarello 2003; Cummings 2006). Instead of an example of the horrors of Japan's 'primitive' feudal past from which it was to be eventually enlightened and civilized (due to modernization), *Onibaba* portrays the abject ('shanty-town') desperation of an informal economy constructed amid the instability created by the warring ('Palace') states. This condition is an allegory for the present, as well as one particular to a historical period.

These notable examples of a post-war engagement with heterogeneous and subaltern alterities reflected the conditions of a sub-class rural and urban poor clustered around US bases, in factory-towns and industrial sites in mainland Japan, Okinawa and elsewhere in Asia. As do the *burakumin* and *hibakusha*, these bodies and their representations destabilized the nationalist meme of the homogeneous, classless and efficient nation-state underpinned by the myth of pure Japanese identity, as they exposed the inner engine of an over-arching 'whiteness'.

Rather than an idealized form of indigenous purity, the awkward eloquence of Hijikata's *butoh* invoked 'blackness', which included the contradictions of bodies immersed in a society recovering from destruction while under continuing occupation by and in deep collaboration with a foreign power. These qualities, often stigmatized as 'savage', reflected the shock and scarcity in burnt cities, displaced populations living in polluted urban spaces under construction and historically exploited peasant–farmer–fisher collectivities. Not a way of life, *per se*, *butoh* ontology suggested 'people [living] by sheer will ... like living corpses, and the scars on their souls manifest themselves somewhere on their bodies' (Ōta in Minear 1990: 272). This condition can also be extended to a vast and uncounted number of villagers exposed to the American wars in Korea and Vietnam (displacement, exploitation, extirpation).

An Aesthetic Analysis of *Ankoku Butoh*

In a period Ohno Yoshito described as the beginning of Hijikata's 'own dance' beginning around 1972, Hijikata developed and recorded a set of études in choreographic notations known as the *Butoh-fu* (Butoh phrases). These helped *butoh-ka* (Butoh dancers) to cultivate degrees of sensitivity and emotional complexity as an antidote to the superficial immediacy of consumerism. It also offered a method to explore the mercurial domain of memory.

Together with his wife Motofuji Akiko, Hijikata opened the dance studio Asbestos Hall in 1974 (*Abestos-kan*). He worked intensively to choreograph sixteen works with his main dancer Ashikawa Yōko, the co-founder of the Butoh company Hakutōbō. Other groups that were set up by students of his workshops include *Harupin Butoh-ha, Genjūsha, Byakkosha,*[1] *Hakutōbō, Muteki-ha, Dairakudakan, Dance Love Machine* and *Ariadne* for whom Hijikata occasionally choreographed (Kuniyoshi 1986a: 127–41; Kurihara 2000b: 29–33). Ashikawa commanded significant respect from other dancers for her strength and skill, and sometimes was even associated with Japanese female shamanism (*miko, itako, yamauba*) and the mythic sun-goddess Amaterasu Ōmikami.

Instead of leaping to the judgement of *butoh* as a reactionary form of heliocentric ethno-nationalism, or 'cultural fascism', as discussed in the previous chapter, the ethno-nationalist *minzoku* ideology, which sacralized the peasant farmer as a core organizing unit in the Empire of Japan was radically distinct from the horizontalist collective ontology expressed by Hijikata and other post-war artists. On 9 February 1985, in his farewell speech 'Collection of an Emaciated Body' (*Suijaku-tai no saishū*, also *Kaze Daruma* or 'Wind Dharma') in the first 'Butoh Festival' 85' in Tokyo, Hijikata described his childhood home of Akita in Tōhoku as a staple supplier of soldiers, geisha, rice and horses to the central government (Hijikata 1985a: 71; Hijikata 1985b; Kurihara 2000a: 21). Hijikata's reference point was the colder northern regions of Tōhoku and its harsh and exposed climate of persistent and bone-chilling winds, its spring mud and rushing rivers. The collectivist ontology of its villager inhabitants was based on pre-State folk Shintō animist traditions that were more localized and less essentialized than within the nationalist frame of the Meiji state. As Hijikata stated, 'Tōhoku also exists in England' (Hijikata 1985a: 17; Hijikata 1985b).

Butoh was also distinct from a 'free world' ideology in which religion served as a lever in the US-led ideological offensive in Asia during the Cold War. In an anecdote in *Kaze Daruma*, Hijikata clarified that rather than any particular spiritual entity, the original source for *butoh* was the mud. He also shared a particularly formative childhood experience of being rescued from the riverbed, where he was trapped by a whirlpool (*uzu*) in a rushing river swollen with melted winter snow. He considered his rescue and release from the riverbed as one re-birth among many, and a core experience the *butoh-ka* must regularly undergo (Hijikata 1985b).

> Sometimes in early spring I would fall down in the mud and my child's body, pitiful to its core, would gently float there...While in the mud, it occurs to me that I could very well end up being prey...It's as if my body had, from its very core, returned to its starting point...But I can, I know, declare that my *butoh* started there with what I learned from the mud in early spring [*shundei*], not from anything to do with the performing arts of shrines or temples. I am distinctly aware that I was born of mud and that my movements now have all been built on that. (Hijikata and Kurihara 2000: 73–74)

Rather than personal trauma as the kernel of Hijikata's *butoh* aesthetic, his allegory addressed both suffering and awakening as a pre-condition for constant transformation (Hijikata 1985b). In Hijikata's experiences of the whirlpool and the mud are transformative because he becomes aware of a pre-existing vulnerability (prior to conscious knowledge) underpinning life's passage. In understanding the vulnerability of the human body exposed to larger forces, Hijikata also allegorized the *hyakushō* condition in particular, as it existed in relation to the structural violence of capital accumulation in the broader projection of state-corporate power.

Such sense-memories were crucial in the creative nourishment of *butoh-ka* in *Ankoku Butoh*. Similar to but with a different intention than Yanagi Muneyoshi's version of grotesque beauty in agrarian communities in the colonies that evoked a 'power deep behind the race' (Kikuchi 2004: 146), Hijikata's 'peasant grotesque' dance was borne from direct experience of generational poverty and exploitation in an internal colony. As distinct from a nationalist narrative, the characteristic low, slow, grounded intensity of *butoh* offered a translocal, ontological structure from below.

Non-linear but certainly not 'off-balanced', *butoh*, as a dance borne out of the earth, embodied a conscious rejection of a 'human'-centred hierarchy and actively sought to recover 'somatic intimacy with nature'. Not striving to separate from earth and attain ethereal elevation and lightness towards the sky, *Ankoku Butoh* is telluric and autochthonous.

Neither scientific nor strictly aestheticized, Hijikata's practice refined a sharp attentiveness to sensory qualities to develop a skilled appreciation of the living world. Outside an anthropocentric order of value, this invested non-human qualities and phenomena such as a duck, the northern wind, darkness or a flower with significance. The inclusion of the irrational, unclean or wild was not gratuitous. It was to include the ephemeral, grotesque and hybrid as ordinary while infusing them with allegorical logic. In this transgressive way then, *butoh* could engage in profoundly humane praxis.

Butoh plays with time, it also plays with perspective if we humans learn to see things from the perspective of an animal, an insect, or even inanimate objects. The road trodden everyday is alive ... we should value everything. (Masson-Sekine and Viala 1988: 65)

In creating radically inclusive spaces, Hijikata undermined the nationalist illusion within the dominant biopolitical order. As I will show in the following, together with an interest in a peripheral vernacular culture drawn from Tokugawa *kabuki*, visual arts and *taishū engeki* (popular theatre), Hijikata's figurations can be better understood through its commonalities with the modern avant-garde movement in Europe between 1890 and 1945.

Fragmentation: Masks, words, bodies

Claude Levi-Strauss in *The Way of Masks* (1972) identified the emergence of modern art as the moment when a human mask came to hide rather than showing the face. Levi-Strauss found that less concerned with revealing an essence than concealing a mistake, modern masks were death-masks which hid deformities, disfigurations and rhinoplasties resulting from the new weapons of the First World War.

The new inventions of aerial weaponry had dramatically re-drawn the scope of military violence and geopolitical relations with it. In 1921, Guilio Douhet predicted the evaporation of the distinction between soldiers and civilians and that the battlefield would dramatically extend beyond the artillery range of guns, so that the repercussions of aerial offensives would be felt directly by all citizens, becoming combatants within the boundaries of the nations at war (Douhet 1942).

Even before the 'Great War', however, the early century European artists anticipated this modern pre-occupation with masking. As distinct from Hieronymous Bosch's masked perversities in the *Garden of Earthly Delights*, James Ensor's symbolist grotesque paintings featured masked figures among swarming crowds and their swirling emotions. Edvard Munch invoked a similar quality in his paintings.

I saw all the people behind their masks – smiling, phlegmatic – composed faces –
I saw through them and there was suffering – in all of them – pale corpses – who without a rest ran around – along a twisted road – at the end of which was the grave. (McShine and Heller 2006: 210)

Dispersed across several major cities on the continent and in New York during the First World War, Dada artists responded to the bodies produced from the conditions of Euro-American modernity as magnified in its industrialized form of warfare, particularly in medical, psychological and technological domains (Ball and Elderfield 1996: 55; Harrison and Wood 2003: 246–72).[2] They recognized a monumental shift that the First World War represented in the history of the human body (Tison-Braun 1977; Melzer 1994: xvii),[3] as reflected in their juxtaposed images of patriotic soldiers rolled out via the 'influencing machines' of the nation-state (Tausk 1933: 519–56) and the hallucinating *les grands motiles* veterans returned from the labyrinthine trenches and craters of the battlefield. From these literally fragmented war veterans, Sigmund Freud developed an analysis of neurosis and trauma (grounded in Daniel Paul Schreber's diaries), and 'prosthetic artists' developed new *plastikos* techniques to re-mask the shattered 'body-in-pieces' (Schreber 2000). As returnee bodies drifted like floating limbs severed from the unified military body, these were some of the early attempts at social reintegration through 'human design' so as to avoid too much disturbance.

> [Transforming] ... torn, mutilated beings, without any faces, who would otherwise be unbearably repulsive and almost certainly economically dependent, into normal men who could live normal lives, as individuals, and be of service to their country. (Haiken 1997)

Despite the impossibility of such a return due to overwhelming damage suffered, a major aim of these therapeutic interventions was to mitigate the growing potential for public objection to the war. Despite the aim to return the veterans to work through cosmetic and internal reform to sell the validity of the war (Eliot 1952: 37–55), the permanent disfigurement and fixed gaze of traumatized veterans overlaid with cosmetic patchwork produced a new living and visible archive. These actual figures and artistic testimonies contained the corrupt ideology of modern 'human' power.

The cyborgian 'humanchine' proto-types indicated the next new evolutionary step. In contrast to F.T. Marinetti's glorification of this war as 'Futurism intensified' (Marinetti and Flint 1972: 123), however, Dada artists developed a corporealized aesthetic as a reflection of the psychological and emotional inscription of the war, which produced 'shocked objects' from the 'paralyzing horror of events' (Tzara 1977: 65).

The cut-up collage of organic, material and environmental elements mirrored the grand-scale battlefield and reiterated its relentless systemic demolishing and re-fusing of in/animated matter in the dynamic of progress (and profit). Dada artists peeled away the respectability of Euro-American societies through 'bizarre and passionate gestures'.

> Dada put everything in question, seriously revising values and confronting all those who participated in it with their own responsibilities. (Tzara in Motherwell 1989 [1951]: 402–15)

Often marked from Alfred Jarry's *Ubu Roi* ('King Ubu', 1896), Dada texts (re)introduced performance into a theatre dominated by modern literary drama (Fell 2005: 53).[4] Resisting the authority of words, these performance texts emphasized everything else: gesture, sound, costume, objects, movement and texture.

Sometimes dismissed as meaningless, 'illegible', 'anti-art' and 'playful',[5] there has been a concerted attempt to defuse Dada as deliberately non-sensical, childish or obscurantist. In the narrow concern for Dada's artful innovations Dada has been de-politicized, serving to re-bury the bodies it had exposed. In *The Gas Heart* (*Le Coeur à gaz*, 1921),[6] Romanian-born co-founder Tristan Tzara likened the play to the war itself: the 'greatest three-act hoax of the century which will satisfy only industrialized imbeciles who believe in the existence of men of genius' (Tzara 1964).

Tzara's bitter satire was a polemical anti-war performance. In his titular allusion to poison gas munitions[7] with the materiality of the war veteran at the play's centre, Tzara recognized the literal embedding of the systemic logic of the war in the human body. For example:

> The woolen lower jaws of our carnivorous plants... In what limitless metal are your fingers of misery inlaid?... breasts of copper and crystal; The beauty of your face is a precision chronometer; or,... his stomach is full of foreign money. (Tzara 1964)

Tzara's dialogue between human facial parts (Eye, Nose, Mouth, Ear, Neck, Eyebrow) indicated the hypocrisy of continuing civil human relations in lieu of the war: 'have you felt the horrors of the war?' asks the Eye; 'I love the young man who makes such tender declarations to me and whose spine is ripped asunder in the sun', proclaims Mouth; Nose addresses a 'man with wounds of chained wool molluscs'; Ear states: 'He is not a being because he consists of pieces' (Tzara 1964 [1922]; Garner 2007: 500–16). If there was unified conviction and purpose in war's beginning, its aftermath was littered with instability and discontinuity in which identity, truths and trust were fragmented, to which these artists responded with the 'purely functional and necessary' (Tzara 1977 [1917]: 57).

> Mouth:... the mirror is blank when I look at myself. (Tzara 1964)

In self-critical style, Tzara admitted that 'DADA remained within the framework of European weaknesses, it's still shit, but from now on we want to shit in different colors so as to adorn the zoo of art with all the flags of all the consulates' (Tzara 1977 [1916]: 1–2).[8]

Richard Huelsenbeck, the founder of the Berlin chapter of Dada, criticized Tzara and his group as being 'bandits who demolished and destroyed the centuries' (Tzara 1977 [1918]: 12).[9] Instead of the play's incendiary effect on Parisian audiences from its 'despair encased in aesthetic destruction... not known since the days of Robespierre', Huelsenbeck proposed a utopian approach.

> The new man was joined by the new art work, made of new material, expressed in a new consciousness of human totality. (Huelsenbeck 1974: 104)

Forming consensus in ridiculing European civility and the slaughterhouses it produced, Dada artists celebrated chance assemblages while refusing authorial hegemony. Duchampian 'ready-mades' availed a whole panoply of objects for artists' use; Jean Arp made 'elementary art' with everyday materials to 'save mankind'; Man Ray fused inorganic materials with figurative representations;[10] Rudolf von Laban's dancers wore satirical masks in soirées; Marcel Janco wove 'primitive' masks from multiple materials (Arp 1948: 39; Motherwell 1989: 236–37).[11]

As Antonin Artaud confirmed, in the diseased modern human condition, the 'face is an empty force, a field of death … one has the impression that it has not yet started to say what it is and know what it knows' (Artaud 1965: 229; Artaud et al. 1995: 275). Artaud named God as the panoptic operation that signed-off on the internalization of painful bodily formations through 'a psycholubricious thrust of the sky'. Disabused of the ego-self as an internalized structure of the broader order, Artaud sought liberation by extracting and expelling this 'animalcule'. Opposed to a unified State subject – a body with organs, or State-organized body – Artaud proposed 'organic' evacuation – 'no mind, no soul, no heart …' – to void the human of the interpellation of its organs wartime propaganda towards organized self-sacrifice for the nation (Artaud 1974: 13; Hewitt 1993: 134–35). Only when the social body, as opposed to the head, 'becomes a mouth', Artaud argued, could society speak (Artaud 1974: 67–118; Weiss 1992b: 197).

Instead, Artaud proposed ritual release of 'intellectual screams from the delicateness of the marrow' to reach an 'elementary consciousness', to sense and recover vibratory pathways of thought through a 'body without organs' (later 'BwO') (Artaud 1974: (2)17). He explored consciousness as dispersed – 'sometimes knee and sometimes foot' – and equated it to being 'a corpse who forgot his own body' (Artaud et al. 1988: 28; Thévenin in Derrida and Thévenin 1998: 150).

Artaud's under-appreciated negative dialectic of 'emptiness' links him to the critical art and theatre of Huelsenbeck, Piscator and Grosz and can be traced to Nietzsche (Taylor 1990: 196–97).

> Today our conscience knows what these uncanny inventions of the priests and the church are really worth, what ends they served in reducing mankind to such a state of self-violation that its sight can arouse nausea: the concepts beyond, Last Judgement, immortality of the soul, and soul itself are instruments of torture, systems of cruelty by virtue of which the priest became master. (Nietzsche and Hollingdale 1968: 150, MX 138)

Putting aside the appropriation of Nietzsche's texts by right-wing nationalist movements that preyed on interwar despair (Lukács 1981: 37–92),[12] Artaud's criticisms were aimed at the mediation of the human body as a mechanism in the industrial war-machine. His critique also extended to 'new American democracy' post-1945. Like the Reich of the 1930s, 'America' also produced 'soldiers, armies and battleships' in preparation for an 'insane machining against all the competition which would inevitably break out on all sides' (Artaud 1974: 70). He turned his admiration to those people 'who eat right out of the earth and who kill the sun in order to establish the kingdom of black night' (Artaud 1974: 145).

In Artaud's 'anti-*kultur*' period, when he underwent electroconvulsive therapy and insulin-shock treatment in the Rodez mental asylum for nine years, he was steadily reduced to 'uncontrollable tantrums and hallucinatory coprophilic' episodes (Artaud 1974: 153). Misunderstood by his contemporaries, who pathologized his 'trances' and 'disjecta membra' as pitiable (Bréton 1969: 110),[13] Artaud was subsequently marginalized. The diet of chemicals, isolation and psychological examinations was clearly painful, and seemingly as an escape he envisioned 'sporadic re-immersion' into a 'theatre of cruelty' – a 'bath of psychic electricity' of theatrical magic, 'primitive' irrationality and 'true horror' (Artaud, 'I Rodez' 1974 [1945]: 321). His brief encounter with 'Bali-dance' and Tarahumara rituals in Mexico held the clue for what this meant, which he considered as having '*electrical* magic' (Artaud 1958: 48–73).[14] In the post-war 'abyss of shattered symbols', this re-signification away from the formulaic modern industrial world-view informed by the false morality of the church was Artaud's alternative (Weiss 1992a: 126).

Artaud's 'foreign irrationalism' as an alternative to 'modern values' presents difficulty as possibly naïve exoticism. When the American artist Nancy Spero dedicated to Artaud an exhibition of her art works that were critical of American military intervention in Vietnam (*Codex Artaud*, 1971–1972),[15] for example, she said:

> Magic disappears in the light of our rationality. [Yet] we can never truly know their art if we do not believe in their gods. (Weiss 1992a: 54; Blocker 2004: 45–47)

By the 1980s, Artaud was considered a 'negatively a-productive individualist' (Stallybrass and White 1986: 119), and his 'mad literature' was critiqued as dangerously fetishistic. Others like Jean Dubuffet, an artistic champion of 'outsider' or 'naïve' art, took up Artaud's defence.

> Where is he, your normal Man?...For me, insanity is super sanity. The normal is psychotic. Normal means lack of imagination, lack of creativity. (Dubuffet in Weiss 1992a: 136)[16]

In answer to Spero's quandary, although embryonic in form when he died, Artaud's recognition, however intuitive, was less a literal belief system and more concerned with his experience of the porous body immersed in and sensitive to organic electrical pulse as distinct from the discrete modern subject (and its violent electrotherapy).

In a stimulating convergence, Allen Weiss's reading of Artaud through the sculpture of Michel Nedjar suggests the function of the surrogate in ritual. Nedjar's dolls of glass, cloth and flesh were mutilated to warn or protect against the return of past or coming future violence.

> Bury it to dig it up again, decaying things, the earth gnawing away, no frontier between decay and its opposite,...in mud...I am the doll, I am making, to remember, so I can forget. (Nedjar in Weiss 1992a: 19)

This use of ritual as a creative action or *karman* in Mauss' conception (Mauss 2001: 23–24) that substitutes and witnesses for the past or potential violence presents the transformative role of the rite (Levi-Strauss 1982: 42). Unlike the literal exchange of bodies, territory, property and sovereign rule in war, the rite (using mud, doll, mask etc.) is performative and preventative. Dada's conscious illogicality and Artaud's escape from rationalized madness were, in fact, accurate assessments of modern sanity as confirmed by the emergence of the hot and proxy wars in Asia and Cold War nuclear security regimes as the norm.

Having outlined some key principles from the inter-war and post-war European avant-garde, we can now further the analysis of the praxis of *Ankoku Butoh* in post-war Japan.[17]

Butoh notation

In his first ten years of *butoh* work, Hijikata 'never set a choreography' (D'Orazi in Scholz-Cionca and Leiter 2001: 338).[18] In the development of *Butoh-fu* in his second decade of work, he and Ashikawa crystallized sensations in movement phrases. Sometimes material was derived from poetry (*haiku* poet Nagata Kōi) in the form of streams of non-sequiturs pasted on the studio walls, used to identify phrases, and printed on performance posters (Nakanishi 1987: 82). Ashikawa described their work together.

> For almost ten years our daily routine began with his drumming on a small drum stretched with animal hide... with his words, which he uttered in a stream-like poetry. When we danced ... it was like following a poem. (Holborn 1986: 16)

Ashikawa's physical sense for the words and Hijikata's use of onomatopoeia and juxtaposition, ungrammatical conjugations and fragmented discombobulations – 'dribbling candy' (*nadare ame*), 'rotting space' (*ma gusare*) – created (im)possible states for dancers to manifest (Kurihara 2000a: 16). These *Butoh-fu* broke open language and released energies in the 'joints' of words to stimulate the languaged body to create a body-language. As meaning learned through words was destabilized, a passage was opened towards hidden memory, and other forms of truth. Exposing the self and the body to the unfamiliar was a staple avant-garde mode since Jarry. Yet a practical encoding to assist the uninitiated to interpret their imagination through abstract poetry into physical experience was particular to the *Butoh-fu* (Waguri 1998).

The embodiment of language in the *Butoh-fu* is a process of 'image induction'. This enhanced the body's sensitivity and softened its socialized and calcified habits. In becoming animals, plants and atmospheres, the sensory manifestation of a poetic text encouraged intimate dialogue between the corporeal condition and the imagination.

It may be suggested that this process was yet another method of removing the impediments to fill empty bodies with the will and ideas of a charismatic leader. As the text was only a cue for the *butoh-ka* to use to practice and attune their bodies to, however, this suggests their greater autonomy. *Butoh-ka* work from a neutral or basic posture. Yet this is not a uniform or identical design for movement in unison. Although Hijikata certainly set choreographies, the *Butoh-fu* is not a set of instructions for a performance. Working from a balance between emphasis and formal posture (*katachi*) (Kurihara 2000a: 21), the lexical prompts repeated as études cultivated a 'sensory fluency'. In performance, *Butoh-ka* condensed imagined and experienced sensations they had refined in practice into a distilled atmosphere in which an audience could 'bathe' (Broinowski 2004: 11–13).[19]

The *butoh* grotesque is often linked to dance histories of expressionism and early psychoanalysis, including Mary Wigman's 'facial and body tics' and 'emotional fits' (*Hexentanz*, 1913) and Laban's notations of spatio-physical models for human movement (Kinetography, 1920s). It also triggered protuberances, hybrids and contractions beyond a logocentric, psychological and scientific shell that contained the 'human'.

Similarly, a hybridized heteroglossia as found in Bakhtin's bucolic Christian socialist aesthetics (Bakhtin 1984: 367–68) may also be invoked with regard to *butoh*.[20] Yet we need to be aware of the Cold War instrumentalization of Bakhtin against totalitarianism (framed as monologue). Like Ensor's carnival, *Commedia dell'arte* and *Opéra bouffe*, and pre-sanitized versions of *Kabuki* and folk *Noh* theatre, the *butoh* landscape was filled with human and non-human masks and senses. In relation to the subaltern collective rural forms in Asia, Ashikawa's deeply etched masks and bent postures in a 'melting limbo' of emotional experience silently magnified the figural archive from communities in the rural north (Kurihara 2000a: 30).[21] In the ugly beauty of morphing deformation, Ashikawa's dance was emblematic of the stubborn tenacity of a courageous woman (*yūfu*) (Kurihara 2000a: 22).

Rather than privileging area or cultural specificity, however, it is fruitful to examine how the grotesque informs our analysis of *butoh*. As Geoffery Harpham observed, 'grotesqueries…[call] into question the adequacy of our way of organizing the world, of dividing the continuum of experience into knowable particles' (Harpham 1982: 3). In the grotesque, earth and living human and non-human beings are blended in the world, in transgression of human laws which mitigate against disruption and contamination. Bakhtin's analysis of Rabelais' bodies describes an open, messy and fecund condition.

> The body discloses its essence as a principle of growth which exceeds its own limits only in copulation, pregnancy, childbirth, the throes of death, eating, drinking and defecation. (Bakhtin 1984: 26)

As evident in Western and non-Western mythic traditions,[22] the disruptive commingling of grotesque human–animal figures breaks open the clean and standardized order of 'human' norms. The ever-present grotesque is suppressed by institutional discipline and surveillance, spatial arrangements, patterns of labour and consumption. In the early performances of *Ankoku Butoh*, grotesque ritual confronted audiences with their concealed memories and primary fears. They also performed substitution.

Abjection as figuratively signified by refuse and corpses (part of grotesque), in Julia Kristeva's reading, 'show me what I permanently thrust aside in order to live' (Kristeva 1989: 3–4). Waste is a performative forestalling of the final loss of 'I' when the body becomes a corpse, or waste. From another perspective, however, waste could be regarded as regenerative of the broader ecological metabolism in which the human is organically re-connected with and mutually strengthens all forms of life. Rather than disgust, waste may be attributed greater value.

As sometimes perceived in variations of disgust, distortion or even deformity, the 'crude' appearance of near-naked and masked *butoh* bodies seemed to substantiate Yanagi Muneyoshi's prediction that modernity would stifle the 'beauty of the grotesque' (Kikuchi 2004: 146). Yet the 'thickness' of masks of white 'mud' that seal the *butoh* face and body could also be seen as protective. The *butoh-ka* is protected, as they approximate emotions and senses that breach taboos and confront fears (i.e. disease and death). With the degree of distortion as proportionate to the social toxicity breached, this substitutive action released potentially disruptive memories of bone-deep abjection. As affectivities are triggered, the *butoh-ka* is shielded with the 'cladding' and 'grounding' of the mask. A double function is performed: unearthing the semi-conscious fears of the audience, while protecting the performer. But this does not mean the *butoh-ka* is detached from the affectivity triggered.

In response to material desire and the demands of efficient productivity in the 'developed world', *butoh* bodies cracked open the narrow mould and repertoire of modern human movement to expand consciousness towards our biological foundation within the living planetary organism. Instead of a stiffly preserved traditional arts archive, *butoh* (along with *angura* theatre) recovered aspects of worker and peasant vernaculars that remained connected to this deeper memory (Mayo et al. 2001: 269–309).

There was notable commonality in the *karman* of *butoh* and Artaud's imagined 'theatre of cruelty'. But instead of a mechanic following a genius' blueprint, Hijikata and his collaborators created a distinct discipline and a lived philosophy, in dialogue with these other artists and their legacies. As an antidote to the crisis of modernity in which human ontology is moulded in the interests of capital accumulation, Hijikata aimed to 'take society's costume off'. In correlation with Artaud's call for 'physiological revolution' (Artaud 1958; 23–24; Artaud 1965: 169–73), and as part of a loose assembly of 'theatres of the body' around the world, Hijikata denoted a 'special passivity' of the animal (*aru tokushū na judōsei*) in his *Butoh-fu* and essays. 'Lifting the sternum', for example, expressed Hijikata's admiration ('jealousy') for the taut skin drawn across the ribs of a stray dog, which can be associated with Giacometti's 'Dog' sculpture (1951). The ontological condition of hunger concentrated in this image indicates the meaning imbued in *butoh* forms.

As a way to shed the negative daily pressures of modern 'rationality' on the body, every rehearsal began with the following phrase:

Walking body (*Hokō-tai*)

A bowl of water rests on top of your head
Eyes are of glass
They reflect rather than see
You cannot see anything but everything is seen
Razor blades are attached to the inner soles of your feet
Pull your sternum up
Joints of the body are hanging on threads of spider web
Relax your hands
Your soul precedes you, your form follows

You want to go out into your body
Walking eyes, walking legs
The space is widened. (Hino and Broinowski 2002)

This posture sensitizes the feet to the floor, lowers the centre of gravity by softening the knees and opening the ankles, and pulls the abdominal wall back against the spine to lengthen it while supporting the centre from which to move. Loosening the jaw and drawing back the chin lengthens the neck, while the chest is softened, so it is neither collapsed nor pushed out. As the shoulders drop, the arms and the head 'float', as the 'bowl of water' placed on the head allows unforced poise. A held core and released body creates space and facility. While based on the Noh principle of *tanden* (centre), or *shin* (core/soul) (Broinowski 2004; Fraleigh and Nakamura 2006: 107), active 'emptying' configured in the *butoh* posture avails to the dancer a greater range of movement through which many 'selves' could pass. As Ashikawa observed of Hijikata:

> In the course of a two-hour performance, he started as a thirty-nine year old, and gradually he became younger and younger. He became thirty-five, then he was twenty-five, eighteen, twelve, and I remember thinking … this must be the secret of dance. (Ashikawa in Holborn 1986: 128)

Enmeshed within alienating urban enclosures, the substitutional work was to create a site in and between bodies in which partial refuge could be inhabited. While not replacing a lost commons, for those suffering consumerist isolation, social exile or restraint and prohibition, some respite could be found through the temporary extraction of the dominant ontology imposed upon the individual on a daily basis.

For Ohno Kazuo, burdened by a strong sense of duty to others and from his eight-year service as a soldier in the Imperial Japanese army, two of which were as a POW in New Guinea, *butoh* functioned as a sort of potlatch.

> Many people die to serve the living … I carry all the dead with me. The soul wears the costume of flesh, universe flesh, speaks for universe, peel off skin, kill flesh on the road, lay them down. The suffering of others have been engraved in us … we survived only because others died in our place. (Ohno and Ohno 2004: 60, 255, 298–99)

Having begun the return to Tōhoku in the early 1960s through several trips and tours (*27 Nights for Four Seasons*, 1972),[23] although part of an entrepreneurial ride upon popular nostalgia, Hijikata was increasingly preoccupied with excavating his personal memories. His second phase of work came to an end when Hijikata withdrew from the *butoh* scene and closed Asbestos-kan around 1976. As *butoh-ka* travelled first to France in the early 1980s, and spread from there, the 'thickness' of the masks notably became smoother, more refined and closer to the texture of *Kabuki* or *Nihon Buyō* make-up. Hijikata's student Nakajima Natsu, among others, produced her solos in this period. Nakajima's adaptation of the 'walking phrase', for example, suggested the shift underway in the approach to *butoh* at the time.

Carrying eternity (your ancestry) with you, your body disappears, you forget to ask, you become nothing, and you walk to the other end … Flowers are sensory organs carried at the center of the body, breathe into your center, be unassuming, give without being asked, let the flower carry you. (Fraleigh and Nakamura 2006: 115)

In dilating analytical focus to expand into a mind–body mediated by a central 'flower', possibly called 'soul', we can perceive a more generous ontology, aware of its connection with a past and to others. In her signature bomb-shelter hood (as in *Kimi no Na ha* in Chapter 1), Nakajima's nuanced 'flower' also suggested a traumatized condition with a *ressentiment* desire.

In the context of a resurgent nationalism and dispersal of the anti-*Anpo* and anti-US bases movements to Okinawa, Hokkaido and overseas in the 1980s, the substitution of the grotesque had a different effect. Inflected with a sense of national victimhood, the emphasis on Japanese suffering of the US area bombing also raised the problem of deflection of blame for suffering inflicted upon populations exposed to Japanese imperial war crimes in Asia. In this way, *butoh* drew closer to an increasingly dominant ethno-nationalist narrative.

In the following, I turn to concept of decay and its associated themes of death, memory, time and disappearance that are fundamental to A*nkoku Butoh*.

Bodies of decay

It is through a state of dementia that we will regenerate our vision … by employing this decay at will. (Dubuffet 1988 (1968): 101)

Hijikata's appreciation of decay recovered the presence of the abject and death in the predominant modern fixation with vitalism and life-oriented aesthetics. In recognition of the labyrinthine intestinal structure and actual lived realities concealed within and beneath the social apex, Hijikata found rich material in children. Not as affirming symbols of hope and the future but as examples of resilience in repressive worldly conditions, Hijikata recalled the community practice of swaddling babies in baskets or tying them to poles in their houses while the parents worked in the rice paddies of Akita. He noted how they played with their 'body parts as if they were not their own'.

I would sneak over to take a peek at those kids. They made strange movements; one fed food to his own hand [as if it were somebody else's] … he must feel that he was somebody else. (Hijikata 1987a: 50)

Instead of pathologizing such behaviour, as found in American wartime and post-war anthropological interpretations of Sioux Indian 'cradle-boarding' or Russian swaddling practices as the root of unremitting rage in adulthood, Hijikata observed the body transformed into a creative object of thought and play for the child. With limited range of movement and sources for attention, after their cries go unheeded, the child turns inward to ask 'what is a hand? what is a foot?

what is walking?'. Hijikata's point was that less stimulus catalysed an imaginative (non-normative) exploration of oneself.

One example is Hijikata's 'Crawling Doll' *Butoh-fu* phrase as performed to the 'The Dying Swan' from Tchaikovskii's *Swan Lake*, '... life [began] when the dried scum on a baby's eyes cracked open'.

Crawling Doll (*Hai-hai Ningyō*)

A baby is crawling on all fours
The baby crawls backwards
The baby becomes a doll
The baby freezes and becomes an object. (Hino and Broinowski 2002)

A 'baby' crawling backwards to one of the most iconic ballet scenes of tragic death seemed to invert the infant as one of the central images of hope, developmentalism and future-orientation in modernity. Learning to crawl in recognition of mortal limits drew nearer to lived reality.

The embrace of decay and death in the *Butoh-fu* undermined the Platonic light–dark binary and the fundamental mistrust of *eikons* ('phantoms') as false consciousness. Populated with dead babies, derelicts, worm-infested bodies, ghosts, *gaki* (dwellers of the first ring of Buddhist hell), rotting plants and dry flowers, neither *pathosformel* nor primitivist 'fetish' (Gombrich and Saxl 1970: 325–58), *butoh-fu* resonated with folk Shintō and popular Buddhist sensibilities.[24]

This embrace of shadow and death in *butoh* could be equated with the 'pathos of melancholic loss and the beauty of death' (Tansman 2009: 15), as a core element of Japanese quasi-fascist aesthetics. Yet, as I have pointed out so far, the embrace of non-nationalist collective rural life in *butoh* appears to be in contrast with the highly aestheticized orientation of self-sacrifice for the nation (Littleton 2005: 71–72).

In his farewell speech, Hijikata also said, 'I may not know death, but it knows me' (Hijikata 2000: 77).

We should keep the dead by our side and live with them.

All we have now is light.
The light was carried on the back of our darkness.
That's why darkness runs away from the night.
We haven't got darkness at night these days.
The darkness of the past was clear and limpid. (Hijikata 1987a: 84)

Advocating a permanent presence for death in social consciousness is not synonymous with a political desire to return to a society of direct imperial or militarist rule. Without romanticizing them, Hijikata's relatives were part of village populations of itinerant workers from Tōhoku who sought seasonal work in trading ports and colonial peripheries in East Asia, South-East Asia and the Pacific. In their vulnerability in insecure conditions, it was as common for such miners and tenant farmers, to be entrapped in prostitution, opium addiction and slave labour as it was for them to find employment and settle. Hijikata's inspiration was drawn from these specific folk sensibilities in pre-electrified rural communities in Tōhoku, as well as their post-war adaptation in newly industrialized urban spaces. Hijikata's embrace of death was less pre-disposed to fascism than it was consistent with pre-modern indigenous traditions as well as it was imbued with wartime experience. Ohno Kazuo, regarded as the 'lighter' side of *butoh*, also reiterated the importance of liminality between life and death, human and cosmos. Similar to indigenous Okinawans, whose graves are shaped as a woman's womb and birth canal,[25] Ohno regarded the womb as both mother and universe that flows through these interwoven realms. Ohno wrote:

> Which is a boat, which is a river? Interwoven life and death, a baby holds onto a mother, a mother onto a baby in the flow of a river. My mother's womb? The womb of the universe? Butoh is the womb of my mother and the universe. Thought is reality, reality is thought. (Fraleigh and Nakamura 2006: 65)

There is also commonality in a Western philosophical tradition that can be traced to Heraclitus, Lucretius, Seneca, Manilus and Montaigne, all of whom acknowledge death's presence at birth. As Montaigne wrote, for example:

> Your death is a part of the order of the universe ... The constant work of your life is to build death. You are in death while you are in life. (Montaigne 1958: 64–66)

While wary of romanticism, the modernist desire to castigate the 'august voices' of spirit possessions and apparitions as atavistic or orientalist superstition (Lehmann 2006: 59) leaves less room for paying serious attention to these modes as forms of thought.[26] The outcome is to render them vulnerable to anthropological instrumentalization, as discussed earlier.

The material effect on the body evident in the *Butoh-fu* was to dilate crystallized clusters of sensation and release fragments of memory. Through a de-rationalized experiential ontology, the internalized will and its rigid classifications that supported the modern *logos* became more ambiguous. The body was re-oriented towards other entities. Immersed in material energies, agentic attention shifted to moving from outside the 'self'.

With homeostasis as a core principle in the *Butoh-fu* and its praxis, the self comes to be informed as much by environmental conditions as by internal volition. In this sense, the *butoh* body is situated in-and-as 'landscape', which includes pasts (selves, memories, atmospheres) that are liberated in the present mediating body ('spirit'). Neither particularly essentialist nor nationalistic, working and thinking through sensations and non-lexical imaginaries naturally drew from and engaged philosophical and socio-political meaning (Yoshimoto in Bhathal 2009).[27]

Spirituality as de-subjectivized time in Butoh

Despite the broad and hybridized practical and conceptual engagement of *butoh*, its analysis has tended to downplay its socio-political associations while emphasizing spirituality. Pivoting on Hijikata's rejection of formal religion and Ohno's embrace of it, *butoh* is often binarized in a light–dark frame. Hijikata's *butoh* is characterized as 'yang' (masculine) and Ohno's *butoh* as 'yin' (feminine). The former is considered energetic, destructive and perverse, while the latter is calm, maternal and regenerative (Fraleigh and Nakamura 2006: 24). Although Hijikata's 'godlessness' has been characterized as his 'dark spot' (Fraleigh and Nakamura 2006: 48), Ohno Yoshito maintained that Hijikata's last words were 'god's light' (Ohno 2004: 137), while for Motofuji Akiko, they were '*banzai*' ('hooray', or lit. 'eternal life') as he danced on his death-bed (Masson-Sekine and Viala 1988: 94).

Where 'overt' *butoh* and 'expressionless Noh' have both been attached to a universal *yūgen* (grace or mystery) (Greiner 2008), *butoh-sei* (*butoh* qualities, or *butoh*-ness) are sometimes de-historicized as an 'aesthetic everywhere'. Fraleigh's detailed attention to the Zen *butoh-ka* is also evocative; an ephemeral soul-body (*konpaku*) who dances in the darkness (*yami*) of a river of desire (*yoku no kawa*) between living (*shigan*/此岸) and dead (*higan*) in a cosmic nothingness (*mu*) (see also Dopfer and Tanerding 1994: 55).[28] But Hijikata's *shigan* (志願), or naked 'volunteer soldier', presumably engaged the present world in non-violent struggle.

In the *Butoh-fu*, the *butoh-ka* engages contradiction so as to make the body receptive to clearer sensation.

People in the dark and light (*Mei-an no Jinbutsu*)

A telepathic girl seen by the falling star-/(You as the girl)/The girl has four holes in her body/So you can see the air behind her/A glove on her right hand/The moment she sees the star her pupils dilate and move slowly/She swoons in the brightness/She becomes dark in the light/The holes open wide in her body and the light hitting her forehead becomes dark/Become the outline of her body, so only the outline is visible/All that is within is dark/Being the falling star, the human girl has disappeared/And as the light hits the forehead in light and darkness, she moves between light and dark in her body. (Hino and Broinowski 2002)

In this poetic map, the *butoh-ka* confronts paradox, or coexisting contradiction (*mujun dōitsu*), in which they are neither subject nor object, *and* both subject and object. In this convergence of subject and object, dark and light, death and life, paradox assists in sensing the body's momentary synthesis in deformation, magnification and dispersal within the cosmos.

Formalized in Zen Buddhist concepts such as *ma* or *yūgen* as found in the Noh treatises of Zeami (1363–1443) (Rimer and Yamazaki 1984: 120–25), William Blake, who features in the *Butoh-fu* as a long beard, also recognized the process of breaking open consciousness by struggling with text (Blake 2000: 88). Dostoyevsky described a character's epileptic seizure leading to sudden illumination of life's synthesis (Dostoyevsky et al. 2002: 237). H. D. Thoreau found a 'sympathy with water as deep as his arteries'. William James, based on the Vedic view of all-enveloping nature, 'reached down to a curious sense of the whole residual cosmos' (James 2007: 261). Stefan Rosenszweig described a 'darkness appears as a light from inside. It is the beginning which is the only enigma in the world' (Rosenzweig and Galli 2005: 261).

In contrast to reified immateriality, the sensory condensations of past experience captured in the *Butoh-fu* phrases focus on materiality but need not be opposed to spiritual experience. Like Nietzsche's epiphany, when he looked past the fetishized ego into the abyss to recognize an 'all-in-all', practicing the *Butoh-fu* unpeeled hardened layers and de-centred the everyday self and memory to transform the *butoh-ka* (Kurihara 2000a: 15). For Nietzsche, a *vogelfrei* (free bird) remembers truth in 'the meaning of the Earth' when divested of a narcissistic *fascinum*, and having defenestrated from guilt and attachment (Nietzsche and Large 1998: 34; Yves Klein, 'Leap into the void', 1961; Nietzsche 2008).

Masking was essential in a *butoh* ontology that was conscious of eternal death in all living things, and that sought non-duality, non-separation and non-identification. Mud (*shundei, doro*), as its crucial element, masked the whole body. Akin to a ritualized live burial, the whole body mask mediated their transformation in a special zone. Becoming materials, merging insignificance and significance, recognizes the eternal reality of the constant flux of everything and nothing.

This provocation of decay towards death was a way to stimulate the *butoh-ka* to reach the limits of modern normative logic. The 'Pollen' phrase that employed an erotic and totemic symbol peeled back layers towards this experience of consciousness.

Pollen (花粉)

One worm moves on your neck,
One worm on the back of your hand,
One worm on the inside of your thigh
One worm on the side of your stomach
And then the worms multiply
Until there are a thousand crawling on you
There are worms crawling on the soft parts of your skin
The worms crawl into your pores
The worms eat this expression you have created
The worms eat this will to be eaten by worms
The worms are the air around you
Your bones are picked clean
You're a bleached skeleton
You have the desire to hold your lover but you can't
You have no purpose. (Hino and Broinowski 2002)[29]

In this evocative combination of eroticism and disintegration, the *butoh-ka* sensitized their skin in degrees of dilation such as pleasure, ticklishness, irritation and pain. As symbolic mediums between earth and bodies, worms can be found in the eighth century Man'yōshū poetry (*Kojiki*, 710) collection in descriptions of ritual orgiastic festivals (*utagaki*). During the *utagaki*, young men slipped into young women's beds in the pitch dark (*yobai*, or 'night-crawling'), which continued until the mid-1950s. *Mimizu-senbiki* ('a thousand twisting earthworms') is also a poetic metaphor for female orgasm (Sato 2008). The phrase offered a path to transform from unconscious numbness to acute un-self-conscious awareness, so as to reach an integrated consciousness.

Hijikata and *butoh-ka* also performed an inversion of this, mummifying themselves in 'dressings' – newspaper, gauze, bandages, plaster, masks – in the abject phenomenon of a worm-riddled corpse (*mushi-tai*). The maggot infested half-dead bodies of *hibakusha* as found in the writings of Ōta Yōko or Hayashi Kyōko (1986) are invoked as a core image in post-war consciousness in Japan. Also with a background in *taishū* (popular) Edo ghost stories (*kaidan*), and vengeful spirits (*shūnen shinri*) and ghosts (*onryō*) of Noh plays and Buddhist and Shintō tales, such 'freakish' imagery was frequently incorporated into 'J-horror' films in the following decades in which *butoh* dancers found minor roles. Delayed in its release for its use of themes such as leprosy (indirectly linked to the *hibakusha* legacy), *Horrors of Malformed Men* (Ishii Teruō, Tōei, 1969) (similar to the cult classic *The Island of Dr. Moreau*) cast Hijikata as the mad malformer of a quarantined community. In *Ringu* (Nakata 2002), a more recent J-horror hit, Ashikawa Yōko played 'movement double' in the role of Sadako.[30]

Present in the 'Pollen' phrase and the commercial horror genre is the sublime. As recognized by Edmund Burke (Ashfield and de Bolla 1996: 101), and later George Bataille, the sublime entailed 'the stuff of life that is also death gorged in life with decomposed substance' (Bataille 1991: 3, 95). Not simply a human awe of death, the sublime as represented by the 'ghost', 'living dead' or the 'dead wet girl' motif in J-Horror reflects a modern anxiety of liminality as being neither alive nor dead. As *revenant* who return to trouble the living from an unresolved past (McRoy 2008: 87), decaying bodies represent the potential to disrupt the social order. If the modern subconscious is based on masking, then the dread of exposure of suppressed reality is built into it. As Hijikata recognized, the creative potency and perseverance of hidden memories lay in the degree in which such 'ghosts' are denied.

> What is memory if not the sum of all those things that have been... erased, eliminated – in a word, all that has ceased to exist? And is it not the world made so as to attend to that sum?... Unless we deal with such problems we will only end up worrying about this straitened world – and thus, putting a lock on the door to the universe. (Hijikata 1993)

Another practical liminality in the *Butoh-fu* is 'wind', as evoked in the 'Smoke' (*kemuri*) phrase. Also featuring in *angura* poetics[31] and inspired by a diversity of winds in Tōhoku, the 'Smoke' phrase suggests a fragile, lithe and non-'human' structure that mediates the body. For Hijikata, 'wind' released from 'every nerve, muscle and joint' suggested different qualities for the dancer to work with. As Nakajima Natsu described, for example,

> [w]alk of smoke... because *butoh* is about disappearing, that is why a form is left behind... the *disappearing history of the flesh trails behind the metropolis of the flesh* .... (Fraleigh and Nakamura 2006: 108, italics mine)

The *Butoh-fu* triggers assisted younger *butoh-ka* in the praxis of transformation by compressing and stretching attention in their movement. Akin to albeit less limited than the centred 'braking' or 'pulling back' in Noh theatre, Hijikata's notion of 'elastic time hidden in each expression, sent by the dead' enabled a broad range of temporalities (mineral, atmospheric, animal, vegetable). In a series of concentrated moments that were melted and stretched into each other, rather than quantified speed or fetishized essence, in what superficially appeared to be 'slowed down', effectively *butoh-ka* separated themselves from the efficient ordering of habituated time. This dilatory effect literally created space to (re)discover less familiar or forgotten ways to move, breathe, sense, feel, think and value.

Maro Akaji's accidental time, Furukawa Anzu's 'Crocodile Time', Yoshioka Yumiko's liquid time of melting cells, Nepal-based Subbody Rhizome Lee's perception of 'living from the dead'.[32] To break open, pause, melt or invert modern 'human' temporality was to allow space to otherwise suppressed or ignored entities. Although such experiential 'histories of the flesh' are buried in the inexorable advance of modern temporality, *butoh* praxis recovered material memory through discrete durations. In Hijikata's 'Dead time' phrase of a woman holding a dried flower, for example, phrases such as 'smoke' or 'pollen' were combined to give a quality of vanishing presence that was detailed to comprise his dead sister, or a quality of 'dead sisterliness' (see Figure 3.3, p. 94). This attunement to materiality so as to hear voices of water, trees, rocks, insects as carried on the wind rather than singularly human words, was to perceive 'the breathing of the dead who have never gone away' (Birago Diop, 'Souffles', quoted in Hughes in Murakami 2005: 110).

As noted by Hijikata in his *Tōhoku Kabuki* series (1984), thought was to disappear in self-forgetting: 'Although called *Tōhoku Kabuki*, ... the utter darkness exists throughout the world doesn't it? To think is the dark' (Hijikata and Shibusawa 1985: 18). In a distracted, over-exposed and amnesic world, Hijikata actively sought an immersion into darkness, or to 'become an object'.

X-Ray Girl (レントゲン少女)

A forgotten cigarette in the left hand
An evening autumn wind blows into the right side of your face
Falling leaves
Don't notice, make your eyes look anywhere
Drop your eyes as if looking down a declining road
Disappear and become the air around you
Black eyes (holes in the face). (Hino and Broinowski 2002)

In exposed stillness, the body of the girl disappears by inverting light to become a shadow. In its stress on 'X-ray', this phrase suggests the momentary 'image-capture' of an all-clearing and exposing atomic flash and the glowing remainder of her body. In this phrase, we can sense a disease continuing in the form of 'hot' radiating particles blowing from past to future, carried both inside and outside the body.

The reiterated link between *butoh* and disease is not accidental. The term *butoh* is lexically associated with 'choreia' (*butoh-byō*),[33] a medical term for an involuntary movement disorder known as dyskenesias (St Vitus' dance) and 'characterized by arrhythmic, rippling, muscular contractions'. While *butoh* reflects the 'traditional' function of hosting the dead through masked ritual, it also elicits a modern return of the repressed. In 'X-ray Girl', it is the memory of the dead who died in the atomic bombings and the curtailed lives of *hibakusha*, but its evocation of disease more generally also suggests an awareness of the stigmatization of sufferers of leprosy (Hansen's disease) and contemporaneous industrial-scale bio-chemical disasters such as Minamata (Ui 1992).[34]

Becoming the object (*Mono ni naru*)

Together with the fragmented, masked, decayed and disappeared bodies, Hijikata also proposed that the body was an 'expressive thing' and 'inorganic substance' (*mukibutsu*), as seen in the phrase 'taxidermied peacock'.

Taxidermied Peacock (*Hakusei Kujaku*)

Being stabbed under the feet by arrows
Crest of the peacock
Four metre long tail-feathers
No shoulders
No muscles
No bones
Inside only cotton
Only nerves relating you to the surrounding space
An infinite number of perspectives of which you are painfully and completely aware, penetrate and stab you
Conscious of wing-feathers sprouting from your fingers and your arms
Fleas all over your body, living with you
Your entire body is aged and worn
Dust purveys the space. Dust is tumbling off you
If you move the slightest inch, you will produce a cloud of dust
An exhibit. (Hino and Broinowski 2002)

As a neglected relic from a past era, an immobile yet neurally active carcass, or an organ-less padded bag penetrated by sensitive fibres, this phrase evokes a particularly painful state. In a combination of rotting beauty and nostalgic pride, the sensitized yet incarcerated exhibit suggests the paradox of the un-dead. Being encased within glass as a stuffed organ-less object while still conscious and rotting, indicates a helpless yet lively paralysis.

In practical terms, this phrase contrasts a certain everyday numbness with qualities of 'nerve' (*shinkei*). Through sensory images of dead branches, dry petals and cobwebbed vegetable roots animated with degrees of 'electricity from the floor' (*chikaden*), the *butoh-ka* undergo varied transformations.

In broader terms, the image of the nation as a musty, flea-ridden taxidermied peacock is empty, yet it continues to be re-animated with shocks of electricity. As Deleuze and Parnet discuss with regard to the modern citizen, 'minor' emotions of love and shame unmake the institutionalized normative 'molar subject' (Deleuze and Parnet 2007: 124–47).[35] In this case, as his own condition weakens in the final stage of his work, Hijikata is focused on a weakened, softened and subtle body (*suijakutai*). As an ageing dancer from a richly embodied peasant–farmer history encapsulated in consumerist urban density, this project of unmaking 'molar' subjecthood through the electricity of 'minor' emotions constituted awakening to death's eternal presence.

Comprehending Hijikata's oeuvre as a choreographic poem is unavoidable. But *Butoh-fu* are not just metaphorical. As poetic 'metaphors for the body', they are not mythic narratives. Nor are they internalized narratives for the audience to scrutinize for psychological meaning. Rather than reifying innate identity or attempting literal representation of immateriality, the practice of the *Butoh-fu* as a set of scores is to heighten sensitivity to other presences. They are triggers for *butoh-ka* to engage in shaping material conditions to be felt within a shared space of evolving atmospheres. Neither separate nor denatured, in contrast to the modern body of tension, alertness and effort (Kuriyama 2001: 23), the *butoh-ka* becomes aware of the *butoh* body as an everything and nothing in itself.

This equilibrious consciousness un-separated from a surrounding environment could be traced to the disciplinary tradition of Chinese medicine and *qi* studies. To do so exclusively, however, is to ignore the socio-historical context in which *butoh* was formed.

In their dynamic of facilitating the recovery of memories of the dead (*shitai*) and materializing immersive disappearance, the liminalities found in the *Butoh-fu* can be read as responses to the psycho-ontological conditions established during Occupation and perpetuated in the post-war period. When we see Hijikata in *Hōsōtan* and in *Shizuka na Ie* sprawled on the stage-floor in a kimono and a wig and barely lifting his head as if only just alive, for example, we witness a figurative and historical condition of local rural village life: marginalized, stigmatized and forgotten in modernity's ongoing drive. Having discussed some of the fundamental elements, principles and motifs in the *Butoh-fu*, we will now turn to the position of *butoh* in the politics of witnessing of historical events.

The Politics of Form in Post-*Ankoku Butoh*: (Not) a Dance of the Nation-State

The *Ganimata* posture (lit. 'crab groin'), based on the 'Walking' phrase (Chapter 4), was hunched, bent and splayed like an agrarian farmer who had descended from generations of farmers who planted rice in the soft wet mud. Rather than an ideological symbol of ethno-nationalist 'being' (Nakajima Natsu in Lee 1998: 11), this posture inferred a real material condensation of farming labour history and the exploitative relations between the capital and its 'internal colonies' (Vlastos 1998: 65–66). Moreover, instead of being cathected to a timeless and closed identity, in the post-war period, the *ganimata* posture invoked a living remainder whose bodies fell foul of the new national image but could not be so rapidly erased. The 'blackness' of *ganimata* offered chimeric potential.

Well after Hijikata had established his approach through the *Butoh-fu*, debate continued over the 'form' of *butoh*. In his improvisatory *butoh*, Ohno Kazuo considered 'form as leading life' (Lee 1998: 18), while for Tanaka Min, improviser and another 'student' of Hijikata, *butoh* is 'for breaking style and form', which ironically suggests pre-existing form (Vermeersch 2002: 30).[1] The poet Ōoka Makoto cited Hijikata as indicating his way was the opposite of 'other kinds of dance', which 'apply an external uniform method to train the dancer' (Ōoka 1987: 10–11). *Butoh-ka* Iwana Masaki claimed that '*Butoh* doesn't and never has existed', while admitting that Hijikata 'created a method' (D'Orazi in Scholz-Cionca and Leiter 2001: 330, 337). For *butoh* director Muramatsu Takuya (Butoh-ha dattan), '*butoh* is *butoh* only if a performer or director says it is *butoh*'. Among the critics, Uchino Tadashi found that it is 'not the concern of the dancer whether it is *butoh* or not', while Fraleigh contended that misappropriation 'keeps *butoh* alive' and D'Orazi denied any 'codified language and that [*butoh*] should not be considered in terms of form' (Scholz-Cionca and Leiter 2001: 331). Baird has argued that in the context of an overriding ideological telos of competition in the 1960s, *butoh* was part of a collective New Left turn away from doctrinaire and obdurate 'Soviet raised-fist style sloganeering' (Baird 2005: 47).

As in any 'theatre of the body', form in *butoh* was inflected with the principles and qualities determined by the artist. Overt politicized debate or ideology were not common features in *butoh* practice, yet the *habitus* they created, and the praxis of working and sometimes living collectively, actively shaped an ontology that reflected their social values and ideals in tension with real conditions. Not against the student-led anti-*Anpo* protests of the 1960s, they recognized and sympathized with the need for significant change. As Hijikata stated:

> My dance lies first and foremost in human revolution. The utopia of the future is reflected in my retina. There is only one method for causing this ideal society to emerge – the remodelling of the human. No matter how much one agitates for such surface things as societal revolution or against the renewal of the Mutual Security Treaty, these will never be anything more than surface revolutions. (Hijikata in Nishi Tetsuo 1960: 64).

Maintaining ambiguity in *butoh* may help the *butoh-ka* remain open to primary questions: 'what is the body?', 'what is identity', 'what is the nation?'. To ignore the politicized consciousness in the artistic process of *butoh* is not only ahistorical but also misses the importance of such questions to human creativity as a mode of participating in society.

The deconstruction of form in *butoh* permits exploration beyond molar norms. To do so is to re-admit that which is excluded – abjection, memory, death, nothingness – and to confront deep-seated fears regarding the de-subjectivized 'void'. Re-making 'chimeric' figures from this basis is regenerative and future-oriented in a way that can be socially transformative.

In this praxis, *Butoh* is situated within a lineage of artists and intellectuals who have understood human form as a topoi for larger socio-historical formations. As Foucault found in the European leprosaria and sanitoria of the eighteenth century, human bodies are disciplinary instruments of social control through their interdiction and confinement as 'abnormal' (Foucault and Khalfa 2006: 130–31). With discoveries in natural and physical sciences, a rational and detached gaze was developed for the edification of the civilized (Foucault and Khalfa 2006: 441–43). No longer subject to the will of an absolute sovereign, pathologizing undesirable mistakes, flaws or 'evils' using 'madness' as the key signifier was central to the production of rational productive 'human' subjecthood. As Schelling observed in the early nineteenth century,

> [t]he constant *solicitation* of madness is the indispensable requirement of the active living understanding. Where there is no madness there is no proper, actual and living understanding. (Schelling 2000: 103–4).

In the new social contract with the sovereign, framed as unstable and harmful to others and/or themselves, the 'mad' were admitted and scrutinized for abnormal symptoms. The threat they posed was the challenge they apparently posed to 'truth'. Importantly, any subject deemed 'mad' was denied the right to give testimony in a court of law. This meant that only subjects deemed to be of good character and endowed with a higher degree of education and social status could be granted full legal recognition. As Artaud found in making the case in 'A man suicided by society' (1963 [1947]: 135–63) that Vincent Van Gogh's suicide was not 'mad' (he had previously burned his own hand and cut off his left ear before apparently shooting himself) but a reflection of the society's abnormal systemic suppression of difference, rather than punishment for heresy modern interrogators simply denied the subject's rationality.

For those who did not reduce Artaud's own persecuted sensibility to madness, it is possible to perceive the new biopolitical techné of re-building the human to conform to efficient and productive modalities in support of the geopolitical and economic drive towards the First World War, one of the most destructive and impacting events in human history. Citizens were offered an ultimatum: '... either do not mention a certain silence or follow the madman down the road of his exile' (Derrida 2001: 42). Those beyond the criteria of legitimate subjecthood were institutionalized or forced into exile beyond the reach of state surveillance.

In a similar vein to Artaud, from the late 1960s on, Jean Dubuffet proposed 'a long operation of progressive deconditioning' of the self as part of 'a machine ... that allows it to function' (Dubuffet 1988: 61). In recognition of deference (to authority) as a core mode in the patriarchal order and the commodification and fetishization of (false) difference, Dubuffet offered a critique of 'culture' institutionalized in the official organs of the 'new empire' through which 'we are mobilised, that we preach crusades' (Dubuffet 1988: 10). In contrast to the sterile and spectacular objects of state sponsored art ('papier-maché hydrangea') that reflected the 'glory of the Emblem', his large, vividly chaotic, 'childish' and 'primitive' works celebrated the impure, corpuscular rawness of 'the chimera' (Dubuffet 1988: 37, 86–88, 78; Weiss 1992a: 73).

Whether *grands motiles*, *hibakusha*, incurables or abject, children or indigenous, these *vogelfrei* 'disposables' in their common *deformé* bodies unstitched 'molar' codes and the modern 'organicity' of narcissistic authenticities, to create space for the return of cacophonous actuality.

Poetic witnessing and cultural politics

Given the disruptive potential in interrogating society's 'waste' and digging up concealed memories, it is clear why such artists and practices have been discouraged. These artists who sought to bear witness to the corrupt order faced the authorities' disciplinary levers of censorship, rationality, national security etc. Given the epistemological controls over 'truth' and admissibility, these bodies, as reflected in the mash-up bodies of Dada, Artaud's voluntary evacuation of an 'I' (BwO) and the clay-masked *deformé* substitutions in *butoh*, stand as poetic witnesses in varying removes from the actual event or structure.

Importantly, as noted by Felman, however, the non-verbal poetic body as 'material evidence for truth' can be considered admissible testimony, or a statement regarding the event (Felman and Laub 1992; Felman in Caruth 1995: 17). Silence has a meaning (Rich 1979: 308), as the embodied condition as marked evidence of a history authenticates both their person and the event itself (Caruth 1995: 151–53). Just as the 'remains of a charred building is witness to a conflagration' (Douglass and Volger 2003: 36), 'a tremor, a shock, a displacement of force can be communicated – that is, transmitted' (Derrida 1977: 173).

Duras' paradox of (non)-iterability in Alain Resnais' film *Hiroshima mon amour* (1960) can be seen in the famous dialogue in a brief liaison between a Japanese architect and a French actress.

He: You saw nothing in Hiroshima. Nothing.
She: I saw *everything*. *Everything*. I've always wept over the fate of Hiroshima. Always.
He: No. What would you have cried about?
She: I saw the newsreels ... History tells, I'm not making it up. On the second day certain species of animals rose again from the depths of the earth and from the ashes. Dogs were photographed. For all eternity. I saw them ...
He: You saw nothing. Nothing.

The 'closed circuit' of this misunderstanding is based on the distinction between having seen documentary photographic footage of the atomic aftermath and the problem of cognizing its meaning, leading to the event's non-'iterability' (Monaco 1979: 44). In the gap existing between the event and its 'incomprehensibility' lies the 'trauma'.

Traumatic experience beyond the psychological dimension of suffering suggests a certain paradox: that the most direct seeing of a violent event may occur as an absolute inability to know it; immediacy may take the form of belatedness. (Caruth in Parker and Sedgwick 1995: 89).

By contrast, Nakano Jiro's *tanka* translations in the anthology *Outcry from the Inferno* 'witnessed' the inscription of the bomb's 'poetry' into the flesh and genetic code of its 'survivors'. Many accounts which included prisoners caught in the scorching heat (Setoguchi Chie) and the bodies of teachers and students reduced to bones (Shoda Shinoe), focused on physical damage: peeling, swollen, cretaceous and maggot-infested flesh in victims, burnt and deranged animals and compulsive and prolonged searches through rubble and bodies for signs of relatives (Jungk 1961: 204–5; Sekimori and Shōno 1986: 46, 74).[2]

I began looking for my mother ... all I had to go by was the fact that she had gold teeth ... I held skull after skull and peered into the jaw ... there were times when, squatting, I even raised fire-blackened heads to look at the teeth. (Nagasaki Akira in Sekimori and Shōno 1986: 74).

These *tanka* artefacts refuse to rely on the sublime, or the failure of representation as evidence of something beyond description, and actively testify to the event as they contain intense significance within them. Their continued 'non-iterability', rather than unintelligible, 'traumatized' or simply 'dark', reflects an apparatus of 'truth' that has been constructed to ensure that the perpetration of greater lies (Foster 1996: 166).

As testified through poetic witnessing, the actuality of these bodies undermined vertiginous 'phantoms' held up as models for responding to a crisis of modernity (i.e. the atomic bombs). Where material evidence is unobtainable or has been ignored, poetic witnessing can step in to refuse closure upon an 'unnameable remainder' and engage in 'trans-memorative' engagement. At the same time, poetic witnessing can protect from the consequences of releasing sensitive information.

To conclusively pursue the cessation of violence and oppression, simply making 'their' horror 'our own' risks perpetuating false moral innocence and ignorance of the root causes of the harm done. In fact, selective attention to testimonies of atrocities, massacres and holocausts can aid the ongoing biopolitical production of state terror and 'the camp'. We must go further to also identify and dismantle the biopolitical caesurae installed in the subject (Derrida 1994: xix; Vogler in Douglass and Volger 2003: 205)[3] and to dismantle totalizing capitalism and its psychoanalytical master discourse (Deleuze and Guattari 2000: 240–261).

In short, as discussed so far, Hijikata's breaking open of space to permit the re-entry of silenced 'ghosts' through masked bodies in *butoh* (as silent movement), negotiated the after-shocks and rapid reconstitution of the new order. The *Butoh-fu* phrase 'Ash walk – bodies walking to execution', for one example, ritualized the ontological memory of (involuntary) human sacrifice (Hijikata in Kayō 1993: 84–91; Fraleigh and Nakamura 2006: 55). As part of an archive of material memories produced from the circuitous production of broken minds and bodies sacrificed in the accumulation of wealth and power from the First World War to the present, these poetic masks expose the concealed while they protect from the socio-political impact intrinsic to the event's memory.

The politics of 'emptiness' in post-war Japanese aesthetics

The sensation of not being human or real, of alienation stems from 'not existing' because one's society does not grant one equal rights. The critical strategy used by those considered as marginal, is to empty out the self. (Ōtori 2004)

In Hijikata's 1963 production of *Anma*, Hijikata's bare back was painted with an image of a flayed human spine by Nakanishi Natsuyuki (based on a painting by eighteenth-century anatomical artist Jacques-Fabien Gautier D'Agoty). Was there more to this image than the anatomical spectacle of the dissected body, or the symbology of a passive, suffering martyr?

The *butoh* of Ohno and Hijikata has been celebrated for its respectful signification of women. In Sorgenfrei's analysis of Terayama Shūji, whose work showed a notable preoccupation with powerful female figures (deity, sorceress, goddess, vampire) (Sorgenfrei 2005: 58–62),[4] such adulation possibly signified a young Japanese male's excessive dependency (*amae*) upon the mother figure. On the other hand, it has also been argued that progressive male post-war desires (i.e. *yakeato-ha* writers) were based upon the rehabilitation of the female body (as an object), as in the case of Abe Sada (Slaymaker 2004: 214; Marran 2007).

In an intensely paranoid nationalist environment in 1936, Abe Sada was publicly villified for her morally depraved killing of her lover and castrating him. In the early post-war, critical of the subordination of the female in evolutionary biology as closer to nature, Abe was publicly rehabilitated by the *yakeato-ha* writers as a paragon of earthy, passionate eroticism. There were even plans for a stage play based on Abe Sada in 1946. Marran argued that this was in order to transform Japanese masculinity from its prior rigid militarist egotism to a 'cult-like' supplication to a powerful deviant female body (Marran 2007: 51–52, 128, 142).[5]

Comparing Ōshima's *In the Realm of the Senses*, which portrays Abe's affair with Kichizō, and Satoh Makoto's *Abe Sada's Dogs*,[6] which portrays loyal imperial soldiers' self-obeisance to the Emperor, Marran finds a common thread in male sacrifice to a dominant figure. In this logic, absolute sacrifice is the shared principle of becoming a dedicated component within a military unit under Imperial command, and relinquishing agency to one's lover.

For Marran, Abe's act was not an expression of love for her lover, and her rehabilitation by the *yakeato-ha* writers was driven by their self-interest in a new political climate. By contrast, Marran sees Abe as neither dominatrix nor maternal and as *the* anti-authoritarian transhistorical figure. Without doubt, Abe's act symbolized a rejection of the unifying and controlling molar norms of the nation and its Empire. Yet, the parallel critique is absent of Abe as a figure who reproduces the totalitarian dynamic of committing a self-inflating act of the total domination of another.

For Ōshima, Abe is treated as an allegory of the military state order. As 'Abe Sada', the jealous and possessive State seduced and entranced its beloved male soldier-bodies ('Kichizō') into total submission before murdering and fetishizing their sacrificial deaths. At the same time, in a potent sign of industrial strike, both Abe and Kichizō as individuals subvert their expected service to Imperial operations as prostitute and soldier, by withdrawing into non-productive 'decadent' love. In this way, the couple's consensual 'commitment' can be seen as a moment of resistance to the dominant nationalist modality.

The post-war recovery of Abe's reputation was also indicative of the way in which mostly middle class Japanese women were upheld as the barometers of success of SCAP-initiated reformist policies and the liberal values of American society. Arguably, Abe Sada represented the infantilization of the mostly working-class Japanese male in his renewed obeisance in an order decreed by the US patriarch. Satoh and Ōshima (and the *yakeato-ha* writers) both aimed to criticize the order of Imperial Japan from below, but as in the earlier discussion, they tactfully avoided any overt reference to the post-war context of the US–Japan alliance. While masochism can be considered as an internalized form of the 'fascistic superego', the patriarchal Japanese militarist order cannot be adequately critiqued without including the biopolitical conditioning inherent to the modern capitalist nation-state as a transnational phenomenon.

Status quo transition: *Otaku* prototypes in the 1970s and 1980s

By the time *butoh* was being exposed to and embraced by international audiences in Paris and the United States with support from Japan's cultural agencies in the early 1980s, Hijikata had withdrawn from the main scene. For a period of seven years until his death, he continued to choreograph *butoh-ka* in small showclubs ('Kitaro', 'Caramel', 'Bruto') in Tokyo high-rises run by Motofuji Akiko from which he could pay for artistic productions. Combining artistic and burlesque elements for show clientele, Hijikata used elements from early neo-Dada performance acts, *butoh* and cabaret in gently subversive commercial entertainment.[7]

From peace-loving tranquil arts such as ikebana and tea-ceremony (1950s) to economic and advanced technological products (1970s) to international cooperation and engagement including art management and production (1980s) (Ogoura 2008), Japan's carefully managed and highly successful programme of cultural diplomacy commodified Japanese culture for non-Japanese audiences.

During the second Cold War (1979–1985) and the rise of the 'bubble economy', the younger generation that grew up in the 1970s had neither experienced the Asia-Pacific War nor the first two decades of the post-war. At the peak of the nation's affluence, while Western responses, primarily in Europe and the United States, ranged across the spectrum from orientalist admiration to inferiority to racialized anger (Huntington 1993: fn. 22; De Coker in Rohlen and Bjork 1998: 191–214), Prime Minister Nakasone Yasuhiro made essentialist claims to explain Japan's economic success (based on mono-racial classless homogeneity grounded in a timeless closed-society of the village) (Roth 2005). Others, such as Ishihara Shintarō (*The Voice of Asia*), spruiked a new and strident brand of nationalism. This new (and retrograde) sense of national pride manifested in notable nostalgia for 1950s and 1960s science fiction, war and anime artefacts (robots/weapons) in a subculture of young mostly male Japanese. Generally, if not unproblematically known as *Otaku* culture (lit. 'of the house'), SF-prone *otaku* took pride in 'made in Japan' products, as cheap, reliable and increasingly sophisticated, which they held to be symbolic of the nation's economic resurgence and which inspired confidence in heroic, mature and authoritative role-models, especially male ones (Azuma 2009: 13, 18). These *otaku* burrowed into early internet fandom prototypes (Bulletin Board Systems – BBS) where they swapped information on their chosen sub-genre, whether early Honda sports cars or Gundam sketches.

With the end of the Shōwa era in 1989, and collapse of the Soviet Union in 1991 and transition to a programme of neoliberal economic 'reform' of intensified deregulation led by the Thatcher and Reagan administrations in the 1980s, ideology was declared to have come to an end. This ruling ideology declared that there was no alternative or outside to capitalism. Covert and proxy American wars were far from over, but with the post-war generation getting older, the nationalist right-wing discourse of triumphal neo-liberalism (despite the continuation of transnational anti-US militarism, socialist, labour and environmental movements), gained traction in the younger generation.

Amid 'globalization' in the 1990s, the surge in popularity of Japan's pop culture products distributed in Asia (manga, anime, video games) and marketed as 'Cool Japan' was seized on by nationalists such as Ishihara, and later Aso Tarō, to explain Japan's special ability to translate Western (American) ideas into Asian sensibilities. Japan, they explained, was replacing the United States as Asia's object of yearning and influence. Okakura Tenshin's goal (*Asia Is One*, 1900) to lead the Asia fraternity had been achieved, they claimed. Nevertheless, Cool Japan seemed to be one of the few successes, as economic stagnation became more than a temporary plunge in GDP.

In two 'lost decades' (1990–2000), as Japan turned increasingly to Asia for trade, its economic stake in common markets was increasingly appropriated by the 'tiger' economies such as South Korea, Taiwan and the PRC. Where careful diplomacy had established governmental level consensus that US–Japan capital investment in the Asian region over decades was Japan's atonement for past aggression, this too was challenged by organized representatives of past victims mainly from South Korea, the PRC and Taiwan, with the tacit support of their governments.

Formal expressions of reflection, regret and sadness were issued by LDP and DPJ representatives, most notably in the Kōno statement (1993) and Murayama apology (1995) for the systematic use of 'comfort women' in sexual slavery by the Imperial Japanese Army to the ROK and PRC in particular, but also to Taiwan, the Philippines, Singapore, Malaysia and Indonesia. At the same time, the LDP led a dedicated programme to re-claim and cultivate national pride in Japan's wartime history. This included high-level semi-official visits to Yasukuni Shrine as the recognized spiritual centre of Japanese militarism and revisionist history; Monbushō revision of school textbooks concerning Japan's war of aggression in the Asia-Pacific; re-introduction of the national flag and anthem ritual in high schools; and regular attempts to mitigate and undermine Article 9 with the ultimate aim of projecting geopolitical power through military means. This was complemented by reinvigorated historical revisionism in popular culture. The popular manga of Kobayashi Yoshinori (*Taiwan-ron*, *Sensō-ron*), among many others examples, celebrated the colonial vestiges of Japanese spirits and values in Taiwan, drawing upon the past Imperial paradigm and applying it to present conditions to inculcate pride in a young mostly male readership.

For Ōe Kenzaburō in 1994, Japan's post-war condition was 'ambiguous', a 'chronic disease' of 'being split between two opposite poles' that was otherwise incurable with prosperity (Ōe 1994). The tensions inherent to post-war Japan's national ontology, with the Emperor at its centre, renewed the debate over conceptions of subjectivity (*shutaisei*) and subjecthood (*shinmin*) (Articles 10 and 19) and its associated molar values (duty, patriotism, family, discipline, uniformity).

In the early 2000s, *otaku* art-stars gained prominence in an expanding global 'J-Pop' industry manifested through avatar or 'cosplay' festivals in large urban venues on important dates in the year's social calendar. Meanwhile, a chorus of Japanese conservatives and mainstream media commentators mainly in the United States seized on the popularity of this sub-genre as an opportunity to castigate Japan for its 'nativist insularity' (village-society) and sluggish post-bubble economy. *Otaku* were cathected with the nation's economic stagnancy and pathologized as lacking 'authentic human intimacy', listless, emasculated, perverse and 'protecting the ego against that which would diminish [it]' (Cohen 2009).

In this context, the sociologist and subculture theorist Azuma Hiroki and a consortium of media and cultural specialists championed *otaku* as a national *cause célèbre* for their symbiotic development of commercial IT technology, software and media.[8] Yet, in his analysis, *otaku* appeared to split into those who formed the engine of the *otaku fantasia* market (IT developers, collectors, publishers, directors, art-stars etc.) and those who retreated into immersive media dependency and anti-sociality.

Making a considerable effort to counter the negative mainstream image of *Otaku* Japan's oneiric voyeurism, Azuma together with the art-star Murakami Takashi promoted the *otaku* sub-culture as anti-naïve and tech-savvy in a cut-throat globalized world. At the same time, Azuma showed particular concern for Japanese youth, particularly young males. In reference to the TV anime *J Saber Marionette*, for example, he found the *otaku* male to be indecisive, socially isolated and over-reliant on the 'database'. He denoted a distinct solipsistic desire for control and 'wholeness' that produced an ironically infantilized and yet nationalistic desire for greater authority in the world (Azuma 2009: 27, 92).

In this early period in *otaku* studies, not enough examined *otaku* as a phenomenon as symptomatic of a broader culture of bullying as evident in structural economic and political policies and conditions. Since the emergence of *karōshi* (death from overwork) that emerged from the system of corporate fealty in the 1980s, the co-temporal emergence of a broad 'precarious' workforce and its new social conditions since the mid-1990s, including *freeter* (partially employed casual labour), *neets* (not in employment, education or training) and *hikikomori* ('shut-ins'), suggests an overlap with the trend in *otaku* tendencies. Coined by psychologist Saitō Tamaki (Saitō 1998), *hikikomori*, initially known as (*rijinshō*), were those who practiced abnormal degrees of social avoidance (inertia, depression, paranoia, voyeurism, agoraphobia, physical violence directed towards the self- and/ or other), and were associated with a heavily techno-mediated lifestyle. Estimates of *otaku* in 2010 ranged broadly from 6,000 to 700,000 people between adolescence and their forties, while the behaviour of 230,000 national citizens was characterized as *hikikomori*-like, of whom 70 per cent were male and 46 per cent were in their thirties (GOJ 2010). In 2003, the Ministry of Health, Labor and Welfare defined this as 'a non-psychotic phenomenal concept denoting avoidance of social participation (school, work, human interaction), and remaining at home for six months or over (including going outside without associating with other people)' (GOJ 2010).[9]

Swinging from benign to dysfunctional, the causes of *hikikomori* withdrawal were traced to bullying and/or both parental over-protectiveness and neglect. Tales of *hikikomori* intimidating their parents, failing in school and relationships, nurturing resentment, and committing varying degrees of violence were widely publicized. (Jones 2006). Well-known cases of violence by young men such as in the 'Neomugicha Incident' (a seventeen-year-old boy held up a bus in 2000) and Takuma Mamoru and Miyazaki Tsutomu reinforced the mainstream narrative.[10]

While it has been convincingly argued that not all *otaku* are anti-social or solipsistic and many are in fact socially engaged and active (Itō in Itō et al. 2012; Condry 2013: 203), we can say that *otaku-hikikomori* behaviour, as in any human behaviour, is produced in relation to a community or society and reflects in varying degrees their treatment in society. Here, I focus on the pressure of not meeting social expectations as reflected in those who are attributed as socially withdrawn *otaku-hikikomori*. In the tight circles of these *otaku* who tend to be exclusive and obsessive in their interests and engaged in intense competition within these groups, those who then 'fail' and are ejected from such groups are left with almost no meaningful or intimate social engagement. Lacking tools for self-help, such isolation can produce irrational acts of resentment. When the young Katō Tomohiro, for example, was arrested in 2008 after having engaged in a random stabbing spree in Akihabara, he said he had been harassed on an *otaku* BBS, the only place he felt he belonged (Editors, *The Japan Times* 2011).[11]

In lieu of the violent self-destruction of the URA cell at Asama-san or the 1995 terrorist attack by Aum Shinrikyō, in which members of the religious sect attacked commuters during morning rush-hour in Kasumigaseki subway station in the heart of Tokyo's bureaucracy, it is possible to associate social isolation and withdrawal with public violence. As part of government 'reform and reintegration' programmes to bring socially withdrawn people back into society in the 2000s, a New Start programme saw trained 'Rental Sisters/Brothers' sent to *hikikomori* dwellings to re-establish some sociality. Instead of seeking the root causes in bullying and structural victimization, the district government increased surveillance in Akihabara (Matsutani 2010) and intensified the paranoid atmosphere in the area. Psycho-pharmaceutical prescriptions also were prescribed to individuals identified with *hikikomori* tendencies. Public media commentary continued to pathologize and vilify *otaku/hikikomori* as 'social pests', and outbursts of *otaku/hikikomori*-type violence did not stop.

While people displaying asocial *otaku* behaviour are responsible for their personal responses to their own situations and should not be regarded solely as passive victims (see Kam in Galbraith et al. 2015: 181), when labelled as social targets (or 'menaces'), such groups also serve to absorb social frustration and become a public distraction from broader conditions. Greater responsibility lies in the creation of structural insecurity (privatizing public assets, market and institutional deregulation, worker retrenchment for 'efficiency' – *risutora*), biopolitical division (structural and institutional discrimination and economic exploitation), securitization and 'disciplinary' education, that can facilitate social intolerance for 'failures' (whether labelled as *otaku*, *hikikomori*, outsiders or otherwise) based on rigid 'molar' categories – self, family, nation. Far from unique to Japanese society, in what we can call an '*otaku*-effect' in this context, this is indicative of the alienating effects of high-density life in technocratic mega urban regions (MUR) of which Tokyo and Osaka are part. In these sprawling urban densities, under increasing police scrutiny and intense pressure of economic austerity and deregulation, with fewer and fewer outlets beyond 'virtual mediation', bullied, isolated and resentful populations are part of a growing 'precariat' underclass who labour in new 'mobile' factory enclosures.

The *otaku-hikikomori* phenomenon also signifies potential for non-violent resistance, however. In the ascetic (*intonsha*) tradition of non-participatory and 'non-productive' self-enclosure, examining the internalized ideological structure can recover core life values. With the potential to surmount physical, social and informational borders through internet access, *hikikomori* could overcome social insularity in greater commonality with empathetic transnational populations.

In a climate of hardening social repression under neoliberal austerity and militarization, this larger mass of public opinion could bring pressure to bear on policy to change modes of structural division and exploitation (Broinowski 2010b).

In actuality, mainstream media commentaries in Japan and the United States on '*Otaku* Japan' were never concerned with resolving *otaku* social problems. Rather, in a striking similarity with early modern European national hygiene studies which found that 'Oblomovian' youth lifestyles (among other mass phobias) increased masturbation ('onania' in 1712) and led to lethargy and premature death (Zizek 1997: 65),[12] the concern was that 'aimless indolence' would obstruct the mobilization of a disciplined youth towards production and military competition with other nation-states (Lacquer 2003: 278). Implicit in this journalistic casting of Japan's 'European condition' of 'Oblomovian' 'immaturity' was the threat that unless Japan lifted its game, China would replace Japan as the United States' preferred 'wise Eastern master' of economic performance.

Otaku and Article 9: The beginning of the security shift

As the *otaku* debate was taking place in the 2000s, following the launch of the War on Terror in 2003, a parallel *realpolitik* debate intensified over Article 9 of the 1947 'peace Constitution', which at least restricted Japan to strictly self-defence of the homeland from invasion and military attack and from settling international disputes through military force. With a climbing PRC military budget and its increased territorial assertiveness, claims of Japan's emasculated and masochistic 'passivity' intensified. Political voices grew louder for Japan to revise Article 9 so as to become a 'normal' nation.

Some view the post-1945 US–Japan relationship as Hobbesian: the citizen (Japan) trades its liberty (autonomous foreign policy) for the protection of the 'Leviathan' (the United States). A strict Schmittian reading – 'the Sovereign is he who decides on the exception' and exercise the right to kill an enemy – would frame the United States as the sovereign of Japan. As the post-1945 US hegemon is itself un-fettered by Article 9, it is entrusted to fill the vacuum of a vacated or incapacitated sovereign to protect this territory on Japan's behalf (Williams in Stockwin et al. 2006: 51–55), making it a proxy sovereign.

In this situation, it is often argued that the US victor took away Japan's military capability and Japan voluntarily assumed a posture of 'self-restraint' and subordination to the US hegemon. Suggestive of negative liberty (Berlin 1969), in this reading, Japan's actions are inhibited by its own Constitution instead by an external force. This condition is sometimes blamed on the theoretical application of negative sovereignty and subjecthood by the post-war and contemporary Japanese intellectual left, who used Foucault's notion of the 'subjectless subject' to define Japanese post-war identity (Takahashi 2005). In this view, in their rejection of an 'innate' Japanese (mostly masculine and martial) predisposition towards violent death (or 'suicide culture'), a 'sadomasochistic' configuration has been established, wherein the US master ('Sword') 'cares' for slave Japan ('Chrysanthemum') and assumes responsibility for their defence. It is crucial in this argument that Japan be seen as voluntarily embracing this role.

Just as in the mediated *Otaku* Japan narrative, this master–slave dialectic frames a 'post-Japan' of neutered 'Japanese' that is emptied of the right and will to defend and therefore define itself as a sovereign nation. The repeated accusation in US commentary that Japan shirks responsibility to defend its sovereign right to belligerency (i.e. 'gets a free ride') projects a Lacanian self-'severance', creating a phantom emptiness where an authentic self once resided. Provoking a desire for suture, those who subscribe to this view seek to re-instate a recognizable (phallic) form of sovereignty so that Japan may exercise its 'normal' right on the world stage once more.

From the 'might is right' position of strategic realism, grounded in a fundamental misreading of Darwinian 'survival of the fittest', the capacity for military belligerence is key to a perceived natural human will to survive and a requirement in the aim to accumulate power, territory and resources. In this logic, the nation's agency (and pride) is vested in its military capacity to protect the nation's physical integrity and enforce civil agreements or pursue any other objective through force in the international arena so long as it remains within norms and legal parameters.

In support of Article 9, on the other hand, Foucault has been useful to problematize subject formation based on the right and capacity to use military force to protect national borders as the quintessential expression of sovereign autonomy. In response to a casus belli (the foreign incursion of national territory or interests), for example, 'self-defense' and 'national security' are invoked to legitimize extra-territorial military action. But self-defence as stipulated in the UN Charter is already a right accorded to every nation in the interests of self-determination, including Japan. This has been the generally accepted bipartisan interpretation of Article 9 for over forty years.

Separating national self-determination (and masculinity) from a capacity for belligerence (as security and sovereignty), however, demystifies the right to use military force so as to perceive it as an industry. When viewed as an industry, it is possible to perceive nation-states facilitating tensions (conflicting territorial claims) so as to create demand for military procurement and spending. While aggravating tensions, growth in transnational corporate contracts for military research and construction increases employment and revenue, boosts investment and stimulates national economic indicators in global financial markets. From this perspective, the Article 9 debate would become more nuanced.

Mainstream media narratives continue to reduce and misrepresent transnational disputes in terms of nineteenth-century statehood as the right to protect oneself, one's family and nation through violence. As multinational corporations and their nation-state supporters compete in a heterogeneous global sphere for influence, assets and resources, transnational alliances resemble an indistinct mixture of state and corporate interests. Such complexity is not conducive to narratives of national pride in sovereign will, integrity and autonomy. In the 2000s, Joseph Nye, Richard Armitage and Chuck Hagel, in a long line of US leaders, reiterated their demands that Japan demonstrate 'responsible maturity' by revising Article 9. As stipulated in the Japan–US security alliance and its strategic role in the US Pacific Command, Japan and Okinawa have long contributed land, economic subsidies (70 per cent), technical knowledge, services, corporate research, development and integration and logistical support and military cooperation. Since the Korean War, in fact, Japan and Okinawa have assumed positive liberty by being participatory agents in American-led wars.

Japan has also functioned as a 'sleeper power'. Since 1955, it has committed to increasing defence budgets in stages of intensive military build-ups. Since the first Persian Gulf War of 1991, Japan's Self-Defense Forces (JSDF) shared integrated weapons technology and participated in 'regional deterrence' exercises with the United States in the region. In its joint-operations in the Second Gulf War from 2003, JSDF ground troops were deployed to Iraq, and its navy (MSDF) assisted in re-fuelling in the Indian Ocean for the war in Afghanistan. The JSDF was also deployed in disaster operations in Japan, Haiti, Indonesia and the Philippines. In the late 2000s, Japan possessed one of the top-ten largest and most highly equipped military capacities in the world, with the second or third most powerful navy and most sophisticated ballistic guided-missile power outside the United States. All of this makes Article 9, and section 2 in particular that Japan never maintain land, sea and air forces so that it does not threaten or use force to settle international disputes, seem absurd.

Having defended its Constitutional right to use tactical nuclear weapons as a minimal requirement of self-defence since 1957, since the mid-1980s and particularly after the collapse of the Soviet Union in 1991, Japan in conjunction with the United States developed ballistic missile defence systems that could be nuclearized 'just in time' if necessary (Mochizuki 2007; Cambell and Sunohara in Campbell and Sunohara 2004: 232). In 1992, it publicly launched its plant to produce highly enriched uranium and plutonium at its Tōkai Recycle Equipment Test Facility (RETF) in Ibaraki and construction of its Rokkasho nuclear processing facilities in Aomori (Tsuchida 1993: 3, 6). Recognized by South Korea, China, North Korea and Russia as Japan's completion of its 'transition to a political and military superpower', these powers responded by renewing nuclear-related development and increasing military spending to deploy in the region.

Realistically, Article 9 has gone hand-in-glove with Japan's military posture. More transparent debate would remove this public mask to expose Japan's military capacity and its strategic intentions within the US–Japan architecture. A more honest discussion would reveal the manipulative hypocrisy in mainstream commentary concerning Japan's emasculation and its lack in a nuclearized East Asian tinderbox. On the other hand, it would also show how other Asia-Pacific nation-states (including Australia, South Korea, Singapore, the Philippines, Taiwan, Vietnam) with military treaties with the United States (or SOFAs) could be similarly considered 'abnormal'.

Moreover, in lieu of the enormity of the symbiotic relationship between the US military industrial complex and US national security state policies which flout international law in its own national interests, sovereignty can be seen to be contingent to US geostrategy. In this context, sustaining Article 9 and a policy of making formal apologies and restitution to victims of Japan's wartime policies in Asia will help reduce the chance of conflict in East Asia based on false pretexts.

Article 9 is a lever with which people can legally obstruct Japan's further entanglement in US-led military belligerencies. It poses a positive and hopeful model from which to re-constitute nation-states in the world order. It would assist in the re-investment of resources away from military towards other pressing security commitments, such as the environment, clean food and water and building renewable energy distribution systems for the region. Japan's reinvestment in the power of its existing Constitution would make it a world leader for future international governance and peaceful coexistence.

As I have argued so far, in Japan's steady re-militarization since 1947, artists and intellectuals who have deconstructed molar forms of national subjecthood have engaged in the formation of alterities that cannot be harnessed to the biopolitical regimes of power. They dismantled 'whiteness' which fetishizes 'national identity' as part of capital accumulation, so as to recover minor modalities of 'blackness'. Rather than seeking a 'post-Western' capitalist world order, which through reversal only repeats the same fundamental contradictions and problems within a modern anthropocentric order, I contend that they sought (from the perspective of the most oppressed, marginal or 'below') decolonial modalities that re-centred the fundamental equality of all human (and non-human) beings.

Many displaced and itinerant workers under new growth regimes, who found themselves cannibalized within new forms of enclosures or ghettos, shared a common experience of being 'emptied' and/or 'doubled' with the molar values of the post-war ideological and institutional structure. Finding truth and meaning in raw materiality, they organized political demonstrations and engaged in artistic and intellectual praxis to ethically and legally ground their lives. Their claim to a people's sovereign responsibility as opposed to sovereignty based on the right to state violence, neither passive nor masochistic, offers potential for a post-'whiteness' world.

The following chapters turn to the theatre of Gekidan Kaitaisha between the mid-1980s and 2006. In the legacy of *Ankoku Butoh* and the cultural politics of the 1960s and 1970s, Kaitaisha continued to focus on the body as it mediated socio-political issues in a globalized economy of Japan in the first decade of the twenty-first century.

Gekidan Kaitaisha: Growing the Seeds of *Butoh*

Gekidan Kaitaisha (lit. 'Theatre of Deconstruction'), an internationally recognized contemporary performance company, formed in Tokyo in 1985. When the playwright left a loose-knit *shōgekijō* (small theatre) group that had been engaged in making adaptations of Greek tragedies, Shimizu Shinjin, one of the actors, volunteered to direct. A renewed membership of younger performers from the same university subsequently re-formed the core of the company. Together, Shimizu and performer-choreographer Hino Hiruko developed their body-centred approach based on their interpretations of *Ankoku Butoh*, which they call *butoh-sei* (derived from *butoh*).

Like other *butoh-ka*, Hino, Hijikata's youngest student before he died, had collected her own *Butoh-fu*. In the late 1970s and early 1980s, Shimizu had also attended workshops at the Asbestos-kan studio. Together with Hino, Shimizu drew from these inspirations to create Kaitaisha's distinctive approach to performance. A significant amount of Shimizu's work has been to re-read Hijikata's practical philosophy through post-structuralist and critical theory, modern history and memory, and contemporary politics. Deconstructing 'what is' at the site of the body, Kaitaisha have sought to expose structural power which constitutes and mediates it, so as to create an ontology that is more predisposed to being in the world together with others. This praxis can be summarized as 'moving the inside out to allow the outside in' (Broinowski in Harvie et al. 2010a: 223–57).

Kaitaisha became active amid socio-political conditions that nurtured the *Otaku* phenomenon. Shimizu's 'de-spectacle' approach was informed by a critique of the mediated body in society as modes of conveying information were expanding on multiple screen platforms. From 1991, with the aid of financialized capital, a neo-liberal programme to globalize the acceleration of production, circulation and investment ran in parallel with the spread of US military ('lilypad') bases and installations. In the systemic quest to rapidly open, penetrate and develop new markets, these transnationally networked operations utilized military platforms to protect optimal business conditions for the flow of goods between zones preferred by corporate and state clients (Harvey 2005; Johnson 2007; Callinicos 2009; Forte 2010: 2–5).

From a workshop in early 2001, I joined Kaitaisha in May that year as a performer/translator. At that time, Kaitaisha were refining an already established practice, in which they adapted pre-existing forms to different contexts and deepened the theoretical relationship to this practice. Between 1999 and 2006, in a series of workshops, Kaitaisha members[1] intensively developed their studio and festival performances known as the '*Bye Bye* series'.[2] Instead of the perpetual fabrication of 'newness', itself an acquisitive and parasitic mode in which artistic methods are acquired and disposed of according to consumer trends in a competitive market, Kaitaisha's incremental refinement of sensory fluency valued a deceptive minimalism. Through the incremental repetition and gradual mutation of form via tiny accumulations of movement, impressions were embedded within the body. In the flow of one production into the next in specific sites and contexts, movements and elements also transformed through their adaptation, and in collaboration with other performers.

As the company prepared for an extensive international tour of *Bye Bye: the New Primitive* (*Baibai – Mikai e*, 2001–3), little time was given to discursive analysis in rehearsals. Outside rehearsals, however, the group engaged in extensive discussion, both theoretical and otherwise. My analysis of Kaitaisha productions in what follows is based on these discussions within a broader corpus of readings. To begin, I outline the primary structures and dynamics of Kaitaisha's method based on the analysis in the previous chapters, which I then discuss with regard to their use in choreography and *mise-en-scene*. This is then contextualized in the socio-historical context.[3]

What is the 'empty body' in Kaitaisha?

Rather than preparing each production anew, the development of form and concepts through accretion over many years is, as Tadeusz Kantor recognized, to engage in the constant re-making of the body (Kantor 1990: 41). Not simply to overlay the body with a newly procured movement form, as if a brand or commodity, this accretive approach recognized that what was already present cannot be concealed. From the shared platform of bodily actuality, the appreciation of which was termed *butoh-sei*, practical performance principles became the subject of communication and negotiation. Less mimetic and more immersive, this practice explored the body and its over-codings in relation to social issues.

Evening rehearsals after work began with light banter and limbering and warm-up exercises of stretching, body-centring and balancing. Once warm, the group performed *hassei* (lit. expressed voice) – controlled breathing and vocalization. When done well, this accessed the body's resonating membranes and re-sensitized neglected parts that were otherwise fixed in habitual form. As sound resonated in and through the body, reached crescendo and fell away, the performer's body grew more responsive to the deeper circulatory flow of breath. The performers then practised *hakobi* ('carrying', as derived from the *hokō* phrase), walking slowly in a neutral posture back and forth across the rehearsal space in lines. Over time (30 minutes to one hour), daily layers unpeeled and increasingly distilled energies 'carried' through the space created atmospheric shifts.

These transformations were not immediate, and the skill in sensing and manipulating such fickle and subtle qualities stems from diligent perseverance over a significant amount of time to develop a relatively unblocked body. This adjustment from habituated and unconscious 'walking' to 'carrying' cultivated a conductive and prismatic medium through which material energies could be sensed and refracted. The primary objective was to heighten the body's receptive sensitivity.

Carrying (*Hakobi*)

Push your soul out in front of you
Let in the atmosphere around you
Push the self outside to become empty
Follow your soul forwards
Follow that energy
Carry the space together with you
Don't walk with your legs
Be carried
The space twists your body. (Hino and Broinowski, 2002)

Becoming 'empty', as if to leave the body while remaining connected to it, enhanced sensitivity to external/internal atmospheres. In prolonged and steady motility in 'silence', this phrase re-structured the body in a 'neutral' posture as such: abdomen pulled back along the spine, released muscle tension in the shoulders, neck, face and head, dilated muscles and cells through increased blood flow and transference of energy. This posture facilitated greater exchange between the body's membranes and less active or locked areas. Regular practice enabled deeper release in unconsciously fixed habits and patterns, to melt the eyes, face, jaw, eyes, neck, shoulders, hips, groin, hands, ankles and feet, softening and extending energetic flow as friction and force are reduced (*gensoku no nagare*). In less frantic or blunt interaction with surrounding atmospheres, energy qualities become distilled and sustained in their distribution. This facilitated more acute receptivity and sharper discernment of vibrations.

   With the diffusion of the force of 'expression', the performer grows less 'internalized' and more aware of 'being seen' and 'being moved'. This is not a purposive act of will to increase inter-subjective awareness and heightened self-consciousness, which cuts out a singular entity from a surrounding atmosphere. Instead, a softer and lighter quality takes hold in which a sense (*kehai*) of the 'self' seems to lift. This takes place in the face, particularly the eyes, the jaw and neck, followed by the shoulders and hips as the lower legs and feet swell in relationship with the floor. In this enlivened relaxation, the eyes as filters of light waves, and the face and skin as surface densities of nerves, pores and blood, become receptive and perceptive pads for a material gaze. In short, instead of plastic and representational masks, the eyes, face and skin surfaces are membra or media to feel the fluctuating atmospheres in a room of energies that include other bodies and their complex qualities.

   With my face relaxed and my weight centred somewhere in my sacrum, I can be attentive in a different way. My floating chin is determined by an extended spine as my eyes are seated in the middle of my head. Dilated, reflecting a horizon, I am seen through. The room moves my body multiply, at once. My body translates and becomes pressures. My weight leads me and my body follows. Weight is not unlike the soul, but is not only 'grave'. (Broinowski journal notes 2001–2005 [2003])

'Carrying' cultivates acuity towards an always already existing course of energy moving within and through the body. With an expanded literacy in these atmospheric qualities, otherwise tacitly accepted bodily perceptions and frames become unstable, or simply fall away. Increasingly 'emptied' and 'opened' in this way, some aspects of psycho-social conditioning that are privileged in our daily ontological understanding and discourse of self become more apparent as blockages. The negative inflection of 'emptiness' as a loss of agency, identity, direction and sometimes faith (or 'nihilism') is misleadingly narrow and does not apply here. Instead, enhancing membranous permeability to flux exposes and reduces habituated tensions.

Specific phases of 'carrying' – self-willed 'following', non-isolated solitariness, expansive diminution, humble confidence, dilated alertness – indicate a complex and subtle 'dialogue' ongoing in the body's immersion within atmospheres as it modulates within the primary dynamic of homeostasis.

As purposive individual will, certainly a formidable force, is re-directed towards greater trust in and attentiveness to these constant manifestations, fluency in drawing sustained sensory nourishment is deepened. Reduced force in volition refines the exploration of energetic exchanges as they pass across and through the body. Not an evacuation of will *in toto*, or its corollary in the possessive occupation of space as an agentic assertion of presence, a conscious fluidity predisposes the body to the imperceptible. Where strenuous effort drowns out quieter yet ever-present catalytic processes, distilled dilation through 'carrying' engages in tactile dialogue with space.

This form of silence and stillness moves below consciously controlled speeds of deliberate expression. 'Relinquishing' to the body (undermining the internalized mind–body divide), an ambient dialogue becomes audible. Becoming an object to itself as well as a subject, a dilated body expands micro-attention to the catalytic effects of objects, energies, qualities and other bodies in an atmospheric envelope. In fact, in transcending agentic choreography as it is generally understood, this practice informs the larger subject (*shutai*)/object (*kyakutai*) in collaborative dialogue with less-perceptible phenomena.

As in Hijikata's 'becoming object' phrase, the initial emptying leads to increasing material fluidity in exchange with other bodies. The performer takes responsibility for creating conditions in which this may transpire as a sculptor of less audible, invisible sensoria. In diluting conceptual binaries of internal and external, mind and matter, invisible and visible forms, performers negotiate energetic concentrations. Based on the common principle of transformation, these performers shared with *butoh-ka* the practice of shaping ambient pressures and temporal densities as they were shaped by them.

If mediated capitalism produces a body over-coded with normative 'molar' representations, then 'carrying' is a resistant practice that re-designs the lived environment in its own logic. This material dissolution of mediatized conditioning, congealed in quotidian attitudinal modes, re-releases blocked energies. In the temporary hiatus, disciplinary dyads internalized in pre-consciousness are made available to the performer for scrutiny. In becoming atmospheres through dilated, sensitive and vibratory media inverting the competitive disciplinary mode of the corporate state, these bodies become more not less capable in the world.

As opening night for *Bye Bye: The New Primitive* drew near, Kaitaisha performers rehearsed set phrases. Compartmentalized and modular, these phrases were divided into individual and partner scenes, or group choreography. The latter entails *mure-kehai* (group sense), 'crash' (throwing and catching), *rensa* (chain-reaction), *gunji* (military grapple) and 'exile' (vectoral compositions of flight and nodal assemblages). Instead of organized inter-subjective patterns, these phrases, particularly in their repetition, become more fluid as they transform into a composition of atmospheres.

These solo and group sequences were adapted to meet contingencies in different performance venues. Dressed in a base costume of lingerie (slips, corsets, girdles), gauze bandaging and black shorts, individual performers also had distinctive clothes to denote roles: schoolboy's shorts, hat (Nakajima); *burqa*, *mino* (grass skirt), *hanbok* (Korean traditional dress) (Hino and Nakajima); black suit or hooded grey coat, broom (Kumamoto Kenjiro); shorts, short black evening dress, black heels (Aota Reiko); torn blue corduroy jeans, long-sleeved collarless grey shirt, grey suit, long coat, suitcase (Adam Broinowski).

The central concepts and scenes were reflected in the textural scenography – image, spoken and written text, sound, light. In the sparse light and ambient sound, puncturing in their sudden and intense bursts of magnification, densities were juxtaposed in a score of gradients. While not vacuous or upbeat, the tone was neither humourless nor morose. Instead, the atmosphere crackled in extremes of light as transforming bodies in phrases and configurations ('chimera', 'pack', '*suishō*', 'sea-dog') sustaining the spine of the production. What historico-cultural dimensions can be read in such atmospheric transformations?

Transformations (*Sei-sei henka*): Becoming-Animal

Since the 1980s, popular media-scapes have paraded a range of hybrid and/or transformed bodies – monsters, avatars, clones, cyborgs, ghosts – to excite a visual smorgasbord of novelty. As discussed, 'chimera' signifies the potential to unsettle the integrity of this system. This can also be identified in the opening scene of *Bye Bye: The New Primitive*.

From the wings of the stage in Frankfurt, I see Hino sitting on a stool covered in a thin veil of white powder and wearing a white corset and white swimming cap. Her lone body has been sitting in profile as the audience enter the theatre. A low ambient rumble fills the dimly lit auditorium. The room falls to a hush. She falls forward from the stool, first crawling, then drawing herself up to two legs, then to her toes, her arms raised and spasmodically twitching as she crosses the stage. Phosphorescent in the pitch-black, Hino improvises with her senses. While thoroughly rehearsed, it is uncertain whether she will be able to enter the quality she has known before, a mode that carries her. The[re is a] tension [in] seeking to subdue anxiety while using a degree of energy required to sustain the sharp quality of her movements. As her movements grow impulsive, anxiety gives way to ease. A 'dilated' texture develops as her confidence becomes subtle. With a habitual armour having melted away, a softened assuredness allows her to move out into space. She embodies electrical thought born from within dark space. (Broinowski 2002: 3–4, 13)

Hino's body became attuned to a spectrum of material atmospheres. In going out into the body, she became a medium or a prism that refracts energy. Not only is a normative reproduction for an audience's interpretation and judgement, the body's singularity is manifest in this approach. Not just a vacant space to be occupied with prescribed meaning, the performer's dilation in real time means that a composition must be actually re-lived each time within a fluid and immediate set of contingencies.

Learning to read the body from within the practice in this way, many of the 'neuro-political' images of (national) identity and psycho-subjectivity are exposed as constructs. As a derivation of the social and peasant *butoh* grotesque, in a similar way the less valued and therefore obscured becomes the focus. In the brutal conditions of capture, consumption, commodification and disposal in ocularcentric hyper-mediated capitalist modernity, this ontology values other agency in the non-visible realm.

In Kaitaisha's *Bye Bye* series, Shimizu projected text on bodies, objects and the back wall: 'be colours, be hybrids, be renewed slaves stripped of the ragged old skin and hold a new weapon' (Shimizu 1999). While possibly inspired by the concept of 'becoming-animal' in Deleuze and Guattari's explorations of 'inhumanities' (Deleuze and Guattari 1987: 191, 240), Shimizu's reading is equally informed by Hijikata's *butoh*. Grounded in energetic principles, the constant appearance of non-human entities in both, either as memories or senses, suggests a shared desire to de-centre and expand the human as isolated from animal, vegetable, atmospheres, and organic and inorganic materials. Importantly, while sharing a similar performance dynamic with Richard Schechner's universal trance, Victor Turner's euphoric 'spontaneous *communitas*' and Jerzy Grotowski's 'holy body' (Grotowski 1969: 16; Turner 1996; Schechner 2002: 166), this work to dismantle the 'human' to 'repossess' the body revealed its hierarchical structures.

If the everyday body is mediated and en-'tranced' with socialized over-codings, then it is the subject as the narrative double of the nation-state and its ontological boundaries that masks or occupies the body's organs and nerves in (false) unity. Grounding material self-awareness in actual bodily processes reduces the irrealizing effects of fetishized identity. In this way, in reference to the critical art of Barbara Kruger, Shimizu claimed the body as a 'battleground' mediated by neurologically impacting narratives that exploit the individual's desires and capacities for identification to shape a false 'humanism'.

[E]veryone is digging holes in the hope of self-realisation... but bodies will always be mediums or screens... power and force are the things that have been intentionally erased. (Shimizu and Ōtori 2001: 25)

The 'chimaeric' forms Kaitaisha performers manifested were not yet commodified. In becoming assemblies of mediating organs which see and are seen through every pore and follicle, the familiar human-inhuman binaries grow less distinct and more textured. As the performer actualizes un-'self'-consciousness qualities, an internalized mode of seeing in the audience is potentially unsettled. Yet, just as a 'surveilled' condition had already proliferated through the surge in urban panopticism in the 1990s, audiences were already pre-mediated and 'seen with' desires that transcended any theatre artists' control. Rather than being able to control what audience members sensed or interpreted, at the very least we can say that an amorphous 'polyphony' – dilated, refracted, mutated, concentrated, secreted – was dispersed across an atmospheric spectrum within which they were de-familiarized and immersed.

The commonality is energy, which mediates living beings, objects and substances. As they were immersed in these pressures and densities, the audience witnessing bodies as they 'de-tranced', however, subtle and subconscious, may have been de-habituated from their everyday mediated capitalist society. From this energetic dynamic then, created from the components of movement phrases, short texts, high-contrasting light and ambient sound, we can turn to the overarching 'conceptual' theme that permeated Kaitaisha's scenography.

Pack (*Mure*)

The distilled atmosphere from Hino's iridescent 'chimera' was broken up by a howling noise-scape, staccato-flesh impacts and cavorting shadows from flurries of group-movements termed *mure-kehai* (pack sense).

> In 'crash', in black shorts and torn army jackets the pack mutate in an amorphous mass: twitching, crouching, throwing, catching, colliding. This branches into *rensa* (chain), wherein bodies link randomly by responding and melding in acute attentiveness. Their inter-relationality anticipates, receives and marks in precise, unforced, poised, centered, trusting and independent unfoldings. (Broinowski, journal notes, 2004)

'The Pack' is also a concept in Deleuze and Guattari's 'nomadic war-machine' which privileges 'difference over uniformity, flows over unities, mobile arrangements over systems, seeing that what is productive is not sedentary but nomadic' (Deleuze and Guattari 1987: 233; Foucault et al. 2000: 3: 108–9). As a group transformed from territorialized (national) identity into mobile anonymity, its 'becoming animal' manifested in a polyphonous 'pack', the ontological structure of which destabilized institutionalized subjective encodings.

Neither militarist, nor militant, nor a totalizing hierarchical (pyramid) structure, this form cannot be reduced to labels such as 'radical' or 'disturbing' that have been over-used so as to have lost their meaning. Nor is it simply 'playful creative dissent' (Eckersall 2006: 164) in a tendency that tends to infantilize performance and render its meanings superficial. To the contrary, it activates a multivalent sensorium that excavates 'traces of fascism' in a group-body. Not an endless chain of self-mediating mirrors, the dilation and transformation into energetic atmospheres in 'Pack', opens unto heterogeneous bodies and forms that generally fall beyond human models. In a field of de-controlled energies, precious, fragile and meaningful sensory constellations are liberated from reified ontological repetitions. In this way, Kaitaisha offer a distinct mode of theatrical praxis and critique.

Discipline

There were two main versions in the *Bye Bye* series of the following scene. In *The New Primitive* (2001) version,

> an older male body (Fueda Uichirō) interrupts the elliptical chaos [of 'pack'], rolling a mirror on-stage. He places a live flame in front of it. The bodies disperse and the shadows melt away. I am left standing facing the mirror with my back to the audience. (Broinowski, journal notes 2004)

In the *Phantom* (*Gen'ei*, 2003) version,[4] the polyphonous atmosphere was re-cut into disciplined martial bodies of diagonal linearity (*retsu*). Simultaneously, a body isolated from the group performed the 'spider' phrase (*kumo*) in a semi-lit spot on the ground. Moving in arrhythmic, swinging circles this body spoke the names of marginalized non-national ethnicities.

Figure 6.1 Gekidan Kaitaisha. *Bye Bye The New Primitive*. Occupation. Photo: Miyauchi Katsu, 2001–2002

A man (Broinowski) wearing an American army jacket stands with his back to the audience in front of a mirror. The light from a flame reflected in the mirror flickers in the space. From the back wall a woman (Nakajima) wearing beige corseted underwear [a *mino* in *Phantom*] walks along a narrow corridor of light bifurcating the stage. As the Greek alphabet is issued from the man like bolts of electricity, the woman shakes with increasing intensity as she slowly progresses toward the front of the stage. As he reaches Omega, the woman arrives at the stage's edge and is shaking violently. She speaks: 'labour not, consume not, reproduce not', and collapses to the floor. (Broinowski, journal notes 2004)[5] (see Figure 6.1)

For Nakajima, transforming the consistency of her skin transpired in infinitesimal gradations along a sustained build to a crescendo of shaking. With little other sound, this prolonged intensity tended to divide audience responses into anxious negation, non-commitment or deeper reflection. Considering Shimizu's interest in photography and the body, the woman's skin can be regarded as a site for territorial inscription. The white male soldier speaking the (Greek) alphabet suggests a set of signifiers of the post-war system in an age of nuclear physics (alpha, beta, gamma).

As discussed earlier, English lessons in the Occupation context can be regarded as an instrument to realign the public mind to the new order. In this scene as well, there is a pattern in which the body of the local inhabitant is overcoded with a universalizing tool of liberal imperialism. As the voice of the US soldier sporadically ruptures the silence with Greek letters from 'Alpha to Omega' while he watches his reflection, the dominant Cold War logic plays out. A biblical reference became apparent: 'I am the Alpha and Omega, the first and the last' (Revelation 1:8, 21:6, 22:13). Clad in the skin of war, his language can be read as a weapon/tool used to 'humanize' the occupied in the victors' image. It can also be regarded as code in an epistemological frame instrumentalized in the process of imperial domination.

Nakajima's bare fragility shaking on a straight white highway is reminiscent of the 1972 photo of Kim Phuc by Huynh Cong 'Nick' Ut as a young girl who cries in pain as she ran down the M1 highway away from her village which had just been bombed with napalm in Vietnam. This jolts our collective memory and makes more intimate the force of the globalizing 'free' market, in the form of state violence and its dispossession of local communities of their land and *habitus*.

Kaitaisha's titular reference to 'primitive' did not exclusively refer to Japanese bodies or identity. As shocks rippled across Nakajima's exposed skin, her body becomes 'doubled' with the language of the colonizer and its gestures as it mediated those who have been exposed to 'primitive accumulation' in Asia in the Cold War and during Japan's modern Imperial project as discussed earlier (Marx 1976: 725, 748). This image of an emaciated body which had been exposed to the violent forces of capital in the peripheries and in urban enclosures, which stared back at the living from the cell or the grave, was central to this production. Whether as *hibakusha* or rural agrarian peasant villager from the Korean peninsula, Okinawa, Manchukuo, China, Vietnam, Cambodia, Laos, the PRC, Taiwan, the Philippines, Indonesia, India, Timor-Leste, Burma or elsewhere coerced or forced to work for the Imperial Japanese Army or the US occupiers, the asymmetrical occupier–occupied dynamic is visible and consistent. Nakajima's phrase, 'labour not, consume not, reproduce not' suggests the harsh proletarianizing conditions imposed on those exposed to colonization, state violence and capital accumulation.

In a refusal of productivity akin to a hunger- or sit-down strike, Nakajima's body dropped to the ground, which she then dragged off stage as if it were a limp body carried off by some state personnel. Used in various ways throughout the *Bye Bye* series, this dynamic was reinforced in Shimizu's projected text – 'Have no beginning, nor end, nor origin, nor telos. Have no concern with production or realisation. Be barren' (Shimizu 1999). Nevertheless, the flickering mirrored light occupied only a fraction of the dark space, and its reach was finite.

Medium (*Baitai*)

Having 'emptied' the body to become both subject and object, the eyes of the performer 'screen' subjectivity. They filter and are affected by mediating 'inhumanities'. Instead of Hijikata's 'smoke' phrase, however, Kaitaisha bodies are mediated by 'water' in the phrase 'crystal discipline' (*suishō*).

Crystal Discipline (*suishō*/水晶)

Shoulders dropped, draw up from the ears, lengthen the back of the neck, suck from the pit of the stomach, knees bent slightly, feel your weight sink into the earth. 'Water' drawn from the earth through the floor, through the soles of your feet, up into your legs, through your sacrum and into your sternum, along your spine and out of the top of your head. Your arms are drawn out in front of the body until outstretched above the head. Passed-through, your body sinks into the earth while it soars in the sky. Move through a series of forms: 'ghost', 'falling star', 'shifting sand', 'execution'. (Broinowski, journal notes 2004)

Watching this exercise over a prolonged period, I was estranged from a familiar 'seeing system'.

Kumamoto's dripping neck, his ambiguous face, translucent skin through which coloured veins pulse, transform Kumamoto into a living, pulsing, sweating object. He becomes plant-like, an organism, something natural. (Broinowski, journal notes 2004)

Suishō was also a staple phrase in the *Bye Bye* series. In the 'Family' (*Kazoku*) scene in *New Primitive*, the performers entered with stools wearing varieties of beige lingerie and bandages. The stools are placed upstage in a V-formation. Facing the audience, they mounted their stools in unison. They reflected a post-war nuclear family, with Kumamoto in a short slip as 'husband' and 'father', Nakajima in a longer slip as wife and mother, Aota as the older daughter in shorts and a singlet, and Ishii as younger brother in trousers. With their straight arms slowly raised, one and then both together, various memes of modern political gestures immediately come to mind: a Nazi *sieg heil*, a Maoist sign to the masses, a Statue of Liberty beacon, an Imperial Japanese *banzai*. In this family-body vector saluted as it gazed impassively beneath a constellation of lights, the bandaged corsetry suggested at once militarized, damaged and/or controlled bodies bound in disciplinary encodings. As the family continued silently in the *suishō* phrase, this family unit as a core unit of exchange reflected the advanced capitalist post-war apparatus of the Japan–US system. The body's distinctive particularity was made more obvious in this unity, however, and like Kumamoto's dripping figure, in its repetition its image-signification gradually distorted into absurdity and then became unrecognizable. Under sustained attention, these bodies steadily mutated from 'human' form to become 'water'.

In *Phantom*, the 'pack' and 'family' sections were followed by 'exile' – a group choreography under strobe light and aural density. When the sound and strobe cut, Kumamoto slowly pushed a broom, Gotō wandered like a ghostly child with her long hair covering her face and Tano, an older woman, carried a bucket.

Ghosts (*Yūrei*)

The second act of the *Bye Bye* series was dedicated to the memories, ghosts and bones of history. *Phantom* was embellished with a new set – a dirty white wall of large squares – and new costumes (Korean *hanbok/chimachogori*, Afghani *burqa/niqab*). As I walked along the back wall performing the 'alphabet sequence', Hino wearing a *hanbok* carried a live flame diagonally across the space which she placed in front of the mirror. Kumamoto pushed a wheelbarrow across the front of the stage and then stopped to shovel earth onto the floor. Nakajima sat on a stool she placed centre-stage. She slowly raised the hem of her *burqa* to her thighs, and began to randomly slap them. By the time I said 'Upsilon', Nakajima's slapping was frenetic and hard. By 'Omega', she had ceased and fallen to the floor, at which point she called out 'Abraham'.

Figure 6.2 Gekidan Kaitaisha. *Bye Bye Phantom*. Colony. Photo: Miyauchi Katsu, 2004

New Primitive was performed in the immediate aftermath of the 9/11 attacks on the World Trade Centre and Pentagon, including a performance at the Japan Society in New York City. *Phantom* was produced during the US-led invasion of Afghanistan and Iraq in the subsequent 'War on Terror'.

I stopped in front of Nakajima's *burqa* enshrouded body. She stood and trailed closely behind me as I walked downstage. Concealed to the audience by my body as we slowly moved towards them, she asked questions.

'Where are you from?', she asks. I speak the pronouns of my personal family history: '1858, Poland, Vjelun, Proszna River, London, Pacific Ocean, Melbourne, Tehran, Tokyo'. (Broinowski, journal notes 2004)

In a desperate 'call' to a prophet by an (presumably) 'Afghan' woman in a *burqa* being answered by an English-speaking man of European descent in modern clothes (overcoat) suggested a renewed occupier–occupied relationship. As the woman is informed of an individual history of migration of the man she follows behind, as in *New Primitive*, alongside the remarkably unlikely nature of the encounter itself, we can see the process of 'liberation' of a 'native' woman from an 'underdeveloped fourth world' context.

This relational dyad was overlapped with Kumamoto and Hino performing the slapping scene, as derived from Kaitaisha's earlier *Tokyo Ghetto: Hard Core* (1995) which addressed the issue of domestic violence in Tokyo (Broinowski 2004: 55).

Hino wears a *hanbok* and Kumamoto wears a suit. He slaps Hino's bare back, as the Emperor's names ('Jinmu, Suizei, Annei…') are forced from her with each blow. (Broinowski, journal notes 2004) (see Figure 6.2)

This scene was used in *New Primitive*, in which I repeatedly slapped the back of Nomoto. Nomoto's entire body was painted grey and she wore grey underwear, a grey tail and a Mars helmet, and held a dagger. Similar to Hino, Nomoto spoke the names of the Japanese emperors, while the 'family' scene was performed in parallel. When I stopped hitting Nomoto, I withdrew saying 'save our souls' as fake blood literally spilled from my mouth. In both scenes, 'family' and 'national' histories were invoked, and the blood spilled from the ventures of colonial imperialism.

These scenes suggested the violent inscriptions of language and history upon human bodies. In *New Primitive*, the Japan–US post-war order reinvigorated the modern militarist nation-state structured by the Emperor system. In *Phantom*, the Emperor system was transplanted onto 'Korea', either during colonial occupation of the Korean peninsula or upon zainichi Koreans in their post-war re-education and/or domestic and social repression (see, for example, Ryang 2012).

Simultaneously, in different temporality, the new site for occupation in Afghanistan as reflected by Nakajima's *burqa* was undergoing similar inscription by US-led neo-colonial coalition forces. Alongside the immediate violence, the longer term violence lay deposited in the infusion of the colonizer's story and language with the Afghani woman's identity as she was 'saved', presumably in exchange for her embrace of the occupiers' system of 'whiteness'.

In *New Primitive*, after being slapped, Nomoto resumed walking and swinging her dagger as she spoke the names of non-state 'primitive' ethnicities (i.e. 'Ainu, Chechen, Yorta Yorta, Chukchi ...'). In *Phantom*, after a somewhat un-tender sexualized coupling with Hino, Kumamoto stood and withdrew scattering yen-notes behind him. He then rushed to place one in Aota's black high-heel.

> He goes to Aota, a modern Japanese 'daughter', who is hitting herself with handcuffs. He restrains her but she breaks from his grasp and stands on a chair and falls backwards. Kumamoto catches her and [carrying her in his arms] shows Aota's rigid upside-down face to the audience. He begins to frantically clutch his pockets and clothes. (Broinowski, journal notes 2004)

Kumamoto's be-suited everyday salaryman with a disposable income in an advanced capitalist urbanized society offered money to Aota's young woman in an evening dress and heels. Then, switching to his role as father of the family unit, he either intervened to prevent the suicide of his tormented 'daughter', or discovered her after it was too late. In this circuit of social dynamics, we see the systemic circulation of capital between gendered workers in conjunction with familial relations. In the commodification of sexual relations as an engine in the overall drive for capital accumulation, we see stress and fatigue reach limit-point in the human components of this system. As the 'father' sank into compulsive repetition and was rendered unproductive and inefficient, I reached the back wall.

> Reaching the white block-wall, I drop my coat saying 'I was born of my mother and this is where I die'. I fall to the floor and crawl into a mound of earth left from Kumamoto's wheelbarrow. (Broinowski, journal notes 2004)

From the side of the stage, both Hino and Gotō performed *suishō*, while Gotō, who stood on a high stool, spoke the Emperor's names from the twentieth-century in a high voice ('Meiji, Taishō, Shōwa, Heisei'). In 'crystallized' temporality, both became mediated by the disciplinary code of the modern *Tennôsei* structure.

In the second act of *Phantom*, a dialogue was held between ghosts in a desert wasteland mediated by live flame. We see thick braided strands of the migration histories of individuals and of entire peoples marked by pronouns, costumes and movements. Each cluster of historical experience, when placed alongside one another, formed a collage of ghosts and the living from distinct periods.

This evoked what Susan Buck-Morss called 'universal history', which she likened to Gustavo Artigas' installation in which different ball games are played on the same field (Buck-Morss in McHugh 2009). By placing specific national and ethnic histories, normally perceived in isolation, in dynamic interplay, the atmosphere thickens with the confluences of interdependent entities from distinct temporal and geographic settings.

Phantom concluded in a third act – 'Everybody In, Everything In'.

As an audio-video of a US military helicopter gunship plays across the back wall, Nakajima in a *mino* shakes at the centre of the stage with her back to the audience [see Figure 6.3]. I perform 'junky' across the upstage half. As Nakajima's shaking grows voluble, she turns to face the audience. Kumamoto grabs and pulls me to the ground, and drags me across the stage as I shout over the wall of sound, repeating 'Everybody In'. The pack enters, twitching, stumbling, clutching, recovering. Nakajima joins them. The video and sound cut. In dim silence, the breath of the bodies can be heard. One by one they disappear from the stage. (Broinowski, journal notes 2004)[6]

As in *New Primitive*, bodies performed 'exile' (*rensa* and 'pack'), rhythmic sound pulses accompanied with footage of USAF carpet-bombing over Vietnam, fire-bombing over Tokyo and in Okinawa, and nuclear tests in the Pacific Ocean. After the audio-visual barrage, they form two lines of a vectoral and disciplinary apparatus as I shout the words of Article 9 in English.

An aporia appeared. Words of peace ('forever renouncing war as a means to settle international disputes and forgoing the right to belligerency') were spoken from within a modern militarized formation that remained engaged in and disciplined by the US alliance system and its violent operations. Each body belongs to a family unit that is bound to a corporate group, which is indivisible from the nation and the state's international alliances. Individuals are alloyed to a potent apparatus that drives a violent machine towards another such apparatus determined as 'enemy'. Three couples are then clustered in the *gunji* ('military') phrase in which contorted limbs bound in beige corsets and bandages squirm in a circuit of restraint and escape. These dyadic knots suggested quasi-eroticized vitalism as imbued in martial training of the state.

Over time, in repetitive muscular fusions, an association with trench warfare of the First World War in which soldiers who 'curled up and hid in deep trenches' became apparent. Pacified and immobilized from exposure to the shock from the impacts of newly mechanized weaponry (Freud et al. 1953: 32–33), these soldiers demonstrated what Freud called the 'death instinct', 'life instinct' and 'repetition compulsion'. Shaken free from the 'soldier-trance' ideals of manhood, fraternity, patriotism and fear of the enemy, which, according to Foucault, 'control, shape and valorise individual bodies according to a particular system', all bodies on these battlefields became abject. They burrowed, clutched, hid and clumped, like a terrified pack of animals (Foucault et al. 2000: 3: 82).

In *New Primitive* I called out 'Massacre!', while in *Phantom*, after howling a sustained and agonized lament, Kumamoto called out '*Minna goroshi da!*' ('Massacre!'). In both versions, Aota, who cried 'Mama!' to the open sky as the progeny born in the ashes of war, was left with the final word. In silence, the group then melted from the stage.

As in the second act of *Phantom*, where 'phantoms' from other pasts converged in the 'desert', the third act comprised assemblages in battlefields – lines, commands, units, drills. The second act suggested generational migratory histories and their interwoven associations that exist beneath the perpetual immediacy of the battlefield

Figure 6.3 Gekidan Kaitaisha. *Bye Bye Phantom*. Target. Photo: Miyauchi Katsu, 2004

as evoked in the third act. In the context of the early stage of the War on Terror, this third act can also connect a contiguous dynamic from the Korean War through the American War in Vietnam to US military operations in Iraq and Afghanistan.

Critical reception

Audience responses to the *Bye Bye* series suggested highly contrasting intensities: 'visceral', 'concentrated', 'absorbing', 'strong', 'weird', 'provocative', 'profound', 'beautiful', 'ugly', 'pointed', 'dark'. Besieged bodies, as the primary theme, as exposed in the military and economic operations of whiteness, resonated strongly in New York city two weeks after the attacks on the World Trade Center and Pentagon on 11 September 2001. The dance critic Klaus Wetzeling recognized it as a 'powerful theatre of war [in which] the performers are war-machines whose bodies are battlefields', while Marga Wolffe regarded its figures as 'sick bodies carrying scars ... deeply stained by all of the century's wars' (Wetzeling 2001: 49; Wolffe 2001: 27). Jack Anderson of the *New York Times* remarked that Kaitaisha's 'scenes of violence and terror provoked shudders ... [but] cannot compete with real events' (Anderson 2001).

Indeed, the endlessly mediated events of 9/11 contrasted starkly with Kaitaisha's sparse production. Both the real and its spectacle certainly trumped any form of theatrical representation in levels of force, scale, effect, technical operation and display, dissemination, public impact, transformation and response.

Alexis Soloski, in the *Village Voice*, criticized *Bye Bye: The New Primitive* for slowness ('glacial'), lack of purpose ('no organizing principle'), naïvety (in that 'war is bad'), lack of entertainment ('doesn't make for much theatre') and lack of reality ('failed to capture what war is like') (Soloski 2001). In stark contrast with their German colleagues, the expressed desire for theatrical performance to be comparable to the 'real' in affect or impact on the viewer of these American critics suggested a deeper philosophical disparity with regard to the performing arts. While Soloski was temporarily appeased when 'filmed explosions leap across the back wall, bright lights shine, actors writhe furiously, and loud electronic music assaults the ear ... [the scene is] clear, cruel, alive', his appetite for a close likeness to the original (war, conflict or 9/11) remained unsatiated: 'If only the rest of *New Primitive* would climb up a few more steps on the evolutionary ladder' (Soloski 2001). Tokyo-based critic Nishidō Kōjin, by contrast, was more perspicacious in reviewing the *Bye Bye* series. Unperturbed by the lack of thrilling or wrenching spectacle, Nishidō identified Nakajima's 'tiny body exposed in the frontier of capitalism as the most fierce battlefield' (Nishidō 1999: 118).

In New York, the 'slapping scene' was alternately received in after-talks and audience responses as 'agonizing ... seat-squirmingly nasty and dull', 'like a heart-beat which makes any other thought irrelevant', or, as possessing a 'particular beauty of suicide and self-sacrifice' (possibly ironic).[7] This scene often elicited responses that were vague and personalized, both in Japan and elsewhere.

Just as some critics recognized the production's implicit critique of the transformation of images of real violence into entertainment, full houses at the Japan Society so soon after 9/11 at least reflected a willingness to engage with artistic reflection (some claimed it was the first time to leave their homes). When parallels were drawn to real events, defensive protests of innocence emerged. One audience member commented, for example, 'We know it's about us, but why us? We're good people' (Broinowski, journal notes 2001).

In this context, the performing body became a conduit of cultural memory and historical events that extended in a continuum to both past and future. Beginning from the inversion of the basis of subjective identity, the passage and interplay of clusters of time-event-experience is made possible through bodies dilated into atmospheres. Causal relations in history flowed through and between these performing bodies as they refracted complexities and allegorized a dense weft of inter-relational memories.

Kaitaisha in Social Context: *Otaku* and Military-Media-Technologies

Considerably affected by the Persian Gulf War (1991), Shimizu reversed the trajectory Kaitaisha had taken until that point. Instead of embracing the fetish for new media technology in theatre at the time, he turned to focus on ways in which the body was 'besieged' by media (Shimizu and Ōtori 2001: 121–23). With reference to critical media theorists such as Baudrillard and Virilio, Shimizu regarded the spectacular 'green dark' displays of the Gulf War battlefield as demonstrative of the latest networked media-weapons systems. His critique concentrated on the wartime reduction of bodies to statistics ('data bodies') evident in the interface between the organic body and the inorganic military-media apparatus.

Shimizu's view was part of a broader critique of broadcast media reporting of the First Gulf War (images of oil-sodden birds; luminescent green missile streaks; destroyed Iraqi tanks in the desert; charred bodies on a highway with no detailed explanation) and the Second Gulf War or the Iraq War (falling twin towers; a statue of Saddam Hussein pulled down with a rope around its neck; the Abu Ghraib prisoner known as 'Gulliver'; President Bush on the USS *Abraham Lincoln*), diverted or distracted public attention from the actual effects of these operations (Iraqi/Afghani total death tolls, military actions and operations, types of deaths). As Badiou observed,

> [W]hat counts – in the sense of what is valued – is that which is counted. Inversely, everything that deals with numbers must be valued…Our soul [sic] has the cold transparency of the figures in which it is resolved. (Badiou 2008: 8)

The explosion of civilian media technology since the 1990s has seen networked military systems re-packaged and re-deployed from military technology that has already been distributed and used as weaponry. As Virilio noted at the turn of the century, components from 'missile defence' systems became 'ubiquitous GPS', television as a military communications network became 'global entertainment', and 'multimedia feedback' systems (hazardous and remote operations) became domestic robots (i.e. 'ASIMO'). Under a 'cyclopean' global tele-surveillance system ('global vision'), military networks have been completely transformed (Virilio 2000b: 22).

Practiced first by marketing corporations and adopted by corporate states, these systems have been used in the civil domain to accumulate bio-data (blood, sex, type) run through an axiomatic grid that collapses individuating differences (historical, cultural, social, biological factors) to make 'objective' profile assessments in demographic management (Thacker 2005: 25; Puar 2007: 169). Statistical analysis of extensive data sets is re-used to target abnormal profiles for national or private security, while the real drivers of social problems and threats are concealed.

In this increasingly penetrating network of surveillance systems, across diverse layers of social interaction, a vast 'data body' of virtual boundaries has been built to shadow ostensible reality (Stadler 2002: 120–24). By 2014, led by the US National Security Agency (NSA) apparatus and its collaborating nations (i.e. 'Five Eyes' – UK, the United States, Australia, Canada, New Zealand), the projected illusion of omniscience makes it seem that is possible not only to know what is not known but also to 'unknow' what is known. In short, media technologies can be used to project 'dreams' beyond which nothing exists. The invisible is increasingly a new terrain of contestation.

Aside from a growth market in databases, this collected data informs legislative and corporate policies on taxation, immigration, insurance, superannuation and investment schemes, health and education programmes, as well as national/military security policies, which are increasingly driven by the logic of profitability and growth. This biopolitical grid divides and filters unsuspecting groups into patriotic citizen agents – 'militarized bodies' – and non-patriotic bodies (Armitage 2003: 1–2).

If the unimaginable is manifested first by the military avant-garde (Virilio and Lotringer 2002: 211), while high-end, sensitive and complex technologies remain highly protected by military, industrial, corporate and academic consortia, as an *après-* or *dernier-garde*, civilian media can be deconstructed to analyse 'perception management' as a liberating action at the site of the body. In this *partage du sensible* or 'partition, or division and distribution of the sensible' across ubiquitous media 'surfaces' (Rancière 2006: 49–50), 'factual evidence' markets to and inscribes the public itself.

Rather than a pluralist democratic platform, through the organoleptic 'surface-substrata' of media technologies, 'politics' or dialogue across the public life of the senses, is regulated into (unilateral) speeds: military, tele-cinematic, techno-scientific (Virilio 2000a: 45). With each new media platform distributed *enmasse*, history shifts with the new temporal mode. As such, bodies are 'dissolved' in cinematic speed via accelerated frame-times and rates of perception. In the confusion of the 'real', 'visual' and 'virtual' through perceptual design and reality curation, the public life of mediated sensation captivates, senses and lives the body to the point of saturated numbness.

While new media technologies promised greater access and connectivity, they have exponentially fragmented real ties to lived worlds. As in the *otaku* phenomenon, these mediating devices accelerate the consumption of targeted illusions, providing a surrogate cocoon against reinforced fears while promoting consumption (Virilio 1989). As discussed, the results are often social paralysis (demotivation, dismemberment, irrealization, isolation, violence).

In a 'cut-up' exercise often used in Kaitaisha workshops, participants wrote their personal memories on paper and chose a correlating gesture. The papers were then torn up and placed in a pile. While performing the gestures, the word fragments would be read collectively. Kaitaisha used this to suggest the mutability of narrative, memory, and more deeply, identity.

The strength of the media image lies in its failure to recognize the 'outside' (Shimizu 2004), and it operates to contain and unify the 'village' or imagined community (of the nation). Deconstructing this 'surface' recovers somatic relations with time and memory in the present. In relation to the stunned 'immediacy' of ecstasy/paralysis produced from mediated news events (mostly violence), we can see how the public mind is captured and controlled through designed and distributed narratives across ubiquitous 'surface' media. In this way, however small in scale, Kaitaisha's praxis has engaged in re-politicizing themselves and their public during the neoliberal fundamentalist turn of the 1990s and 2000s.

Global conceptualism and the body

In Kaitaisha's performance praxis, critical readings of socio-political and historical problems are combined with somatic discipline and practice. In 2002, for example, Shimizu laid out a 'map of globalized operations' to situate the human body as mediated through images of 'physical expression' within a system of global capitalism. According to this axiomatic map, a global regime of networked transnational capitalism, divides into four interlocking categories: nationalism, capitalism, physicalism, the media image.

Nationalism as a narrative is deployed through media networks to prescribe, interpellate and anticipate public narratives on selected issues. Capitalism accelerates the rate of consumption through convenient communications devices widely distributed by IT-entertainment network providers. One effect is to reduce 'the body' to biopolitical data used for surveillance ('national security').

Nationalism and capitalism overlap in a mutual objective: worker management production to engineer optimal conditions for economic growth. In the national and corporate sponsored image projected to excite and exalt the 'flesh' (*nikutai*) and team (*sōtai*), 'physicalism' in large-scale mass rituals (i.e. Olympic Games, World Cup, EXPOs, etc.) inculcates 'vitalism' through a 'theatre of life' (Bergson 1998 [1907]: 26–28).[1] This rehearses a population for competition, and ultimately war.

These four concepts formed an axiomatic 'global regime' – nationalism, capitalism, physicalism, the mediated image. Shimizu then appended Kaitaisha's movement phrases to each concept, as follows:

- Capitalism – 'Transformation/*Seisei Henka*'
- Media Image – 'Repetition/*Hanpuku*'
- Nationalism – 'Nervous System/*Shinkeisei*'
- Physicalism – 'Phantom Pain (or limb)/*Gen'ei-shi*' (Shimizu 2002: 142).

'Transformation' is for the de/construction of mediated stereotypes through 'parasitism' (appropriation) and 'reversal' (inversion). 'Repetition' was to break open habituated patterns and release trapped energies through repetitive movement. 'Nervous system' permitted sensitivity ('excess') otherwise repressed by daily modes of spatial organization and labour production. 'Phantom Pain' recovered 'missing limbs' of occluded or neglected memories from a permanently future oriented 'theatre of life' (Shimizu 2002: 141–48).

To extrapolate these categories, the 'media image' captures and pacifies a consumer public while a transformative operation occurs beneath the surface image stream. Designed to individualized tastes and trends and distributed across multiple social layers, form mutates as it is commodified. In the relentless drive to create demand, a 'database' of model types offers an archive for the reproduction of affect whenever consumer desires flag.

Physicalism, or fitness capitalism, is cultivated co-extensively within the sovereign right to kill. State-sanctioned killing is carried out in the name of protecting life of citizens of that state and its allies. Deeply ingrained biopolitical categories are used to excite the 'human will to survive' reinforced as a core modern value which legitimates and standardizes state violence (Foucault 1991 [1976]: 52–60). Portrayed as a 'necessary evil' and natural human behaviour, sustaining 'our way of life' is made contingent upon the death of others (and some of 'us'). This 'cost' is putatively reduced in the perception of a population or demographic of 'already dead' whose lives are somehow cheaper or worth less (Mbembé and Meintjes 2003: 40).

As nation-states and transnational corporations co-axially develop and deploy disciplinary regimes of police/military, law, taxation and population management (including media control), under neoliberal deregulation, national assets are floated on the financialized market. Fitness capitalism reinforces a biopolitical ideal (not necessarily racialized) of a superior transnational class, and conceals those undesirable populations who bear the burden to support this privileged population.

In the merger in the mid-1980s of networked financialization and cybernetic feedback systems designed to improve labour inefficiencies, while such tools are regarded as 'a-political' and practical, their functional design reflects the organizing principle of a globalized database for more effective social control and market reach. At this point, it was no coincidence that *otaku* prototypes and multimedia entertainment technologies became prevalent. As 'poly-harmonious' subjectivities were modelled across screen media, they were largely overlooked as products of private global banks of human data used for social control.

Shimizu took up these images and bodies so as to re-think these conditions in neoliberal society. Instead of a transcendent medium of transformation as often discussed in *butoh* (Hijikata 1977: 125), Shimizu regarded the body as a mediating screen or 'magic mirror' for memories, self-projections and reflexivity in a market-driven world (i.e. Takahashi and Bruer 1984: 46). Just as Hijikata described a sense of 'being watched' in the city by a past Tōhoku life-world, Kaitaisha's praxis was consistent with *butoh* in that it 'de-tranced' the body to become sensitive to being 'watched' by present 'pasts'. If Hijikata's concern was with the body from the colonial peripheries of Empire as a 'corpse being stood up' (by earth, atmosphere, elements, energy, memory), then Shimizu's was with those marginalized bodies surviving in the globalized media operation.

Shimizu noted how multicultural cosmopolitanism of the 1990s was replaced with a hardened binary of same (human)/difference (animal) within a tightened mesh of biopolitical indicators in the post-9/11 setting (Shimizu 2004).[2] In fact, this dyad of a unified us and excluded them was already in operation. But Shimizu's analysis referred to how biopolitical profiling across a spectrum of behaviours in networked media determined 'humanness' from which to excise and exclude suspicious 'non-human' behaviours in the public imagination.

Evident in the stunningly blunt statements and security clamp-downs by the Bush administration in the mid-2000s, followed by other nations of the global North, new security systems appeared to justify racialized violence, vilification and discrimination in the name of securing the population against terrorism.

The world was again distinctly divided, but this time power was far less symmetrical. A global multi-state corporate force was pitted against collections of guerrilla fighters (mujahideen) who had once been funded, armed and organized by the United States to fight the Soviet Union in Afghanistan. This new war offered an opportunity to unveil the new capacity of topographic (satellite) imagery to convey an apparent totality within the target scope, and to strike from invisible vantage points (unmanned aerial vehicles, UAVs). The dynamics of geopolitical negotiation was altered once again. New satellite-networked weapons systems reduced negotiation and deliberation time even further. As propaganda too, this technology rendered the enemy as a virtual abstraction (heat-producing screen objects to be hit). While the pilot's vulnerability and sense of responsibility was reduced to that of a banal if secretive office worker, the power to kill over great distances increased. As Virilio observed, 'telecommand [remote] replaces immediate command and ethics' (Virilio and Der Derian 1998: 117–33).

Mapped in a 'temporal-topography' of digital satellite nodal points, the 'real' was augmented so as to form the 'virtual'. But despite this hyper-mediated and semi-cocooned existence where the violence of capital accumulation is out-sourced to less protected populations, the inconvenient emergence of actualities cannot be completely stifled.

The *Dream Regime* collaborations

The *Dream Regime* project (2004–2008) travelled from Wales to Timor-Leste to Tokyo over a three-year period,[3] beginning with a three-week workshop residency conducted by Kaitaisha in Cardiff in January 2004. A group of twenty-seven performers, visual artists, academics and activists gathered from around the UK and further afield – Indonesia, East Timor, Australia, the United States, Japan – to participate. *Dream Regime* was an artist-led collaborative investigation of globalization, war and memory and how these phenomena could be analysed in and through the performing body. Subtitled 'politicising the actual body/actualising the political body',[4] the performances conducted in Cardiff and Dili engaged in re-framing and re-thinking dominant reporting on the 'Global War on Terror' in the first decade of the twenty-first century.

In Cardiff, participants were introduced to the conceptual map of the performing body within a global system discussed earlier. Then, while engaging with the participants' depictions of their ancestral and personal journeys as a whole, the workshop focused on key tensions between participants from Timor-Leste and Indonesia, and an Australia documentary that portrayed East Timor's transition to independence. The central problems raised in Cardiff, informed a subsequent workshop trip to post-occupation Timor-Leste, and further research into the realities of Timorese transition from military occupation informs the rest of this chapter.

In this sort of workshop between virtual strangers, it is typical to begin with sharing personal stories in a convivial environment to establish trust. In this case, the participants were asked what they thought performance was for. The consensus was that performance was a creative response to significant problems, such as the War on Terror, as a means of social change. In response, Shimizu declared that he did not intend to change anything. Perceived by some members as negative and passive, they advocated 'hope' from the 'belief' that change was possible through performance, no matter how minor or abstract. Perceiving this as 'righteous positivity', Shimizu contended that it was more honest to engage critical action through theatrical methods (Broinowski, journal notes 2004). But what was being negotiated was less how to effect social change through performance. It was more a split in perspectives concerning the War on Terror itself.

The most clear expression of this split came in the form of a written response, which was subsequently published, to a short performance early in the workshop that addressed the invasion of Afghanistan in October 2001 as part of Operation Infinite Justice (later named 'Operation Enduring Freedom' in the War on Terror).

An essayed response

The writer (Allinson) analysed a ten-minute solo I performed together with some video footage. Played on a laptop, a USAF bombing raid (most likely by a Predator drone) of an unnamed Afghani village in 2002 as one of tens of thousands launched, played in a single monochromatic shot. The perspective was through the coordinated view-finder with heat-sensing optics attached to the military aircraft and connected via live video feed via satellite to viewers in chat rooms. These included operators, commanders, and military lawyers (Central Command Combined Air and Space Operations Center, Al Udeid Air Base, Qatar) and data analysts and technicians (Distributed Common Ground System, Langley Air Force Base, Virginia, USA) (Gregory 2010: 40). Anything that emitted heat was rendered white.[5] The audience could hear the interconnected polyvocality of directives and expletives, breath and action, and became aware of the collective effort that went into conducting military strikes through this remote air (in-flight/via-satellite) and ground (on-base) apparatus (unmanned aerial system, UAS).

Initially Allinson responded to the performance in the form of surprise.

> Having discussed 'globalisation' in an abstract, non-specific way until this point the 'real world' hadn't intruded into the performance space. I wasn't prepared and was surprised. (Allinson 2007)

Significantly moved, after the performance Allinson drew a series of captioned pictures ostensibly to detail her emotional arc. This is a method often used to encourage children to describe a traumatic event. Following initial surprise and shock ('unaware that I was crying'), the arc progressed through anxiety and pain ('endless', 'unbearable'), awakening ('real'), exposure ('something has been ripped open'), knowledge and alienation ('some are visibly upset, some are not'), *communitas* ('we are here') and subjective closure (Broinowski, journal notes 2004).

Allinson then analysed the performance, establishing a 'whole' of bodies in the 'space' (objects, possessions, bodies) that she divided into three parts: screen (fiction), live ('Adam'), audience ('we').

> Adam, the performer, waited silently in the space. No explanation was given. (Allinson 2007: 2)

Following the surprise, the initial shock was a 'sudden intrusion' of 'white blobs' on the video screen.

> I was disconcerted by the [transformation of the] 'real' into the comfort of the 'fictional' .... (Allinson 2007: 3)

The next shock was the transgression of the convention of suspending disbelief with the audiovisual glitches on the DVD and the performer's incursion into the audience space.

> Adam, seemingly unaware of the proximity of the audience, almost fell into them, causing some spectators to quickly shift position. (Allinson 2007: 5)

Allinson was de-habituated from her familiar mode as audience by witnessing actual deaths on-screen and a live presence that did not follow the 'rules'. Instead of an opportunity to understand why this experience was confronting to her, however, as if in revenge for the intrusion upon her *illusio*, Allinson inverted the terms to return to her pre-performance condition.

First, she framed the live performer as a menacing figure who disrupted the peaceful whole. 'Off-balanced' with a 'hollow face' and 'hanging' body that 'falls against the wall', the performer was rendered suspect in an insinuated association with the bodies on-screen. With the aid of 'media-event' theory (Birringer 1998: 157–58), Allinson then made the actual space virtual, co-habited by audience ('we') and live performer ('Adam'), and made the virtual on-screen real. In doing so, Allinson concluded *cogito ergo sum*, that solitary affective experience was the 'only firm basis' from which to determine reality. Conducted over roughly three years, this analysis was justified as necessary to overcome her shock and to 'reset' her condition.

It is of interest for this discussion that Allinson adopted the role of 'traumatised witness', and utilized theory that irrealized the event so as to recover her earlier 'innocent' self. As an over-determined 'terrorist' signifier was mediated in a blizzard of fears across the globe during the early 'War on Terror', this self-fortifying response was precisely the reaction that precluded further interrogation of the socio-historicity of the actual victims (in the video), the production of 'terrorists' and of the political motivations underlying the USAF operations. Such an inquiry would have exposed the fact that one of the UAS operators described in the recorded video used in the performance the targeted bodies as hiding in 'a mosque' before they were 'extra-judicially' killed.

Allinson's response missed an opportunity to self-reflexively comprehend the way in which populations, which include her, have become complicit in their nations' involvement in an illegal war that has left more than 1 million dead. She demonstrated the mental contortions necessary to avoid ethical recognition of the murder of dubiously or fallaciously named 'illegal combatants' in such US-led operations. As if to bandage the knife instead of the wound that it had been used to inflict, in the inversion of the perpetrator and victim of the crime, Allinson's response reflected the greater corruption of international law caused by these actions of the United States and its coalition nations. But there were other responses to these creative tensions.

Collaborative tensions

Another perspective on the War on Terror was introduced in the interactions of Indonesian actor/activist Tony Brouer and Filipino scholar/Timorese advocate Jacqueline Aquino Siapno. Tony focused on the difficulties in being an Indonesian male amid the security clampdown since 9/11 in historical context, while Jacqueline concentrated on the unsettled grievances left from the Indonesian military occupation of Timor-Leste. The making of Tony's 'Arena' scene began with an exercise.

> The black-box theatre in Cardiff has heavy, cold walls. During a group discussion, Shimizu asked Tony and I to 'run through the wall'. Left unexplained, I run then stop short of the wall, and try to merge with it as if it were thick wet concrete. By contrast Tony throws himself at the wall, slapping it on impact. He seems to sink halfway in, as if the wall had set around his limbs, leaving them half-buried. The 'walls are black now, not white', said Shimizu. (Broinowski, journal notes 2004)

This scene was eventually performed in front of a video backdrop of the entire group drawing the maps and lines of their personal and ancestral migratory routes and telling stories about these journeys (as derived from 'cut-up' exercise).[6]

> Tony extracts himself from the wall and turns to face us, a group of 'first world' interrogators who move in with a barrage of questions. Howling and crouching, he calls out 'hitam!, hitam!, hitam!' (lit. 'black'). (Broinowski, journal notes, 2004)

Carrying a heavy rock into the space, Tony then delivered a monologue on his participation in the student-led Reformasi movement following the 1997 Asian financial crisis in which they demanded the dissolution of the New Era Soeharto regime and the return to democratic process that had been banned.

The Arena scene suggested the victimized condition of a young Indonesian Muslim male in a post-9/11 atmosphere of biopolitical profiling implemented across the global north. In his monologue, Tony interpreted this new regime as a continuation of 350 years of Dutch, and briefly Japanese, colonization in Indonesia. In the interests of space, for this discussion it is worth noting that rather than the nation's population as a whole, the brunt of institutionalized violence experienced on the Indonesian archipelago over this period was borne by subaltern peasant farmer–fisher people until the nation's independence in 1949.

Jacqueline Siapno, an academic and activist residing in Timor-Leste, followed with her monologue. With her baby son Hadomi on her hip, she delivered a critical lecture in front of a backdrop of an inverted world map with East Timor at the top and centre. Siapno contested Tony's performance, and claimed that he had not taken adequate responsibility for Indonesian aggression in Timor-Leste during the military occupation. Telling him 'not to leave his rock here' (in Timor-Leste), she concluded her speech with a video document showing an old Timorese woman clutching the freshly exhumed bones of her lost son to her chest as she lamented at a mass grave site. In the final production, Hino accompanied this talk with a dance.

Tony's scene drew a stark dichotomy between his 'blackness' and his 'white' interrogators to address the contemporary condition of the Indonesian Muslim male during the War on Terror, which he then traced to colonial history in Indonesia. Siapno's critique aimed directly at unresolved issues from the recent occupation of Timor-Leste by Indonesia. There was too little time in rehearsal to engage the problems in detail and these political tensions manifested in personal ways. Siapno questioned the competence of Tony's translator Komuro. Tony and Komuro accused Siapno of elitism and Komuro argued that the dominant use of English was a form of cultural imperialism, and so on.

When the entire group attended François-Michel Pesenti's *The Paesinae* in the adjacent theatre,[7] the themes only reinforced the differences in cultural politics among group members. Reminiscent of Oscar Wilde's Romans in *Salome*, Pesenti's near-naked bodies and grotesque tableaux of masturbating, drooling and flagellating bodies suggested the Bacchanalian tenor of neo-imperialist ventures in 'Oriental' territories.

When asked the next day about his impressions of the performance, Tony stated that he had enjoyed the performance but had sought forgiveness from God (Allah) when he returned home (Broinowski, journal notes 2004). Declaring that 'others' gods' should be respected, Shimizu used the opportunity to state that 'blackness' as used in the 'Arena scene' introduced a perspective otherwise ignored in productions intended for non-Muslim audiences in theatres in advanced capitalist countries. These sorts of discussions reflected the effects of mediated neo-orientalist binaries that were so pervasive in the early stages of the 'War on Terror'. They also culminated in two hours of performance to a predominantly local theatre-going Cardiff audience. The unusual convergence of perspectives offered an unfamiliar experience and hopefully communicated how particular narratives are privileged while others are neglected.

The *Dream Regime* production opened with a rear projection of the Charter of the United Nations signed on 26 July 1945 in the establishment of the United Nations. This was formed with the purpose of maintaining international peace and security

UNIVERSITY OF WINCHESTER
LIBRARY

Figure 7.1 Gekidan Kaitaisha. *Dream Regime: Era of the Sick*. Photo: Miyauchi Katsu, 2011

through collective measures to settle international disputes (collective security) and to prevent threats to and breaches of peace, in conformity with the principles of justice and international law (Article 1: 1). Peace would be strengthened through equal rights based on self-determination of peoples and their fundamental freedoms, and international cooperation to solve international problems (Article 1: 2–4).

In front of this projection, performers lined one side of the stage with a single microphone placed in front of them. Each one stepped out to speak the places and dates of predominantly Euro-American initiated wars from the early nineteenth century to the present. At the core of the scene lay the paradox of a legally constituted universalist pacific ideal agreed to by a chorum of modern nations whose wealth and power had been derived from the accumulations of imperialist conquest and exploitation since 'new world' expansion in the fifteenth and sixteenth centuries.

From the new world order established in 1945 to the contemporaneous 'War on Terror', both the solo performance and the Arena scene hardly reflected 'hope that could be believed in' and the means through which to effect social change. Nevertheless, perhaps it is in the exposure to this paradoxical condition through which we may recognize the actual sources of violence.

Mediated surfaces

Another perspective came from an Australian documentary filmmaker, who was invited to the workshop to discuss his documentary *Birth of a Nation* (2001).[8] The film followed two main subjects, Rosa and Lu'Olo, in the lead-up to the first national elections in Timor-Leste in August 2001. 'Rosa' is a single mother of six and Lu'Olo is an ex-guerrilla who ran for President of Parliament as part of the national electoral campaign for Constituent Assembly run by FRETILIN (*Fretilin–Frente Revolucionária do Timor-Leste Independente*).

Unlike *Xanana: The Man, The Nation* (2003),[9] *Birth of a Nation* avoided the 'great leader and his nation' narrative. Siapno, nevertheless, criticized its use of a hetero-normative couple to symbolize the freshly minted nation: a male freedom fighter, a mother of six. Siapno observed the gendered binary in the small corpus of Australian documentaries on East Timor in which men were 'heads of the nation' while women were 'mothers' who were responsible for birth, child-rearing and domestic duties beyond the public sphere.

> Lu'Olo gets to be a revolutionary, nationalist, citizen, and nation-builder ... [while Rosa as] wife and mother [gets] conflated with domesticity. (Siapno in Broinowski, journal notes 2004)

Yet Siapno also had her stereotyped biases. For leadership she preferred Rosa's 'soft and beautiful survivor-visionary' burdened with children over Lu'Olo's undomesticated guerrilla persona. Obviously, the Timorese view of themselves and the formation of their nation could not be reduced to a couple. It is also ironic, that Siapno's critical view cleaved to Xanana Gusmão's vision for Timor-Leste as stated in 2001, in which the former FALINTIL commander (Forças Armadas de Libertação de Timor-Leste) proposed that the nation's principles be derived neither from its neighbours' 'modern values' nor from a 'royal' couple but on those of Timor-Leste communities (Gusmão 2001: 10–11).

In addition, as the filmmakers' choices were made within the financial and political remit of the national broadcaster to reflect 'Australian viewers' sensibilities, it was also clear that 'soft-power' editorial policy had guided this representation of the new Timorese nation. This is instructive as it denotes how an extremely complex history of military occupation and covert struggle experienced by diverse Timorese peoples is simplified based on unrelated competing factors. Although a truism, documentaries like *Birth of a Nation* reflect how some people see their nation and some filmmakers (and their executive producers) want this nation to be seen.

It is also a truism that there is no fixed and verifiable 'truth' of a nation in its entirety. As artefacts, however, documentary representations can be placed in dialogue with other voices to expose underlying tensions and competing interests. When these truth claims are situated in the context of centuries of colonial occupation and decades of military occupation and civil war, for example, we become more attuned to a legacy of paternalistic narratives which frame Timor-Leste and more powerful nations in a child–parent relationship. Certainly, the violent history in Timor-Leste has created great suffering and left generations of impoverished and traumatized men, women and children. With no independent capacity to project itself to domestic and international audiences, however, Timor-Leste remains vulnerable to being 'occupied' by other means, whether framed as a 'basket-case' or otherwise.[10]

As in both the solo performance and Siapno-Tony dialogue, *Birth of a Nation* revealed more through what was not spoken and demanded further scrutiny from the perspective of Timorese communities themselves. As argued by historian Clinton Fernandes, for example, Australia's conflict with the Japanese Imperial Army in Portuguese Timor in 1942 was framed as a 'duty to protect' mission (Fernandes 2010: 213–33). Usually understood as the effort to expel an invading Japanese force (to protect Australia and save the indigenous inhabitants), in fact, a combined Dutch and Australian force coordinated by the British compromised Portuguese neutrality by landing in Timor to draw Japanese forces into an engagement. In this way, the Australian government was complicit in the deaths of 40,000–60,000 Timorese, or 13 per cent of the territory's total population (Levy and Sidel 1998). No restitution, however, was paid either by the relevant Allied forces or Japan to the Timorese.

Similarly, as in *Birth of a Nation*, what is commonly left out in historical narratives of this period is that the Soeharto government decided to invade and occupy Timor-Leste in 1975, with the approval of other governments. As John Pilger exposed in *Death of a Nation (1994), the* Australian government tacitly approved of the invasion and serial massacres of Timorese under Indonesian rule. As these facts complicate government and corporate interests, the 'subaltern' histories of Timorese people (FALINTIL veterans, students, teachers, NGO workers) have been written out of the nation's official history. Not only is it important to recognize the actual perpetrators of violence, it is also crucial to grasp what criteria informed and drove the framing of the official narrative.

Grounded truths: Timor-Leste and the return to the Pacific

In early 2005, Kaitaisha visited Dili to conduct a one-week workshop with a local theatre company (Bibi Bulak), orphans, survivors of torture and NGO workers. This coincided with the launch of the Commission for Truth and Friendship between Indonesia and Timor-Leste.

Like many locations in South and South-East Asia, wealth disparity between the local population and foreign aid officials was markedly visible every day in Dili in 2005 (Wigglesworth 2013: 51–74). Such material contrasts in a harsh environment made a colonial residue difficult to avoid. Once in South-East Asia, however, the dynamics in Kaitaisha also seemed to shift. At one point, for example, having joked that I 'didn't look as good in shorts [as Japanese men]', the producer made a point of informing me that 'Australia was part of the Pacific Rim but not part of Asia' (Broinowski, journal notes 2001–2005 [2005]).

Had the 'Asian values' espoused twenty years ago by conservative 'Asianist' politicians such as Nakasone Yasuhiro, Lee Kuan Yew, Mahatir Mohammed, among others, re-emerged with a shift in hemispheres? Could national and ethnic identity encoded under monolithic terms such as 'Asia' and 'the West' be so ineluctably tied to personal behaviour? Would this undermine the critical traction established by a group of putatively independent artists in this project? What of the common purpose to create a forum for voices otherwise silenced and occluded from official narratives so as to openly recognize our nations' complicity in crimes against humanity? What did this imply for the project of dismantling molar encodings in the body? As the following discussion shows, local Timorese perspectives could offer a new frame.

Pinto's story

Just as our minds were setting around respective biases, 'Pinto', the owner of 'Vila Accordia' where Kaitaisha stayed while in Dili,[11] graciously offered a succinct overview of the historical experiences of Timorese people in a specially convened session in his backyard. Pinto identified as a veteran of FALINTIL, as he proved with a number tattooed on his forearm. His English accent was hewn from his professional years of translation for Australian geologists, mining employees and journalists who had visited Timor-Leste during Indonesian occupation.

To indicate the depth of the imprint from nearly 300 years of Portuguese colonial rule (1702–1975), Pinto equated the degree of servility of a Timorese with the amount of Portuguese spoken (Broinowski, journal notes 2005). In the twentieth century alone, direct interference and occupation came from Portuguese, Australian, Dutch, Japanese (1942–1945), Indonesian (1975–1999) and from Australian-led United Nations forces. His irony was not lost when he knowingly described contemporary Timorese as shy, gentle and deferential, happy and helpful with strong family ties and who rarely fight.

In contrast to the popular image of Papuans and Timorese 'angels' in the Second World War history (Lal and Fortune 2000: 542), Pinto described a deeply compromised and desperate situation in which indigenous Timorese under occupation were coerced to work for both sides – Japanese and Allied. When exposed to Japanese anti-European colonial ideology and its martial regime, the latter to which he likened Indonesian military training, Pinto described how Japanese soldiers had forced people from his village to dig caves into mountain-sides to house munitions and provide food and sexual services to them.

As for many under Japanese Imperial rule, those residing in Japanese-occupied areas of Portuguese Timor adopted Japanese names and learned Japanese to avoid accusations of enemy collaboration that could lead to public execution. Pinto's account included stories he had been told by his father who had experience as a translator for the Japanese occupiers of his village (Broinowski, journal notes 2005).

Pinto confirmed that the Timorese people, unlike defeated Japan, received little or no restitution for their losses during the war. Instead, Timor-Leste was reincorporated as a Portuguese province after the San Francisco Treaty in 1952, and life was sealed within a Portuguese worldview. Until the Carnation Revolution ended the Salazar-Caetano dictatorship in 1974, the Timorese remained a twilight colony with few paved roads or schools and an illiterate majority (99 per cent) (Christalis 1995: 19–20; Jardine 1995: 67).

As Portuguese rulers prepared to flee in April 1974, in October, a group led by Indonesian General Benny Madani plotted the annexation of Timor-Leste. In January 1975, pro-independence forces formed a coalition (Fretilin and UDT – Timorese Democratic Union) but were infiltrated by Indonesian operatives. In February, Indonesian forces staged a mock island invasion on Sumatra, and supplied the pro-Indonesian integration forces (APODETI) to engage in 'civil war'. In July 1975, Lisbon legislated for home-rule by a Timorese popular assembly until Portuguese sovereignty completed in October 1978. Following strong local electoral support for Fretilin (55 per cent), UDT staged a military coup. Fretilin counter-attacked and assumed control of most of Timor-Leste. Portuguese administrators took refuge on Ataúro island and UDT moved to the Indonesian side of Timor while Fretilin petitioned the UN for international recognition of Timor-Leste independence, which they declared on 28 November.

When the Whitlam government assumed formal relations with the Soeharto government in 1972 and after Whitlam's visit to Jakarta in 1974, despite Whitlam's support for decolonizing nations, Australia recognized Indonesian policy on Timor-Leste. Directly following a visit by US President Ford to Jakarta on 7 December 1975, the Indonesian military (ABRI) armed with US weapons and assisted by Australian and British logistics launched Operasi Komodo.[12] Installing a pro-Indonesia elite (Apodeti and UDT) in Timor-Leste, Indonesian integration was declared (MacDonald 1980: 202–15). Indonesian mixed forces unleashed a brutal crackdown that drove FALINTIL into the mountains and terrorized the civilian population (Taylor 1999; Dunn and Dunn 2003; CAVR 2006). With the then US Secretary of State Henry Kissinger's open consent, the Australian ambassador to Jakarta Richard Woolcott advised Canberra that East Timor be regarded as too poor for 'viable' independence. This should not be surprising given past political interference in the Soeharto anti-communist coup against Sukarno and support for the US-led engagement in Vietnam (CAVR 2005: 92). The Fraser government showed 'understanding' for Indonesia's *de jure* and *de facto* sovereign claim to East Timor in 1978 and undermined the independence movement as official policy until 1999.

The Australian and Indonesian governments began negotiation over the ownership of the Timor Sea gas and oil reserves valued at roughly $30 billion over the following three decades (Pilger 2004: 13–14).[13] The talks were concluded in 1989, when foreign minister Gareth Evans signed the 'truly, uniquely historical' Timor Gap treaty (Aarons and Domm 1992: 77–80; Carey and Bentley 1995: 80; Henry 2010).

Like many other Timorese, Pinto described a gradualist occupation policy of creating 'a land without a people', by 'razing Timorese homes' and 'filling deep holes' with Timorese bodies across a 'scorched landscape' to be filled with settlements of Indonesian migrants (see Jardine 1995: 139; Broinowski, journal notes 2005).

> Some pretended to be dead as they lay amongst the dead. Some raked through the ashes for body parts belonging to their relatives. Some crawled to churches for safety, or into the jungle to fight, or they were dragged to jail to be tortured. Some starved. The starving would wave any flag for something to eat. There were children with empty stomachs filled with hungry worms, which crawled into their lungs, ears and throats until they choked. (Broinowski, journal notes 2005)

In the fragmentation of Timorese society under a toxic occupation, many East Timorese joined the underground resistance. Pinto, for example, vowed to never forget 'the courage of ordinary people [to resist]' such terror. Yet he maintained that some secrets would remain privy to the Timorese (Broinowski, journal notes 2005).

However unsubstantiated, Pinto's perspective has been confirmed by many scholars. The legal scholar Ben Saul, for example, concluded that the 'crimes against humanity, war crimes and other gross violations of human rights' under the Indonesian occupation of Timor-Leste constituted 'cultural genocide' against a 'political group' (Saul 2001: 477). Since the end of occupation, neighbourly transnational state-corporate interests appear to have overridden any enforceable legal recognition.

In August 1999, Indonesian troops were permitted to remain as overseers until the UN-sponsored (UNAMET) referendum (Cotton 2004: 90–98). As forewarned by President Habibie, following an overwhelming pro-independence electoral majority, pro-integration militia (TNI) and ABRI soldiers carried out a rampage, leaving 1,400 Timorese dead, 300,000 displaced, 280,000 refugees deported to West Timor, and the infrastructure in ruins (Stahl 2002; Nevins 2005: 91, 104–10; Robinson 2010).[14] Only in mid-September 1999 was the Australian-led InterFET intervention launched as a 'proud stand for peace' (Scott 2009).

After the election of Fretilin led by Prime Minister Mari Alkatiri and President Xanana Gusmão in 2002, having anticipated sovereign claims to its legal territories in the Timor Sea, the Australian government withdrew from the International Court of Justice (ICJ) and the International Tribunal on the Law of the Sea (ITLOS) (Brennan 2004). The costs (Timorese lives) of Indonesia's aggression were weighed against the benefits of the promised largesse from mining the Greater Sunrise Field (in the Timor Sea) (Brennan 2004; Editors, *The Guardian*, 2004a, 28 April; Editors, *The Guardian*, 2004b, 28 December). This equated to a reward for abetting mass murder (MacDonald et al. 2002; Kehi 2004). This official 'realism' undermined international law with regard to Timorese sovereign rights (Alkatiri 2004, 3 November; Holmes 2004, 10 May; Khamsi 2005).[15] While Indonesian politicians publicly denied 'negative' stories (about the occupation) (Vickers 2005: 215), Australia's 'partial responsibility' for the events was rarely acknowledged (Jolliffe 2004).

The paradox of a sovereign people hailed by the 'international community' and newly attributed rights under the UN Charter, while organized theft conducted in the interests of powerful nations and transnational corporations is blinding (Editor, *Agence France Presse*, 2004c).[16] This collective failure to recognize the right to self-determination of a newly decolonized nation has been a central pattern of the original violence of imperialist power that has continued since post-war 1945. It evokes Rey Ileto's observation that 'the masses are the ones who make history, but the masses are not allowed to speak' (Ileto 1979: 4–5). But there is another even more troubling aspect.

'Truth and reconciliation' and the marked body

It is not surprising that Timorese refer to their land as a national burial mound. The 'Santa Cruz Massacre' (12 November 1991) (Ramos-Horta 1992; Martinkus 2001; Jolliffe 2009) was only one of a series of massacres to have tormented the Timorese people during the Indonesian occupation (Jardine 1995: 50–76; Tanter et al. 2001: 260; Kiernan 2003: 594; CAVR 2005: 593–94).[17]

Timorese 'independence' presented the opportunity to mourn, commemorate the dead and to create a Timorese narrative of its colonial history. Yet this was compromised by the need to alleviate eviscerating poverty after Fretilin leaders formed government on 20 May 2002. In 2001, Gusmão noted the importance of geography and trauma to Timorese identity. The nation's disruption owed to its geostrategic value – a deep-sea trench rich in mineral wealth, a suitable passage for submarines, a strategic 'choke point' – as recognized in the installation of a US military base in Darwin in 2012 following President Obama's announcement of the 'US Asia pivot' in Canberra in 2011. To honour the 'bones of martyrs' which fill the land, Gusmão vowed to prosecute the 'ruling Indonesian military elite' and their local Timorese collaborators under two legal systems – traditional Timorese 'justice' (public confession and apology), international juridical process (evidential truth and proportional sentencing) (Gusmão 2001: 2–9).

While prioritizing indigenous protocols over financial inducements to elicit admissible evidence, however, the promise to prosecute a broad range of crimes including official conspiracies to invade, occupy and destroy Timor-Leste did not come to fruition (Editors, *La'o Hatumuk*, 2001; Kingston 2006).[18]

By 2010, transited from guerrilla leader to technocrat, President José Ramos-Horta in his vision for the new Timor-Leste likened the nation to the 'Singapore or Dubai of South-East Asia'. His entreaty typified the attitudes of an elite who were no longer burdened with the effects of the past. In a familiar formula, Ramos-Horta promised material productivity and wealth to families and victims to 'heal the wounds, reconcile, and move on'. Central to this vision were deals with Indonesia, Portugal and Australia, as well as the IMF and Asian Development Bank (Editor, *ELBT*, 2010; Fitzgerald 2010).[19]

As Raulston Saul noted, modern corporatist wisdom values professionalism and efficiency, and distinguishes between immorality of the individual and amorality of and for 'the team'.

Amorality … involves denying our responsibility and therefore our existence as anything more than an animal. (Saul 1992: 26)

As seen from the military occupation and economic recovery in post-war Japan, without proper foundations, a sky-scraper future built on economic imperatives would leave troublesome problems in Timorese society unresolved. As land acquisitions, rationalization, evictions from city slums and speculation for development projects took hold, the denial of the instrument of redress has ensured that self-determination would be ambiguous. With the subordination of 'truth and reconciliation' to the economic priorities of a managerial class, in 2006 in Dili, waves of violence and displacement threatened a *krisis* that would negate the sacrifices people had made for a new nation. This also affected Jacqui Siapno, whose house in Dili was burned down in an act of 'random violence' (Editor, *The Age*, 2006; Perlez 2006).[20] Such conditions have the potential to create 'criminogenic' spaces and 'transnational' profligacies, which over the longer term may lead to further destabilization and intervention (Armitage 2000: 25–56).

The birth of Timor-Leste seems to be founded on a miscarriage of justice. Independence is defined as based on national integrity, territorial sovereignty, international recognition and participation, mutual non-aggression, non-interference in internal affairs, and equality under international law. In the transition from occupation to economic dependency, the independence of Timor-Leste has been stunted as it is contingent upon submission to neo-liberalizing directives from powerful state-corporate and institutional interests in the broader system (Pilger 2006).

Embracing the dead: Making a body re-inhabitable

By 2010, Dili was a mass of construction sites in preparation for a tourist boom. As the ruins disappeared with the new foundations, financial injections from foreign investors for development projects did not erase troublesome memories entirely. This was evident in the peculiar treasures yielded from occasional 'sink holes' around Timor-Leste (Editors, *ETLJB*, 2010d; *Tempo Semanal*, 2010b).

When one end of the Dili airport runway sank during flooding in 2008, five bodies were recovered. Bullet holes were found in their skulls. In Hera in 2009, sixteen bodies were uncovered. Excavations for the foundations of a luxury hotel development in Tubir in 2010, revealed two graves containing nine bodies (husbands, brothers, sons). The Australian/Argentine forensic team named the '12 November Committee' revealed that these bodies belonged to Timorese student activists executed by the ABRI (Jolliffe 2010).

Gregorio Saldanha, a political prisoner for eight years in Indonesian prisons and representative of an organization to commemorate the student resistance under occupation, called for a memorial at the site to honour the students' sacrifice. He demanded more information on other graves for 2,000–3,000 families who continued to search for missing bodies (Belo 2010). While guerrillas, activists and political leaders have received commemorative attention, less has been paid to villagers and their countless unmarked and minor graves (Grenfell 2012).

To the embarrassment of Timorese technocrats, customary agrarian village life has remained a dominant modality for the majority of Timorese people. Impoverishment and indigeneity are often confused in foreign 'Aid' drives while severing ties to land and tradition has been proposed as the solution to attract large-scale corporate investment. In contrast to the imported epistemology of colonial elites, indigenous customary knowledge in the form of embodied cultural practices in Timorese village communities (oral, aural, dance, food etc.), have helped re-suture broken relations (Babo-Soares 2004: 22). The primacy of the dead in traditional Timorese society is key in this process (Howard 2003: 4; UNESCO 2003).[21] As Max Stahl, long-term observer of East Timor observed:

> Nowhere have I seen greater care, greater respect, greater love for the dead than in East Timor. They grieve for the people they love who die, not less than the people in the West, but more. (Inbaraj 2004)

Although 'animism' has been portrayed as a rapidly declining belief system, while 90 per cent of East Timorese identify as Catholic, roughly 70 per cent practice *lulik* (sacred), *lisan* or *adat* (custom and law that attend to the spiritual realm) interwoven with other religions (Catholicism, Hinduism, Islam) (Soares in Niner 2000: 40; Tylor 1913). Central to this system is the proper burial of the dead, without which settlement cannot be achieved. To do so, bodies must be returned to their birth-village and rites that 'remove' the *klamar* (spirit) from the corpse are necessary for its successful 'return' to an infinite ancestral constellation. Washing the bones, dispatching the spirit, reorganizing co-habitation and redistributing property are actions which allow the living community to repay their debt, let go of the dead and re-order social relations (Hicks 2004; Traube 2007: 9–25).

In a rite of reciprocity, gifts such as *tais*, animal parts and prayers are given. To restore order between the secular living and the spiritual dead, these practices return conditions to equilibrium, without which disaster may occur in the living world. The Mambai people of central Timor, for example, send a 'ship of the dead' laden with buffalo horns along the river to negotiate the exchange – 'we do not know you anymore, you do not know us anymore' (van Gennep 1960: 190). If accepted, the spirit of the newly deceased no longer troubles the living (Traube 1986: 201–3). *Lulik* objects placed at the *lulik* site (burial grounds) recognize ancestral continuity with the living which is vital for community integrity (Metcalf 1992: 242).

As village communities were denied their relatives' bodies during occupation, which were either scattered or piled in mass graves and mixed kinship ties, mourning could not be performed (Editor, *ETLJB*, 2012b). Due to improper separation from the material body, villagers feared a 'bad death' as the spirit would be impure, be denied entry to the spirit realm and would wander in a suspended state between realms of the living and the dead (Moss 1925: 141; Smart 1984: 58). As they are denied sanctuary, they grow toxic and vengeful and can disturb the living through repeated appearances in dreams, as illness or deaths, producing more 'unquiet souls' (*bo'ok/bulak*) (Hertz 1960: 46). Shared by communities throughout South-East Asia (Barnes 1974; Kwon 2012: 227–37), in the case of unjust, grievous death (i.e. from massacre), it is not only the suffering of the individual as they died as much as their right to release from their pain in the living world. It is with this aim that rites are performed to recognize and appease the grievance of the 'wandering ghost', and prevent their return to the village (Metcalf 1992: 127; Yi 1992: 18–19).

As the suffering of the lonely remainder is often diagnosed as 'trauma', in its narrowly defined psychiatric application, individuals have been treated for personal issues. The blight of domestic and gang violence and other alienated behaviours since 2002 has not been treated with reparative justice in both juridical and customary forms to the communities as a whole. Foreign investment and techno-managerial mass mobilization of rural village communities will only further conceal the injustice for those who continue to be troubled by wronged spirits, and will only encourage dependency and intensify social fragmentation (Silva and Kendall 2002).

In answer to the question raised in Cardiff at the start of the *Dream Regime* project, customary ritual and Timorese performing arts[22] and knowledge rooted in the land can help to recover agency and collective memory at the site of the body. While the demands for the recovery of relatives' bodies are not abandoned, these living traditions offer surrogate practices when there is little alternative. In short, performance can help empower communities to confront and negotiate causation of conflict beyond official narratives (McWilliam 2008: 217–40).

Between Cardiff and Dili, 'shock' is a common response to human conflict. A distinction must be made, however, between the 'shock' of viewing a military video on a computer in a short live performance, and the shock of those whose relatives have disappeared (among other experiences of military violence). Actual bodies provide the evidence and catalyst to disabuse the mediated individual of fabricated truth-claims. They compel us to declare our collective responsibility to properly remember the dead and how and why they died as a fundamental practice of living.

The projection of the UN Charter in the first scene of the *Dream Regime* workshop stood in high contrast to the litany of crimes against humanity and war crimes by Indonesia together with complicit foreign powers, and those in Afghanistan and Iraq (and elsewhere) by the Coalition forces in the War on Terror that were touched on in scenes from the production. As shown in Japan's post-war experience of nation formation and rapid economic growth in alignment with the US alliance system and Americanized market capitalism, much was left unresolved in terms of regional relations and internal contradictions. The spread of a state-corporate monoculture during Cold War modernization created great losses in cultural knowledge in agrarian-fisher communities in Japan, and across decolonizing nations in Asia and Africa. Timor-Leste has faced similar problems. Instead of repeating the problems from seeking to modernize 'backward economies' such as Timor-Leste, perhaps Timor-Leste could assist in re-thinking the norms and priorities of modern nations and societies. It could set a precedent, for example, for resolving unsettled issues of justice and responsibility for crimes against humanity through indigenous epistemologies and practices of reconciliation.

In the final chapter, I introduce some recent *butoh* practitioners in Japan who have engaged with the historical legacy of the Pacific War in Japan before concluding with an analysis of my solo performance in the context of the War on Terror.

8

Occupied Bodies in the Twenty-First Century: Continuing the *Butoh* Legacy

After Hijikata's death, *butoh* mushroomed in several transnational reconfigurations. Too many to engage here, most groups chose to freely aestheticize, decontextualize and instrumentalize *butoh* to their own ends. Kaitaisha delved further into the potential Hijikata's body concepts offered, and continued to critically engage with the changing modes of embodiment in society in cultural and regional contexts. Notably, some *butoh* artists took up the *Ankoku Butoh* practice of witnessing and protesting against war and violence in the legacy of twentieth-century anti-war art and aerial warfare.

Suzuki Ikkō (*Butoh*) and Kawachi Kirara (visual artist) re-convened every year from 2009 in an old warehouse in Tokyo, itself the survivor of many fires, to perform *3.10*, and to commemorate the '*iki-jigoku*' Tokyo firebombing on 9–10 March 1945 (Vallaincourt-Matsuoka 2008, 2009). In juxtaposing the wartime slogans on both sides – '*Amerika wa kanarazu katsu!*' ('America will win!'), '*Nippon wa zettai ni makenai!*' ('Japan will not be defeated!') – in the context of the US-led War on Terror, the artists inferred a timeless present. In Takuya Ishide's *A Timeless Kaidan* ('A Timeless Staircase/Ghost Story', New York, 2007), a projection of 'Hiroshima' on a gauze scrim was reiterated for, as the critic Lori Ortiz wrote 'as long as war rages' (Ortiz 2008). At the same *butoh* festival in New York in 2009, Kō Murobushi and the Garnica Leimay ensemble produced *Furnace*, which described a 'ball of movement born in a furnace blast is a great hybrid,... we are at the center of the furnace again ...' (Kō and Leimay 2009). In 2008, *butoh-ka* worked with Yoko Ono and several younger visual artists in an exhibition based on Article 9 in New York (Watanabe 2008). In the same year, *butoh-ka* Iwana Masaki released *Vermillion Souls* (2008), a fiction film set in Tokyo in 1952. Filmed in Normandy and employing dance, it tells of a boy who follows a trail of leaflets dropped from a low flying plane to a medieval castle on restricted land owned by the Imperial family on the periphery of Tokyo. As the castle's residents await their day of execution, they are afflicted by an unnamed disease: Hizume has fused fingers and uses his teeth to paint calligraphy; Ne'an is a prostitute who bears the scars of a failed double suicide with her lover; Maria is a mysterious, wheelchair-bound oracle; Kakera is a corpse; Hinomaru, a

UNIVERSITY OF WINCHESTER
LIBRARY

former kamikaze pilot, guards the motley group. Employing 1960s vaudevillian grotesque surrealism, Iwana's post-Occupation allegory suggests memories in permanent decay. As post-war Japan persists in the collective imagination through the endless and destabilizing presence of hybrid revenant and chimera, so too will those in Timor-Leste (and others elsewhere) continue to be re-visited by these 'inhumanities'.

In concluding, the following offers an analysis of my own solo performance produced in the context of the War on Terror as poetic witnessing to the injustice of state-corporate violence in the first decade of the twenty-first century.

Vivisection Vision: Animal Reflections (VVAR)

In May–June 2004, in response to the launch and expansion of the 'War on Terror' since 11 September 2001, I made a solo performance entitled *Vivisection Vision: Animal Reflections* that was first performed at the Kaitaisha studio in Tokyo (for poster image see Figure 8.1). Versions of this production were subsequently performed in Sydney (2006) and Denmark (2008).

Created during a concentrated collaborative period with Kaitaisha (2001–2005), this solo was concerned to conceptualize the phenomenon of the Global War on Terror (GWoT, since 2003) through the 'logic of movement and its performance' (Franko 2007: 35). Rather than any particular event in this ongoing war, I engaged the interpellated rationale as mediated by the Bush administration leading up to and during the military operations in Iraq and Afghanistan during the early phase of GWoT (2003–2005). An edited film version can be found online (Broinowski 2011).

Contextualizing the performance (of 'evil')

On the evening of 11 September 2001, US president George W. Bush announced 'today, our nation saw evil' (Bush 2001a). On many occasions since then, *realpolitik* has been combined with Manichean logic to polarize the world as 'good or evil', or in the Schmittian logic of friend and enemy. In the case of the invasion of Iraq and Afghanistan, the War on Terror was begun with the premise that it would 'go on for decades', not only to defeat the terrorist group 'Al-Qaeda' but 'every terrorist group of global reach' (Bush 2001b) so as to rid the world of 'evil-doers' (Bush 2002).

In apparent ignorance of Arendt's warning of the moment when a politician removes their public mask by associating policy and action with personal belief, Bush and his advisers assumed the 'tyrant's need to appear to possess uncommon devotion' to God so they move less easily against him, believing that he has the gods on his side (Aristotle 2008). Instead, Bush declared America's righteous authority to lead the world in 'confronting and opposing evil and lawless regimes' (Bush 2002). In launching a distinctly non-secular doctrine, Bush made his view of the world and his role in it very clear:

Figure 8.1 *Vivisection Vision: Animal Reflections.* Poster image. Photo: Adam Broinowski, Hino Hiruko, 2004

I believe God wants me to be President. (Bush in Rich 2004)

I trust God speaks through me ... God told me to strike at al Qaeda ... to strike at Saddam which I did. (Bush to Mahmoud Abbas, Regular 2003)

I will not forget ... I will not relent ... I will not yield ... I will not rest until I have
built a world of divine prayer ... (based on Isaiah 62: 6–7; Bush 2001b)

[O]ur nation has been chosen to be the model of history and justice, ... The liberty
we prize is not America's gift to the world, it is God's gift to humanity ....(Bush 2003)

This threat cannot be ignored. This threat cannot be appeased. Civilization
itself ... is threatened. (Bush 2001c)

This confrontation is willed by God who wants to use this conflict to erase His
people's enemies before a New Age begins. (Bush to Jacques Chirac, Hamilton 2009)

Go gentle now, I know many have fears tonight, live your lives, have your children,
be calm, ... (Bush 2001)

Exploiting the opportunity presented in 9/11, Bush re-loaded the charismatic
popular nationalism of the Reagan years and, as a 'moralizing agent', invoked the
spirit Douglas MacArthur had sought to spearhead in Occupied Japan and project
further into Asia. While renewing Cold War psychological warfare techniques,
Bush II's theocratic posture also appealed to America's Republican heartlands by
exploiting the founding myths of the New World: 'Manifest Destiny' and Christian
dispensationalism (Belmonte 2008: 1). In doing so, he replaced the bio-mediated
'have a nice day' Reaganite ideology of the late 1980s with a more muscular political
modality that was intended for 'our' post-9/11 civilization. The intractability of the
Bush doctrine, which cast anything that was against 'our' (US) values and interests as
against us and was therefore non-negotiable (Cheney in MacDonald 2003), echoed a
level of alarmism more akin to the political rhetoric of the Second World War.

The terrorists who struck America are ruthless, they are resourceful, and they hide
in many countries. They came into our country to murder thousands of innocent
men, women and children. There is no doubt they wish to strike again and that
they are working to acquire the deadliest of all weapons. Against such enemies,
America and the civilized world have only one option ...' (Cheney 2002; Cerf
2003: 298–300; Kelley 2007: 101)

In the exhortation of 'mystical violence' upon a mythical 'them', 'terrorists' or 'evil',
public support could be mobilized through fear (of the unknown). The appeal to the
molar codes of a target constituency, through religious faith, national patriotism,
family survival and the like, as authenticated in the personal assurance of the president
(via the 'fireside' chat), the people's unquestioned trust was reinforced in the vital
importance of the matter and legitimacy of the official response to it (Neilson in Sakai
and Solomon 2006: 165). In effect, internal fear and anger from the shock and suffering
of the 9/11 attack was quickly re-directed towards an external enemy, serving to unite
the polity against existential threat. That decades of US-funded and coordinated covert
and proxy wars had contributed to the attacks was the kind of context that was stifled
as the months stretched into years after 9/11.

As Robert J. Lifton observed, the militarization of apocalyptic impulses was part of a US neo-conservative strategy to instrumentalize popular religious dogma to support the 'grandiose megalomania' of US foreign policy (Lifton 2003: 122). The warrant from God not only reduced the leaders of designated countries or groups to targets but also de-humanized them as 'evil' and prepared them for extermination with impunity. The targeted constituency of American citizens (i.e. Christians) were forced to decide between the integrity of their faith (and of any moral principle they held) and a vaguely defined group of 'Muslim terrorists' who were 'responsible' and were hiding somewhere in the state of Afghanistan.

Just as Dante conceded to place Mohammed at the core of his *Inferno*, however, Edward Said recognized that Islam lay not at the fringes but at the centre of Western cultures and societies (Said 2001: 9). The threat as conceived by the neo-conservative ideologues identified the enemy not based on precise fact but on biopolitical, theological, cultural and moral terms. The details were occluded while the threat was deterritorialized and magnified almost as a pathological inversion of its own violent legacies.

Self-appointed as a prophet-medium who spoke for God, Bush escalated the nation's response to a 'crusade' (which he later retracted), to anoint it as a holy and blessed mission transcending the juridical foundations of the modern civil state. In this logic, not only could dissenting or denouncing this position be interpreted as quasi-apostasy, it could potentially make Bush and his advisers unimpeachable as their decisions were expressions of God's law. This insurmountable frame for the War on Terror was also adopted by Tony Blair who led the UK as the next major contributor among the Coalition of the Willing to the War (Wynne-Jones 2009).

Together with a worldwide call for support for its mission, as part of the Bush doctrine after 2001, the US Homeland Security strategy to wage unilateral pre-emptive war expressed an exceptionalist right of the United States to intervene far beyond its own borders to defend its national security and interests. Although it remains indeterminate whether the war in Afghanistan amounts to a war of aggression, the US and UK governments perpetrated crimes against humanity beginning on 7 October 2001 when it launched 'Operation Enduring Freedom' (originally Operation Infinite Justice) with aerial and long-range (disproportionate) missile attacks on ill-defined Taliban forces and 'Al Qaeda' training camps killing non-combatants in the process. This was followed by a ground invasion and occupation with some of the largest military bases in the world.

Under a false pretext that Saddam Hussein's Iraq state possessed 'Weapons of Mass Destruction' (WMDs), following a 2002 Congressional resolution to authorize the use of military force against Iraq as part of a 'Global War on Terror', on 18 March 2003, Bush declared the start of Operation Iraqi Freedom to attack and invade Iraq without the mandate of the United Nations. The blistering destruction of the initial offensive ('Shock and Awe') campaign was followed by military occupation and the use of urban warfare tactics ('Counter-insurgency', COIN). The indiscriminate kidnappings, torture and killing of civilians that followed, in prisons but not limited to Abu Ghraib and Guantanamo Bay,[1] breached the Geneva Conventions. At the time of writing, no responsible commanding officer of the United States or any other nation in the Coalition has been tried in a non-military court. This established a precedent for standardized military operations and foreign policies in the post-9/11 era, which has made it more difficult to enforce international law as other nations point to this precedent to justify their own military and security operations. If President Clinton could be impeached for sexual misconduct and lying under oath (Article 11, Section 4), then legal inaction for this war of aggression makes a mockery of the existing judicial system.[2]

Knowledge has also been a casualty during the War on Terror. Many scholars assumed a deferential and apologetic tone after the invasion of Afghanistan. In this context, philosopher Susan Neiman, for example, wrote that 'reason stumbles when confronted by the pain of Evil' (Neiman 2002). Others refused to be duped. Cornel West described the Bush administration as 'evangelical nihilism drunk with power' (West 2004: 25–62), while Said regarded Lewis's 'Churchillian rhetoric and vocabulary of gigantism and apocalypse [as] designed not to edify but to inflame "Western" readers' indignant passions about what we need to do' (Said 2001: 4).

Said criticized the simplistic use of labels like 'Islam' and the 'West' drawn from key texts like T. E. Lawrence's *Seven Pillars of Wisdom*, Samuel Huntington's *Clash of Civilisations* and Bernard Lewis's *The Roots of Muslim Rage* by 'self-appointed combatants in the West's war against its haters'. In observing a fundamentalist strain within both Jewish and Christian discursive traditions, Said concurred with Ahmad's critique of the politicization of Islam (Ahmad 1995) and argued how easily civilization could collapse into barbarity through practices of invasion and occupation. He pointed out that borders of present national territories have never been fixed and have long been transgressed and re-drawn in a history of transnational relations, making the definition of 'terrorism' used by Bush, Obama and others contingent upon whether the actor is 'us' or 'them', whoever 'they' may be.

Complexity that ran counter to the aims of a war president was deemed impractical, whose role was to define the enemy ('who we fight') and the threat ('why we fight') in simple terms for a confused and insecure constituency. As discussed earlier, objectifying the enemy is to mobilize public support and erase uncertainty for killing to proceed. The reduction of Afghani and Iraqi societies to tribal warrior cultures and feuding religious sects in which all civilians are potential insurgents appears to have justified in the minds of the invaders and occupiers their own barbaric practices, as these are only what 'tribals' understand. In short, 'we' behave like 'they' do when 'they' don't behave like 'we' do. In actuality, however, 'they' serve as a construct for those who wish to carry out other objectives indirectly related to the cause for military aggression declared in 'our' name.

Since the discovery of the 'New World', the 'savage'/'civilized' (animal/human) binary that was then refined and applied through a biopolitical system of governance through the Enlightenment has augmented the idea of America's rightful claim to North American lands and territories and expansion further west. The vision of a modern materialist 'Judeo-Christian' civilization that shone the light of knowledge into dark Asiatic dwellings and cultures underpinned the American invasion of Puerto Rico, Guam, Cuba and the Philippines in the contest with Spain in the Spanish–American War of 1898–1901. This acquisition of colonies and resources through renewed primitive accumulation reinvigorated Anglo-American global enterprise as imperial Europe was exhausted from inter-state warring.

In parallel with the US official response after 9/11, some populist evangelical leaders told their flocks that US foreign policy in the Middle East was a continuation of the biblical claims to old Jerusalem (Phillips 2006: iii). In the 1980s, as part of the New Right televangelist movement (Billy Graham, Pat Robertson, Reverend Jerry Falwell, Jimmy Swaggart, Reverend Jim Bakker), in the tradition of taking up the cross against the infidels by identifying threat, predicting chaos and promising reward for sacrifice, Falwell, for one, predicted 'a nuclear holy war over Jerusalem in which the Russians would come out second best ... if we are ready for it. The issue is survival. Jesus was not a pacifist' (Pilger 2010: 149). After 9/11, preachers reiterated Revelations to impose an ultimatum on people in the Middle East: either 'cooperate' and join in the 'purification' of Mount Zion and Jerusalem, or join the 'Arab terrorist' and be bankrupt and crushed by American might, 'your flesh dissolving where you stand' (LaHaye 1984; Evans 2004).[3]

For these preachers, Babylon is modern-day Iraq, Lebanon, Syria, Libya, Sudan, Somalia and Iran; Mount Zion is Jerusalem and Israel; American Christians (especially Republicans) are God's chosen ones and the Iraq War is a 'rehearsal' for a greater conflagration that is pre-ordained. To them, the War on Terror is simply the path to usher in the 'second coming' of Jesus Christ. In this context, it is not unreasonable to reiterate Sinclair Lewis's prediction that 'when fascism comes to America, it will be wrapped in a flag and carrying a cross' (Lewis in Hedges 2006: 1). It begs the question of just what is 'evil'?

Bush's 'cowboy' swagger underscored the fact that despite the shift in register from pre-television oratory to affective micro-expressions of innuendo in casual or tele-prompted speech (Massumi 2005: 34), the economy of threat through core (Christian) beliefs and dark truths privy to insiders to enlist contemporary Americans (particularly an anti-intellectual popular right while keeping the rest ambivalent) was as effective as it had been over the past century.

The 'War on Terror' is an accumulated aggregate of standardized operations in foreign territories by the US state (in competition with other imperial powers) through the nineteenth and twentieth centuries. In a litany of proxy and covert (CIA and other agencies) interventions including support for the Hussein regime in Iraq and the mujahedeen in Afghanistan (Stockwell 1978; Coll 2004),[4] and overt (US forces) conflicts based on dubious pretexts conducted since the 1950s, the WMD in Iraq, fabricated sarin-use by the Syrian government on 'freedom fighters' (Hersh 2014: 21–24) and the *coup d'etat* in Kiev on 21–22 February 2014 (Cohen 2015) after years of staged destabilization are all too familiar.

This latest reiteration of the US intervention has refined its tactics to combat the old guerrilla warfare formula of becoming indiscernible from local civilian populations. Known as the Tactical Ground Reporting Network (TIGR), 'human terrain' visual technologies have been deployed to create a hyper-visible battle space. This is a system of constant data reports of enemy movements to discern and analyse the 'fluid target' within the broader population (using biometrics, demography) by the Command Post of the Future (CPOF) (Croser 2007: 38). As a major step away from the USSBS within the Napoleonic legacy of total warfare, this merger of horizontal (ground reporters) and vertical (drones) filtered through a grid of forensic networked data technologies to control a 'multi-dimensional battle space' as it changes in real time permitted 'capillary' analysis by the occupier. However, sophisticated utility of capture and modelling this tracking and weeding out of undesirable bodies as determined by biopolitical profiles and applied trans-nationally and trans-culturally – different (barbaric), unpredictable, non-productive – ignores anything that might identify them as human individuals. It is not within the ambit of trained military operatives to do so. Meanwhile, the master illusions that underpin these operations remain the same.

Since the Reverse Course doctrine and Eisenhower's uncharacteristic warning in 1961 (Eisenhower, 17 January 1961),[5] the largest military industrial complex in history has continued to grow exponentially as its totalizing visions have continued relatively unquestioned and unchecked. Despite enormously costly programmes such as Total Information Awareness, Full Spectrum Dominance and Prompt Global Strike, the ongoing 'failures' in the Middle East demonstrate that the core objective is not regional stability. To the contrary, it is to create demand for weapons trade and reconstruction and to continue unfettered access to cheap resources for the US and multinational corporate contractors, which circuitously affects domestic elections and foreign policy. This project aims to exploit and aggravate conditions for perpetual war, particularly in 'Third World' nations, for large-scale profit, to further the US geostrategic command and control, and to further erode the foundational principles of the UN Charter. Yet this method of diplomacy, which has long underpinned international relations, now threatens to distract and delay from coordinated international cooperation on the anthropogenic depletion of the Earth's ecosystems.

Theorizing the performance

In the following reading of *Vivisection Vision: Animal Reflections* (2004) made during the early stages of the 'War on Terror', my aim is to situate my body and its 'point of view' so as not to assume a universal transparency. In doing so, I appreciate that 'what I am' is inseparable from inter-subjective and trans-local relations – I prismatically refract environmental conditions. While sensory immersion within an ecology makes my inside also outside, and the reverse, to infinity, this was to recognize a 'black body' to which I had been blinded by an over-coded identity which I thought was myself. This 'I' is an accretion of hegemonic 'whiteness' – a global neoliberal late capitalist system – and yet offers a tool with which to dismantle its oppressive modalities (Yancy 2005: 215–41). In performance, my body transformed from a relatively ahistorical and naturalized 'I', into a historicized contingency so as to recognize what was absent, or at least not yet visible.

In the director's notes, I defined the evangelist preacher as one who placed the image of 'evil' between the trigger (human/soldier/hunter) and the target (animal/enemy). I wanted to identify the composition of this image, its function and the structure contained and produced in it. 'Evil' by its very nature, I reasoned in lay terms, also had to exist within my body. In knowing it intimately, I could take responsibility for its operative semblances and affects. In these notes, I described the problems I set out to explore.

To vivisect is to use surgical techniques to dissect and analyse that which is (still) alive. A professional detachment inherent to the forensic technologies of science, medicine, policing and the military has been historically cultivated for peering into the face of death. In the significant desire to distance and ascend, empathy, currently known as 'mirror-neuron function', is subdued. Thoroughly immersed in the commercial arena of advanced industrial societies, embodied screen-lens-object networks create distance from the subject–object of analysis. This way of seeing, augmented and refined over time, confuses reality with representation and ultimately, often intentionally, the nexus between body, space and object. Yet, in periods of crisis, faults in this 'seeing apparatus' reveal what previously was invisible to the guided eye.

Wandering the roads that slice through the wilderness, I transform into subject and object. I step outside myself to sense, in radical dilation, the abject hidden behind screens that blind me. In a steroidal, super-flat reality, avoiding the diluted pleasures of narcissistic confession, how can layers of delusion be peeled away to recognise complicity? How can the misguided, righteous violence in support of capital accumulation for very few be interrupted?

Moving through states of captive consumption, de-control, renewal and repetition I search for the invisible in the cracks in the surface. In deconstructing the body and its representation within architectures of over-production, what is the source of violence? How is a structural anatomy of violence inverted? (Broinowski 2006b)

Vivisection Vision: Hunting 'evil'

This exploration was manifest in the performance as described in the following.

A room of night-vision green. A figure in a fake fur blue suit with a mangled face caked in dirt drifts across the space like a ghost. Taking off the mask, it reveals another mask (white) pulled tightly over its eyes and nose. It cannot see. A camera is in its mouth [see Figure 8.2]. It walks to the edge of the stage and falls off. The body is prevented from moving further by two lengths of sharp metal wire, one vertical, one horizontal, spanning the width and height of the theatre, between the audience and the stage. It pauses as if sensing the presence of the audience. Withdrawing to the stage again, it slips, and writhes on the floor, as if trapped in a discrete nightmare. Quietening, it unplugs and extracts the camera from its mouth, peels the blind from its head, to see for the first time. It exits. (Broinowski 2011)

The cross-hair wire established a binary relationship between audience and performer and its associated antinomies – human and animal, normal and exotic, soldier and enemy, observer and observed. It constructed the architecture of an image-machine, within which a living organism could be measured visually in height, width and depth as it changed over time. In the scopic regime of a microscope, endoscope, rifle-scope, camera-scope or a game-radar-drone-screen, as a device for calibrated targeting it reflected a cool modality of objective precision (see Naaman 2012).

Figure 8.2 Adam Broinowski. *Vivisection Vision: Animal Reflections*. Suit-camera-target.
Photo: Heidrun Löhr, 2006

This perspective, derived from the inception of modern anatomy in sixteenth-century Europe the original purpose of which was to search for the physical location of the 'soul' in the body (Denomme 1998), had developed into a 'cognitive revolution' by the nineteenth century in the systematic ordering of objects in an ocular-centric hierarchy in which the observer was refitted for the task of 'spectacular consumption' (Crary 1990: 19; Jay 1993). In this 'power/knowledge' regime of modernity, vision as the faculty of clarity encouraged abstracted, dematerialized and totalizing tendencies. Other forms of knowing the non-visible (touch, smell, taste, intuition, emotion) were subordinated in the struggle to control hegemonic space in global communications (Virilio 1989: 4). 'Slower-poorer-weaker' localized societies framed in stadial levels of development were those that had less access to 'see' the world.

In colonial Australia, the modern scientific gaze was harnessed for administrative, economic, territorial and cultural dominance to manifest the new world. In the process of transforming the physical landscape – mining, livestock, private enclosures, roads, railways, ports – the original inhabiting peoples were exposed, disciplined, ordered and regulated through a regime of vision. This optical discourse, propagated by European scientists, missionaries and artists, realigned the Aboriginal order of the senses that were intrinsic to knowledge of specific land, waters and pathways. Naturalized as an 'evolutionary' step, forced displacement threatened if not erased entire practices, cultures, values and law (*kanyini*). Despite being premised on visibility, colonial occupation sought to deny the physical presence of Aborigines in the legal concept of *terra nullius* as a form of self-blinding (Brantlinger 1985: 185; Gibson 2008).

Supported by this reductionist epistemology, which comprehends only reflections of itself, the mechanized prosthetic gaze was then rapidly developed to further detach the subject from its object of 'study' so as to perceive it as if it were already dead. This gaze eventually manifested in atomic physics and the production of the 'world target' of the Cold War and its nuclear weapons, targeting and delivery systems and their spectacular mediation (Chow 2006: 25–43). Phenomenology and embodiment offer a perspectival counter-point to this scopic regime.

> [E]xperience is not arrayed before me as if I were God, it is lived by me from a certain point of view; I am not the spectator, I am involved, and it is my involvement in a point of view which makes possible both the finiteness of my perception and its opening out upon the complete world as a horizon of every perception. (Merleau-Ponty 2002: 354)

The ontology that dilates to become atmospheres resonant with differences is neither a discrete enclosure nor a universalizing representation. It is an ongoing process of recognizing the invisible in a regime of the visible. As explored in this discussion, the invisible (abject, banned, past, 'black') already exists within 'our' bodies. As Derrida wrote of Merleau-Ponty's notion of the visible, in order to be absolutely foreign to the visible and even to the potentially visible, this invisibility would still inhabit the visible, or it would come to haunt it to the point of being confused with it, in order to assure from the spectre of this very impossibility, its most proper resource. (Derrida and du Louvre 1993: 51)

This bifurcation of the theatre space with the wire cross-hair conflates the cross, camp and rifle- or gun-scope of the hunter/soldier. The blinding masked body behind the wire approximates an animal condition in making the follicles on my skin grow acutely sensitive, as if to see with them. Blindness, watched in a 'target', suggests exposure and potential sacrifice, in an exchange in the logic of equivalence or payment for something. As Derrida writes:

Punishment may annul the evil or produce a benefit ... revenge also re-establishes equivalence or equity. Turning to martyrdom, and thus into witnessing, blindness is often the price to pay for anyone who must finally open some eyes. (Derrida and du Louvre 1993: 101)

Blindness can also be the un-representable, un-picturable, inconceivable and un-seeable. In short, blindness can signify ambition, absolutism, madness or ignorance. This blinded figure with a camera in its mouth may invoke the US military's 'vision machine' (Virilio 1994: 49), in which an intense blindness or sightless vision (non-gaze) frames 'every image as a manifestation of an energy, an unseen power' (Virilio 1994: 72). This is evident, for example, in the heat-targeting of drone (UAV) seeing systems.

My body, as distinct from the 'black' (*ankoku*) body, is a 'carrier' or 'receptacle' of the modern scopic regime, conditioned to see in a limited way. The white vinyl blinds the eyes and masks the face. Facelessness, especially in modernity, signifies erasure of identity and is a primary fear. Commonly symbolizing dehumanization, through which the subject can be disposed of, facial exposure is considered (one of the only) sites to scrutinize identity and internal, private truth (or soul). While masking provides anonymity from an interrogating gaze, unmasking is necessary for social inclusion, agency, recognition and protection. While light and sight (visibility) are equated with knowledge, the blinded and blinding state of 'whiteness' suggests a contradictory demand for knowledge through the production of the 'animal' to be hunted.

Although masking affords the stage performer the latitude to shape other identities (Kierkegaard 1849; Garff 2005: 59; Westfall 2007: 9, 154–71), here it is primarily used to demonstrate a condition, of acquiring knowledge without self-knowledge or responsibility. This masked condition was to reflect the insouciant sense of freedom arrogated to the US leaders in an apparatus of 'whiteness' as they decided to invade Afghanistan and Iraq. As the late US Republican senator Robert Byrd stated:

[i]t is business as usual, ... we are truly sleepwalking through history, ... I must truly question the judgment of any President who can say that a massive unprovoked military attack on a nation whose population is comprised of over fifty percent children is in the highest moral traditions of our country. (Byrd 2004)

Self-examination

*In the second scene I re-enter with a white balloon that it is filled with liquid and
which I trail slowly on a string like a pet or a sole belonging across the space lit
deep-red. My torso is bare and I am wearing grey factory pants that are too small
and held up with string. Immersed in a silent conversation with a balloon, the
balloon grows heavy and recalcitrant and I let go. With the arm that had pulled the
balloon, I begin to hit my body, as if it were separated and moving with a mind of its
own. After a few blows, this arm pulls my head sideways and downwards as if to pull
it off.* (Broinowski 2011)

As a membranous bladder, a skin-like bag, a soft organ akin to a heart or stomach,
the balloon is, as Adorno described, 'what philosophers once knew as life, having
become the sphere of private existence and now mere consumption, dragged along as
an appendage of the process of material production, without autonomy or substance
of its own, … estranged (by) the objective powers that determine individual existence
even in its most hidden recesses' (Adorno 2005 [1951]: 15). Like a heart transplant that
Jean Luc Nancy evoked in *L'Intrus* (Nancy 2002), I am a semi-naked émigré worker
dragging my replaceable organs/belongings along, in permanent precariousness
between past and future.

As I hit my body, its subjective boundaries are unsettled. Dilating the skin and
enlivening sensitivity to energetic atmospheres, the habituated border between self
and other becomes permeable in greater fluidity. Magnifying senses beyond sight, the
sense of de-personalization unsettled molar encodings and unlocked the potential for
different perspectives..

In the artistic tradition of rejecting normativities that prop up martial homosocial
structures (Norse in Kaufman 1999: 133), this was to dismantle the dominant ego
apparatus and hierarchy of life internalized in the body. An initial impression of
masochism, or being 'at war with oneself', dissipates with repetition as the action
actively peels away mediated images that saturate the body. In this case, the limb turned
upon the body to open out into nothingness is to de-trace the body of its 'internalized
chemistry' (levy in Kaufman 1999: 26). Is this evil?

Kierkegaard found that 'evil as defiance' was divided into active and passive types
(Roberts 2006: 134). In the vainglory of the charismatic leader, the active defiant
magnifies the self as master with promises of 'bread and love' to the spiritless (Roberts
2006: 129–36). The passive defiant refuses God's help and chooses lustful rage but
ultimately leads a fragmented and paradoxical life without transcendent order. While
the former used a distorted concept of love to seek dominion over the mass in the ends
of which are wilful destruction, the latter, which Kierkegaard referred to as 'sickness
unto death', sought to control the mode through which help comes as opposed to
accepting helpfulness on God's terms (Kierkegaard 1989: 66). Both, however, refuse to
give up the last vestiges of self.

Not to be confused with various mediations of self-denial and sacrifice including
those used by guerrilla insurgents, in the context of the War on Terror, this scene can
be regarded as forced confession. It critically reflected an extensive and systematic
programme of abuse and torture as an intrinsic tool of US-led warfare.

Not restricted to the sensory deprivation of masking, this programme of torture has employed a variety of methods to expose the subject to intolerable pain. Indelibly destructive, it forces the body to turn on itself. As in the function of sadism, the inflated thrill to the ego in inflicting suffering and exploitation and the suppression or absence of empathy in taking life in incremental degrees is the occupier's modality.

In contrast, the occupied experience the disintegration of accreted and core layers of identity, agency, customary knowledge, sensuality, trust, belief and memory. Framed as necessary for national security as self-preservation, this process steadily strips the victim of volition until they are under total control of the torturer. The occupied, caged in a box, uncontrollably shaking with shock from sudden and repeated assaults without the reassuring knowledge of limits, assume unequivocal compliance and obeisance. No longer 'human', the occupied embody the will and command of the occupier. As a condition of live burial, the occupied have no option but to become accomplices in their own demise. Death comes as a welcome release.

In this context, renouncing self-love, that is love of the self that has been constructed within 'whiteness', is to shed that self to embrace another or many 'othered' selves. This shedding and going out into those other selves could be considered as part of a larger decomposition and re-composition of the world.

Mirror: Death

> *I carry a mirror on my back, the light reflecting on the roof as I slowly spin beneath it. I lie the mirror down and kneel at its edge, as if at an open grave, my body trembling in incrementally increasing intensity in a single light reflecting from the mirror in the surrounding darkness. Folding quietly, my head is placed on its crown on the mirror until it teeters and rolls like a ball. Sliding my sweaty joints across the surface, I come to lie face up, a body on a table.*
> (Broinowski 2011)

In an act of 'sousveillance', or surveillance from below, the mirror reflected light while it shielded the body. Kneeling and shaking was a liminal moment of humble apology for the disproportionate exercise of power as signified in my reproduction of the identity and apparatus of whiteness. At the same time, drained of any hope or resistance, this shaky body joined a long line of bodies who had lain there before (Hoschchild in Schulz 2007: 101–2).

Even in this moment, the historical impotence and folly of power incapable of relenting is reflected. 'Evil' is perhaps most concentrated here, in the greatest possible distance of power from the actual body exposed in its most intimate and vulnerable condition. This moment, innumerably repeated in a network of secret prisons operated by the US military officers and private contractors, is not unique to the War on Terror. It is a reiteration of a historical pattern that can be traced across a spectrum of periods and contexts: the bravura rendition by the seventeenth-century anatomist with the stricken beast; the agonized slave exposed to the European colonizer's whip or *chicotte*; the live experiments of German and Japanese medical scientists in the Second World War; and the torture gangs in Latin and South America trained at the School of the Americas (SOA), among others.

This power relation is reiterated in the 'video game' operated by a drone pilot who dispatches their heat-sourced ant-targets from a comfortable chair in a mobile unit on a USAF base somewhere in the continental United States. In each case, the body is transformed into an illusion as a signifier of 'evil' before execution takes place. As Adorno observed, 'Auschwitz begins whenever someone looks at a slaughterhouse and thinks: they're only animals' (Ryder 2000: 10; Adorno in Patterson 2002: 109; Best 2014: 8–11). As discussed earlier, the biopolitical split of human and animal status is central to propaganda. No matter how precisely an object can be targeted, the rationale for the act of killing is unlikely to be consistent with the motivations of those who are ultimately responsible.

The potential to de-stabilize dominant and normative encodings through vulnerability and opening is in the return to an always already present body. Instead of illusions of strength, pride and dynamic self-will, when Bush declared that God spoke through him, he would have done well to consult those moral philosophers who proposed ways to offer a self without authority through becoming desire in the void (Weil 2002: 12–13), or emptying out to nothing to maximize sensitivity (Eckhart in Roberts 2006: 119; Kierkegaard in Roberts 2006: 123).

This is not to proselytize any particular religion, or to prescribe passive asceticism. This is to counter the righteous ontology proclaimed and prescribed by Bush and his cohort in the name of 'freedom loving people' to conduct the criminal operation of the Global War on Terror to further other discrete interests. This also arrives at an embodied actuality that inhabits a tiny rock spinning amid a mass of burning gases in a vast nothingness known as space.

Transformation: Humanimal

The bones of my arm are the first to lift off the glass, followed by my body that gathers itself up and crawls off the slab. The light reflects on my back which is streaked in black paint. Retrieving the balloon, unconcerned, unashamed, I am a humanimal *with a bag of water clenched in my teeth. As I carry the water, I am stood and my arm is moved through a variety of salutes, straight and bent, my finger coming to rest at my temple. Walking along the mirror I speak.*
There is no animal as cruel as human
There is no animal as bright
A thousand suns, each one brighter than the last
A desert full of empty shells
All is gone, all is gone, all …

Only death can ensure immortality, in a resurrection and re-packaging of the original body in serial simulacra. Here, the body is returned to repeat an apocalyptic vision. From carrying the mirror, a black stain marked my back as if burnt from an incendiary heat. Another layer was exposed in a subcutaneous memory of historical oppression. Darkness could return through an opening in my blackened back. A chimera, released from the policed and occupying normativities of whiteness, drew the body nearer to the excluded or enclosed in the centre's reserves and ghettos.

As undocumented aliens, homeless *sans-papiers*, permanent refugees and detainees, the *humanimal* suggests a biopolitically produced class of people on a mass scale in the Cold War and after. Scrutinized for potential subversion in the paranoid narcissism of the polis and denied inalienable human rights, the *humanimal* is rendered in varying degrees of abjection: dirty, ugly, wild, vicious, immature, primitive, uneducated, medieval, untrained, lazy, sick, etc.

Familiar with this ritualized schema, Amiri Baraka observed in America how 'after so many years of trying to enter their kingdoms, now they suffer in tears, these others, saxophones whining, through the wooden doors of their less than gracious homes. The poor have become our creators. The black. The thoroughly ignorant. Let the combination of morality and inhumanity begin. Is power the enemy?' (Baraka in Kaufman 1999: 75). The civilized present affords no less brutal discriminatory practices, although with more sophisticated mediations (West 2007). Neither exoticized nor permitted full-residency, the *humanimal* drifts in temporal suspension from earth, people and language, attracting cursory fascination while reflecting enviable lives within the polis walls. This ontology inhabits grey zones in and beneath polis-surveilled surfaces. Fixed in ontological lowness within the state's stratified epidermis, the *humanimal* exists in permanent temporariness amid high density, disrepair and limited mobility.

Despite the efficiency of a ubiquitous command system, the *humanimal* in experimental zones upon which we test and refine our control methods, our pathological hypocrisy is known not just to the *humanimal* but to us.

As the *humanimal* is 'saluted', a system of law and sovereignty founded upon violence and its denial is distilled in posture and gesture. In the growing indistinction between human and animal, combatant and non-combatant, battlefields and non-conflict zones, and reality and illusion in dominant mediated discourse, the Global War on Terror signifies a massive effort to complete the post-1945 US-led imperial project.

In an avalanche of 'end-game narratives', viewers have been conditioned to accept and respond to post-9/11 violence through survivalist modes. Typically producing denial, deferral, equivocation, fear or disempowerment, repeating scenes of destruction both capture and numb viewers to produce political consensus in former liberal democracies. While ideology itself is denied and projected onto other systems, the praxis of public and critical debate about the most important issues is neglected. As economic health and growth remains the primary object of protection in advanced nations, the majority remain uncertain and terrified of losing their remaining material comforts.

Suspension, labour, flame

> *I leave the mirror, suspend the balloon above it and resume work, crushing tin cans in the corner. A recorded image of the audience is projected through the wire onto the back wall of the stage. I place a lit candle under the balloon, as the only remaining light in the space.* (Broinowski 2011)

Suspending the balloon near the end of the performance, as if in an impermanent and perpetual state of exception, I became a body returned to the naked reality of global capitalism. This body, exploited in the 'advanced' accumulation and concentration of capital and power, inverted the image of 'evil' reproduced by Bush in a legacy of modernity.

In the present rejection of evidence that contradicts our self-image in the dominant mediated discourse of perfection and success, perspective may be regained through questioning blind obedience to the triumphalist drums of war that beat in time with a global financial system in an 'arrogant and warlike ordering of the universe' (Cohen in Kaufman 1999: 437).

The audience recorded through the camera inside my mouth at the beginning of the performance is re-projected at the end. First, the audience are the hunters as they pursue the tracked animal. Yet as they are lured by the hunted it seems that they too are watched. The hunted may also become the hunter. Furthermore, the time-gap between capture and dissemination of the video-recorded image of the audience invited reflection on what may lie in the black-box of memory in our mirrored lives. Finally, reflecting the audience to themselves suggested an equivalence of participation in the performance, and a call for reciprocity in testimony, apology and restitution to resolve underexamined violence.

The live flame beneath the balloon creates a tension but also potential. The body – a tremulous liquid-filled bladder determined by gravity – is an object of fragile value that carries millennia of evolutionary relations. In answer to the millennial tendency in the Global War on Terror, perhaps Derrida's claim that 'without a messiah, (is the) anticipation of what might be, a vision of potential, a promise, eternal and incomplete, but not waiting for incarnation or the coming, that which *in itself* is enough, the failure to manifest which does not matter' (Derrida 1994: 182).

Instead of exclusively quantitative evaluation, the potential of the body is in its inextricable relation within a broader ecology of unquantifiable value the recognition of which does not need to be delayed. The empty venue, cross-wire and stage remained at the conclusion of the performance.

Conclusion: Occupied Conditions and Re-Shaping Public Consciousness

Without recognition and acceptance of the real issues which underlie the constructs that ideologically framed, masked and mobilized national populations towards war in the Pacific between the Allies and Japan and Japan and its East Asian neighbours, neither the governments of Japan nor the United States have been able to properly recognize, convincingly admit and effectively compensate for the wrongdoings consciously and systematically ordered by high officials.

'Hiroshima' remains a deep scar that has not been given appropriate expressions of remorse, apology and restitution by official representatives either of the perpetrator nation or by the Japanese government. Despite a series of 'deep regrets' offered by successive Japanese leaders for crimes against humanity committed by the Japanese Imperial Army, individual and multi-national claims for reparations have been neglected, particularly to Asian nations, as part of a broader revisionist approach in modern Japanese history (Pilling 2009). This has been most evident under the second Abe administration since 2012, but it is part of a phenomenon since the 1990s. While the Japanese government has received the greater share of international criticism for not taking appropriate responsibility for such crimes in the past two decades, the US government has received comparatively little criticism for its part in this. Nor has it been recognized enough that Japan's official reticence towards apology and restitution has been determined by its alliance with the United States under the post-1945 system formalized in the San Francisco Treaty.

In 2010, while the US president did not attend himself (although he may have wanted to), following his April 2009 'disarmament speech' in Prague, Obama ended a 65-year hiatus by sending the first official US representative to attend the Hiroshima memorial ceremony on 6 August. This precedent continued with a visit by US ambassador Kennedy to Hiroshima in August 2014.

On the other hand, while criticized as apologist by conservative Republicans and veterans and their families who recall joining up to fight fascism in the Pacific, Obama's 'Pivot to Asia' in a changing geopolitical climate to contain China's apparent military threat has bolstered the security alliance with Japan.

The sustained official consensus that the bombings ended the war and saved lives, pacified the inhabitants and deterred the Soviet Union from invading Japan, has been consistent with the US–Japan centred alliance system which has served America's post-1945 wars in Asia. The game-changing development of atomic weapons in the pursuit of geostrategic interests, which accrued enormous power to the United States, was calculated as well worth the anguish suffered by generations who have been exposed to the effects of radiation released into the environment in atomic and nuclear detonations in the United States, Japan, the Pacific and elsewhere.

In the overriding ambition to forge a US-led new world order, in Japan, MacArthur's military response to organized protests, the expediency of the Tokyo Trials, the Truman Doctrine expanded under Eisenhower, political interference and the crushing of popular dissent towards the Japan–US security alliance, undermined the processes of democratic self-determination since the nation's post-war inception.

The demise of the Soviet Union and the Shōwa emperor's passing presented a unique opportunity for a thaw in the East–West paradigm and a draw-down in US military basing and occupation in East Asia and elsewhere. Due to the dominant perspective of the Japan–US alliance, despite diplomatic relations having steadily resumed in the region, tensions with Japan over unresolved territorial disputes and historical issues, particularly with North Korea, South Korea, China and Russia, have remained.

The US–Japan alliance system extended Cold War thinking into a different climate. As the dynamics of global capitalism intensified in reach, scale and speed, beyond an ideological conflict encoding the Cold War, the tensions in the early 1990s exposed the underlying geopolitical competition between nation-states and their alliances over energy and access to trade routes. Instead of relinquishing its role as global hegemon, the United States continued to expand its economic and military pacts, weapons and bases as if to complete total dominion. Beginning with the Persian Gulf War, which eventually metastasized as a post-9/11 Global War on Terror, an Islamist insurgency served as justification for the continuation of global US military operations and corporate growth. A thorough reconciliation of relations in East Asia has not occurred as the 'post-war' status quo set by the US hegemon has been reinforced.

In parallel, conservative nationalists in Japan have called for the realization of their long-held ambitions for Japan to resume 'great power' status. Since the 1950s, this political faction have used the 'imposition' of the pacifist Constitution (Article 9), and an un-reflexive combination of victimhood and righteousness with regard to the war, as cover behind which to carry out Japan's military build-up. With US urging, the original security agreement for US protection of Japan from 'existential threat' in proximate conflicts has gradually been stretched to permit Japan to provide greater military support to US-led military operations (Ebata 2005). This has produced further scepticism in the region for official reiterations of apology for Japan's wartime conduct and for its intentions to remain a pacifist state.

Since 1957, when Prime Minister Kishi mooted to the Diet the legality of possessing tactical nuclear weapons as a minimum deterrent, the LDP has maintained the possibility of Japan's nuclearization. This was re-confirmed in a Cabinet Legislative Bureau debate which found nuclearization constitutional if it could be proven that they were the 'minimal level of armed force necessary' for 'self-defence'.

Following several military build-ups (Welfield 2013: 364–70), the Nakasone administration in the late 1980s renewed the push for this eventuality. Even though it only marginally exceeded the 1 per cent cap on military spending, by this stage Japan's economy had grown so vast that its military capacity was easily placed within the top ten nations. In the late 1980s security realists in Japan claimed that US nuclear deterrence could not be guaranteed as credible and that non-nuclear status was no longer viable with regard to nuclear threats posed by North Korea, China and Russia. These were the years that the Japan Nuclear Fuel Services (JNFS) began construction of a nuclear reprocessing plant and storage facility on land bought near Rokkasho village, Aomori prefecture for the production of enriched and depleted uranium (Broinowski 2014b: 26–55).

In 1991 during the Persian Gulf War the JSDF shared integrated weapons technology and participated in 'regional deterrence' exercises with the United States. In July 1992, Japan formally announced the plan to reprocess spent nuclear fuel into small quantities of high-grade plutonium (98 per cent Plutonium 239) from the cores of Japan's Fast Breeder Reactors (Jōyō and Monju) at the Tōkai Recycle Equipment Test Facility (RETF) in Ibaraki operated by the Power Reactor and Nuclear Fuel Development Corporation (PNC). This was recognized by several regional nations as bringing to fruition Japan's 'transition to a political and military superpower' (Tsuchida 1993: 3, 6), and signalling an arms race in North-East Asia. As the United States continued to develop smaller nuclear warheads, in May 1993, North Korea test-fired a Sodon 1 missile into the Japan Sea.

By June 2002, the United States announced its withdrawal from the Anti-Ballistic Missile Treaty (ABM) of 1972. In 2003, high-level US officials suggested that Japan's nuclearization could be supported if its policy complemented US deterrence (Mochizuki 2007: 314), whether through shared tactical missiles, as in Europe, or fuelled with indigenous plutonium.

In the Second Gulf War, on 9 December 2003, JSDF ground troops were deployed to Iraq, and its navy (MSDF) assisted in re-fuelling for the war in Afghanistan. In 2004, the US military deployed the Aegis Anti-Ballistic Missile Defense (ABMD) and satellite system after a decade of development under the President Reagan's Strategic Defense Initiative (SDI). Japan officially joined the US Anti-Ballistic Missile Systems (ABMS) programme in 2006 (following joint research since the 1980s) and contributed to its technical development (Furukawa 2003: 120). This was to create a multi-layered 'fence' of SMIII and PAC-3 missiles for missile interception in flight or before launch in coordination with US nuclear and conventional extended deterrence (Dawson, 9 December 2012).

After North Korea resumed missile tests in July 2006, Japan imposed strict sanctions. It was argued by an Institute for International Policy Studies report commissioned by Nakasone Yasuhiro that in lieu of an imminent security threat Japan would need to alter its defence status to permit 'pre-emptive' strikes on enemy bases (IIPS 2006: 6). This was followed by the first nuclear test by North Korea on 9 October 2006.

According to the Nuclear Non-Proliferation Treaty (NPT), if Japan were to nuclearize it would be required to return all nuclear materials 'to the original exporting country'. Sanctions by its uranium suppliers could be expected if it did not comply (the United States, UK, France, Canada, Australia) (Hisane 2006). Over the 2000s, however, as seen in the US–India Civil Nuclear Agreement of 2008 and the decision of the Nuclear Suppliers Group (including Canada and Australia) to export uranium to India (and nuclear reactors while overlooking its intention to reprocess nuclear fuel) as a non-NPT signatory, the NPT is not sacrosanct. So, while some states are shown lenience (Israel, a non-NPT state, possesses between 200 and 400 nuclear weapons), others like Iran, an NPT signatory since 1970 with no weapons, are strictly sanctioned (Potter 2005: 343–54; Tellis 2005: 33; Blix, 12 May 2014a).

Realists in the United States and Japan have exacerbated and taken advantage of hostile relations with North Korea and China to justify expanding the joint security regime and its military and technology industries (Nishihara, 14 August 2003; Nakanishi and Nishioka, December 2006: 60–61; Smith, 7 October 2013).

Japan's consistent refusal to abandon its full-scale fuel fabrication and reprocessing programme of spent fuel from light-water reactors (LWRs) indicates its commitment to closing the nuclear fuel cycle. Although Japan returned a symbolic amount of separated plutonium received from the United States in 2014 due to expressed concerns over its security policy, its existing stockpile of 44–48 tonnes of separated plutonium (out of a total of 150 tonnes), the fourth largest stockpile of 'civilian' plutonium and the largest of any non-nuclear weapons state, was overlooked (Johnston, 15 November 2005; Johnston, 6 January 2006; Okuyama, 13 April 2014). Unlike France, Britain and Russia, all of which reprocess plutonium for nuclear fuel, Japan is the only NPT non-nuclear weapons state to be granted permission in the Japan–US nuclear cooperation agreement to reprocess 'US origin' fuel, which represents the total inventory as this includes any fuel irradiated in US-made reactors (Pomper and Toki 2013). Its nuclear recycling and pluthermal programmes (use of mixed oxide fuel in power reactors) would increase Japan's plutonium inventory roughly by 800 tonnes of uranium and 8 tonnes of separated plutonium annually (Tabuchi, 9 April 2014).

Other nations, principally in the region, are concerned that 'energy autonomy' would make Japan invulnerable to sanctions from suppliers. With this capability, Japan could divert plutonium towards deployment on nuclear armaments, which would overcome its reliance on the US nuclear umbrella, although it would be unlikely to de-couple from it. With both Rokkasho and the Monju FBR operational, and with fuel fabrication by no means beyond Japanese technicians, the weapons potential from the current stockpile is conservatively estimated at 1,000 warheads, and could amount to as many as 5,000 warheads (based on the IAEA estimate of 8 kg of plutonium per nuclear weapon) (Johnston, 10 May 2014). This would provide Japan the leverage for greater geopolitical authority its LDP leaders have coveted for so long. This would trigger an even more rapid nuclear arms race in the region with China, South Korea and Taiwan, and possibly the Philippines and Vietnam.

As part of collective defence, the ABMS is networked with F-35 aircraft, a new fleet of aircraft carriers, amphibious crafts and submarines, and satellites in real conditions. The ABMS is built to be interoperable with US military operations. This ties JSDF operations to a larger and broader US 'global missile shield' and 'global nuclear strike force' (Aegis-class destroyers, super-stealth nuclear bombers and satellite and space weapons)[1] (Jimbō in Self and Thompson 2003: 33, 41–44; Okazaki, 23 April 2006).

Following the founding of the National Security Council in December 2013, the Abe government unveiled its intention to 'upgrade' to 'pro-active' status with the United States (on par with Britain), with a sharp increase in military spending and the lift on a self-imposed ban on international weapons export (Editor, *UPI*, 18 December 2013).

On 1 July 2014, the Abe government approved the alteration of the Constitution to permit it to conduct 'collective security' operations with the United States and other allies, including pre-emptive and retaliatory strikes across a range of platforms. In the aim for an unequivocal 'self-defense military' (*ji-ei gun*), this system is designed for the use of (offensive) force beyond defence of the homeland in rapid deployment and interoperability with the US military and other allies, and is arguably unconstitutional

Should Japan decide to 'nuclearize', high-enough grades of plutonium (or enriched uranium) would be required for deployment on deliverable missile warheads. For this purpose, nuclear reprocessing and fabrication of spent fuel into highly concentrated fissile material is essential. Whether Japan constructed its own tactical nuclear missiles, 'shared' them with the United States, or continued to rely on the US nuclear umbrella, the intimacy of Japan–US military operations, and the fact that they could be used to achieve 'nuclear primacy' and force compliance to its will (Lieber and Press 2006: 42–54), contravenes Japan's obligations to the NPT as a non-nuclear weapons state. In general, this propels the militarization of the region and undermines international stability.

As it is known that the results of a nuclear exchange between nuclear weapons states would be so catastrophic as to undermine the very economic and national security aspects they are said to defend, as well as the biological health of exposed populations, whichever strategic calculus is deployed, their actual use cannot be justified (Robock and Toon 2010: 74–81; Helfland 2013). In this way, nuclear weapons and their operational architecture, which includes their fuel production systems, contradict their stated aim of protecting, or even defending, the people of the nation against harm.

As the Abe administration has at least mooted the re-appointment of the emperor as the head of state (*genshū*), implemented national internal security measures (including a broadly defined secrets law), strengthened and extended external military pacts (*heiwa shien hō*) and trade agreements with allies, boosted military spending, reigned in national broadcasting and fortified territorial borders, the defence of the nation is increasingly being framed as a 'natural' function. In this logic, institutions, citizens, properties and goods become the life-blood and organs of the national body, and which includes their integrity beyond national borders (trading routes, access etc.). To protect this greater whole, the necessity for the sacrifice of a portion of the internal population is inculcated in public consciousness. Nations are not organic bodies, however, and the priorities behind such preparations, given the reality of radiation dispersed by weapons and reactors, are more than likely not to be for the defence and protection of the national population.

As I have argued, it is precisely because of the foundational formations of new Japan as inextricable from the Occupation and broader US geo-strategy that Japan has sought to bolster its security in the early decades of the twenty-first century. Japanese sovereignty and national identity has been based on a contradiction, if not an aporia. In a fundamental turn which shook every domain; military, economic, political, socio-cultural and even ecological and physiological, Japan was re-aligned to further US military and economic interests in East and South-East Asia over the following decades. To expedite this transition, the Japanese economy was placed on an exclusive fast-track, while the slower social processes of mourning and reflection after significant loss and defeat were overridden in a campaign of false optimism in techno-material progress.

Guided by SCAP and a rehabilitated government, popular narratives of uplift and recovery tended to ignore thorough analysis of the causes for the war in public discourse. Just as Creon had reinforced the friend/enemy distinction by punishing Antigone for honouring her brother in death, the antagonisms with the PRC, North Korea and the Soviet Union aggravated by US-led foreign policy denied ordinary people in Japan the opportunity to reconcile with former enemies and re-think decades of policy and education which had reinforced Japan's superiority. Instead, national Japanese identity was quickly re-planted and reified within the US-led 'new order'.

But just as the Dada artists had found critical potential in *les grande motiles* as the core signifiers of the absurdity of industrialized slaughter, a sub-stream of artists turned to their bodies as the most reliable ground from which to face the conditions in new post-war Japan. As the painful and inconvenient memories dissipated and the business of reconstruction towards the future occupied the present, their works reflected, both directly and in abstract form, the divided condition of semi-colonized peoples.

The disfigured and weakened *hibakusha* bodies remained the shadow symbol in a shiny new narrative. Marginalized bodies in Japan – *hibakusha*, prostitutes, orphans, homeless, returnee war veterans, displaced rural villagers, zainichi Koreans and Chinese – reflected the foundational instability in terms like 'Japan', 'democracy' and 'human'. They embodied and refracted the actuality of modern state oppression over time – in the Asia–Pacific in the Meiji period and in the 'hybrid' US-led new order policies.

As I have developed through this book, it is in these bodies and their artistic reflections that we can perceive, destabilize and challenge the occupied condition. As demonstrated in *Ankoku Butoh* during the 'golden period' in the mid- to late 1950s, artists engaged in re-making the human condition in parallel with the return of the largest mass political left movement in Japanese history. This period was one of the most creative in devising praxes of organization, assemblage, debate and demonstration. Together with like-minded international movements during the 1960s, the body came to be understood as the locus of power and identity, through which oppressed heterodox minorities could speak.

Along with the significant black power movement as part of the movement for civil rights in the United States in the same period, 'blackness' in particular also signified war's aftermath, rural village life under the modern industrialized state, urban exploitation and commodification under the gaze of 'whiteness'. It also reflected a mode of empowerment to re-negotiate self-determination in a generally semi-colonized condition.

This analysis of *Ankoku Butoh* revealed how a series of masks offered protective cladding for the performer in transgressive 'surrogate actions'. As in any rite carried out in a discrete space, as found in the *butoh-fu*, the *butoh* performer dilated habituated rational will and temporal modalities to become sensitized to others, both past and present, and approach elements and atmospheres beyond 'human' – animal, vegetable, mineral, elemental. In doing so, this theatre of the body operated as a mnemonic device and a praxis for re-making the human.

The socio-political resonance in this work should not be disregarded. In the genealogy of an 'avant-garde' movement that critically responded to modern state militarism, Hijikata introduced an urbanized *hyakushō* form that counter-posed the instrumentality of consumer culture as well as modern ethno-nationalism. In reflecting a subaltern rural émigré culture in post-war Japan, *Ankoku Butoh* tapped a commonality shared with similar communities in East and South-East Asia, particularly during the Korean and Vietnam wars.

With the ascent of the Japanese economy together with resurgent nationalist pride amid globalized neoliberal financial systems in the 1980s, the *otaku* emerged as a prototypical ontology of the new post-Cold War and post-Shōwa era. As *butoh* was orientalized for transnational markets, Gekidan Kaitaisha re-worked *butoh-sei* principles. Recognizing the body as a conduit of history and memory, Kaitaisha productions, such as the *Bye Bye* series, deconstructed the body mediated by surfaces of state-corporate capitalism. Physical forms, phrases and scenes were constructed to situate the body within the violating dynamic of the modern *Tennō-sei* system, and in its renewed condition under the US hegemon in the 'post-war' nuclear age.

Performed in an historic post-9/11 moment, the *Bye Bye* production extended into *Dream Regime*, an international collaboration in the early years of the War on Terror. With the body enmeshed within a set of 'globalized operations', by de-trancing the body, at least temporarily, from its networked data-feed to re-sensitize it to the 'outside and other', this served to de-stabilize and expose the internalized master illusions. As a political ontology, this is a praxis of recovering self from an avalanche of masked attachments.

As participants recalled their personal histories of migration in *Dream Regime*, it became clearer how dominant mediated narratives create excluded and marginal histories and narratives, such as those in Indonesia and Timor-Leste. While emergent tensions between participants from Timor-Leste and Indonesia could only be briefly touched on in this production, they prompted further research into the recurrent theme of occupation, apology, reparation and justice.

Echoing the problematic formation of post-war Japan, this reiterated how people exposed to state violence became collateral in inter-state and regional power relations. Yet the bodies exhumed from the foundations of Timorese skyscrapers and resorts signify the broader need in Timorese communities to recover the dead to conduct mourning, community bonding and reconciliation. In the rush to convert Timor-Leste into a tourist paradise, Timorese will continue to be occupied by 'wandering ghosts'. That is, unless subaltern and customary knowledge can find ways to make peace with past injustices and reinhabit life beyond the homogenized values of global capitalism.

The Global War on Terror has introduced a nodal network of surveillance, forensic profiling and bio-data collection, to dissect territories and intimate capillaries of communities in a highly detached, prostheticized, neo-colonial modality. In response, in a solo performance, I explored how responsibility could be taken for the war crimes and crimes against humanity committed by states in our name. By dismantling the use of 'evil' as a primary interpellating tool used in support of this war, by assuming those aspects associated with 'evil', I explored a bodily condition that is isolated, purged and exposed to the dominant gaze of power. This was to perceive an apparatus of violence that reinforces 'whiteness' while it continues to scar the commons of tissue and earth.

In analysing a select body of artistic works in post-1945 Japan that reflected the effects, both physical and psychic, from war, occupation and capital accumulation, I have sought to formulate a translocal condition of being 'under occupation' beyond fixed concepts of race, identity and national culture to form new lines and planes of collaborative relations.

Although it often is defined as such, an occupied condition need not necessarily depend upon such molar denominations. Experienced individually or by groups of people, more often than not, its identification and exposure typically relies upon the reality of the body. Although artistic expression offers some relief from the occupied condition, it can also be misrepresented. In the context of socio-political engagements within world-historical change, we can better understand what these particular artistic works do and have done, and why they are crucial in re-making human consciousness in positive ways for future societies.

Notes

Introduction

1   For example, 'If they imitate they should imitate, not any meanness or baseness, but the good only; for the mask that the actor wears is apt to become his face...' (Plato 2010). For Aristotle's purpose of aesthetics, see Davies et al. (2009: 148).

2   For Asian influences in Greek tragedy see Martin Lichtfield West's oeuvre on the Orphic traditions.

3   'The endeavour ("conatus") wherewith everything endeavours to persist in its own is nothing else but the actual essence of the thing in question' (Spinoza and Yessleman 2006: VII, 136, Book XIX, 233: I: 1.5a).

4   Many Western–non-Western artistic exchanges took place in the modern period including Japanese performer Sadayakko and Western opera, Eguchi Takaya, Itō Michio, Ishii Baku, W. B. Yeats and Ezra Pound, Brecht, Meyerhold and Peking opera actor Mei Lan Fang, Artaud and Balinese and Tarahumara dances and Henry Black in Rakugo.

5   The genetic danger inherent to the properties of radioactive radium were known since 1928 with Müller's discovery of mutations in flies from X-ray exposures and the 'Radium Girls' successful case for occupational health against the US Radium Corporation. Between 1939 and 1941, Drs Pecher, Hamilton, Lawrence and Stone of the Manhattan Project observed that uranium fission products (such as I131, P32, Sr 89 and 90) emitted photons, neutrons and particulate radiation. They discovered that strontium was a calcium analogue and studied its metabolic effects from ingestion and the carcinogenic effects in the unborn. In October 1943, a subcommittee of the S-1 Committee for 'Use of radioactive materials as military weapons' comprising of Drs J. Conant, A. Compton and H. Urey wrote to General Groves advising on weaponising such uranium products collected from nuclear pile rods and dispersed into enemy territory as an environmental weapon (dust, smoke, liquid distributed by ground-fired projectile, land vehicle or aerial bomb). The objective was to protect US troops and civilians with potassium, vitamin D and calcium concentrate doses and contaminate enemy food and water supplies, making the land uninhabitable, including airports and railroad yards, and cause casualties in military and civilian urban populations. See Conant, J. B., Compton A. H., Urey H., 'Groves Memo', 30 October 1943, Manhattan District, Oak Ridge, Tennessee; declassified 5 June 1974, http://en.wikipedia.org/wiki/File:Groves_memo_30oct43_p1.GIF, accessed October 2013.

6   Russell found in *Leatherneck*, a US Marines magazine showing a creature labelled 'Louseous Japanicas' and described its 'breeding grounds around the Tokyo area... must be completely annihilated'. A chemical industry journal also published an illustration of the fumigation of axis powers as beetles.

7   Harry Truman to Irv Kupcinet (1963), *Chicago Sun Times*, 5 August.

8   Mizuta-Lippit (2005).

9   Others who actively developed 'social Darwinism' or 'scientific racism' were Georges Cuvier, James Cowles Pritchard, Louis Agassiz, Charles Pickering, Herbert Spencer and Francis Galton.

10 Although the numbers continue to be debated, in August 2014 Hiroshima city recorded more than 450,000 *hibakusha* at the average age of seventy-five years:

Deaths from bombings –
      292,325 in Hiroshima (Sindhu, 8 August 2014).
      165,409 in Nagasaki (Yamamoto, 9 August 2014).
The total certified *hibakusha* from the Second World War by Government of Japan peaked in 1980 at 372,264 which dropped to 183,519 by 1 July 2015, and the average age reached 80 (Ministry of Health, GOJ, 1 July 2015 in Okamoto, 2 July 2015).

Chapter 1

1   The transliteration of Japan's first Emperor Jinmu (神武) is holy military.
2   As demonstrated in their production and trade of wooden tools, lacquer, pottery, iron and copper implements, clothes from silk, hides and their associated products from horses and cows, and alternative cultivation of mulberries, hemp, ramie, fruits and nuts.
3   Kant (1991: 110–11), Hegel and Brown (2009) and Marx and Engels (2001: 488).
4   Blumenbach (1865), de Gobineau (1915 [1853–55]), Haeckel (1883: 1, 2) and Hall (1904).
5   Ainu were nomadic but put in reservations and educated in Japanese schools. Some served in the Imperial Army but upon return were still denied Japanese citizenship and compensation (see Suzuki and Oiwa 1996).
6   Several of these feature films included racist epithets. See, for example, *Guadalcanal Diary, The Fighting Seabees, Objective Burma, Bataan, Gung Ho!, China Girl, Blood on the Sun* and *Air Force*.
7   The journalists put him in a pose for a photograph which caused Tōjō to haemorrhage and prevented his suffocation.
8   Koshiro Yukiko describes a 1947 radio station skit which lampooned the remark but which was cut before broadcast:
      A solemn voice: The Japanese are only twelve-year-old children.
      The crowd: You are quite right, your Highness.
      A solemn voice: But the Japanese have to re-arm themselves.
      A man: Holy cow! You mean the world's first children's army?
9   Schaller cites the Forrestal diary, 10 July 1946, Forrestal Papers.
10 Cl. Raymond Harrison, Army Service Forces, Office of the Surgeon General, 11 March 1946, 'Japanese food situation 1946', NDL PHW 02039, 1 May 1946.
11 Johnson cites Omori Minoru, *Postwar Hidden History, Bōryoku to reisen no jūjiro* [Plots and the Crossroads of the Cold War], vol. 7, 1981.
12 Anpo or AMPO are acronyms for 'An' for 'Anzen' (security) 'Po' for 'Hoshō' (protection or security).

Chapter 2

1   Translated by Saika Tadayoshi, Hiroshima University.
2   100 mSv/y is understood to be underestimated by between 100 and 1,000 times (see ECRR 2003). The ICRP dose regime continues to inform international radiation policy (IAEA/UNSCEAR/WHO) and informed radiation emergencies at Windscale, Sellafield, Three Mile Island, Chernobyl, Fukushima and elsewhere.
3   Kurosawa's early post-war films include *One Wonderful Sunday* (1947), *Drunken Angel* (*Yoidore tenshi*, 1948), *The Quiet Duel* (*Shizukanaru kettō*, 1949) and *Stray Dog* (*Nora inu*, 1949).
4   This was expanded to Four Pillars Nuclear Policy permitting nuclear power for peaceful purposes, promoting global nuclear disarmament and relying upon US deterrence.
5   Inspired by the La Villette slaughterhouse in George Bataille's *Documents* (where Franju later shot his film), Francis Bacon's abattoir carcasses and Kurt Vonnegut's *Slaughterhouse Five*, a vivisectionist Dr Genessier kidnaps young women, steals their faces and grafts them on the ruined face of his daughter.

Chapter 3

1   Among others, Nicolas Villodre, curator of La Cinémathèque de la Danse, traces *butoh* and Iimura Takahiko's *butoh* films to German Expressionism.
2   As KuroDaRaijee pointed out, there were also many other performance art groups outside of the well-known ones mentioned above.
3   Such as Ōshima Nagisa, Imamura Shōhei, Yoshida Yoshihide, Hani Susumu, Okamoto Kihachi, Wakamatsu Kōji, Adachi Masao, Shinoda Masahiro (film); Hosoe Eikoh and Moriyama Daidō (photography); Terayama Shji, Suzuki Tadashi, Satoh Makoto and Kara Jūrō (theatre).
4   Miyazawa's Buddhist inspiration is considered 'vitality in morbidity', as *joie de vivre* in nature's decay and fall (see Pulvers 2008).
5   Gōda made the 'strangulation' reference. Kuniyoshi reiterated it, but pointed to a tendency for exaggeration. Ohno Yoshito and Motofuji Akiko denied that Yoshito killed the chicken (see Motofuji 1998: 19; Kurihara 2000a 44.1: 26, fn. 13).
6   Lafcadio Hearn (*Glimpses of Unfamiliar Japan*, vols. 1–2, 1894), Okakura (Tenshin) Kakuzō (*Ideals of the East*, 1903; *The Awakening of Japan*, 1904; *The Book of Tea*, 1906).
7   French citizenship for Algerians in French-Algiers (1830–1962) was contingent upon their conscription to the French army.
8   These included *Horrors of a Malformed Man* (*Kyōfu kikei ningen: Edogawa Rampo zenshū*, 1969 incorporating *Anma*), *Strange Tales of Dragon Tattoo* (*Kaidan nobori ryū*, 1970, incorporating *Nikutai no hanran*) and *Love Crime* (*Meiji, Taishō, Shōwa ryoki onna hanzaishi*, 1969), featuring the famous Abe Sada, who was the subject of Ōshima's *In the realm of the senses*.
9   Akin to Jean-Luc Godard, Jack Smith, Maya Deren, Jonas Mekas, Yoko Ono and Fluxus, Iimura's visual 'cine-dance' poems moved onstage with the performers at Hijikata's encouragement used time-jumps, tight close-ups and abstractions in a free-style collagist approach. His main film is *Dance Part in the Kingdom of Lilliput* (1964).

10   Iimura moved from 16 mm in the 1970s, to digital media in the 1980s, and released a new version of *Anma* in 2007 with a score by Adachi Tomomi.

11   Hijikata T., 'Naka no sozai/sozai', or 'Inner material/material' in *Hijikata Tatsumi Dance Experience no kai* pamphlet.

12   *Kamaitachi*: a mercurial, invisible animal from local folklore with sharp-claws that causes tiny cuts in human skin. Other photographers – Moriyama Daido, Suda Issei, Kitai Kazuo – also pursued quotidian Tōhoku life with the project *Tōhoku e* (1974–77).

13   These are part of a series of butoh dancers entitled 'Man and Woman/*Otoko to Onna*' (1961); 'Sickle Weasel/ *Kamaitachi*' (1969); 'Hoyō/Embrace', 1971.

14   Terayama Shūji, 'Ierō niiguro datta koro' in Terayama (1978: 260–62).

15   In his play *Dutchman*, Baraka described the distilled black rage as the genius of the United States, and blues and jazz as an alternative for murder. 'Bird would've played not a note of music if he just walked to East Sixty Seventh Street and killed the first ten white people he saw … Just murder! Would make us all sane'. See Bermel (1996).

16   'Hanran', sometimes translated as 'deluge', varies between 'rebellion' and 'revolt'.

17   According to artist-collaborator Wakamatsu Miki, Dunham visited with the Katherine Dunham Group in 1957.

18   See James Baldwin (1985), Richard Wright (1954) and Malcolm X (1971).

19   Simmel opposes emotionally based sensory life of the rural and sophisticated individuated metropolitan life.

20   Imamura made several documentary films, including *A Man Vanishes* (Imamura Productions, 1967), *The Profound Desire of the Gods* (Imamura Productions, 1968), *A History of Postwar Japan as Told by a Bar Hostess* (Imamura Productions, 1970), and *In Search of Unreturned Soldiers* (Imamura Productions, pt. 1–2 1971, pt. 3 1975).

21   Shindō's *Onibaba* (Toei, 1964) is also known as *The Hole* or *The Demon* (lit. 'Demon Hag') and his *Yabunonaka no Kuroneko/Black Cat* (Toei, 1968) negotiates similar terrain.

Chapter 4

1   The parents of the director of *Byakkosha*, Osuka Isamu, were in Hiroshima at the time of the bombings (Baird 2012: 265, fn. 43).

2   Kurt Schwitters, Otto Dix, George Grosz, Hannah Hoch, Heinrich Hoerle, Franz Jung, John Herzefelde, Alfred Stieglitz, Otto Gross, Francis Picabia, Raoul Hausmann, Man Ray, El Lissitzky, Max Ernst, Hugo Ball, Richard Huelsenbeck, Marcel Janco and Jean Arp.

3   Dada flourished in several locations – New York, Berlin, Hanover, Cologne, Barcelona, Paris – culminating in the Cabaret Voltaire on February 1916 in Zurich. The Cabaret closed five months later, but Dadaists continued with Galerie Dada (March 1917), *Dada* magazine and a Zurich soirée in April 1919, after which Tzara moved to Paris.

4   Alfred Jarry, founder of 'pataphysics' (science of imaginary solutions), is considered one of the progenitors of modern avant-garde theatre.

5   Leonard Pronko described *The Gas Heart* as 'cute', Martin Esslin characterized it as rhythmic nonsense that foreshadowed Ionesco, Michel Sanouillet called it 'a sketch', Jacques Baron saw it as 'nothing more nor less than a poem ... perfectly dishevelled dialogue'.

6   Performed at *Soirée Dada*, Galerie Montaigne, 10 June 1921; published as *The Gas Heart* in *Der Sturm*, March 1922; restaged on 6 July 1923 at the *Soirée du Coeur à barbe* at the Theatre Michel, where it was disrupted by a group led by Andre Bréton to protest its conventional theatre accommodation.

7   The First World War saw chlorine, phosgene and mustard gas deployed by the Germans, French and British resulting in over 1,240,000 casualties and over 91,000 deaths. The use of such gases was banned in the 1925 Geneva Protocol.

8   T. Tzara, 'The First Celestial Adventure of M. Antipyrine', 'Monsieur Antipyrine's Manifesto' (1916).

9   T. Tzara, 'Dada Manifesto 1918'.

10   See, a metronome with the cut-out photograph of an eye on its pendulum entitled 'Object to Be Destroyed' (1923–1932).

11   In the *Zurich Chronicle*, Tzara adopted a vaudevillian tone: '... last proclamation!! invention dialogue!! DADA!!! latest novelty!!! bourgeois syncopé, brutist music, latest rage, song Tzara dance protests – the big drum – red light, policemen ...'.

12   See Georg Lukaćs, who regarded Nazism as reactionary bourgeois proto-fascism and associated it with a Nietzschean 'triumph of the will'.

13   Bréton mistrusted the unhealthy potential in the trance Artaud and Desnos were proposing. Weiss described these abnormalities as 'possession trance' and dysfunctional 'disjecta membra'.

14   See Artaud's two essays, 'On Balinese Theatre' (1931) and 'Oriental and Occidental Theatre' (1934).

15   Nancy Spero, 'Codex Artaud' (1971–1972), Jean Hubert-Martin (Dir.), *Magiciens de la Terre*, Paris: Pompidou Centre, 1989.

16   Deleuze compares Guernica to Francis Bacon's deformative work in the 'Three Studies for Figures at the Base of a Crucifixion' (1944) (Deleuze 1990: 47).

17   For example, the clay ceramicist group Sodeisha ('Crawling through Mud Association' – Osamu Suzuki (1926–2001), Kazuo Yagi (1918–1979), Hikaru Yamada (1923–2001)) (see Yellin, 2013).

18   Kasai Akira, unpublished interview.

19   I translated and relied on the practical movement phrases in the *Butoh-fu* compiled by Hijikata's youngest and last *butoh-ka* student before he died, Hino Hiruko. Waguri's *Butoh-Kaden* features 'Hijikata's poetry' and Waguri's choreography from his own *butoh-fu* transcribed from Hijikata's sessions.

20   In Rabelais' images, Bakhtin finds the dynamic in popular grotesque realism as directed towards the bowels of the earth. He argues that the lower body stratum gives birth to a 'new, concrete, and realistic historic awareness' which is 'not abstract about the future but the living sense that each man belongs to immortal people who create history'.

21   Kurihara N., 'Lover of Mr. Bakke/ Bake sensei no koibito' in 'Hijikata Tatsumi Chronology'.

22   Hybrid figures such as the harpy bird-women, snake-haired crones, and dog-headed black bodies with bats wings of the Furies/Eumenides, have been traditional expressions of unease in Western mythology.

23 This included a performance series entitled *Hōsōtan, Susamedama, Gaishi-kō, Nadare-ame, Gibasan.*

24 *Pathosformel* is Aby Warburg's aesthetic and emotive formula of pathos which identified suffering with beauty in Western art (Gombrich and Saxl 1970: 325–38).

25 See, for example, Shikina Cemetery.

26 This includes Maeterlinck, Mallarme, Artaud, Brecht, Wilson, Kantor, Müller and Castellucci.

27 Veteran *butoh* dancer Yoshimoto Daisuke described his 'naked body as a landscape in flux' in *Ruined Body* (2009).

28 These relate to the following concepts: *chokkan* (direct insight), *soku* (implicit in the particular), *funi* (non-duality), *bishū mibun* (beautiful-ugliness), *shogyōmujō* (impermanence), *muga* (no self), *kū* (pain), *issai kaikū* (emptiness), *sekai banbutsu* (worldliness), *shohōmuga* (material insubstantiality), *jiriki* (self-power), *tariki* (other power) and *arijigoku* (ant hell).

29 A staple phrase used by *butoh-ka* (i.e. Katsura Kan's 'Nerve walk' 'worms' crawled over and ate the body; personal correspondence, 23 December 2007).

30 Other 'J-horror' films include *Kwaidan* (Kobayashi M. (dir.), 1964), *Uzumaki* (Higuchinsky, 2000) and *Ju-on, Dark Water* (Nakata, 2004, 2005).

31 See Terayama Shūji and Kishida Rio (*Saraba Hakobune*), Kara Jūrō (*Kaze no Matasaburō*), Ōta Shōgo (*The Tale of Komachi as told by the wind*).

32 Yoshioka Yumiko, Herbst Tanzimpulse, Salzburg, 2009. Also, Maro Akaji: 'If someone tries to prepare food and cuts his finger, this moment of surprise is the first door of Butoh. Time is stopped' (Vermeersch 2002: 31).

33 *Khoreia* ('dancing in unison'), the root word for choreography, occurs alongside a neurological disorder called choreoathetosis, which is characterized by twisting, writhing and twitching movements. See http://www.oxforddictionaries.com/view/entry/m_en_gb0146940#m_en_gb0146940, accessed 10 January 2011.

34 This includes pollution from the Ashio copper mine from the late 1890s; the Okusawa mine collapse of 1936; the Shin-Chisso mercury releases into Minamata bay from the 1930s; asthma problems from petrochemical processing in Yokkaichi between 1957 and 1973; the Miike coal mine explosion 1963.

35 Based on Nietzschean thought, Deleuze and Parnet developed three kinds of lines – molar, segmentary, molecular – in which the first two overcode the individual's existence through a system of binaries established by institutions (as explored in Foucault). The third presents a line of flight and escape through deterritorializing and decoding towards immanence.

Chapter 5

1 Tanaka Min took a few of Hijikata's workshops and asked him to choreograph one of his performances. At *Mai-Juku Body Weather Farm*, Tanaka continues to describe his form of dance as *butoh*, the core of which he considers as being a farmer and working the soil.

2 Hosaka Sakae in 'A nurse in Hiroshima' describes the bodies as follows:

> … the burns covered more than half of his body, and maggots were breeding in them … a moving mass beneath his pale skin …. (Sekimori and Shōno 1986)

3 See also Langer (1995) and Forche (1993).

4 Carol Sorgenfrei acknowledges *amae* as Doi Takeo's most significant contribution to psychoanalysis in Japan but traces the bond of mother–son to Kosawa Heisaku's notion of Ajase complex.

5 According to this discourse, women are described as 'instinctive', 'uncontrollable', 'messy', 'sentimental', 'unprogressive', 'innocent'. As Marran notes, Abe Sada was described by the psychologist Ōtsuki Kenji as 'animalistic, or insect-like, more organism than animal, more insect than organism …' (Seishin bunseki kenkyūjō, 1937).

6 Part of Satoh's trilogy spanning Shōwa colonial history called *The World of Comedic Shōwa* (*Kigeki Shōwa no sekai*). Satoh was the leader of Black Tent Theatre, one of the main *angura* (post-*shingeki*) theatres of the 1960s and 1970s, which made absurdist indigenous narratives in mobile tent theatres its signature (modelled on Edo entertainment).

7 According to Hino Hiruko, dancers with buffalo horns on their heads would parade through the audience. They would then take the stage and move their hips along the horns until they reached their limit of physical endurance or dancers would 'cheek-dance' with members of the audience, transgressing the boundary of no contact. Author's conversation with Hiruko Hino, 25 August 2001. Author's notes 2001.

8 Azuma's consortium was called GLOCOM, and was for academic research into networked communications. See 'ISED', http://www.glocom.jp/ised/, accessed 9 January 2010.

9 See Cabinet Office, Government of Japan (GOJ), 'Survey of young people's consciousness (*hikikomori* conditions), *Policy on Cohesive Society*, July 2010 *hikikomori* – http://www8.cao.go.jp/youth/kenkyu/hikikomori/pdf_index.html, accessed 25 July 2010.

10 Miyazaki, noted for his brutality when he raped, filmed and cannibalized four children, was depicted as an *otaku* because his room was filled with videos, *anime* and manga.

11 Katō Tomohiro was a construction worker who committed a pre-meditated stabbing spree in Akihabara in 2008 killing seven and wounding ten. The prosecution found that he suffered insecurity regarding his employment, his appearance and his inability to find a girlfriend. Subsequently, fifty security cameras were installed and the pedestrian zone was closed for two years. Katō was sentenced to death on 24 March 2011.

12 Ivan Goncharov's novel *Oblomov* (1859) depicted a figure who refuses to leave his bed for the novel's first 150 pages, symbolizing the stagnation of Russian nobility.

Chapter 6

1 In 2010, the core artists of the company comprised Shimizu Shinjin, Hino Hiruko, Kumamoto Kenjirō, Nakajima Miyuki, Aota Reiko and Amemiya Shirō.

2 *De-control: Cell* (1999), *Bye Bye: Into the Century of Degeneration* (1999), *Bye Bye: The New Primitive* (2001–2), *Death Is Living* (2002), *Bye Bye: Phantom* (2003), *Drifting View X: Bodies of War* (2003) and *Dream Regime* (2004–6).

3 Premiered at Morishita Studios, Tokyo in 2001, toured five UK cities, three German cities, performed in New York city (October 2001) and Singapore (2002).

4 Performed in Tokyo, Keosang, South Korea and Kaoshiung, Taiwan.
5 First performed in Kaitaisha's *Bye Bye: Into the Century of Degeneration* (Setagaya Public Theatre, 1999) informed by Hijikata's *Butoh-fu*.
6 'Junky mode' (or *datsu-ryoku*) was derived from witnessing 'public heroin dances' in a period of high heroin distribution in Smith Street, Melbourne in the late 1990s. In the Kaitaisha production, it suggested a narcotic-affected US marine in Afghanistan and/or Iraq.
7 The first comment is in Broinowski (2002: 15); the second is from a post-performance discussion at Morishita Studios, Tokyo, June 2001; the third at the Storehouse Theatre, Tokyo, 31 January 2003.

Chapter 7

1 Henri Bergson's *Creative Evolution* inspired Georges Sorel's notion of violence as a creative act. Sorel theorized the general strike, but this was later used by the Italian Futurists to justify reactionary violence.
2 *Bye Bye: Phantom* poster, Tokyo: Gekidan Kaitaisha, 2003.
3 Gekidan Kaitaisha, *Dream Regime* workshop #1, Cardiff: Chapter Arts Centre, 7 February 2004.
4 Kaitaisha workshop title, Sydney: Performance Space, 2002.
5 Adam Broinowski, untitled performance, Cardiff: Chapter Arts Centre, 2004. The video was from USAF selective documentation of a single bombing run during 'Operation Anaconda', the first US mission in Afghanistan of the War on Terror in 2002, accessed 8 August 2003.
6 Used by Gekidan Kaitaisha and five Australian artists in *Bodies of War*, Tokyo: Australian Embassy/Gekidan Kaitaisha, 2003.
7 Pesenti (2004).
8 Luigi Acquisto (dir.), Stella Zammataro (prod.), Andrew Sully (dir.), *Birth of a Nation*, Melbourne: ABC TV, 2001.
9 *Xanana: The Man, the Nation* (2002), M. Rivette (dir.), ACMI, Melbourne: Talking Heads Productions, 20 May 2003.
10 Timor-Leste receives aid from TimorAid, World Food Program, US Aid, the International Monetary Fund, Asian Development Bank, and private investors.
11 Names have been changed.
12 Convention for Reception, Truth and Reconciliation Convention, (2005: 92).
13 The 1989 Treaty was made with full knowledge of East Timorese territorial rights to the Zone of Co-operation Area (ZOCA), and was based on the obsolete U.N. Convention on the Continental Shelf, 1958. The reserves include Greater Sunrise, Laminaria/Coralina, Buffalo, Elang-Kakatua, Bayu-Undan. Under international law East Timor is entitled to 80 per cent of the resources as opposed to roughly 20 per cent it received as of 2011.
14 Indonesia's spokesperson Francisco Lopes de Cruz declared: 'If people reject autonomy there is the possibility blood will flow in East Timor'. On 4 September 1999, 78 per cent of the 438,000 voters in favour of independence out of 98 per cent of registered voters, with 21 per cent voting for autonomy.
15 Foreign Minister Alexander Downer feigned 'surprise…after all we've done for East Timor', and then described Prime Minister Mari Alkatiri as greedy, naïve and 'ungrateful' for the 'costs' of the 1999 intervention. See Holmes (2004); Alkatiri (2004).

16   Alkatiri invited the assistance of former UNTAET director Peter Galbraith and
     Downer threatened to bring his own friends (the United States), or end the
     friendship altogether.
17   In 1975, between 60,000 and 100,000 Timorese were killed and several international
     journalists. By 1978, elimination and forced relocation of village populations,
     sterilization, disease and starvation in camps had reduced the population to 500,000.
     The UN Commission for Reception, Truth and Reconciliation (CAVR, 2005)
     estimated 102,800 deaths (18,600 unlawful executions, 84,200 starvation),
     while Kiernan estimated between 103,000 and 145,000–150,000 (not including
     Indonesian lives).
18   In 1999, following the UN Security Council resolution, a Serious Crimes Unit
     (UNTAET) was limited to crimes committed in 1999; cases of torture, rape,
     kidnappings and killings exposed during the Indonesia-Timor-Leste 2005
     Commission of Truth and Friendship (where Pinto gave testimony) could not be
     prosecuted; it is unlikely that calls will be heard for an international tribunal to
     address 'crimes against humanity' between 1975 and 1999 (like Yugoslavia, Rwanda,
     and Sierra Leone).
19   Ramos-Horta refused to 'play Don Quixote de la Mancha to pursue every seen or
     unseen culprit of the past', and opposed UN/NGO 'peace workshops' run by 'midget
     intellectuals who conduct experiments and dispense academic judgements on poor
     little us'.
20   Siapno and her husband Fernando de Araujo were accused by Prime Minister Mari
     Alkatiri and Foreign Minister José Ramos-Horta of inciting unrest following the
     killings in Taci Tolu, Suai on 28 April 2006. Siapno reported subsequent intimidation
     by armed civilians employed by the Alkatiri Government in 2006.
21   NGOs included Bibi Bulak (lit. 'crazy goat') (2001–2009), Permaculture Development
     Institute (PDI), East Timor Community Computer Project, Many Hands
     International.
22   The male sword 'Likurai' dance from Suai, and others from Railako Leten, Ermera,
     Mehara, Los Palos, Lautem, Hatubilico, Ainaro, Atauro, Oecussi, Suai, Manatuto,
     Maliana and Viqueque are some examples.

Chapter 8

1   The US-led war in Iraq was officially ended on 15 December 2011, but operations
    continued beyond this point. At the time of writing, Iraq remains highly unstable
    and the US occupation of Afghanistan continues. Estimations of Iraqi casualties and
    deaths vary widely. A Johns Hopkins study in *The Lancet* estimated 655,000 Iraqis
    (2.5 per cent of the population, double the baseline mortality rate) had died by June
    2006, above the average number of deaths in non-conflict conditions. 601,000 of
    these deaths were through conflict-related violence. The nature of weaponry used
    (i.e. depleted/uranium shells) also suggests that there will be longer term casualties
    that are unaccounted for (Burnham et al. 2006: 1421–28).
2   The US Constitution Article 11, Section 4 maintains that 'the President, Vice
    President and all civil officers of the United States shall be removed from office
    on impeachment for, and conviction of treason, bribery or other high crimes and
    misdemeanors'. Leaders in the Bush administration were not impeached for illegal
    invasion (war of aggression) based on a false premise, and for lying at the United
    Nations to justify it.

UNIVERSITY OF WINCHESTER
LIBRARY

3   Revelations predicts the rapture in which followers are 'swept up to heaven' followed
     by seven years of the Antichrist in Jerusalem under Babylon's rule, followed by the
     annihilation of most of the world's humanity, and Jesus' return as King of Mount
     Zion to restore law and order and everlasting peace. This sort of evangelical discourse
     in the United States recently captured an audience of roughly 65 million people.
4   For example, in Iran, Granada, Panama, Guatemala, Egypt, Syria, Congo, Iraq,
     Indonesia, Chile, Nicaragua, El Salvador, Venezuela, Lebanon, Afghanistan,
     Somalia, Sudan, Cuba, Vietnam, Korea, Laos and Cambodia.
5   See, an excerpt:

> The conjunction of an immense military establishment and a large arms
> industry (whose) influence – economic, political, even spiritual – is felt
> in... every office of the Federal government... we must guard against the
> acquisition of unwarranted influence... by the military–industrial complex.
> The potential for the disastrous rise of misplaced power exists and will
> persist.... (Eisenhower 1961)

Conclusion

1   In 2014, US missile shield deployments were in Alaska and the Aleutian Islands,
     Greenland, Britain, Norway, Japan, South Korea, Australia, Poland, the Czech
     Republic, Georgia, Turkey and possibly in Ukraine.

Bibliography

Aarons, M. and R. Domm (eds.) (1992), *East Timor: a western made tragedy*, Ann Arbor: Left Book Club, University of Michigan.

Abe, K. (1966), *The face of another*, New York: Knopf.

Abram, D. (1997), *The spell of the sensuous: perception and language in a more-than-human world*, New York: Vintage Books.

Acquarello (2002), 'Kaneto Shindō', *Strictly Film School*, http://www.filmref.com/directors/dirpages/shindo.html#children, accessed September 2008.

Acquarello (2003), 'Kaneto Shindō', *Strictly Film School*, http://www.filmref.com/directors/dirpages/shindo.html, accessed August 2009.

Acquisto, L. and A. Sully (2002), *East Timor: birth of a nation*, Sydney: ABC.

Adachi, M. (2003), *Eiga-kakumei*, Tokyo: Kawade Shobō Shinsha.

Adorno, T.W. and E. Jephcott (2005 [1951]), *Minima moralia: reflections on a damaged life*, London: Verso.

Adorno, T. W. and M. Horkheimer (1991), *Dialectic of enlightenment*, London: Verso.

Agamben, G. (1993), *The coming community*, Minneapolis: University of Minnesota Press.

Agamben, G. (1998), *Homo sacer: sovereign power and bare life*, Stanford, CA: Stanford University Press.

Agamben, G. (1999), *Remnants of Auschwitz: the witness and the archive*, New York, London: Zone Books; MIT Press.

Agamben, G. (2004), *The open: man and animal*, Stanford, CA: Stanford University Press.

Agamben, G. (2005), *State of exception*, Chicago: University of Chicago Press.

Ahagon, S. (2010), 'I Lost My Only Son in the War: Prelude to the Okinawan Anti-Base Movement', *The Asia-Pacific Journal*, http://japanfocus.org/-CDouglas-Lummis/3369, accessed February 2010.

Ahmad, E. (1995), 'In a Land without Music', *Dawn*, July.

Ai, N. (1997), *Haisen taiken no sengo shisō: 12 nin no kiseki*, Tokyo: Ronsōsha.

Aldous, C. (2010), 'Contesting Famine: Hunger and Nutrition in Occupied Japan, 1945–1952', *Journal of American-East Asian Relations*, 17(3): 230–56.

Alexander, J. (2003), 'Obscenity, Pornography, and Law in Japan: Reconsidering Oshima's "In the Realm of the Senses"', *Asian-Pacific Law & Policy Journal*, 4: 148–68.

Alkatiri, M. (2004), 'All East Timor Seek is a Fair Go', *Age*, 3 November.

Alkatiri, M. (2006), 'Lecturer "Sexed up" East Timor Violence', *The Age*, 15 May.

Allen, J. (2008), *Vietnam: the (last) war the U.S. lost*, Chicago, IL: Haymarket.

Allinson, J. (2007), 'Cross-Media Audience Experience: Objectivity through Subjectivity', *Body, Space & Technology Journal*, 06/02, http://people.brunel.ac.uk/bst/vol0602/jodieallinson/home.html, accessed December 2007.

Amino, Y. (2012), *Rethinking Japanese history*, Ann Arbor: University of Michigan.

Anderson, J. (2001), 'An Experimental Work, Overwhelmed by Topicality', *The New York Times*, 9 October.

Arakawa, A. (1956), 'Yūshoku jinushō, sono ichi', *Ryūdai Bungaku*, 2(1): 39–43.

Aristotle (2008 [350 B.C.]), *Politics*, Chapter V, http://en.wikiquote.org/wiki/Aristotle, accessed 3 April 2008.

Aristotle, B. Jowett, and S. Butcher (1964), *Politics and poetics*, New York: Heritage Press.

Armitage, J. (2000), *Paul Virilio: from modernism to hypermodernism and beyond*, London: Sage.

Armitage, J. (2003), 'Militarized Bodies: An Introduction', *Body & Society*, 9(4): 1–12.

Arp, J. (1948), *On my way: poetry and essays 1912–1947*, New York: Wittenborn, Schultz.

Artaud, A. (1947), *The theatre and its double*, New York: Grove Press.

Artaud, A. (1963), *Antonin Artaud anthology*, San Francisco: City Light Books.

Artaud, A. (1968), *Collected works*, London: John Calder.

Artaud, A. (1974), *Œuvres completes d'Antonin Artaud*, Paris: Gallimard.

Artaud, A. and C. Schumacher (1991), *Artaud on theatre*, London: Methuen Drama; Heinemann Educational Books.

Artaud, A., C. Eshleman, and B. Bador (1995), *Watchfiends & rack screams: works from the final period*, Boston, MA: Exact Change.

Artaud, A., S. Sontag, and H. Weaver (1988), *Antonin Artaud, selected writings*, Berkeley: University of California Press.

Ashfield, A. and P. De Bolla (1996), *The sublime: a reader in British eighteenth-century aesthetic theory*, New York: Cambridge University Press.

Aubrey, C. (1982), *Nukespeak, the media and the bomb*, London: Comedia Pub. Group.

Auer, J. and T. Watanabe (2006), *From Marco Polo Bridge to Pearl Harbor: who was responsible?* Tokyo; California: Yomiuri Shimbun, JP Trading USA.

Avenell, S. (2008), 'From the "People" to the "Citizen": Tsurumi Shunsuke and the Roots of Civic Mythology in Postwar Japan', *Positions: East Asia Cultures Critique*, 16(3): 711–42.

Azuma, H. (2009), *Otaku: Japan's database animals*, Minneapolis: University of Minnesota Press.

Babo-Soares, D. (2004), 'Nahe Biti: The Philosophy and Process of Grassroots Reconciliation (and Justice) in East Timor', *The Asia-Pacific Journal of Anthropology*, 5(1): 22.

Badiou, A. (2008), *Number and numbers*, Cambridge: Polity Press.

Baird, B. (2005), *Butō and the burden of history: Hijikata and Nihonjin*, Diss.: University of Pennsylvania.

Baird, B. (2012), *Hijikata Tatsumi and Butoh: dancing in a pool of gray grits*, New York: Palgrave Macmillan.

Baker, N. (2008), *Human smoke: the beginnings of World War II, the end of civilization*, New York: Simon & Schuster.

Bakhtin, M. (1984), *Rabelais and his world*, Bloomington: Indiana University Press.

Baldwin, J. (1985), *The Price of the Ticket: Collected non-fiction, 1948–1985*, New York: St. Martins' Press.

Balibar, E. and I. Wallerstein (1991), *Race, nation, class: ambiguous identities*, London; New York: Verso.

Ball, H. and J. Elderfield (1996 [1974]), *Flight out of time: a Dada diary*, Berkeley: University of California Press.

Ball, W. M. (1948), *Japan, enemy or ally?* London; Sydney: Cassell.

Ball, W. M. (1952), *Nationalism and communism in East Asia*, Carlton: Melbourne University Press.

Barber, S. (1993), *Antonin Artaud: blows and bombs*, London; Boston, MA: Faber and Faber.

Barber, S. (2004), *Jean Genet*, London: Reaktion Books.

Barber, S. (2005), *Hijikata: revolt of the body*, London: Creation Books.

Barker, R. (1986), *Hiroshima Maidens: a story of compassion, courage and survival*, UK: Penguin.

Barnes, R. H. (1974), *Kédang: a study of the collective thought of an eastern Indonesian people*, London: Oxford, Clarendon Press.

Barnouw, E. (1978), *The Sponsor: notes on a modern potentate*, New York: Oxford University Press.

Barshay, A. E. (1992), 'Imagining Democracy in Postwar Japan: Reflections on Maruyama Masao and Modernism', *Journal of Japanese Studies*, 18(2): 365–406.

Bataille, G. (1962 [1957]), *Erotism: death and sensuality*, New York: City Lights Books.

Bataille, G. (1987), *Eroticism*, London: Marion Boyars.

Bataille, G. (1988), *The accursed share: an essay on general economy*, New York: Zone Books.

Bataille, G. (1991), *The accursed share, vols. 2 and 3*, New York: Zone Books.

Bataille, G. and M. Foucault (1970–1988), *Oeuvres completes*, Paris: Gallimard.

Bataille, G. and A. Stoekl (1985), *Visions of excess: selected writings, 1927–1939*, Minneapolis: University of Minnesota Press.

Bateson, G. (1979), *Mind and nature: a necessary unity*, New York: Dutton.

Bazin, A. (1967), *What is cinema?* vol. 1, Berkeley: University of California Press.

Belmonte, L. (2008), *Selling the American way: national identity, propaganda, and the Cold War, 1945/1959*, Philadelphia: University of Pennsylvania Press.

Bell, D. (2007), *The first total war: Napoleon's Europe and the birth of warfare as we know it*, Boston, MA: Houghton Mifflin.

Belo, T. (2010), 'East Timor Hotel Development Reveals Multiple graves', *East Timor Law and Justice Bulletin*, 11 March, http://easttimorlegal.blogspot.com/2010/03/east-timor -hotel-development-reveals.html, accessed 27 March 2010.

Benedikt, M. and G. Wellwarth (1964), *Modern French plays: an anthology from Jarry to Ionesco*, New York: E. P. Dutton.

Benjamin, W. (1931), 'The Destructive Character', *Frankfurter Zeitung*, 20 November, Frankfurt.

Benjamin, W. (1968), *Illuminations: essays and reflections*, vol. 2, New York: Random House Digital.

Benjamin, W. (1969), *Illuminations*, vol. 2, New York: Random House.

Benjamin, W. (1985), *The origins of German tragic drama*, London: Verso.

Bennington, G. (1993), *Jacques Derrida*, Chicago: University of Chicago Press.

Berger, J. (1980), *About looking*, New York: Random House Digital.

Berger, J. (2008), *Ways of seeing*, London: Penguin.

Bergson, H. (1998 [1907]), *Creative evolution*, London: Dover Publications.

Berlin, I. (1969), *Four essays on liberty*, Oxford: Oxford University Press.

Bermel, A. (1996 [1973]), *Contradictory characters: an interpretation of the modern theatre*, New York: Dutton.

Bernays, E. and M. Miller (2005), *Propaganda*, Brooklyn, NYC: Ig Publishing.

Best, S. (2014), *The Politics of Total Liberation*, London: Palgrave Macmillan.

Bettelheim, B. (1961), *The informed heart: autonomy in a mass age*, London: Thames And Hudson.

Bhabha, H. K. (1990), *Nation and narration*, London; New York: Routledge.

Bhabha, H. K. (1994), *The location of culture*, London; New York: Routledge.

Bhathal, R. K. (2009), 'Cave New York Butoh-kan Masters Series', *News Blaze*, 3 October. http://newsblaze.com/story/20091031112243jnyc.nb/topstory.html, accessed January 2013.

Bird, R., J. Ramos-Horta, X. Gusmão, and C. Belo (1999), *Inside out East Timor*, East Melbourne: Herman Press.

Birringer, J. (1998), *Media & performance: along the border*, Baltimore and London: John Hopkins University Press.

Bix, H. P. (1972), 'Report from Japan 1972: Part II', *Bulletin of Concerned Asian Scholars*, 4(4): 17–30.

Bix, H. P. (1986), *Peasant protest in Japan 1590–1884*, New Haven: Yale University Press.

Blackwood, T. (2008), 'Bushidō baseball? Three "Fathers" and the Invention of a Tradition', *Social Science Japan Journal*, 11(2): 223–40.

Blake, W. (2000), *The selected poems of William Blake*, Hertfordshire: Wordsworth Editions.

Blix, H. (2014a), 'Israel Possesses Nuclear Weapons: Former IAEA Head', *Press TV*, 12 May 2014, http://www.presstv.ir/detail/2014/05/12/362349/israel-possessesnuclear -weapons/, accessed 13 May 2014.

Blix, H. (2014b), 'International Nuclear Body to Curry Favor with Israel: Exposed', *Press TV*, 15 April 2014, http://www.presstv.ir/detail/2014/04/15/358676/nuclear-body-to -curry-favorwith-israel/, accessed 13 May 2014.

Blocker, J. (2004), *What the body cost: desire, history, and performance*, Minneapolis: University of Minnesota Press.

Blum, W. (1986), *The CIA, a forgotten history: US global interventions since World War 2*, London; Atlantic Highlands, NJ: Zed Books.

Blumenbach, J. F. (1865), *The anthropological treatises of Johann Friedrich Blumenbach*, London: Longman, Roberts and Green.

Borton, H. (1957), *Others: Japan between east and west*, New York: Council on Foreign Relations, Harper.

Bourdieu, P. (1990), *The logic of practice*, California: Stanford University Press.

Box, M. and G. McCormack (2004), 'Terror in Japan: The Red Army (1969–2001) and Aum Supreme Truth (1987–2000)', *Critical Asian Studies*, 36(1): 91–112.

Boyer, P. (1985), *By the bomb's early light: American thought and culture at the dawn of the atomic age*, New York: Pantheon.

Brandt, L. (2007), *Kingdom of beauty: mingei and the politics of folk art in Imperial Japan*, Durham: Duke University Press.

Brantlinger, P. (1985), 'Imperial Gothic: Atavism and the Occult in the British Adventure Novel, 1880–1914', *English Literature in Transition, 1880–1920*, 28(3): 243–52.

Braw, M. (1991), *The atomic bomb suppressed: American censorship in occupied Japan*, Armonk, NY: M.E. Sharpe Inc.

Brcak, N. and J. Pavia (1994), 'Racism in Japanese and US Wartime Propaganda', *Historian*, 56(4): 671–84.

Brecht, B., (1964), 'Theatre for Pleasure and Theatre for Instruction', in Willet, J. (ed.), *Brecht on Theatre: the development of an aesthetic*, New York: Hill and Wang.

Brecht, B. (2002), 'Brecht, Bertolt', *Microsoft Encarta Online Encyclopedia, 1997–2002*, http://encarta.msn.com, accessed February 2014.

Brecht, B. and J. Willett (1992), *Brecht on theatre: the development of an aesthetic*, New York: Hill and Wang.

Brecht, B., R. Grimm, and C. Molina y Vedia (eds.) (2003), *Bertolt Brecht: poetry and prose*, New York: Continuum.

Brennan, F. S. (2004), 'Closing the Timor Gap Fairly and in a Timely Manner', *The Australian*, 3 September, http://www.timorseaoffice.gov.tp/journals.htm, accessed September 2009.

Brennan, F. S. (2004), 'The Timor Sea's Oil and Gas: What's Fair', *Catholic social justice series*, 15.

Bretlinger, J. and S. Groden (1970), *The Symposium of Plato*, Cambridge: University of Massachusetts Press.

Bréton, A. (1969), *Entretiens 1913–1952, avec André Parinaud [et al.]*, Paris: Gallimard.

Bréton, A. (1972), *Manifestoes of surrealism*, Ann Arbor: University of Michigan Press.

Broderick, M. (1996), *Hibakusha cinema: Hiroshima, Nagasaki, and the nuclear image in Japanese film*, London; New York: Kegan Paul International; Columbia University Press.

Broinowski, A. (2001–2005), Journal notes. Unpublished.

Broinowski, A. (2002), 'The Body in Avant-Garde Theatre in Japan', *Japan Foundation Newsletter*, 29(3–4): 12–15, 20.

Broinowski, A. (2004), 'Untitled: Performance with Operation Anaconda', *Vivisection vision: animal reflections*, performance series, Cardiff: Adam Broinowski.

Broinowski, A. (2004–2011), *Vivisection vision: animal reflections*, Tokyo; Sydney: Gekidan Kaitaisha, Performance Space, A. Broinowski, www.youtube.com/watch?v=75BDR2xu02I, accessed May 2015.

Broinowski, A. (2006a), 'Yaneura–The Attic', *NEW Voices*, 5–6: 56–61.

Broinowski, A (2006b), *Vivisection Vision: animal reflections*, director's notes, 1–3 June, Sydney: Performance Space.

Broinowski, A. (2007), *Know no cure*, Melbourne; Kuala Lumpur: Adam Broinowski, Dramalab.

Broinowski, A. (2008), 'The Performance of War Images', *Being there: then*, Sydney: University of Sydney, ADSA conference.

Broinowski, A. (2009b), 'A Rebellion of Being/Tatsumi Hijikata's Ankoku Butoh', *SOME/THINGS*, 001, www.someslashthings.com/broinowski, accessed December 2010.

Broinowski, A. (2010a), 'Gekidan Kaitaisha – *Bye Bye: The New Primitive* (2001) – Theatre of the Body and Cultural Deconstruction', in Harvie, J. and A. E. Lavender (eds.), *Making contemporary theatre: international rehearsal processes*, Manchester; New York: Manchester University Press, Palgrave Macmillan.

Broinowski, A. (2010b), 'Otaku: Resistance and Conformity', *Double Dialogues: In/Stead, Expositions & Revelations*, Issue 3, http://www.doubledialogues.com/in_stead/in_stead_iss03/Broinowski.html, accessed July 2012.

Broinowski, A. (2011 [2008]), 'Vivisection Vision: Performing the "humanimal"', *Dance dialogues: Conversations across cultures, artforms and practices*, Brisbane: World Dance Alliance Global Summit, http://ausdance.org.au/articles/details/vivisection-vision-performing-the-humanimal, accessed December 2011.

Broinowski, A. (2014a), 'Sovereign Power Ambitions and the Realities of the Fukushima Nuclear Disaster', in Nadesan, M., T. Boys, A. McKillop, and R. Wilcox, *Fukushima: dispossession or denuclearization*, The Dispossession Publishing Group, 28–55, http://www.amazon.com.au/Fukushima-Denuclearization-Nadesan-McKillop-Wilcox-ebook/dp/B00NT65OK8, accessed 1 November 2014.

Broinowski, A. (2014b), 'Global Power Shift: A USA–Japan–Australia–India Nuclear Chain', *Journal of Oriental Studies Australia (JOSA)*, 46, 118–142.

Broinowski, A. R. G. (2004), *Theatre of Body in Japan: Ankoku Butoh (Dance of Darkness)-Gekidan Kaitaisha (Theatre of Deconstruction)*, M.A. diss., Melbourne: University of Melbourne.

Buck-Morss, S. (1989), *The dialectics of seeing: Walter Benjamin and the Arcades Project*, Cambridge: MIT Press.

Burch, N. (1979), *To the distant observer: form and meaning in the Japanese cinema*, London: Scholar Press.

Burchett, W. (1945), 'The atomic plague: I write this as a warning to the world', *Daily Express*, 5 September.

Burchett, W. (1983), *Shadows of Hiroshima*, London: Verso.

Burchett, W., G. Burchett, and N. Shimmin (2005), *Memoirs of a rebel journalist: the autobiography of Wilfred Burchett*, Sydney: UNSW Press.

Burnham, G. et al., (2006), 'Mortality after the 2003 invasion of Iraq: a cross-sectional cluster sample survey', *The Lancet*, 368(9545), 21 October: 1421–1428.

Burkman, T. (1988), *The Occupation of Japan: arts and culture: the proceedings of the sixth symposium*, Norfolk, VA: The MacArthur Memorial Foundation, Old Dominion University.

Burr, W. (ed.) (2004), 'The Creation of SIOP-62: More Evidence of the Origins of Overkill', *National Security Archive Electronic Briefing book No. 130*, 13 July 2004, http://www2 .gwu.edu/~nsarchiv/NSAEBB/NSAEBB130/, accessed 30 January 2014.

Burr, W. and J. Kimball (2015), *Nixon's nuclear specter: the secret alert of 1969, madman diplomacy and the Vietnam War*, Texas: University of Kansas.

Buruma, I. (2003), *Inventing Japan, 1853–1964*, New York: The Modern Library.

Buruma, I. (2007), *Drunken angel*, New York: Criterion Collection.

Bush, G. W. (2001a), 'Presidential Evening Address to the American People', *Geoge W. Bush Whitehouse Archives*, 11 September, http://georgewbush-whitehouse.archives .gov/news/releases/2001/09/20010911-16.html, accessed December 2014.

Bush, G. W. (2001b), 'US President's Veterans Day speech', *Whitehouse News Releases*, 20 September, http://www.whitehouse.gov/news/releases/2001/09/20010920-8.html, accessed 1 May 2009.

Bush, G. W. (2001c), 'Remarks to Department of Labor Employees', in Cerf, C., 2003.

Bush, G. W. (2002), 'West Point Commencement address', *George W. Bush Whitehouse Archives*, 1 June, http://georgewbush-whitehouse.archives.gov/news/ releases/2002/06/20020601-3.html, accessed 12 December 2008.

Bush, G. W. (2003), 'State of the Union Address', *Washington Post*, 28 January.

Butler, J. (1990), *Gender trouble: feminism and the subversion of identity*, New York: Routledge.

Byrd, R. (2004), *Losing America: confronting a reckless and arrogant presidency*, New York: W.W. Norton.

Bywater, H. I. (2013), *The fragments of the work of Heraclitus of Ephesus on nature*, Hong Kong: Forgotten Books.

Calarco, M. and S. DeCaroli (2007), *Giorgio Agamben: sovereignty and life*, Stanford, CA: Stanford University Press.

Calichman, R. (2005), *Contemporary Japanese thought*, New York: Columbia University Press.

Callinicos, A. (2009), *Imperialism and global political economy*, Cambridge: Polity Press.

Campbell, R. H. (2005), *The silverplate bombers: a history and registry of the Enola Gay and other B-29s configured to carry atomic bombs*, North Carolina: McFarland Publishing and Co.

Campbell, K. and T. Sunohara (2004), 'Japan: Thinking the Unthinkable', in Campbell, K., R. Einhorn, and M. Reiss (eds.), *The nuclear tipping point: why states reconsider their nuclear choices*, Washington: Brookings, 2004.

Capra, F. (1971), *The name above the title; an autobiography*, Library of Congress, New York: Macmillan.

Carey, P. and G. Bentley (1995), *East Timor at the crossroads: the forging of a nation*, Honolulu: University of Hawai'i Press.

Caruth, C. (1995), *Trauma: explorations in memory*, Baltimore, MD: Johns Hopkins University Press.

Catry, J. (2004), 'Quand l'Australie spoile le Timor-Oriental', *Le Monde Diplomatique*, 10 Novembre.

Cavell, S. (2008), *Philosophy and animal life*, New York: Columbia University Press.

Cavin, S. E. (2007), 'The Use of Social Scientists in World War II Prisoners of War Camps', *American sociological association*, New York: New York University, Conference Proceedings.

Cecil, P. (1986), *Herbicidal warfare: the ranch hand project in Vietnam*, New York: Praeger.

Cerf, C. (2003), *The Iraq war reader: history, documents, opinions*, New York: Simon and Schuster.

Césaire, A. (1972 [1955]), *Discourse on colonialism*, New York: Monthly Review Press.

Chandler, J. (2008), 'Scientists and Villagers Summon Spirits of the Dead in Bid to Heal Old Wounds', *The Age*, 23 August.

Chang, G. H. (1988), 'JFK, China, and the Bomb', *The Journal of American History*, 74(4): 1287–1310.

Chatterjee, P. (1986), *Nationalist thought and the colonial world: a derivative discourse?* London: Otowa, N. J., Zed Books, United Nations University.

Cheney, R. (2003), 'Remarks by the Vice President to the Veterans of Foreign Wars 103rd National Convention', 26 August 2002, in Cerf 2003: 298–300.

Cheng, Y. (2010), 'Orphan Okinawa and the Japan-U.S. Alliance', *Takungpao*, 10 May, http://watchingamerica.com/News/55641/orphan-okinawa-and-the-japan-u-s -alliance/, accessed 23 July 2010.

Chernus, I. (2002), 'Eisenhower's Atoms for Peace', *Library of presidential rhetoric*, College Station, TX: A&M University Press.

Chomsky, N. (2006), *Failed states: the abuse of power and the assault on democracy*, New York: Metropolitan Books.

Chow, R. (2006), *The age of the world target: self-referentiality in war, theory and comparative work*, NC: Duke University Press.

Chow, R. (2007), 'A Filmic Staging of Postwar Geotemporal Politics: On Akira Kurosawa's No Regrets for Our Youth, Sixty Years Later', *Boundary 2*, 34(1): 67–77.

Christalis, I. (1995), *Bitter dawn: East Timor, a people's story*, London: Zed Books.

Clark, R. S. (1992), 'Legality of the Timor Gap Treaty: An interview with Professor Roger Clark, Professor of International Law at Rutgers University in the United States', in Aarons, M. and R. Domm (eds.) 1992: 77.

Clark, R. S. (1995), 'Timor Gap: The Legality of the 'Treaty on the Zone of Cooperation in an Area between the Indonesian Province of East Timor and Northern Australia', in Carey, P. and G. Bentley (eds.) 1995: 73–96.

Clarke, G. (2008), 'Row that demonized China', *The Japan Times*, 12 May, http://search.japantimes.co.jp/cgi-bin/eo20080512gc.html, accessed June 2009.

Cohen, R. (2009), 'Unusual Obsessions', *The New York Times*, 15 December, http://www.nytimes.com/2009/12/15/opinion/15iht-edcohen.html, accessed December 2009.

Cohen, S. (2015), 'The Ukrainian Crisis: A new Cold War?' Fairfield University, 5 February, http://off-guardian.org/2015/04/06/stephen-cohen-deconstructs-the-historical -fallacies-and-political-myths-behind-the-current-crisis/, accessed 29 May 2015.

Colebatch, T. (2003), 'How They Fooled Us on East Timor', *The Age*, 11 March, www.theage.com.au/articles/2003/03/.../1047144918616.html, accessed March 2010.

Coll, S. (2004), *Ghost wars: the secret history of the CIA, Afghanistan, and Bin Laden, from the Soviet Invasion to September 10, 2001*, New York: Penguin.

Committee for the Compilation of Materials on Damage Caused by the Atomic Bombs in Hiroshima and Nagasaki (1981), *Hiroshima and Nagasaki: the physical, medical, and social effects of the atomic bombings*, New York: Basic Books.

Conant, J., A. Compton, and H. Urey (1943), 'Groves Memo', Manhattan District, Oak
    Ridge, Tennessee, 30 October, declassified 5 June 1974, http://en.wikipedia.org/wiki/
    File:Groves_memo_30oct43_p1.GIF, accessed October 2014.
Condry, I. (2013), *The soul of anime: collaborative creativity and Japan's media success story*,
    Durham: Duke University Press.
Convention for Reception, Truth and Reconciliation Convention ('Chega!' Report) (2005),
    CAVR Timor Leste 2001–2005, Dili: CAVR, http://www.cavr-timorleste.org/, accessed
    4 July 2010.
Corea, G. (1986), 'The Mother Machine: Reproductive Technologies from Artificial
    Insemination to Artificial Wombs', *MCN: The American Journal of Maternal/Child
    Nursing*, 11(5): 357–63.
Cornell, D., M. Rosenfeld, D. Carlson, and N. Benjamin (1992), *Deconstruction and the
    possibility of justice*, New York: Routledge.
Cornyetz, N. (1999), *Dangerous women, deadly words: phallic fantasy and modernity in
    three Japanese writers*, Stanford, CA: Stanford University Press.
Cotton, J. (2004), *East Timor, Australia and regional order intervention and its aftermath in
    Southeast Asia*, London; New York: RoutledgeCurzon.
Coughlin, W. J. (1952), *Conquered press: the MacArthur era in Japanese journalism*, Palo
    Alto, CA: Pacific Books.
Crary, J. (1990), *Techniques of the observer: on vision and modernity in the nineteenth
    century*, Cambridge, MA: MIT Press.
Cribb, R. (2004), *Nomads in archaeology*, Oxford: Cambridge University Press.
Cristalis, I. (2002), *Bitter dawn: East Timor, a people's story*, London; New York: New York,
    Zed Books, Palgrave.
Croser, C. (2007), 'Organising Complexity: Modes of Behaviour in a Networked Battlespace',
    Canberra: Australian Army, Land Warfare Studies Centre, working paper 133.
Cross, S. (1996), 'Prestige and Comfort: The Development of Social Darwinism in Early
    Meiji Japan, and the Role of Edward Sylvester Morse', *Annals of Science*, 53(4): 323–44.
Cull, L. (2009), 'How Do You Make Yourself a Theatre without Organs? Deleuze, Artaud
    and the Concept of Differential Presence', *Theatre Research International*, 34(3,
    October), 243–55.
Cumings, B. (1964), 'Why Did Truman Really Fire MacArthur?... The Obscure History of
    Nuclear Weapons and the Korean War Provides the Answer', *New York Times*, 9 April,
    http://hnn.us/articles/9245.html, accessed December 2010.
Cumings, B. (2002a), *Parallax visions: making sense of American-East Asian relations*,
    Durham, NC: Duke University Press.
Cumings, B. (2002b), 'Boundary Displacement: The State, The Foundations, and Area
    Studies during and after the Cold War', in Miyoshi, M. and H. Harootunian (eds.)
    Learning places: the afterlives of area studies, Durham: Duke University Press.
Cummings, D. (2006), 'Onibaba', Shindō, Kaneto (dir.), *Masters of cinema series*. London:
    Eureka.
D'Cruz, J. V. and W. Steele (2003), *Australia's ambivalence towards Asia: politics, neo/post-
    colonialism, and fact/fiction*, Victoria: Monash Asia Institute.
Daisuke, Y. (2009), *Ruined Body*, New York: CAVE.
Davies, S., K. Higgins, and R. Hopkins (eds.) (2009), *A companion to aesthetics*,
    Chichester, UK; Malden, MA: Wiley-Blackwell.
De Landa, M. (1991), *War in the age of intelligent machines*, New York: Zone Books.
De Man, P. (1984), *The rhetoric of romanticism*, New York: Columbia University Press.
De Seversky, A. P. (1942), *Victory through air power*, New York: Simon and Schuster.

Defense Industry Daily (2014), 'Serious Dollars for AEGIS Ballistic Missile Defense',
    10 August, https://www.defenseindustrydaily.com/serious-dollars-for-aegis-ballistic
    -missile-defense-modifications-03091/, accessed August 2014.

Deleuze, G. (1990), *The logic of sense*, New York: Columbia University Press.

Deleuze, G. and C. Boundas (1993), *The Deleuze reader*, New York: Columbia University
    Press.

Deleuze, G. and F. Guattari (1987), *A thousand plateaus: capitalism and schizophrenia*,
    Minneapolis: University of Minnesota Press.

Deleuze, G. and F. Guattari (2000), *Anti-Oedipus: capitalism and schizophrenia*,
    Minneapolis: University of Minnesota Press.

Deleuze, G. and C. Parnet (2007), *Dialogues two*, New York: Columbia University Press.

Denomme, J. (1998), 'Leonardo da Vinci: The Search for the Soul', *Journal of Neurosurgery*,
    November, 89(5): 874–87.

Der Derian, J. (2001), *Virtuous war: mapping the military-industrial-media-entertainment
    network*, Boulder, CO: Westview Press.

Derrida, J. (1977), 'Signature Event Context', *Glyph*, vol. 1 in *Margins of philosophy*, vol. 307.

Derrida, J. (1982), *Margins of philosophy*, Chicago: University of Chicago Press.

Derrida, J. (1986), *Glas*, Lincoln: University of Nebraska Press.

Derrida, J. (1994), *Specters of Marx: the state of the debt, the work of mourning, and the new
    international*, New York: Routledge.

Derrida, J. (2001), *Writing and difference*, London: Routledge, Kegan Paul.

Derrida, J. and Musée du Louvre (1993), *Memoirs of the blind: the self-portrait and other
    ruins*, Chicago: University of Chicago Press.

Derrida, J. and P. Thévenin (1998), *The secret art of Antonin Artaud*, Cambridge, MA: MIT
    Press.

Descartes, R. (1972), *The treatise of man*, Cambridge: Harvard University Press.

Desser, D. (1988), *Eros plus massacre: introduction to the Japanese new wave cinema*,
    Bloomington: Indiana University Press.

Dixon, W. (2003), *Visions of the apocalypse: spectacles of destruction in American cinema*,
    London: Wallflower Press.

Dobbins, J. (2003), *America's role in nation-building: from Germany to Iraq*, Santa Monica,
    CA: RAND.

Dollimore, J. (2001), *Sex, literature, and censorship*, Cambridge; Malden, MA: Polity Press,
    Blackwell.

Dopfer, U. and A. Tanerding (1994), 'Dance on the Borderlands between life and death',
    Ballet International, August/September.

Dore, R. P. (1966 [1959]), *Land reform in Japan*, Oxford: Oxford University Press.

Dostoyevsky, F., R. Pevear, and L. Volokhonsky (2002), *The idiot*, New York: Everyman's
    Library.

Douglas, M. (1969), *Purity and danger: an analysis of concepts of pollution and taboo*,
    London: Routledge & Kegan Paul.

Douglass, A. and A. Volger (2003), *Witness and memory: the discourse of trauma*, London
    and New York: Routledge.

Douhet, G. (1942), *The command of the air (Il domino dell'aria (1921))*, New York:
    Coward-McCann.

Dower, J. W. (1986), *War without mercy: race and power in the Pacific war*, New York:
    Pantheon Books.

Dower, J. W. (1995), 'The Bombed: Hiroshimas and Nagasakis in Japanese Memory',
    Diplomatic History, 19(2): 275–95.

Dower, J. W. (1999), *Embracing defeat: Japan in the wake of World War II*, New York: W.W. Norton/New Press.

Dowsey, S. J. (1970), *Zengakuren: Japan's revolutionary students*, Berkeley, CA: Ishi Press.

Druker, J. (2009), *Primo Levi and humanism after Auschwitz: posthumanist reflections*, UK: Palgrave Macmillan.

Du Bois, W. E. B. and B. Edwards (2007 [1903]), *The souls of black folk*, Oxford, England and New York: Oxford University Press.

Du Bois, W. E. B. and D. Lewis (1995), *W.E.B. Du Bois: a reader*, New York: H. Holt and Co.

Dubro, A. and D. Kaplan (1995), 'A Question of Intelligence: Forty-five Years of the CIA in Japan', *Tokyo Journal*, March, 32–37.

Dubuffet, J. (1952), 'Letter to Michel Tapie', *Prospectus*, 2 (21 December): 308.

Dubuffet, J. (1988), *Asphyxiating culture and other writings*, New York: Four Walls Eight Windows.

Dulles, J. F. (1951), 'Speech at the San Francisco Peace Conference', *The world and Japan database project*, Tokyo: Institute of Oriental Culture, 5 September.

Dunn, J. and J. Dunn (2003), *East Timor: a rough passage to independence*, Double Bay, NSW: Longueville Books.

Dusevic, T. (2004), 'Hands off My Petroleum!', *Time*, 10: 38–41.

Easlea, B. (1983), *Fathering the unthinkable: masculinity, scientists, and the nuclear arms race*, London: Pluto Press.

Ebata, K. (2005), *Beigun saihen*, Tōkyō: Bijinesusha.

Eckersall, P. (2006), *Theorizing the angura space avant-garde performance and politics in Japan, 1960–2000*, Vol. 23, Leiden; Boston, MA: Brill.

Editor (2001), 'Time to Get Serious about Justice for East Timor', *La'o Hamutuk Bulletin*, 2 October, accessed 21 February 2008.

Editor (2003), 'Australia and East Timor: A Squabble over Oil', *The Economist*, 13 March, http://www.economist.com/node/1633471, accessed March 2010.

Editor (2004a), 'East Timor in Row over Oil Reserves', *The Guardian*, 28 April, http://www.guardian.co.uk/world/2004/apr/28/oil.australia, accessed March 2008.

Editor (2004b), 'East Timor's The Road to Recovery', *The Guardian*, 28 December. http://www.guardian.co.uk/print/0,3858,5092767–115023,00.html, accessed March 2010.

Editor (2004c), 'East Timor Accuses Australia of Robbery in Sea Border Dispute', *Agence France Presse*, 28 April.

Editor (2009a), 'U.S. Pushed Japan on Nuke Pact in '64', *The Japan Times*, 3 November, http://search.japantimes.co.jp/mail/nn20091103a9.html, accessed 11 November 2009.

Editor (2009b), 'A-bombings "Were War Crimes": Mass Killing of Civilians by Indiscriminate Bombing Condemned by International Peoples' Tribunal', *The Japan Times*, 9 August 2009, http://search.japantimes.co.jp/cgi-bin/fl20090809x4.html, accessed August 2009.

Editor (2010a), 'Remains of Nine Found in Timor Graves', *ETLJB*, 6 March, http://easttimorlegal.blogspot.com/2010/03/remains-of-nine-found-in-timor-graves.html, accessed 28 March 2010.

Editor (2010b), 'Pelican Paradise Is Building on Remains of Indepedence Heroes', *Tempo Semanal Husi Imiba Imi*, 25 February, http://temposemanaltimor.blogspot.com/2010/02/pelican-paradise-is-building-on-remains.html, accessed 29 March 2010.

Editor, Associated Press (2010c), 'Soviet Attack Trumped A-bomb Role: Historian', *The Japan Times*, 16 August, http://search.japantimes.co.jp/cgi-bin/nn20100816a4.html, accessed 17 August, 2010.

Editor (2010d), 'Luxury Hotel Development under Construction of Site of Remains of Victims of Indonesian Genocide in Timor-Leste', *ETLJB*, 26 February, http://easttimorlegal.blogspot.com/2010/02/luxury-hotel-development-under.html, accessed 28 March 2010.

Editor (2010e), 'Ramos Horta Savages Timor's Donors as 'Intellectual Midgets'", *ETLJB*, 10 March, http://www.easttimorlawandjusticebulletin.com/2010/03/ramos-horta -savages-timors-donors-as.html, accessed 25 March 2010.

Editor (2011), 'Akihabara rampage verdict', *The Japan Times*, 29 March, http://search .japantimes.co.jp/cgi-bin/ed20110329a1.html, accessed 29 March 2011.

Editor (2012a), 'Huge scale of A-bomb gene study revealed', *The Japan Times*, 23 April, http://www.japantimes.co.jp/news/2012/04/23/national/huge-scale-of-a-bomb-gene -study-revealed/#.U_GB1UisPPk, accessed July 2014.

Editor (2012b), 'Remains of hundreds of East Timorese murdered by Indonesian military buried in mass grave', *ETLJB*, 10 November, http://www .easttimorlawandjusticebulletin.com/2012/11/remains-of-hundreds-of-east-timorese .html, accessed July 2014.

Editor (2013a), 'Japan discussed acquisition of "defensive" nuclear weapons in 1958', *The Japan Times*, 17 March, http://www.japantimes.co.jp/news/2013/03/17/national/ japan-discussed-acquisition-of-defensive-nuclear-weapons-in-1958/#.UUT_hhllw-a, accessed 17 March 2013.

Editor (2013b), 'Japan unveils new defense strategy amid Chinese military expansion', *UPI*, 18 December 2013, http://www.upi.com/Top_News/World-News/2013/12/18/ Japan-unveils-new-defense-strategy-amid-Chinese-military-expansion/UPI -91111387348905/#ixzz34wuT24sR, accessed 14 April 2014.

Editors (1967), 'Hakunetsu suru Kuroi Yuki saiban: Hōtei ha sengo eiga wo dō sabaku', *Eiga Geijutsu*, 14(May): 236.

Editors (1970), *The Indochina story; a fully documented account*, New York: Bantam Books.

Editors (1972), *The Pacific rivals: a Japanese view of Japanese-American relations*, New York: Weatherhill/Asahi.

Edwards, R. (2005), 'Edwards Hiroshima bomb may have carried hidden agenda', *The New Scientist*, 21 July, http://www.newscientist.com/article/dn7706-hiroshima-bomb-may -have-carried-hidden-agenda.html#.U1CRfsdbLhQ, accessed January 2014.

Eisenhower, D. (1961), 'Farewell Speech', *Eisenhower archives*, Washington: US Government.

Elam, H. and D. Krasner (2001), *African-American performance and theater history a critical reader*, Oxford; New York: Oxford University Press.

Eliot, T. S. (1952), *Complete poems and plays, 1909–1950*, New York: Harcourt.

Ellsberg, D. (2002), *Secrets: a memoir of Vietnam and the Pentagon papers*, New York: Viking.

Eto, J. (1989), *Tozasareta gengo kūkan: senryōgun no kenetsu to sengo nihon*, Tokyo: Bungei Shunjū.

European Committee on Radiation Risk (ECRR) (2003), *Recommendations of the European Committee on radiation risk: health effects of ionising radiation exposure at low doses for radiation protection purposes regulators*, Brussels: ECRR, http://www. euradcom.org/.

Evans, J. A. (1998), *Celluloid mushroom clouds: Hollywood and the atomic bomb*, Boulder, CO: Westview Press.

Evans, M. D. (2004), *The American prophecies: Ancient Scriptures reveal our nation's future*, New York: Warner Books.

Fanon, F. (1963), *The wretched of the earth*, New York: Grove.

Fanon, F. (1967), *Black skin, white masks*, New York: Grove.

Federici, S. (2004), *Caliban and the witch*, New York: Autonomedia.

Fell, J. (2005), *Alfred Jarry: an imagination in revolt*, Fairleigh: Dickinson University Press.

Felman, S. and D. Laub (1992), *Testimony: crises of witnessing in literature, psychoanalysis, and history*, New York: Routledge.

Fernandes, C. (2004), *Reluctant saviour: Australia, Indonesia and the independence of East Timor*, Carlton North: Scribe Publications.

Fernandes, C. (2010), 'Are we really East Timor's heroes?', *New Matilda*, 24 February, http://newmatilda.com/2010/02/24/are-we-really-east-timors-heroes, accessed 30 February 2010.

Finburgh, C., C. Lavery, and M. Shevtsova (2006), *Jean Genet: performance and politics*, Basingstoke; New York: Palgrave Macmillan.

Fitzgerald, M. (2010), 'So much money wasted by donors says Ramos Horta', *The Irish Times*, 9 March.

Fleming, E. (2009), 'The 64th Anniversary of USA Terrorism Enlightened by the Wisdom of Nonviolence', *Opednews*, http://www.opednews.com/articles/The-64th-Anniversary -of-US-by-Eileen-Fleming-090731-847.html, accessed January 2010.

Forché, C. (1993), *Against forgetting: twentieth-century poetry of witness*, New York: W.W. Norton.

Forte, M. (ed.) (2010), *The New Imperialism: militarism, humanism and occupation*, vol 1, Montreal: Alert Press.

Foster, H. (1996), *The return of the real: the avant-garde at the end of the century*, Cambridge, MA: MIT Press.

Foucault, M. (1972), *The archaeology of knowledge*, London: Tavistock Publications.

Foucault, M. (1973), *Madness and civilization: a history of insanity in the age of reason*, New York: Vintage Books.

Foucault, M. (ed.) (1977), *Language, counter-memory, practice: selected essays and interviews*, Oxford: Blackwell.

Foucault, M. (1978), *The history of sexuality*, vol. 1, New York: Pantheon Books.

Foucault, M. (1991), 'Faire livres lesais mourir: le naissance de raicisme', *Les Temps Modernes*, 46(535), February: 37–61.

Foucault, M. and C. Gordon (1980), *Power/knowledge: selected interviews and other writings, 1972–1977*, New York: Pantheon Books.

Foucault, M. and J. Khalfa (2006), *History of madness*, New York: Routledge.

Foucault, M., J. Faubion, and R. Hurley (2000), *Power*, New York: New Press.

Foucault, M., et al. (2003), *Society must be defended: lectures at the Collège de France, 1975–76*, New York: Picador.

Foucault, M., et al. (2007), *Security, territory, population: lectures at the Collège de France, 1977–78*, Basingstoke; New York: Palgrave Macmillan, République Française.

Fraleigh, S. and T. Nakamura (2006), *Hijikata Tatsumi and Ohno Kazuo*, New York: Routledge.

Franko, M. (2007), *Ritual and event: interdisciplinary perspectives*, New York: Routledge.

Freeman, L. J. (1981), *Nuclear witnesses: insiders speak out*, New York: Norton.

French, T. (2013), *From Allied Landings to the Land Cruiser: Jeeps and the Postwar Revival of the Japanese Automotive Industry*, Kyoto: Ritsumeikan University, 1–17.

Freud, S., et al. (1953), *The standard edition of the complete psychological works of Sigmund Freud*, London: Hogarth Press.

Friedman, L. J. (1999), *Identity's architect: a biography of Erik H. Erikson*, New York: Scribner.

Fujitani, T. (2001), 'The Reischauer Memo: Mr. Moto, Hirohito, and Japanese American Soldiers', *Critical Asian Studies*, 33(3): 379–402.

Fukuyama, F. (2006), *The end of history and the last man*, New York: Free Press.

Furukawa, K. (2003), 'Nuclear Option, Arms Control, and Extended Deterrence: In Search of a New Framework for Japan's Nuclear Policy', in Self and Thompson (eds.) 2003: 95–147.

Galbraith, P., T. H. Kam, and B.-O. Kamm (2015), *Debating Otaku in contemporary Japan: historical perspectives and new horizons*, London: Bloomsbury.

García, M. a. E. (2005), *Making indigenous citizens: identities, education, and multicultural development in Peru*, Stanford, CA: Stanford University Press.

Garff, J. (2005), *Soren Kierkegaard – a biography*, Princeton: Princeton University Press.

Garner, S. B. (2007), 'The Gas Heart: Disfigurement and the Dada Body', *Modern Drama*, 50(4): 500–16.

Gatens, M. (2009), 'Spinoza and Philosophers Today – Gabor Boros, Herman De Dijn, Moira Gatens, Sylviane Malinowski-Charles, Warren Montag', *Kritika & Kontext*, 38–39.

Gekidan Kaitaisha (1995), *Tokyo Ghetto: hard core*, Tokyo.

Gekidan Kaitaisha (1999), *De-control: cell*, Tokyo.

Gekidan Kaitaisha (1999), *Bye Bye: into the century of degeneration*, Tokyo.

Gekidan Kaitaisha (2001–2002), *Bye Bye: the new primitive*, Tokyo, UK, Germany, New York.

Gekidan Kaitaisha (2002), *Death is living*, Tokyo.

Gekidan Kaitaisha (2003–2004), *Bye Bye: phantom*, Tokyo, Aarhus, Germany.

Gekidan Kaitaisha (2003), *Drifting view X: bodies of war*, Tokyo.

Gekidan Kaitaisha (2004), *Dream regime*, workshop #1, Cardiff: Chapter Arts Centre.

Gekidan Kaitaisha (2005), *Dream regime*, workshop #2, Dili: Artemoris.

Gekidan Kaitaisha (2004–2008), *Dream regime*, Cardiff, Tokyo.

Gelb, J. and M. Palley (1994), *Women of Japan and Korea: continuity and change*, Philadelphia: Temple University Press.

Genet, J. (1964), 'The Funambulists', *Evergreen Review*, 32, April–May: 45–49.

Genet, J. (1971), *Funeral rites*, London: Panther.

Genet, J. (1973), *Our lady of the flowers*, New York: Grove Press.

Genet, J. (2003), *Prisoner of love*, New York: New York Review Books.

Genet, J. (2004), *The thief's journal*, New York: Olympia Press.

Gennep, A. v. (1960), *The rites of passage*, London: Routledge & K. Paul.

Gibson, R. (2008), *Visual cultures and colonialism: indigeneity in local and transnational imagery*, Melbourne: Monash University, Keynote speech.

Giddens, A. (1979), *Central problems in social theory: action, structure and contradiction in social analysis*, London: Macmillan.

Gillespie, I. (1988), 'Mishima and the archaic mind', *Adam–International Review*, 487–92.

Gilmartin, W. and W. Ladejinsky (1948), 'The Promise of Agrarian Reform in Japan', *Foreign Affairs*, 26(2): 312–24.

Girard, R. (1986), *The scapegoat*, Baltimore, MD: Johns Hopkins University Press.

Gluck, C. (1985), *Japan's modern myths*, New Jersey: Princeton University Press.

Gobineau, A. de (1915 [1853–55]), *An essay on the inequality of the human races*, London: William Heinemann, Howard Fertig.

Goldberg, D. T. (1993), *Racist culture: philosophy and the politics of meaning*, Oxford, MA: Blackwell.

Gombrich, E. and F. Saxl (1970), *Aby Warburg: an intellectual biography*, London: The Warburg Institute.

Gorer, M. G. (1943), 'Anthropology Division: Themes in Japanese Culture', *Transactions of the New York Academy of Sciences*, 5(5) II: 106–24.

Gorō, Hani (1946), *Meiji Ishin*, Tokyo: Iwanami Shoten.

216 *Bibliography*

Government of Japan (GOJ) (2010), 'Survey of young people's consciousness (*hikikomori* conditions)', *Policy on Cohesive Society*, Tokyo: Cabinet Office, http://www8.cao.go.jp/youth/kenkyu/hikikomori/pdf_index.html, accessed 25 July 2010.

Gregory, D. (2010), 'Dis/Ordering the Orient: scopic regimes and modern war', Unpub., 1–54.

Greiner, C. (2008), 'Yūgen and the Artist's Body in the Contemporary World – a Communicational Process', *Semiotics of culture and cultural uses*, Lyon: University of Lyon, Conference.

Grenfell, D. (2012), 'Remembering the Dead from the Customary to the Modern in Timor-Leste', *Local-Global: Identity, Security, Community*, 11(2): 86–108.

Grotowski, J. and E. Barba (1969), *Towards a poor theatre*, London: Methuen.

Groves, Gen., Lt Col. Rea (1958 [1945]), 'Memo of telephone conversation', 25 August, US Department of Defense, http://www2.gwu.edu/~nsarchiv/NSAEBB/NSAEBB162/76.pdf, accessed July 2014.

Guha, R. (1982), *On some aspects of the historiography of colonial India*, Delhi; New York: Oxford University Press.

Guha, R. (1982), *Subaltern studies, vol. 1*, Delhi: Oxford University.

Gunther, J. (1950), *The riddle of macarthur*, New York: Harper & Brothers.

Gusmão, X. (2001), 'East Timor in Transition: Reconciliation and Conflict Prevention', *Weatherhead policy forum report*, New York: East Asian Institute, Columbia University.

Gusmão, X. and S. Niner (2000), *To resist is to win!: the autobiography of Xanana Gusmão with selected letters & speeches*, Richmond, Vic.: Aurora Books with David Lovell Publishing.

Gusterson, H., (1998), *Nuclear Rites: A weapons laboratory at the end of the Cold War*, Berkeley: University of California Press.

Gusterson, H. (2004), *People of the bomb: portraits of America's nuclear complex*, Minneapolis: University of Minnesota Press.

Guthrie-Shimizu, S. (2012), *Transpacific field of dreams: how baseball linked the United States and Japan in peace and war*, Chapel Hill: University of North Carolina Press.

Güven, F. (2005), *Madness and death in philosophy*, Albany: State University of New York Press.

Haeckel, E. (1883 [1868]), *The history of creation*, London: Kegan Paul Trench & Co.

Haiken, E. (1997), *Venus envy: a history of cosmetic surgery*, Baltimore: Johns Hopkins University Press.

Hajimu, M. (2012), 'Fear of World War III: Social Politics of Japan's Rearmament and Peace Movements, 1950–3', *Journal of Contemporary History*, 47(3): 551–71.

Hall, G. S. (1903), 'The Relations between Higher and Lower Races', *Massachusetts Historical Society*, 16 January.

Hall, G. S. (1904), *Adolescence: its psychology and its relations to physiology, anthropology, sociology, sex, crime, religion and education*, New York: Appleton.

Hall, G. S. (1911), 'Eugenics: It's Ideals and What It's Going to Do', *Religious Education*, 6(2): 152–59.

Halsey, Admiral W. (1945), *politics 2* (August): 226.

Hamilton, C. (2009), 'Bush's Shocking Biblical Prophecy Emerges: God Wants to "Erase" Mid-East Enemies "Before a New Age Begins"', *Counter Punch*, 24 May.

Hammond, M. and J. Ruyak ([1990] 2008), 'The Decline of the Japanese Diet: From Macarthur to Mcdonalds', *East West Journal*, October.

Hanaga, M. (1983), *Butō: nikutai no shūru rearisuto-tachi: Hanaga Mitsutoshi shashinshū = The butoh*, Tokyo: Gendai Shokan.

Hane, M. (1982), *Peasants, rebels, and outcastes: the underside of modern Japan*, New York: Pantheon.

Hane, M. (2003), *Peasants, rebels, women, and outcastes: the underside of modern Japan*, Lanham, MD: Rowman & Littlefield.

Hara, T. (1983), *Nihon no genbaku bungaku*, Tokyo: Horubu Shuppan.

Hardt, M. and A. Negri (2000), *Empire*, Cambridge, MA: Harvard University Press.

Harootunian, H. D. (1988), *Things seen and unseen: discourse and ideology in Tokugawa nativism*, Chicago: University of Chicago Press.

Harpham, G. (1982), *On the grotesque: strategies of contradiction in art and literature*, Princeton; Guildford: Princeton University Press.

Harrison, C. and P. Wood (2003), *Art in theory, 1900–2000: an anthology of changing ideas*, Malden, MA: Blackwell Pub.

Harrison, R. (28 March 1946), 'Final report on food situation in Japan', Memo for Secretary of Agriculture, Secretary of State, in Aldous, C. 2010: 12.

Harrison, T. (1992), *The gaze of the gorgon*, Newcastle upon Tyne: Bloodaxe Books.

Harvey, D. (2005), *The new imperialism*, Oxford; New York: Oxford University Press.

Hasegawa, T. (2005), *Racing the enemy: Stalin, Truman, and the surrender of Japan*, Cambridge, MA: Belknap Press of Harvard University Press.

Havens, T. R. H. (1987), *Fire across the sea: the Vietnam War and Japan 1965–1975*, Princeton, NJ: Princeton University Press.

Havens, T. R. H. (2006), *Radicals and realists in the Japanese nonverbal arts: the avant-garde rejection of modernism*, Honolulu: University of Hawaii Press.

Hayashi, K. (1986), 'Two Grave Markers (Futari no bohyō)', *Bulletin of Concerned Asian Scholars*, 18(1): 18–35.

Hayashi, K. (2005), 'Masks of Whatchamacallit: A Nagasaki Tale (Nanjamonja no men)', *The Asia-Pacific Journal: Japan Focus*, http://www.japanfocus.org/-Hayashi-Kyoko/1668, accessed February 2007.

Hayes, D. (2005), *The Japanese disease: sex and sleaze in modern Japan*, Lincoln, NE: iUniverse.

Hecht, G. (2012), *Being nuclear: Africans and the global uranium trade*, Cambridge, MA and London: MIT Press.

Hedges, C. (2006), *American fascists: the Christian Right and the war on America*, New York: Free Press.

Hegel, G. W. F. and R. Brown (2009), *Lectures on the history of philosophy, 1825–6*, Oxford, New York: Clarendon Press; Oxford University Press.

Heidegger, M. and D. Krell (1993), *Basic writings: from being and time (1927) to the task of thinking (1964)*, New York: Harper Collins.

Hein, L. and M. Selden (1997), *Living with the bomb: American and Japanese cultural conflicts in the nuclear age*, Armonk, NY: M.E. Sharpe.

Helfland, I. (2013), 'Nuclear Famine: Two Billion People at Risk: Global Impacts of Limited Nuclear War on Agriculture, Food Supplies and Human Nutrition', *International Physicians for the Prevention of Nuclear War, Physicians for Social Responsibility*, November, Somerville, MA: IPPNW.

Henry, A. H. (2010), 'The pebble in Gareth's shoe', *New Matilda*, 3 February, http://newmatilda.com/2010/02/03/pebble-gareths-shoe, accessed 3 February 2010.

Hersey, J. (2009 [1946]), *Hiroshima*, London: Penguin.

Hersh, S. (2014), 'The Red line and the Rat line', *London Review of Books*, 36(8), 17 April: 21–24.

Hershberg, J. G. (1995), *James B. Conant: Harvard to Hiroshima and the making of the nuclear age*, Stanford, CA: Stanford University Press.

Hertz, R. (1960), *Death and the right hand*, Glencoe, IL: Free Press.

Hewes, L. I. (1955), *Japan–land and men; an account of the Japanese land reform program–1945–51*, Ames, IA: Iowa State College Press.

Hewitt, A. (1993), *Fascist modernism: aesthetics, politics, and the avant-garde*, Stanford, CA: Stanford University Press.

Heymann, P. (2011), 'Muslims in America after 9/11: The legal situation', *Harvard Law School*, www.ces.fas.harvard.edu/conferences/muslims/Heymann.pdf, accessed 10 April 2011.

Hicks, D. (2004 [1976]), *Tetum ghosts and kin: fieldwork in an Indonesian community*, Long Grove: Waveland Press.

Higashi, M. (1972), *Okinawa no shōnen*, Tokyo: Bunshun bunkō.

Hijikata, T. (2004 [1968]), 'Nikutai no Hanran', *CD-ROM Hijikata Tatsumi no Butoh*, Kawasaki: Okamoto Taro Museum of Art, October, 12 mins.

Hijikata, T. (1977), 'Tatsumi Hijikata, Tadashi Suzuki, Senda Akihiko: Lacking language=Body Hypothesis', *Gendai-shi Techō*, Tokyo: Shichō Press.

Hijikata, T. (1985a), 'Wind Dharma: Collections of an Emaciated Body', *Gendaishi techō*, 28(6), 28 May.

Hijikata, T. (1985b), 'Nikutai no Hyōgensha tachi', *Zen'ei Hōsō Inroku*, Tokyo: NHK.

Hijikata, T. and T. Shibusawa (1985), 'The Extreme Luxury: Interview of Mr. Hijikata Tatsumi', *W-Notation* (July): 2–27.

Hijikata, T. (1987a), *The body on the edge of crisis*, Tokyo: PARCO.

Hijikata, T. (1987b), *Bibō no Aozora*, Tokyo: Chikuma shobō.

Hijikata, T. (1993), *Hijikata Tatsumi Butoh Daikan*, Tokyo: Yūshisha, unpag.

Hijikata, T. and N. Kurihara (2000 [1960]), 'Inner Material/Material', *TDR: The Drama Review*, 44(1): 34–42.

Hijikata, T. and N. Kurihara (2000 [1961]), 'To Prison', *TDR: The Drama Review*, 44(1): 43–48.

Hijikata, T. and N. Kurihara (2000 [1985]), 'Wind Daruma', *TDR: The Drama Review*, 44(1): 71–81.

Hijikata, T. and N. Kurihara (2000), 'On Material II Fautrier', *TDR: The Drama Review*, 44(1): 60–61.

Hindmarsh, R. (ed.) (2013), *Nuclear disaster at Fukushima Daiichi: social, political and environmental issues*, New York: Routledge, 2013.

Hilgartner, S., R. Bell, and R. O'Connor (1983), *Nukespeak*, New York: Penguin Books.

Hino, H. and A. Broinowski (2002), *Butoh-fu*, Tokyo (unpublished).

Hirano, K. (1992), *Mr. Smith goes to Tokyo: the Japanese cinema under the American occupation, 1945–1952*, Washington, DC: Smithsonian Institute.

Hirschman, C., S. Preston and V. Manh Loi (1995), 'Vietnamese Casualties during the American War: A new estimate', *Population and Development Review*, 21(4): 783–812.

Hisane, M. (2006), 'Japan Joins the Race for Uranium Amid Global Expansion of Nuclear Power', *Japan Focus*, 22 April, http://japanfocus.org/-hisanemasaki/1626, accessed June 2014.

Hobbes, T. and R. Tuck (ed.) (1991), *Leviathan*, Cambridge: Cambridge University Press, 145: 149.

Holborn, M. (1986), *Black sun: the eyes of four: roots and innovation in Japanese photography*, New York: Aperture.

Holborn, M. and E. Hosoe (1999), *Eikoh Hosoe*, Cologne: Könemann.

Holmes, J. (2004), 'Rich Man, Poor Man', *Four corners*, Sydney: ABCTV.

Homei, A. (2012), 'The contentious death of Mr. Kuboyama: Science as politics in the 1954 Lucky Dragon incident', *Japan Forum*, http://dx.doi.org/10.1080/09555803.2012.745585, accessed 3 January 2013.

Honda, K. (1972), *Vietnam war: a report through Asian eyes*, Tokyo: Mirai-sha.

Hook, G. and G. McCormack (2001), *Japan's contested constitution: documents and analysis*, London and New York: Routledge.

Horton, D. (1946), *The return to Japan: report of the Christian deputation to Japan, October–November, 1945*, New York: Pub. for the Federal Council of the Churches of Christ in America and the Foreign Missions Conference of North America, Friendship Press.

Hoschchild, A. (1999), *King Leopold's ghost: a story of Greek, terror and heroism in colonial Africa*, New York: Houghton Mifflin.

Hosoe, E. (1985), *Ba-ra-kei = Ordeal by roses: photographs of Yukio Mishima*, New York: Aperture.

Howard, B. R. (2003), *Indigenous peoples and the state: the struggle for native rights*, DeKalb, IL: Northern Illinois University Press.

Howland, D. (2000), 'Society reified: Herbert spencer and political Theory in Early Meiji Japan', *Comparative Studies in Society and History*, 42(1): 67–86.

Huelsenbeck, R. (1974), *Memoirs of a Dada drummer*, New York: Viking Press.

Hughes, T. H. (2012), *Literature and film in Cold War South Korea: freedom's frontier*, New York: Columbia University Press.

Huntington, S. (1961), *The common defense: strategic programs in national politics*, New York: Columbia University Press.

Huntington, S. (1993), 'The Clash of Civilisations?', *Foreign Affairs*, 72(3, Summer): 23–49.

Husserl, E. (1980), *Ideas pertaining to a pure phenomenology and to a phenomenological philosophy*, The Hague; Boston, MA: M. Nijhoff; Kluwer Publishing.

Hutchinson, P. (1947), 'Japan – A Laboratory Test', *Christian Century*, 64, 30 July: 918–19.

Hutchinson, R. (2007), 'Kurosawa Akira's One Wonderful Sunday: Censorship, Context and "Counter-discursive" Film', *Japan Forum*, 19(3): 369–89.

Ienaga, S. and R. Minear (2001), *Japan's past, Japan's future: one historian's odyssey*, Lanham, MD: Rowman & Littlefield Publishers.

Igarashi, Y. (2000), *Bodies of memory: narratives of war in postwar Japanese culture, 1945–1970*, Princeton, NJ: Princeton University Press.

Igarashi, Y. (2007), *Haisen no kioku: shintai, bunka, monogatari 1945–1970*, Tokyo: Chūō Kōron Shinsha.

Ikegami, Y. (2011), 'Introducing Post-war History in the Nuclear Accident Debate', *jfissures*, 7 May, https://jfissures.wordpress.com/2011/05/07/introducing-post-war -history-in-the-nuclear-accident-debate/, accessed July 2012.

Ileto, R. (1979), *Pasyon and revolution: popular movements in the Philippines, 1840–1910*, Quezon City Manila: Ateneo de Manila University Press.

Imamura, S. (2000), *Kanne kara Yamiichi e*, Tokyo: Kōsaku-sha.

Inbaraj, S. (2004), 'Filmmaker Max Stahl wants to drive away past devils', *East Timor and Indonesia Action Network*, http://www.etan.org/et2004/july/08-14/08filmkr.htm, accessed 3 March 2010.

Israel, J. (2001), *Radical enlightenment: philosophy and the making of modernity 1650–1750*, Oxford; New York: Oxford University Press.

Itō, M., D. Okabe, and I. Tsuiji (eds.) (2012), *Fandom unbound: Otaku culture in a connected world*, New Haven: Yale University Press.

Iwabuchi, K. (1994), 'Complicit Exoticism: Japan and Its Other', *Continuum*, 8(2): 49–82.

Iwasaki, A. (1971), 'Gishiki no Shinri', *Art Theatre*, 87 (June): 8–16.

Jacobs, R. (2015), 'Anthropogenic Fallout: The *Bravo* Test and the Death and Life of the Global Ecosystem', *Hiroshima Peace Research Journal*, 2: 77–96.

Jager, S. and R. Mitter (2007), *Ruptured histories: war, memory, and the post-Cold War in Asia*, Cambridge, MA: Harvard University Press.

James, W. (2007 [1902]), *Varieties of religious experience: a study in human nature: lecture II*, New York: Cosimo Classics.

Jameson, F. (1986), 'Third-world Literature in the Era of Multinational Capitalism', *Social Text*, 15: 65–88.

Jardine, M. (1995), *East Timor: genocide in paradise*, Tuscon, AZ: Odonian Press.

Jay, M. (1993), *Downcast eyes: the denigration of vision in twentieth-century French thought*, Berkeley: University of California Press.

Johnson, C. (1972), *Conspiracy at Matsukawa*, Berkeley: University of California Press.

Johnson, C. (1993), *A phenomenology of the black body*, Ann Arbor: University of Michigan.

Johnson, C. (ed.) (1995), 'The 1955 System and the American Connection: A Bibliographic Introduction', *JPRI*, (11), July.

Johnson, C. (1999), *Okinawa: cold war island*, San Francisco: Japan Policy Research Institute.

Johnson, C. (2007), *The sorrows of empire: militarism, secrecy and the end of the republic*, New York: Metropolitan Books.

Johnston, E., (2005), 'Rokkasho Drawing Proliferation Flak: Multinational Controls Urged to Deter Nuclear Arms-Seeking Copycats', *Japan Times*, 15 November.

Johnston, E. (2006), 'Rokkasho Tests Break Plutonium Pledge, Activists Tell IAEA', *Japan Times*, 6 January.

Johnston, E. (2014), 'Going nuclear: how close has Japan come? We examine the historical debate on the country's atomic ambitions', *Japan Times*, 10 May.

Jolliffe, J. (2004), 'Australia Blamed in East Timor Report', *Sydney Morning Herald*, 5 April.

Jolliffe, J. (2006), 'Compromising Justice in East Timor', *Far Eastern Economic Review*, 169(3): 54–7.

Jolliffe, J. (2009), 'Graves may give answers to Dili massacre', *The Age*, 1 April.

Jolliffe, J. (2010), 'Remains of nine found in Timor', *The Age*, 5 March, http://news.theage.com.au/breaking-news-world/experts-examine-timor-massacre-victims-20100305-pork.html, accessed March 2010.

Jones, A. (1998), *Body art/performing the subject*, Minneapolis: University of Minnesota Press.

Jones, M. (2006), 'Shutting themselves in', *New York Times Magazine*, 15 January, http://www.nytimes.com/2006/01/15/magazine/15japanese.html?ei=5088&en=7b1fdacbeb794332&ex=1294981200&pagewanted=all, accessed June 2006.

Jungk, R. (1961 [1959]), *Children of the ashes; the story of a rebirth*, London: Heinemann.

Kamala, V. (2012), 'Occupier/occupied', *Identities: Global Studies in Culture and Power*, 19(4): 1–12.

Kant, I. (1991), *On the different races of man (1775) in observations on the feeling of the beautiful and the sublime*, Berkeley: University of California Press.

Kantor, T. (1990), *Wielopole/Wielopole: an exercise in theatre*, London; New York: M. Boyars, Rizzoli International Publications.

Kase, T. (1986), *Kase Toshikazu kaisō-roku (ge)*, Tokyo: Yamate Shobō.

Katzenstein, P. J. and Y. Tsujinaka (1991), *Defending the Japanese state: structures, norms and the political responses to terrorism and violent social protest in the 1970s and 1980s*, Ithaca, NY: Cornell University.

Kaufman, A. (1999), *The outlaw bible of American poetry*, New York: Thunder's Mouth Press.

Kawai, K. (1950), 'Mokusatsu, Japan's Response to the Potsdam Declaration', *Pacific Historical Review*, 19(4): 409–14.

Kawamura, T. (2003), *Nippon wars (remix)*, Tokyo: Daisan Erotica.

Kayō, M. (1993), *Utsuwa toshite no shintai: Hijikata Tatsumi Ankoku buto giho e no apurochi*, Tokyo: ANZ-DO.

Khamsi, K. (2005), 'A Settlement to the Timor Sea Dispute?', *Harvard Asia Quarterly*, 9(1): 6–23.

Kehi, B. (2004), 'Australia's Relations with East Timor: People's Loyalty, Government's Betrayal', *Borderlands e-Journal*, 3(3), http://www.borderlands.net.au/vol3no3_2004/kehi_timor.htm, accessed 12 Jun 2009.

Kelly, W. (1998), 'Blood and Guts in Japanese Baseball', in Linhart, S. and S. Frühstück (eds.), *The culture of Japan as seen through its leisure*, New York: State University of New York Press.

Kelley, C. (2007), *Post-9/11 American presidential rhetoric: a study of protofascist discourse*, Lanham: Lexington Books.

Kelley, F. and C. Ryan (1947), *Star Spangled Mikado*, New York: Robert F. McBride.

Kelman, P. (2001), 'Protesting the national identity: the cultures of protest in 1960s Japan', PhD Diss., Sydney: University of Sydney.

Kerner, A. (2007), *Representing the catastrophic: coming to terms with 'unimaginable' suffering and 'incomprehensible' horror in visual culture*, New York: Edwin Mellen Press.

Kerner, A. and T. Iimura (2009), 'The Media Art of Takahiko Iimura: Iimura's Butoh films by Aaron Kerner', 13 June, takahikoiimura.sblo.jp/article/33280794.html, accessed October, 2009.

Kerr, A. (2001), *Dogs and demons: tales from the dark side of Japan*, New York: Hill and Wang.

Kersten, R. and D. Williams (eds.), *The left in the shaping of Japanese democracy: essays in honour of J.A.A. Stockwin*, London, New York, Leiden: Routledge.

Kierkegaard, S. (1989 [1849]), *The sickness unto death: a Christian psychological exposition for edification and awakening*, London; New York: Penguin Books.

Kiernan, B. (2003), 'The Demography of Genocide in Southeast Asia: The Death Tolls in Cambodia, 1975–79, and East Timor, 1975–80', *Critical Asian Studies*, 35(4): 585–97.

Kiernan, B. and O. Taylor (2007), 'Bombs over Cambodia: New Light on US Air War', *The Asia-Pacific Focus*, 12 May, http://japanfocus.org/-Ben-Kiernan/2420/article.html, accessed April 2015.

Kiernan, B. and O. Taylor (2015), 'Making More Enemies Than We Kill? Calculating U.S. Bomb Tonnages Dropped on Laos and Cambodia, and Wighing Their Implications', *The Asia-Pacific Journal: Japan Focus*, 13(16), No. 3, 27 April, accessed April 2015.

Kikuchi, Y. K. (2004), *Japanese modernisation and Mingei Theory: cultural nationalism and oriental orientalism*, London; New York: RoutledgeCurzon.

King, P. (2009), *Undermining proliferation: nuclear winter and nuclear renunciation*, Sydney: The Centre for Peace and Conflict Studies, University of Sydney, No. 9/1, October.

Kingston, J. (2006), 'Balancing Justice and Reconciliation in East Timor', *Critical Asian Studies*, 38(3): 271–302.

Kiyose, I. (1986), *Hiroku Tōkyō Saiban*, Tokyo: Chūō Kōronsha.

Klein, S. B. (1988), *Ankoku Butō: the premodern and postmodern influences on the dance of utter darkness*, Ithaca: Cornell East Asia Series, 49.

Kō, M. and X. G. Lemay (2009), *Furnace*, New York: CAVE Butoh Festival, 5–8 November.

Koga, Y. (1956), 'Konketsuji no chōsa-jōhō', *Monbushō Shotō Chūtō Kyōikukyoku Konketsuji shidō kiroku*, 3(April).

Koikari, M. (2002), 'Exporting Democracy?: American Women, "Feminist Reforms", and Politics of Imperialism in the U.S. Occupation of Japan, 1945–1952', *Frontiers: A Journal of Women Studies*, 23(1): 23–45.

Kojima, N. (1954), *American school*, Tokyo: Misuzu Shobō.

Kolin, P. C. (2007), *Contemporary African American women playwrights: a casebook*, London; New York: Routledge.

Kosaka, K. (2009), 'Forget the Suicide Stereotype', *The Japan Times*, 18 June, http://search .japantimes.co.jp/cgi-bin/fl20090618a2.html, accessed 19 June 2009.

Koschmann, J. (1996), *Revolution and subjectivity in postwar Japan*, Chicago: University of Chicago Press.

Koshiro, Y. (1999), *Trans-Pacific racisms and the U.S. occupation of Japan*, New York: Columbia University Press.

Koshiro, Y. (2003), 'Beyond an Alliance of Colour: The African-American impact on modern Japan', *positions*, 11(1): 183–215.

Kozak, W. (2010), 'A Hiroshima Apology?', *The Wall Street Journal*, 6 August, http://online .wsj.com/article/NA_WSJ_PUB:SB10001424052748703748904575411123599873634 .html, accessed 6 August 2010.

Kristensen, H. (ed.) (2005), *The nuclear information project: a history of U.S. nuclear weapons in South Korea*, 28 September, www.nukestrat.com, July 2015.

Kristeva, J. (1989), *Black sun: depression and melancholia*, New York: Columbia University Press.

Kroker, A. (1985), *Technology and the Canadian mind: Innis/McLuhan/Grant*, New York: St. Martin's Press.

Kuniyoshi, K. (1985), *An overview of the contemporary Japanese dance scene*, Tokyo: Japan Foundation, Office for the Japanese Studies Center.

Kuniyoshi, K. (1986a), 'Butoh Chronology: 1959–1984', *TDR/The Drama Review*, 30(2): 127–141.

Kuniyoshi, K. (1986b), 'Butoh in Late 1980s', *Performing Arts in Japan Now*, 1 (Spring).

Kuniyoshi, K. (2006), 'Two Kinjiki: Diametrical Oppositions', *TDR/The Drama Review*, 50(2): 154–158.

Kunkle, T. and B. Ristvet, (2013), *Castle Bravo: fifty years of legend and lore: a guide to offsite radiation exposure*, New Mexico: Defense Threat Reduction Agency, GOUS.

Kuno, O. (1960), 'Seijiteki shimin no seiritsu', *Shisō no kagaku* 19(July): 9–17.

Kurihara, N. (2000a), 'Introduction: Hijikata Tatsumi: The Words of Butoh', *TDR/The Drama Review* 44(1): 10–28.

Kurihara, N. (2000b), 'Hijikata Tatsumi Chronology', *TDR/The Drama Review*, 44(1): 29–33.

Kuriyama, S. (1999), *The expressiveness of the body and the divergence of Greek and Chinese medicine*, New York: Zone Books.

Kuriyama, S. (2001), *The imagination of the body and the history of bodily experience*, Kyoto: IRCJS.

Kurosawa, A. (1983), *Something like an autobiography*, New York: Vintage Books.

Kutler, S. (ed.) (1996), *Encyclopedia of the Vietnam War*, New York: Scribner's.

Kuznick, P. (2007), 'The Decision to Risk the Future: Harry Truman, the Atomic Bomb and the Apocalyptic Narrative', *Asia-Pacific Journal: Japan Focus*, 23 July, http://japanfocus .org/-Peter_J_-Kuznick/2479, accessed December 2010.

Kwon, H. (2012), 'Rethinking Traumas of War', *South East Asia Research*, 20(2): 227–37.

La Cerda, J. (1946), *The conqueror comes to tea: Japan under MacArthur*, New Brunswick: Rutgers University Press.

Lacan, J. and B. Fink (2006), *Ecrits: The first complete edition in English*, New York: W.W. Norton.

Laclau, E., J. Butler, and S. Žižek (2000), *Contingency, hegemony, universality: contemporary dialogues on the left*, London: Verso.

Ladejinsky, W. (1938), 'Agrarian Unrest in Japan', *Foreign Affairs*, 17: 426.

Ladejinsky, W. (1959), 'Agrarian Revolution in Japan', *Foreign Affairs*, 38(1): 95–109.

Ladejinsky, W. and D. Berrigan (1949), 'Japan's Communists lose a battle', *Saturday Evening Post*, 8 January.

LaHaye, T. F. (1984), *The coming peace in the Middle East*, Grand Rapids, MI: Zondervan.

Lal, B. and K. Fortune (2000), *The Pacific Islands: an encyclopedia*, Honolulu: University of Hawai'i Press.

LaMothe, K. (2006), *Nietzsche's dancers: Isadora Duncan, Martha Graham, and the revaluation of Christian values*, New York and Houndsmills: Palgrave Macmillan.

Langer, L. (1995), *Art from the ashes: a Holocaust anthology*, New York: Oxford University Press.

Langley, P. (2009), *Medicine and the bomb: deceptions from Trinity to Maralinga*, South Australia: Paul Langley ebook.

Lanzmann, C. (1995), *Shoah*, New York: New Yorker Films.

Laqueur, T. (2003), *Solitary sex: a cultural history of masturbation*, New York: Zone Books.

Lapp, R. E., (1957), *The voyage of the Lucky Dragon*, New York: Harper and Brothers.

Leach, E. (1976), *Culture & communication: the logic by which symbols are connected: an introduction to the use of structuralist analysis in social anthropology*, Cambridge; Melbourne: Cambridge University Press.

Lee, C. K. (1998), *Hijikata Tatsumi and Ankoku Butoh: a body perspective*, M.A. diss.; Singapore: National University of Singapore.

Lee, C.-S. (1967), 'Counter-insurgency in Manchuria: The Japanese Experience 1931–1940', RM-5012, January, Advanced Research Projects Agency, Santa Monica: RAND Corporation.

Lee, J.-B. (2009), 'U.S. Deployment of Nuclear Weapons in 1950s South Korea & North Korea's Nuclear Development: Toward the Denuclearization of the Korean Peninsula', *The Asia-Pacific Journal*, 8(3), http://www.japanfocus.org/-Lee-Jae_Bong/3053/article.html, accessed January 2010.

Lee, S. (2013), 'The Korean Armistice and the End of Peace: The US-UN Coalition and the Dynamics of War-Making in Korea 1953–76', *Journal of Korean Studies*, 18(2): 183–224.

Lefebvre, H. (2003), *The urban revolution*, Minneapolis: University of Minnesota Press.

Legacies of War (2010), 'Legacies of War: Unexploded Ordnances in Laos Congressional Hearing', 22 April, http://legaciesofwar.org/resources/congressional-hearing-uxo-laos/, accessed July 2014.

Lehmann, H.-T. (2006), *Postdramatic theatre*, Abingdon; New York: Routledge.

Leo, V. (1985), 'The Mushroom Cloud Photograph: from Fact to Symbol', *AfterImage*, 13(Summer): 6–12.

Leonard, G. (2011), 'The 1954 Shunkotsu-maru Expedition and American Atomic Secrecy', *Kokusai Kōi Seisaku Kenkyū*, 15(2).

Levi, P. (1989), *The drowned and the saved*, New York: Vintage International.

Levi-Strauss, C. (1982), *The way of the masks*, Seattle: University of Washington Press.

Levy, B. and V. Sidel (1998), *Social justice and public health*, London: Oxford University Press.

UNIVERSITY OF WINCHESTER
LIBRARY

Levy, I. (1981), *The ten thousand leaves: a translation of the Man'yōshū, Japan's premier anthology of classical poetry*, Princeton, NJ: Princeton University Press.

Lewis, S. (1935), *It can't happen here: a novel*, Garden City, NY: Doubleday, Doran & Company, Inc.

Lieber, K. and D. Press (2006), 'The Rise of U.S. Nuclear Primacy', *Foreign Affairs*, March –April, https://www.foreignaffairs.com/articles/united-states/2006-03-01/rise-us -nuclear-primacy, accessed 19 April 2013.

Lifton, R. J. (1987 [1967]), *Death in life: survivors of Hiroshima*, North Carolina: University of North Carolina Press.

Lifton, R. J. (2003), *Superpower syndrome: America's apocalyptic confrontation with the world*, New York: Thunder's Mouth Press/Nation Books.

Lifton, R. J. and G. Mitchell (1995), *Hiroshima in America: fifty years of denial*, New York: Putnam's Sons.

Lin, Y. (1996), *The importance of living*, New York: W. Morrow.

Lindee, M. S. (1994), *Suffering made real: American science and the survivors at Hiroshima*, Chicago: University of Chicago Press.

Lindqvist, S. and J. Tate (1996), *Exterminate all the brutes*, New York: New Press, W.W. Norton.

Linhart, S. and S. Frühstück (1998), *The culture of Japan as seen through its leisure*, Albany: State University of New York Press.

Littleton, C. S. (2005), *Gods, goddesses, and mythology*, New York: Marshall Cavendish.

Löwith, K. and R. Wolin (1995), *Martin Heidegger and European nihilism*, New York: Columbia University Press.

Lukács, G. (1981), *The destruction of reason*, Atlantic Highlands, NJ: Humanities Press.

MacArthur, D. (1946-1947), *Statements to U.S. congress*, Washington: PRJ.

MacArthur, D. (1951), 'Hearings to Conduct an Inquiry into the Military Situation in the Far East and the Facts Surrounding the Relief of General of the Army Douglas MacArthur from His Assignments in that Area', *U.S. Senate, Committee on Armed Services and the Committee on Foreign Relations*, 82nd Congress, 1: 1.

MacArthur, D. and G. Lang (1947), Record Group 5, Box 34, 20 August, Norfolk, VA: MacArthur Memorial Library (MML).

MacDonald, H. (1980), *Suharto's Indonesia*, Blackburn, Vic.: Fontana.

MacDonald, H. (2003), 'Cheney's tough talking derails negotiations with North Korea', *Sydney Morning Herald*, 21 December, http://www.smh.com.au/ articles/2003/12/21/1071941611806.html, accessed September 2008.

MacDonald, H., et al. (2002), *Masters of terror: Indonesia's military & violence in East Timor in 1999*, Australian National University: Strategic and Defence Studies Centre, 145.

Mackie, V. (2003), *Feminism in modern Japan: citizenship, embodiment, and sexuality*, Cambridge; New York: Cambridge University Press.

Mackie, V. (2011), 'Embodied Memories, Emotional Geographies: Nakamoto Takako's Diary of the Anpo Struggle', *Japanese Studies*, 31(3): 319–31.

Maier, C. (1977) 'Politics of Productivity: Foundations of American International Economic Policy after World War II', *International Organization* 31(4): 607–32.

Mackinder, H. (1969 [1919]), *Democratic ideals and reality: a study in the politics of reconstruction*, New York: W.W. Norton.

Mailer, N. (1957), 'The White Negro: Superficial reflections on the hipster', *Dissent* (Summer), New York: University of Pennsylvania Press.

Mailer, N. (1998), *The naked and the dead*, New York: Picador.

Malcolm X (1971), *The End of White World Supremacy: Four Speeches by Malcolm X*, B. Karim (ed.) New York: Monthly Review Press.

Mann, J. (1994), 'C.I.A. Spent Millions to Support Japanese Right in 50's and 60's', *New York Times*, 9 October.

Mann, J. (1995), 'CIA Keeping Historians in the Dark about Its Cold War Role in Japan', *Los Angeles Times*, 20 March.

Marable, M. and L. Mullings (2009), *Let nobody turn us around: voices of resistance, reform, and renewal: an African American anthology*, Lanham: Rowman & Littlefield.

Marcuse, H. (1972), *Eros and civilization: a philosophical inquiry into Freud*, London: Abacus.

Marinetti, F. and R. Flint (1972), *Marinetti, selected writings*, New York: Farrar.

Marotti, W. (2009), 'AHR Forum Japan 1968: The Performance of Violence and the Theater of Protest', *The American Historical Review*, 114(1): 97–135.

Marran, C. (2007), *Poison woman: figuring female transgression in modern Japanese culture*, Minneapolis: University of Minnesota Press.

Marqusee, M. (1999), *Redemption song: Muhammad Ali and the spirit of the sixties*, London: Verso.

Martinkus, J. (2001), *A Dirty Little War*, NSW: Random House Australia.

Maruyama, M. (1963), *Thought and behaviour in modern Japanese politics*, London, New York: Oxford University Press.

Marx, K. (1976), *Capital, vol. 1, a critique of political economy*, New York: Penguin Books.

Marx, K. and F. Engels (2001), *The collected works of Karl Marx and Friedrich Engels*, vol. 6, Charlottesville, VA: InteLex Corporation.

Masco, J. (2012), 'The End of Ends', *Anthropological Quarterly*, 86(4): 1107–24.

Masson-Sekine, N. and J. Viala (1988), *Butoh: shades of darkness*, Tokyo: Shufunotomo.

Massumi, B. (2005), 'Fear (the spectrum said)', *Positions: East Asia Cultures Critique*, 13(1): 31–48.

Matsui, M. (1994–1995), 'Panel-D-Japan: Amerika tai Nichi sennō kōsaku no zenbō', *Views*, November–March.

Matsumoto, T. (2009), 'Revealing "Secret U.S.-Japan Nuclear Understandings": A Solemn Obligation of Japan's New Government', *The Asia-Pacific Journal: Japan Focus*, 1 March, www.japanfocus.org/-Matsumoto-Tsuyoshi/3273/article.html, accessed 21 December 2009.

Matsushita, K. (1956), 'The formation of the Mass State and Its Problems', *Shisō*, 389, November, 31–52.

Matsushita, K. (1964), 'Nippon Konchūki to Nihon Seiji', *Eiga Geijutsu*, 12(2): 196.

Matsutani, M. (2010), 'Akihabara Gets Bank of Security Cameras', *The Japan Times*, 27 January, http://www.google.com.au/search?q=japan+times%2C+akihabara%2C+cameras, accessed January 2010.

Mauss, M. (2001), *A general theory of magic*, London; New York: Routledge.

Mautner, T. (1997), *The Penguin dictionary of philosophy*, London; New York: Penguin Books.

Mayo, M., J. Rimer, and H. Kerkham (2001), *War, occupation, and creativity: Japan and East Asia, 1920–1960*, Honolulu: University of Hawai'i Press.

Mbembé, J.-A. and L. Meintjes (2003), 'Necropolitics', *Public Culture*, 15(1): 11–40.

McCormack, G. (1971), 'The Student Left in Japan', *New Left Review*, 1: 65.

McCormack, G. (2007), *Client state: Japan in the American embrace*, London; New York: Verso.

McFarland, H. (1967), *The rush hour of the gods: a study of new religious movements in Japan*, New York: Macmillan.

McGee, M. (1986), 'An Avant-Garde Becomes an Institution', *High Performance*, 33: 49.

McHugh, L. (2009), 'The History of Haiti Is Relevant to the World', *Cornell Chronicle*.

McLelland, M. (2005), *Queer Japan from the Pacific war to the internet age*, Lanham: Rowman & Littlefield.

McRoy, J. (2008), *Nightmare Japan contemporary Japanese horror cinema*, Kenilworth: Rodopi.

McShine, K. and R. Heller (2006), *Edvard Munch: the modern life of the soul*, New York: Museum of Modern Art.

McWilliam, A. (2008), 'Fatakulu Healing and Cultural Resilience in East Timor', *Ethnos*, 73(2): 217–40.

Mears, H. (1948), *Mirror for Americans*, Boston: Houghton Mifflin.

Melzer, A. (1994), *Dada and surrealist performance*, Baltimore: Johns Hopkins University Press.

Merchant, B. (2013), 'A Brief History of Godzilla, Our Walking Nuclear Nightmare', *Vice*, 23 August.

Merleau-Ponty, M. ([1962] 2002), *Phenomenology of perception*, London: Routledge.

Metcalf, P. (1992), *A Borneo journey into death: berawan eschatology from its rituals*, Philadelphia: University of Pennsylvania Press.

Minear, R. H. (1990), *Hiroshima: three witnesses*, Princeton, NJ: Princeton University Press.

Ministry of Health, Labour and Welfare (2010), *Hikikomori survey*, Tokyo: Japanese Government, http://www8.cao.go.jp/youth/kenkyu/hikikomori/pdf_index .html, accessed July 2010.

Mishima, Y. (1951), *Forbidden colours*, Tokyo: Shinchōsha.

Mishima, Y. (1976), 'Bunka bōei-ron (In defence of culture)', *Mishima Zenshū*, 33.

Mishima, Y. (1985), *The sea of fertility*, New York: Penguin.

Mitchell, G. (1983), 'Japanese Nuclear Film Suppressed', *Nuclear Times*, 12 March.

Mitchell, G. (2005), 'Hiroshima Cover-up Exposed', *Alternet*, 4 August, http://www .alternet.org/story/23914/hiroshima_cover-up_exposed, accessed August 2014.

Mitchell, J. (2012), '"Seconds Away From Midnight": U.S. Nuclear Missile Pioneers on Okinawa Break Fifty Year Silence on a Hidden Nuclear Crisis of 1962', *The Asia-Pacific Journal: Japan Focus*, 28(1), http://www.japanfocus.org/-Jon-Mitchell/3800/article .html, accessed 23 July 2012.

Mitchell, J. (2015), 'Vietnam: Okinawa's Forgotten War', *The Asia-Pacific Journal: Japan Focus*, 13(1), 20 April, http://www.japanfocus.org/-Jon-Mitchell/4308/article.html, accessed 18 May 2015.

Miyoshi, M. (1991), *Off center: power and culture relations between Japan and the United States*, Cambridge, MA: Harvard University Press.

Mizuta-Lippit, A. (2005), *Atomic Light (Shadow Optics)*, Minneapolis: University of Minnesota Press.

Mochizuki, M. (2007), 'Japan Tests the Nuclear Taboo', *Non-Proliferation Review*, 14(2), July, 303–28.

Moen, D. (1997), 'The Japanese Organic Farming Movement: Consumers and Farmers United', *Bulletin of Concerned Asian Scholars*, 29(3): 14–22.

Moen, D. (1999), 'The Postwar Japanese Agricultural Debacle', *Hitotsubashi Journal of Social Studies*, 31(1): 29–52.

Molasky, M. (1999), *The American occupation of Japan and Okinawa: literature and memory*, London; New York: Routledge.

Monaco, J. (1979), *Alain Renais: the role of imagination*, Oxford: Oxford University Press.

Montag, W. (1999), *Bodies, masses, power: Spinoza and his contemporaries*, London; New York: Verso.

Montag, W. (2009), 'Imitating the Affects of Beasts: Interest and Inhumanity in Spinoza', *Differences*, 20(2–3): 54–72.

Montaigne, M. (1958), *The complete essays of Montaigne*, Stanford: California University Press.

Moore, R. (1990), *Japanese agriculture: patterns of rural development*, Boulder Colorado: Westview Press.

Morris, F. (1945), 'Rise and fall of Japan's Empire', *Senior Scholastic*, 17 September, 3.

Morris, I. (1969), *Thought and behaviour in modern Japanese politics*, Oxford: Oxford University Press.

Morris, I. (1980), *The nobility of failure: tragic heroes in the history of Japan*, Harmondsworth: Penguin.

Morris, M. (1988), *The pirate's fiancée: feminism, reading, postmodernism*, London; New York: Verso.

Morris-Suzuki, T. (1998), *Re-inventing Japan: time, space, nation*, New York: M. E. Sharpe.

Morton, R. (1937), 'Japan and China: A War of Minds', *Pacific Affairs*, X: 305–14.

Moss, R. (1925), *The life after death in Oceania and the Malay Archipelago*, London; New York: Oxford University Press, H. Milford.

Motherwell, R. (1989 [1951]), *The dada painters and poets: an anthology*, New York: Wittenborn, Schultz.

Motofuji, A. (1998), 'Otto toshite no Hijikatai, shi toshite no Hijiakata', *Geijutsu Shincho*, Tokyo: Shincho Press, 49.

Mumford, M. (2009), *Bertolt Brecht*, New York, NY: Routledge.

Murakami, F. (2005), *Postmodern, feminist and postcolonial currents in contemporary Japanese culture: a reading of Murakami Haruki, Yoshimoto Banana, Yoshimoto Takaaki and Karatani Kōjin*, New York: Routledge.

Murthy, M., et al. (2000), 'The Amoral Scientists – The Tragedy of Hiroshima', *Current Science*, 78: 19–22.

Mutō, I. and R. Inoue (1985), 'Beyond the New Left: In Search of a Radical Base in Japan (Part1)', *AMPO: A Review of the New Left in Japan*, 17: 20–35.

Naaman, O. (2012), 'It's Mostly Punishment': Testimonies by Veterans of the Israeli Defense Forces from Gaza', *Tom Dispatch*, http://truth-out.org/news/item/12956 -it%E2%80%99s-mostly-punishment-testimonies-by-veterans-of-the-israeli-defense -forces-from-gaza28, accessed November 2012.

Nagata, H. (1982), 'Jiko hihan: Rengo Sekigun no ayamachi o kurikaesanai tame ni', *Impakushon*, 20(2): 104–19.

Nagatomo, S. (1992), *Attunement through the body*, Albany, NY: State University of New York Press.

Nakagami, K. (1990), 'Jazu kyōsaha', *Fūkei no mukō e*, Tokyo: Fuyukisha.

Nakagami, K. (1999), *The cape and other stories from the Japanese ghetto*, Berkeley, CA: Stone Bridge Press.

Nakagami, K. (2000), *Chinohate, Shijo no toki*, Paris: Fayard.

Nakajima, N. (1997), *Feminine spirituality in theatre, opera and dance*, Taipei: Fu Jen University, Conference Presentation.

Nakamura, N. (2006), 'Genetic Effects of Radiation in Atomic-bomb Survivors and Their Children: Past, Present and Future', *Journal of Radiation Research*, 47: B67–73.

Nakamura, A. (2008), "We Did Not Leave Anything Positive", Says Ex-radical, *The Japan Times*, 20 March, http://search.japantimes.co.jp/cgi-bin/ff20080320r2.html, accessed 21 March 2009.

Nakanishi, N. (1987), 'Hijikata Tatsumi', *Bijutsu Techō*.

Nakanishi, T. (ed.) (2006), '*Nihon Kaku Busō*' no Ronten.

Nakanishi, T. and C. Nishioka (2006), 'Anpō kara Hajimaru 'Sengo kara no Dakkyaku' to Nihon no Kaku Busō', *Seiron*, December: 60–61.

Nakano, J. (1995), 'Outcry from the Inferno: Atomic Bomb Tanka Anthology', *Hawaii Writer's Quarterly*, 67–68.

Nancy, J.-L. (2002), *L'Intrus*, East Lansing: Michigan State University Press.

Nathan, J. (1974), *Mishima: a biography*, New York: Da Capo Press.

Negri, A. and T. Murphy (2004), *Subversive Spinoza: (un)contemporary variations*, Manchester; New York: Manchester University Press, Palgrave.

Neilands, J. B., G. Orians, E. Pfeiffer, A. Vennema, and A. Westing (1972), *Harvest of death: chemical warfare in Vietnam and Cambodia*, New York: Free Press.

Neiman, S. (2002), *Evil in modern thought: an alternative history of philosophy*, Princeton, NJ: Princeton University Press.

Nelson, D. (2008), *The war behind me: Vietnam veterans confront the truth about U.S. war crimes*, New York: Basic Books.

Nevins, J. (2005), *A not-so-distant horror: mass violence in East Timor*, Ithaca: Cornell University Press.

Nietzsche, F. (1982), *The Portable Nietzsche*, New York: Viking Penguin.

Nietzsche, F. (2008), *Thus Spoke Zarathustra*, MobileReference.

Nietzsche, F. and R. Hollingdale (1968), *Twilight of the idols; and, the Anti-Christ*, Harmondsworth: Penguin.

Nietzsche, F. and D. Large (1998), *Twilight of the idols, or, How to philosophize with a hammer*, Oxford; New York: Oxford University Press.

Nietzsche, F. and D. Smith (1996), *On the genealogy of morals: a polemic: by way of clarification and supplement to my last book, Beyond good and evil*, Oxford; New York: Oxford University Press.

Niner, S. (2000), *To resist is to win! The autobiography of Xanana Gusmão*, Richmond, Vic.: Aurora Books.

Nishi, T. (1960), 'Kore ga makoto no geijutsu da: Gaitō ni odori deta ankoku buyō', *Sekai Shashin Jōhō*, 34(10): 62–64.

Nishido, K. (1999), 'Bye Bye: Into the Century of Degeneration', *Theatre Arts*, Tokyo, June.

Nishihara, M. (2003), 'North Korea's Trojan Horse', *Washington Post*, 14 August.

Nishimura, S. (1989), 'Medical Censorship in Occupied Japan, 1945–1948', *Pacific Historical Review*, 58(1): 1–21.

Nishimura, S. (2009), 'Promoting Health in American-Occupied Japan Resistance to Allied Public Health Measures, 1945–1952', *American Journal of Public Health*, 99(8): 1364–75.

Nixon, R. (1960), 'The Meaning of Communism to Americans: August 21, 1960', http://watergate.info/nixon/60-08-21_communism.shtml, accessed 20 January 2010.

Nixon, R. (2011), *Slow violence and the environmentalism of the poor*, Cambridge, MA: Harvard University Press.

Nōma, H. and Y. Yukiyama (1968), 'Zadankai: Kome sōdō to burakku pawā: Buraku kaihō kokujin kaihō to bunka', *Asahi Journal*, November, 24: 82–89.

Nornes, A. M. (2003), *Japanese documentary film: the Meiji Era through Hiroshima*, Minneapolis: University of Minnesota Press.

Ōda, M., S. Tsurumi, and Beheiren (ed.) (1968), *Hansen to henkaku: Teikō to heiwa e no teigen*, Tokyo: Beheiren, Gakugei Shobō.

Ōe, K. (1977), *Teach us to outgrow our madness: four short novels*, New York: Grove Press, Random House.

Ōe, K. (1996 [1981]), *Hiroshima notes*, New York: Grove Press.

Ōe, K. (1994), *Japan, The Ambiguous, and Myself*, Nobel Media AB 2014, accessed 23 May 2015, http://www.nobelprize.org/nobel_prizes/literature/laureates/1994/oe-lecture .html.

Office of Intelligence Research (1957), 'The Outlook for Nuclear Weapons Production in Japan', *US State Department*, Washington: Division of Research for Far East, 2 August.

Office of the Historian (1946), 'The Acheson, Lilienthal & Baruch Plans, 1946', *US State Department*, 14 July, http://history.state.gov/milestones/1945-1952/baruch-plans, accessed January 2014.

Ogawa, T. (1970), 'Eros + Gyakusatsu', *Art Theatre*, 75 (March): 4–10.

Ogino, M. (2007), *Scams and sweeteners: a sociology of fraud*, Melbourne: Trans Pacific Press.

Ogoura, K. (2008), 'Japan's Postwar Cultural Diplomacy', *CAS Working Papers*, Berlin: Frei University.

Oguma, E. (2002a), *A genealogy of 'Japanese' self-images*, Melbourne: Trans Pacific Press.

Oguma, E. (2002b), *'Minshu' to 'aikoku': sengo Nihon no nashonarizumu to kokyōsei*, Tokyo: Shin'yōsha.

Ohno, K. (1988), 'Japanese Agriculture Today: Decaying at the Roots', *AMPO: Japan-Asia Quarterly Review*, 20(1, 2): 14–28.

Ohno, K. and Ohno, Y. *Kazuo Ohno's world: from without & within*, Chicago, IL: Wesleyan University Press.

Ohnuki-Tierney, E. (1990), 'The Ambivalent Self of the Contemporary Japanese', *Cultural Anthropology*, 5(2): 197–216.

Ohnuki-Tierney, E. (1993), *Rice as self: Japanese identities through time*, Princeton, NJ: Princeton University Press.

Ohnuki-Tierney, E. (2006), *Kamikaze diaries: reflections of Japanese student soldiers*, Chicago: University of Chicago Press.

Ōi, S. and I. Kawamoto (1954), 'Bikini suibaku kanja no shoshinji rinshō shoken ni Tsuite', *Kagaku ryōhō kenkyūjo ihō*, 8 (1–4): 61–65.

Oiwa, Y. and M. Tsuzuki (2013 [29 August 1945]), 'Medical Records of World's First Radiation Victim from A-bomb Recovered', *The Japan Times*, 4 August.

Oka, T. (1970), 'Japan Fears Reaction Abroad to Writer's Suicide', *New York Times*, 25 November, http://www.nytimes.com/books/98/10/25/specials/mishima-suicide .html, accessed 10 January 2011.

Okada, Y. (2011), 'Race, Masculinity, and Military Occupation: African American Soldiers' Encounters with the Japanese at Camp Gifu, 1947–1951', *Journal of African American History*, 96(2): 179–203.

Okamoto, G. (2015), 'Average age of certified hibakusha tops 80 for 1st time', *Asahi Shimbun*, 2 July.

Okazaki, H. (2006), 'Time to Change Our National Security Strategy', *Daily Yomiuri*, 23 April.

Okuyama, T. (2014), 'U.S. Alarmed about Plutonium Stockpile Growing from Rokkasho Plant', *Asahi Shimbun*, 13 April.

Omori, M. (1981), *Bōryaku to reisen no jūjiro*, Tokyo: Kōdansha Bunkō.

Ōoka, M. (ed.) (1987), 'Tatsumi Hijikata's Philosophy of Butoh', *The Body on the Edge of Crisis*, Tokyo: PARCO.

Ōoka, M., T. Fitzsimmons, and M. Yoshioka (1987), *A Play of mirrors: eight major poets of modern Japan*, USA: Katydid Books.

Operations Coordinating Board (1948–61 [22 April 1954]), 'Outline Check List of US Government Actions to Offset Unfavorable Japanese Attitudes to the H-Bomb and Related Developments', *OCB Central Files*, Japan (1) Sept 56–June 57(3), Box 46, WHO: NSC Staff Papers.

Orr, J. (2001), *The Victim as Hero: Ideologies of Peace and National Identity in Postwar Japan*, Honolulu: University of Hawaii Press.

Ortiz, L. (2008), *Attitude: A Dancer's Magazine*, 21(4).

Orwell, G. (1995), *Animal Farm*, New York: Harcourt, Brace and Co.

Ōsawa, M. (1999), *Sengo no shisō kūkan*, Tokyo: Chikuma Shinsho.

Ōshima, N. and A. Michelson (1992), *Cinema, censorship, and the state: the writings of Nagisa Oshima, 1956–1978*, Cambridge, MA: MIT Press.

Ota, M. (2015), 'US Veterans reveal 1962 nuclear close call dodged in Okinawa', *Kyodo*, 27 March, http://english.kyodonews.jp/news/2015/03/343924.html, accessed 6 April 2015.

Ōtori, H. (2004), *Revolt, dysfunction, dementia – toward the body of 'Empire'*, Hamburg: Laokoon Festival, Keynote.

Packard, G. (1978), *Protest in Tokyo: the security treaty crisis of 1960*, Westport, CT: Greenwood Press.

Pal, R. (1999), *Dissentient judgement of Justice Pal*, Tokyo: Kokusho-Kankōkai.

Parker, A. and E. Sedgwick (1995), *Performativity and performance*, New York: Routledge.

Patterson, C. (2002), *Eternal Treblinka: our treatment of animals and the Holocaust*, New York: Lantern Books.

Pearce, M. and R. Woodford-Smith (2012), 'The (dis)location of Time and Space: Trans-Cultural Collaborations in Tokyo', *Journal of Media Practice*, 13(3): 197–213.

Perlez, J. (2006), 'East Timor's Capital Spirals into Violence', *The New York Times*, 28 May, http://www.nytimes.com/2006/05/28/world/asia/28timor.html?fta=y, accessed August 2009.

Pesenti, M. (2004), *The Paesinae (we used to know how to sing)*, Cardiff: Chapter Arts Center, Pesenti.

Phillips, K. (2006), *American theocracy: the peril and politics of radical religion, oil, and borrowed money in the 21st century*, New York: Viking.

Picchione, J. (2004), *The new avant-garde in Italy: theoretical debate and poetic practices*, Toronto: University of Toronto Press.

Pilger, J. (1994), *Death of a Nation: The Timor Conspiracy*, http://johnpilger.com/videos/death-of-a-nation-the-timor-conspiracy, accessed July 2010.

Pilger, J. (2004), 'Of the Token Hangers-on Who Make up the Anglo-America "Coalition of the Willing", Only Australia Remains True to the Uber-sheriff in Washington', *New Statesman*, 5 April.

Pilger, J. (2006), 'Australia Builds Its Empire', *The New Statesman*, 26 June, http://www.newstatesman.com/200606260026, accessed November, 2009.

Pilger, J. (2010 [1986]), *Heroes*, London: Vintage.

Pilling, D. (2009), 'Beijing Finds Fine Words for Its Old Enemy', *The Financial Times*, 16 December, http://www.ft.com/cms/s/0/0b636690-ea7a-11de-a9f5-00144feab49a.html?catid=14&SID=gc, accessed 11 August, 2010.

Pilling, D. (2010), 'Hiroshima Still Clouds a Postwar Friendship', *The Financial Times*, http://www.ft.com/cms/s/0/eba142ba-a57b-11df-a5b7-00144feabdc0.html, accessed 11 August, 2010.

Pinto, C. and M. Jardine (1997), *East Timor's unfinished struggle: inside the Timorese resistance*, Boston, MA: South End Press.

Piven, J. (2004), *The madness and perversion of Yukio Mishima*, Connecticut: Praeger Publishers.

Plato (2010), *The republic book III*, Adelaide: University of Adelaide ebooks.

Plunka, G. (1992), *The rites of passage of Jean Genet: the art and aesthetics of risk taking*, London; New Jersey: Fairleigh Dickinson University Press.

Polanyi, M. (1958), *Personal knowledge: towards a post-critical philosophy*, Chicago: University of Chicago Press.

Pomper, M. and M. Toki, 'Time to Stop Reprocessing in Japan', *Arms Control Today*, Jan/Feb 2013, https://www.armscontrol.org/act/2013_01-02/Time-to-Stop-Reprocessing-in-Japan, accessed 2 February 2014.

Potter, W. (2005), 'India and the New Look of U.S. Nonproliferation Policy', *Nonproliferation Review*, 12 (July): 343–54.

Potter, E., R. Fredland, and H. Adams (1981), *Sea power: a naval history*, Annapolis, MD: Naval Institute Press.

Price, D. (2008), *Anthropological intelligence: the deployment and neglect of American anthropology in the Second World War*, Durham: Duke University Press.

Puar, J. (2007), *Terrorist assemblages: homonationalism in queer times.*, Durham: Duke University Press.

Publishing Committee for 'Children of Hiroshima' (1980), *Children of Hiroshima*, Tokyo: 'Children of Hiroshima' Publishing Committee.

Pulvers, R. (2008), 'A Japanese Poet Who Found His True Nature through Nature Itself', *The Japan Times*, 26 October, http://search.japantimes.co.jp/cgi-bin/fl20081026rp.html, accessed October 2008.

Pulvers, R. (2009), 'Politically Incorrect Maybe, But Also Some Trenchant Home Truths', *The Japan Times*, 6 December, http://search.japantimes.co.jp/cgi-bin/fl20091206rp.html, accessed December 2009.

Pulvers, R. (2010), 'For All His Failings, MacArthur Was a Fine Precursor of Obama's Bow', *The Japan Times*, 24 January, http://search.japantimes.co.jp/cgi-bin/fl20100124rp.html, accessed January 2010.

Quandt, J. (2001), *Kon Ichikawa*, Toronto: Cinemateque Ontario Monographs, no. 4

Rabson, S. (2010), '"Secret"1965 Memo Reveals Plans to Keep US bases and Nuclear Weapons Options in Okinawa after Reversion', *The Asia-Pacific Journal*, 1 February, http://www.japanfocus.org/-Steve-Rabson/3294, accessed 1 February, 2010.

Rabson, S., T. Ōshima, and M. Higashi (1989), *Okinawa: two postwar novellas*, Berkeley: University of California, Center for Japanese Studies.

Raddeker, H. (1997), *Treacherous women of imperial Japan: patriarchal fictions, patricidal fantasies*, London; New York: Routledge.

Ramos-Horta, J. (1992), *East Timor after Santa-Cruz: Indonesia and the international order*, Lisbon: A Paz e Possivel em Timor Leste.

Rancière, J. (2006), *The politics of aesthetics: the distribution of the sensible*, London; New York: Continuum.

Regan, D. (1988), *For the record: from Wall Street to Washington*, San Diego: Harcourt Brace Jovanovich.

Regular, A. (2003), '"Road Map Is a Life Saver for Us", PM Abbas tells Hamas', *Ha'aretz*, 27 June, http://www.haaretz.com/hasen/pages/ShArt.jhtml?itemNo=310788&contrassID=2&subContrassID=1&sbSubContrassID=0&listSrc=Y, accessed September 2008.

Reid, I. (1963), 'Taidan: Kokujin sabetsu to buraku mondai', *Buraku*, 164, August: 44–48.

Reischauer, E. (1942), 'Memorandum on Policy toward Japan', 14 September, in Iwanami shoten, https://www.iwanami.co.jp/sekai/2000/03/146.html, accessed July 2015.

Rich, A. (1979), *On lies, secrets, and silence: selected prose, 1966–1978*, New York: W. W. Norton.

Rich, F. (2004), 'Now on DVD: The Passion of the Bush', *New York Times*, 3 October.

Richie, D. (1998), *The films of Akira Kurosawa*, Berkeley: University of California Press.

Richie, D. (2009), 'The Pure Horror of Hiroshima', *The Japan Times*, http://search.japantimes.co.jp/cgi-bin/fb20090816dr.html, accessed 9 August, 2009.

Ricklefs, M. (2008), *A history of modern Indonesia since c.1200*, Basingstoke: Palgrave Macmillan.

Rimer, J. and M. Yamazaki (1984), *On the art of the Nō Drama: the major treatises of zeami*, Princeton: Princeton University Press.

Roberts, D. (2006), *Kierkegaard's analysis of radical evil*, London, New York: Continuum International Publishing Group.

Roberts, M. (2007), 'Suicide Missions as Witnessing: Expansions, Contrasts', *Studies in Conflict & Terrorism*, 30(10): 857–87.

Robinson, G. (2010), '*If you leave us here, we will die': how genocide was stopped in East Timor*, Princeton: Princeton University Press.

Robock, A. and O. Toon (2010), 'Local Nuclear War', *Scientific American*, January, 74–81.

Roden, D. (1980), *Schooldays in imperial Japan: a study in the culture of a student elite*, Berkeley: University of California Press.

Rohlen, T. and C. Bjork (1998), *Education and training in Japan*, London, New York: Routledge, 2.

Rolf, R. and J. Gillespie (1992), *Alternative Japanese drama: ten plays*, Honolulu: University of Hawaii Press.

Rosemont, F. and C. Radcliffe (2005), *Dancin' in the streets!: anarchists, IWWs, surrealists, Situationists & Provos in the 1960s (The rebel worker & Heatwave)*, Chicago: Charles H Kerr.

Rosenzweig, F. and B. Galli (2005), *The star of redemption*, Madison, WI: University of Wisconsin Press.

Roth, J. (2005), 'Political and Cultural Perspectives on Japan's Insider Minorities', *The Asia-Pacific Journal: Japan Focus*, 10 April, http://www.japanfocus.org/-Joshua-Roth/1723, accessed November 2008.

Russell, E. (1996), '"Speaking of Annihilation": Mobilizing for War against Human and Insect Enemies, 1914–1945', *The Journal of American History*, 82(March): 1505–29.

Ryang, S. (2002), 'Chrysanthemum's Strange Life: Ruth Benedict in Postwar Japan', *Asian Anthropology*, 1(1): 87–116.

Ryang, S. (2004), 'Chrysanthemum's Strange Life: Ruth Benedict in Postwar Japan', San Francisco: JPRI, 32, July http://www.jpri.org/publications/occasionalpapers/op32.html, accessed 10 July 2010.

Ryang, S. (2012), 'The Denationalized Have No Class: The Banishment of Japan's Korean Minority–A Polemic', *CR: The New Centennial Review*, 12(1): 159–188.

Ryder, R. (2000), *Animal revolution: changing attitudes towards speciesism*, London: Bloomsbury.

Saaler, S. (2007), 'Pan-Asianism in Modern Japanese History: Overcoming the Nation, Creating a Region, Forging an Empire', *Pan-Asianism in Modern Japanese History: Colonialism, Regionalism and Borders*, 1–18.

Saaler, S. and W. Schwentker (2008), *The power of memory in modern Japan*, Folkestone, UK: Global Oriental.

Saffer, T. and O. Kelly (1983), *Countdown zero*, New York: Penguin Books.

Said, E. (1978), *Orientalism*, New York: Pantheon Books.

Said, E. (1995), *Peace and its discontents: essays on Palestine in the Middle East peace process*, New York: Vintage Books.

Said, E. (2001), 'The Clash of Ignorance', *The Nation*, 22(10), http://www.thenation.com/article/clash-ignorance/, accessed March 2010.

Said, E. and G. Viswanathan (2001), *Power, politics, and culture: interviews with Edward W. Said*, New York: Pantheon Books.

Saito, T. (1998), *Shakaiteki hikikomori: owaranai shishunki*, Tokyo: PHP Shinsho.

Sakaguchi, A. (1975), *Sakaguchi Ango shū*, Tokyo: Chikuma Shobo.

Sakaguchi, A. (2000), *Darakuron*, Tokyo: Shinchōsha.

Sakai, N. and J. Solomon (2006), *Translation, biopolitics, colonial difference*, Hong Kong: Hong Kong University Press.

Sakaki, A. (1999), *Recontextualizing texts: narrative performance in modern Japanese fiction*, Cambridge, MA: Harvard University Asia Center, Harvard University Press.

Sams, C. (1998), *Medic: the mission of an American military doctor in occupied Japan and wartorn Korea*, New York: M.E. Sharpe.

Sandler, M. (1997), *The confusion era: art and culture of Japan during the Allied Occupation, 1945–1952*, Washington: Arthur M. Sackler Gallery, University of Washington Press.

Sartre, J.-P. (1988), *'What is literature?' and other essays*, Cambridge, MA: Harvard University Press.

Sasaki, Y. (ed.) (1954), *Scenes of a bomb explosion Hiroshima photograph*, Hiroshima: unknown.

Sasaki-Uemura, W. (2001), *Organizing the spontaneous: citizen protest in postwar Japan*, Honolulu: University of Hawai'i Press.

Sasaki-Uemura, W. (2002), 'Competing Publics: Citizens' Groups, Mass Media, and the State in the 1960s', *Positions: East Asia Cultures Critique*, 10(1): 79–110.

Satō, T. (1982), *Currents in Japanese cinema: essays*, Tokyo, New York: Kodansha International.

Sato, H. (2008), 'Hailing the Sensual Night Crawler', *The Japan Times*, 13 April, http://search.japantimes.co.jp/cgi-bin/fb20080413a1.html, accessed 20 April 2009.

Saul, J. R. (1992), *Voltaire's bastards: the dictatorship of reason in the West*, New York, Free Press: Maxwell Macmillan International.

Saul, B. (2001), 'Was the Conflict in East Timor Genocide and Why Does It Matter', *Melbourne Journal of International Law*, 2: 477–522.

Savona, J. (1984), *Jean Genet*, New York: Grove Press.

SCAP (1951), *History of the nonmilitary activities*, Tokyo: SCAP Price and Distribution and Financial Stabilization Program, 35.

Schaller, M. (1985), *The American occupation of Japan: the origins of the Cold War in Asia*, New York: Oxford University Press.

Schaller, M. (1995), 'America's Favorite War Criminal: Kishi Nobusuke and the Transformation of US-Japan Relations', in Johnson, C. (ed.) 1995, 11, July.

Schaller, M. (2004), 'The Korean War: The Economic and Strategic Impact of Japan, 1950–1953', in W. Stueck (ed.) *Korean war in world history*, Lexington: The University Press of Kentucky, 145–76.

Schechner, R. (2002), *Performance studies: an introduction*, London; New York: Routledge.

Schelling, F. (2000), *The ages of the world: Third version*, Albany: SUNY Press.

Schlei, N. A. (1991), 'Japan's "M-Fund" Memorandum', 7 January, in Johnson, C. (ed.), 1995, 11 July.

Scholz-Cionca, S. and S. Leiter (2001), *Japanese theatre and the international stage*, Leiden; Boston: Brill.

Schreber, D. (2000), *Memoirs of my nervous illness*, New York: New York Review Books.

Schulz, W. (2007), *The phenomenon of torture: readings and commentary*, Philadelphia: University of Pennsylvania Press.

Scott, M. (2009), 'A Global ABC: Soft Diplomacy and the World of International Broadcasting', Bruce Allen memorial lecture, Sydney: Macquarie University.

Scott-Stokes, H. (1974), *The life and death of Yukio Mishima*, New York: Farrar, Straus and Giroux.

Seagrave, S. and P. Seagrave (2003), *Gold warriors: America's secret recovery of Yamashita's gold*, London; New York: Verso.

Seishin Bunseki Kenkyūjō (ed.) (1937), *Abe Sada no seishin bunseki shindan*, Tokyo: Tokyo Seishin Bunseki Kenkyūjo Shuppan-bu.

Sekimori, G. and N. Shōno (1986), *Hibakusha: survivors of Hiroshima and Nagasaki*, Tokyo: Kōsei Publishing Co.

Selden, M. (2007), 'Forgotten Holocaust: US Bombing Strategy, the Destruction of Japanese Cities and the American Way of War from World War II to Iraq', *Asia-Pacific Journal: Japan Focus*, 2 May, http://japanfocus.org/site/view/2414, accessed November 2012.

Selden, M. and A. So (eds.) (2004), *War and state terrorism: the United States, Japan, and the Asia-Pacific in the long twentieth century*, Lanham: Rowman & Littlefield.

Self, B. and J. Thompson (eds.) (2003), *Japan's nuclear option: security, politics, and policy in the 21st century*, Washington, DC: Henry L. Stimson Center.

Shabot, S. (2007), 'The Grotesque Body: Fleshing Out the Subject', *Thamyris/Intersecting: Place, Sex & Race*, 15(1): 57.

Shackleton, S. (2009), 'East Timor: Massacres and Miracles', *East Timor Law and Justice Bulletin*, 9 April, http://www.etan.org/et2009/03march/29/01graves.htm#East_, accessed 10 April 2009.

Shapiro, S. (2008), 'God, or the Body without Organs', http://www.shaviro.com/Othertexts/articles.html, accessed December 2009.

Sharf, R. H. (1993), 'The Zen of Japanese Nationalism', *History of Religions*, 33(1): 1–43.

Shibusawa, N. (2006), *America's geisha ally: reimagining the Japanese enemy*, Cambridge, MA: Harvard University Press.

Shillony, B. A. (2005), *Enigma of the emperors: sacred subservience in Japanese history*, Folkestone, Kent: Global Oriental.

Shimazu, N. (1998), *Japan, race, and equality: the racial equality proposal of 1919*, London, New York: Routledge.

Shimizu, I. (1953), *Kichi no ko, kono jijitsu wo dō kangaetara yoi ka*, Tokyo: Kōbun-sha.

Shimizu, S. (1999), *Tokyo Commands*, Bye Bye performance series, Tokyo: Gekidan Kaitaisha.

Shimizu, S. (2002), 'A System of 'dream': Annihilated Bodies', *'Media Technology'*, *performing arts*, 2: 141–48.

Shimizu, S. (2004), 'A Map of Operations', *Dream regime*, Cardiff: Gekidan Kaitaisha.

Shimizu, S. (2012), 'The Significance of Koshien Baseball in Postwar Okinawa: A Representation of "Okinawa"', *The International Journal of the History of Sport*, 29(17): 2421–34.

Shimizu, S. and H. Ōtori (2001), 'The Birth of a Theatre and the Besieged Body: A Strategy for Globalization', in *Gekidan Kaitaisha 1991–2001*, Tokyo: Gekidan Kaitaisha, 68–87.

Shimizu-Guthrie, S. (2012), *Transpacific field of dreams: how baseball linked the United States and Japan in peace and war*, Chapel Hill: University of North Carolina Press.

Shindō, K. (2001 [1952]), *Genbaku no ko*, Tokyo: Kindai Eiga Kyōkai, Gekidan Mingei, Asumikku Esu.

Shorrock, T. (2004), 'Red Flags and Christian Soldiers: American Missionaries in Cold War Japan', *The interpreter*, Colorado: The US Navy Japanese/Oriental Language School Archival Project, 72.

Siddle, R. (1996), *Race, resistance, and the Ainu of Japan*, London; New York: Routledge.

Silva, M. da and S. Kendall (2002), 'Issues for Women in East Timor: The Aftermath of Indonesian Occupation', *Expanding our horizons*, Sydney: University of Sydney, February, 22.

Simmel, G. and K. Wolff (1950), *The sociology of Georg Simmel*, Glencoe, IL: Free Press.

Simpson, C. (2003), 'Immigration Crackdown Shatters Muslims Lives', *Chicago Tribune*, 16 November 2003, http://www.chicagotribune.com/news/watchdog/chi -0311160374nov16,0,6814408.story, accessed 16 March 2011.

Sindhu, J. (2014), 'Hiroshima Commemorates 69th Anniversary of Nuclear Bomb', *NewsPakistan*, Retrieved 9 August 2014.

Slater, L. (1986), 'The Dead Begin to Run: Kazuo Ohno and Butoh Dance', *Dance Theatre Journal*, 4(4): 6–10.

Slaymaker, D. (2004), *The body in postwar Japanese fiction*, New York: RoutledgeCurzon.

Smart, N. (1984), *The religious experience of mankind*, New York: Scribner.

Smith, J. (2005), *Economic democracy: the political struggle of the twenty-first century*, Radford, VA: Institute for Economic Democracy Press.

Smith, S. (2013), 'North Korea in Japan's Strategic Thinking', *The Asan Forum*, 7 October, http://www.theasanforum.org/north-korea-in-japans-strategicthinking/, accessed October 2013.

Soares, D.-B. (2001), 'East Timor: Perceptions of Culture and Environment', *Sustainable development in East Timor conference*, Melbourne: RMIT.

Sobchack, V. (1996), *The persistence of history: cinema, television, and the modern event*, New York: Routledge.

Sodei, R. and J. Fukushima (1985), *Haikei MacArthur Gensui-Sama: Senryōka no Nihonjin no tegami*, Tokyo: Otsuki Shoten.

Sodei, R. (1992), *Senryo shita mono sareta mono: Nichibei kankei no genten o kangaeru*, Tokyo: Simul Press, 1986.

Soloski, A. (2001), 'Bodies of Evidence', *Village Voice*, 10 October.

Sontag, S. (2003), *Regarding the pain of others*, New York: Farrar, Straus and Giroux.

Sorel, G. and J. Jennings (1999), *Reflections on violence*, United Kingdom; New York: Cambridge University Press.

Sorgenfrei, C. (2005), *Unspeakable Acts: the avant-garde theatre of Terayama Shuji in postwar Japan*, Honolulu: University of Hawaii.

Spaight, J. M. (1924), *Air power and war rights*, London; New York: Longmans, Green and co.

Spinoza, B. de and J. Yessleman (2006), *Ethics* 3: VII, 136, Book XIX, 233, www.yesselman. com/e3elwes.htm, accessed July 2014.

Spivak, G. C. (1988), *In other worlds: essays in cultural politics*, New York: Routledge.

Spivak, G. C. (1993), *Outside in the teaching machine*, New York; London: Routledge.

Spivak, G. C. and S. Harasym (1990), *The post-colonial critic: interviews, strategies, dialogues*, New York: Routledge.

Spivak, G. C. and E. Rooney (1989), 'In a Word: Interview', *Differences*, 1(2): 124–56.

Stadler, F. (2002), 'Opinion i: Privacy Is Not the Antidote to Surveillance', *Surveillance and Society*, 1(1): 120–24.

Stahl, M. (2002), *In cold blood: the massacre in East Timor*, London: ITV.

Stallybrass, P. and A. White (1986), *The politics and poetics of transgression*, London: Methuen.

Standish, I. (2011), *Politics, porn and protest: Japanese avant-garde cinema in the 1960s and 1970s*, New York: Continuum International Publishing Group.

Starrs, R. (1994), *Deadly dialectics: sex, violence, and nihilism in the world of Yukio Mishima*, Honolulu: University of Hawaii Press.

Steinhoff, P. G. (1989), 'Hijackers, Bombers, and Bank Robbers: Managerial Style in the Japanese Red Army', *Journal of Asian Studies*, 48(4): 724–40.

Steinhoff, P. G. (1999), 'Student Protest in the 1960s', *Social Science Japan*, 15: 3–6.

Stewart, F. and K. Yamazato (2011), 'Living Spirit: Literature and Resurgence in Okinawa', *Manoa: A Pacific Journal of International Writing*, 23(1).

Stewart, F., K. Yamazato, and J. Shirota (2009), *Voices from Okinawa: featuring three plays by Jon Shirota*, Honolulu: University of Hawai'i Press.

Stiegler, B. (1998), *Technics and time*, Stanford, CA: Stanford University Press.

Stockings, C. and J. Connor (2010), *Zombie myths of Australian military history*, Sydney: University of New South Wales Press.

Stockwell, J. (1978), *In search of enemies: A CIA story*, New York: W. W. Norton.

Stoler, A. (1995), *Race and the education of desire: Foucault's History of sexuality and the colonial order of things*, Durham: Duke University Press.

Stone, I. F. (1989), *The haunted fifties: 1953–1963*, Boston: Little Brown and Co.

Sugita, Y. (2004), *Pitfall or Panacea: The irony of U.S. power in Occupied Japan, 1945–52*, London and New York: Routledge.

Sussan, H. (1983), 'Why the Atomic Bomb didn't Hit Home', *Nuclear Times*, March, 10–15.

Suzuki, D. T. and K. Ōiwa (1996), *The Japan we never knew: a journey of discovery*, St Leonards: Allen & Unwin.

Svoboda, T. (2009), 'US Courts-Martial in Occupation Japan: Rape, Race, and Censorship', *The Asia-Pacific journal: Japan Focus*, 21 January, http://www.japanfocus.org/-terese -svoboda/3148, accessed September 2010.

Tabuchi, H., et al. (2014), 'Japan Pushes Plan to Stockpile Plutonium, Despite Proliferation Risks', *New York Times*, 9 April, http://mobile.nytimes.com/2014/04/10/world/asia/japan-pushes-plan-tostockpile-plutonium-despite-proliferation-risks.html, accessed 9 April 2014.

Takahashi, T. (2005), *War responsibility*, Tokyo: Kodansha Gakujutsu-Bunkō.

Takahashi, Y. and L. Bruer (1984), *Theatre of Escape: an interview with Lee Bruer*, Eureka, Tokyo: Seido Publishing.

Takekawa, S., (2012), 'Drawing a Line between Peaceful and Military Uses of Nuclear Power: The Japanese Press 1945–1955', *The Asia-Pacific Journal: Japan Focus*, www .japanfocus.org/-Shunichi-TAKEKAWA/3823/article.html, accessed 3 January 2013.

Takemae, E. (2002), *The allied occupation of Japan*, New York: Continuum International Publishing Group.

Tamamoto, M. (1995), 'Reflections on Japan's Postwar State', *Daedalus*, 124(2): 1–22.

Tamanoi, M. (2009), *Memory maps: the state and Manchuria in postwar Japan*, Honolulu: University of Hawai'i Press.

Tamura, T. (1947), 'Nikutai ga ningen de aru', *Gunzō* (May).

Tanabe, H. (1964), *Tanabe Hajime zenshū 1963–1964*, Tokyo: Chikuma-shobō.

Tanaka, K. (1973), *Building a new Japan: a plan for remodeling the Japanese Archipelago*, Tokyo: Simul Press.

Tanaka, T. (2002), *Japan's comfort women*, London: Routledge.

Tanaka, T., T. McCormack, and G. Simpson (2011), *Beyond Victor's justice?: The Tokyo war crimes trial revisited*, London: Martinus Nijhoff Publishers.

Tanaka, Y. and P. Kuznick (2011), 'Japan, the Atomic Bomb and the "Peaceful uses of nuclear power"', *The Asia-Pacific Journal: Japan Focus*, http://www.japanfocus.org/ -yuki-tanaka/3521/article.html, accessed 4 July 2012.

Tanaka, Y. and M. Young (2010), *Bombing civilians: a twentieth-century history*, New York: New Press.

Tanizaki, J. (2001 [1977]), *In praise of shadows*, New York: Random House.

Tansman, A. (2009), *The aesthetics of Japanese fascism*, Berkeley: University of California Press.

Tanter, R., M. Selden, and S. R. Shalom (2001), *Bitter flowers, sweet flowers: East Timor, Indonesia, and the world community*, Lanham: Rowman & Littlefield Publishers.

Tatara, M.(1998), 'The Second Generation of Atomic Bomb Survivors: A Psychologist's View', in Danieli, Y. (ed.), *International handbook of multigenerational legacies of trauma*, New York: Plenum Press.

Tatlow, A. (2001), *Shakespeare, Brecht, and the intercultural sign*, Durham, NC: Duke University Press.

Taurog, N. (1947), *The beginning or the end*, Editor's note, USA: MGM.

Tausk, V. (1933), 'On the Origin of the "Influencing Machine" in Schizophrenia', *The Psychoanalytic Quarterly*, 2: 519–56.

Taylor, J. (1999), *East Timor: the price of freedom*, London; New York: St. Martin's Press.

Taylor, S. (1990), *Left-wing Nietzscheans: the politics of German expressionism, 1910–1920*, Berlin; New York: W. de Gruyter.

Tellis, A. (2005), *India as a New Global Power: an action agenda for the United States*, Washington, DC: Carnegie Endowment for International Peace.

tenBroek, J., et al. (1970 [1954]), *Prejudice, war and the constitution*, Berkeley: University of California Press.

Terashima, J. (2010a), 'The US-Japan Alliance Must Evolve: The Futenma Flip-Flop, the Hatoyama Failure, and the Future', *The Asia-Pacific Journal: Japan Focus*, 20 August, http://www.fpif.org/articles/the_us-japan_alliance_must_evolve, accessed August 2010.

Terashima, J. (2010b), 'The Will and Imagination to Return to Common Sense: Toward a Restructuring of the US-Japan Alliance', *Asia-Pacific Journal: Japan Focus*, 15 March, http://japanfocus.org/-Terashima-Jitsuro/3321http://japanfocus.org/-Terashima-Jitsuro/3321, accessed August 2010.

Terayama, S. (1978), *Ōgon jidai: Terayama Shūji hyōronshū*, Tokyo: Kyūgei shuppan.

Thacker, E. (2005), *The global genome: biotechnology, politics, and culture*, Cambridge, MA: MIT Press.

The Hague Report, Commission of Jurists on the Laws of War (1923), 'General Report of the Commision of Jurists at the Hague', *American Journal of International Law*, XVII, Supplement, October.

The Institute for International Policy Studies (IIPS) (2006), 'A Vision of Japan in the 21st Century', 5 September, www.iips.org/National%20Vision.pdf, accessed June 2008.

The International Peoples' Tribunal on the Dropping of Atom Bombs on Hiroshima and Nagasaki Executive Committee (2007), *The International Peoples' Tribunal on the Dropping of Atom Bombs on Hiroshima and Nagasaki*, Peace Memorial Museum, Hiroshima, 16 July, www.k3.dion.ne.jp/~a-bomb/indexen.htm, accessed 18 June 2008.

Thévenin, P. (1969–1970), 'Entendre/voir/lire (Hearing/Seeing/Reading)', *Tel Quel*, 39–40 (Fall–Winter).

Thompson, A. (2008), *Performing race and torture on the early modern stage*, New York: Routledge.

Thompson, E. P. and D. Smith (1981), *Protest and survive*, New York: Monthly Review Press.

Tipton, E. and J. Clark (2000), *Being modern in Japan: culture and society from the 1910s to the 1930s*, Honolulu: University of Hawaii Press.

Tison-Braun, M. (1977), *Tristan Tzara, inventeur de l'homme nouveau*, Paris: A.-G. Nizet.

Tomishige, H. (2010), 'Hikikomori – Social withdrawal in Japan', *nhjournal*, http://nhjournal37.blogspot.com/, accessed July 2010.

Totani, Y. (2008), *The Tokyo War crimes trial: the pursuit of justice in the wake of World War II*, Cambridge, MA: Harvard University Press.

Totani, Y. (2011), 'Tokyo War Crimes Trial', in *The Encyclopedia of War*, Wiley Online, 1–6, http://onlinelibrary.wiley.com/doi/10.1002/9781444338232.wbeow637/pdf, accessed March 2012.

Traube, E. (1986), *Cosmology and social life: ritual exchange among the Mambai of East Timor*, Chicago: University of Chicago Press.

Traube, E. (2007), 'Unpaid Wages: Local Narratives and the Imagination of the Nation', *Asia-Pacific Journal of Anthropology*, 8(1): 9–25.

Treat, J. (1996), *Writing ground zero: Japanese literature and the atomic bomb*, Chicago: University of Chicago Press.

Truman, H. (1945), 'Presidential Statement', Eben A. Ayers papers, 'Army press notes', box 4, 6 August, Missouri: Harry S. Truman Library.

Tsuchida, A. (1993), 'The Nuclear Arming of Japan', *Japan Society of Physics*, Tokyo: conference paper, August, 1: 1–10.

Tsuchiya, Y. (2002), 'Imagined America in Occupied Japan: (Re-)Educational Films Shown by the U.S. Occupational Forces to the Japanese, 1948–1952', *The Journal of American Studies*, 13, 193–213.

Tsuitsui, W. (2004), *Godzilla on my mind: Fifty years of the King of the Monsters*, London: Palgrave Macmillan.

Tsurumi, E. (1988), *The other Japan: postwar realities*, New York: ME Sharpe.

Tsurumi, S. (1969), *Kataritsugu sengoshi*, Tokyo: Shisō no Kagakusha.

Tsurumi, S. (1987), *A cultural history of postwar Japan, 1945–1980*, London; New York: KPI, Methuen.

Tsurumi, S. (1992), *Kigō-ron shū*, Tokyo: Chikuma shobō.

Tsurumi, S. (2010), *An intellectual history of wartime Japan: 1931–1945*, Abingdon: Routledge.

Turim, M. (1998), *The films of Oshima Nagisa: images of a Japanese iconoclast*, Berkeley: University of California Press.

Turkle, S. (1984), *The second self*, New York: Simon & Schuster.

Turner, B. (1996), *The body and society: explorations in social theory*, London; Thousand Oaks, CA: Sage Publications.

Turner, V. W. (1982), *From ritual to theatre: the human seriousness of play*, New York City: Performing Arts Journal Publications.

Tylor, E. B. (1993 [1913]), *Primitive culture: researches into the development of mythology, philosophy, religion, language, art, and custom*, London: J. Murray.

Tzara, T. (1964 [1922]), *The gas heart*, trans. M. Benedikt, http://www.english.emory.edu/DRAMA/TzaraGas.html, accessed 24 June 2009.

Tzara, T. (1977), *Seven Dada manifestos and lampisteries*, London: Calder.

Tzara, T. (2008), *The gas heart: the Dada anti-masterpiece of drama*, North Syracuse: Gegensatz Press, 2008.

Ueno, C. (2009), *The modern family in Japan: its rise and fall*, Melbourne: Trans Pacific Press.

Ueno, H. (ed.) (1996 [1960]), *Koe naki no Koe no Tayori: 1960–1970*, Tokyo: Shisō Kagaku no Kenkyūsha.

Ui, J. (ed.), (1992), *Industrial pollution in Japan*, Tokyo: United Nations University Press.

UNESCO (2003), 'Convention for the Safeguarding of intangible Cultural Heritage', *UNESCO Constitution*, Paris: UNESCO, October. http://portal.unesco.org/en/ev.php URL_ID=17716&URL_DO=DO_TOPIC&URL_SECTION=201.html, accessed March 2010.

United States Government Joint Chiefs of Staff (1961), 'Berlin Contingency Planning', National Security Archives, July, http://nsarchive.files.wordpress.com/2011/11/1961 -06-26a.pdf.

United States Government Whitehouse (2015), '*National Security Strategy*', http://www .whitehouse.gov/sites/default/files/doc/2015_national_security_strategy_2.pdf, 11.

United States Government, State Department (1976), *FRUS, 1949 Vol 1, national security affairs, foreign economic policy*, Washington: US Government Printing Office.

United States Strategic Bombing Survey (1946), *USSBS*, Summary Report (Pacific War), 1 July, Washington: US GPO.

Uzawa, Y. (2008), *Hashimura Tōgō: ierō feisu no Amerika ijinden*, Tokyo: Tokyo Daigaku Shuppankai.

Vallaincourt-Matsuoka, A. (2008), 'Using Dance to Understand Tokyo Bombings', *The Daily Yomiuri*, 14 March, http://sites.google.com/site/suzukiikko/review2, accessed December 2009.

Vallaincourt-Matsuoka, A. (2009), 'Dancing to the Rhythm of Destruction', *The Japan Times*, 6 March, http://search.japantimes.co.jp/cgi-bin/fq20090306a2.html, accessed March 2010 Tokyo.

Van Kirk, W. (1946), 'The Future of Christianity in Japan', *Christian Century 63*, 6 February, 169–171.

Vermeersch, P. (2002), 'Interview with Min Tanaka', *Contact quarterly: Biannual journal of dance and improvisation*, 1: 22–33.

Vickers, A. (2005), *A history of modern Indonesia*, Cambridge, UK: Cambridge University Press.

Victoria, B. (2004), 'When God(s) and Buddhas go to War', in Selden and So 2004: 91–118.

Virilio, P. (1989), *War and cinema: the logistics of perception*, London; New York: Verso.

Virilio, P. (1994), *The vision machine*, Bloomington: Indiana University Press.

Virilio, P. (2000a), *Strategy of deception*, London; New York: Verso.

Virilio, P. (2000b), *Polar inertia*, London; Thousand Oaks, CA: Sage.

Virilio, P. (2002), *Desert screen: war at the speed of light*, London; New York: Continuum.

Virilio, P. (2005), *City of panic*, Oxford; New York: Berg.

Virilio, P. and J. Der Derian (1998), *The Virilio reader*, Malden, MA: Blackwell Publishers.

Virilio, P. and S. Lotringer (2002), *Crepuscular dawn*, Los Angeles, CA: Semiotext(e).

Visweswaran, K. (2012), 'Occupier/occupied', *Identities*, 19(4): 440–51.

Vlastos, S. (1998), *Mirror of modernity: invented traditions of modern Japan*, Berkeley: University of California Press.

Von Eschen, P. (1997), *Race against empire: Black Americans and anti-colonialism, 1937–1957*, Ithaca: Cornell University Press.

Waguri, Y. (1998), *Butoh Kaden*, CD Rom, Tokyo: Justsystem.

Waln, N. (1950), 'Can the Communists Take Japan from within?' *Saturday Evening Post*, 9 December, New York.

Wampler, R. A. (2009), 'Nuclear Noh Drama: Tokyo, Washington and the Case of the Missing Nuclear Agreements', 13 October, http://www.gwu.edu/~nsarchiv/nukevault/ ebb291/index.htm, accessed 10 January 2011.

Ward, E. (1990), *Land reform in Japan 1946–1950: the allied role*, Tokyo: Nōbunkyō.

Washburn, D. (2007), *Translating Mount Fuji modern Japanese fiction and the ethics of identity*, New York: Columbia University Press.

Watanabe, M. and Y. Ose (1968), 'General Academic Trend and the Evolution Theory of Late Nineteenth Century Japan: A Statistical Analysis of Contemporary Periodicals', *Japanese Studies in the History of Science*, 7–8: 129–142.

Watanabe, S. (2008), *Into the Atomic Sunshine – Post-War Art under Japanese Peace Constitution Article 9*, Tokyo: spikyart.com.

Weil, S. (2002), *Gravity and grace*, London; New York: Routledge.

Weiner, M. (2009 [1997]), *Japan's minorities: the illusion of homogeneity*, London: Routledge.

Weiner, T. (2007), *Legacy of Ashes: the history of the CIA*, New York: Doubleday.

Weiss, A. (1992a), *Shattered forms: art brut, phantasms, modernism*, Albany: State University of New York Press.

Weiss, A. (1992b), 'Radiophonic Art: The Voice of the Impossible Body', *Discourse*, 14(2): 186–200.

Weiss, A. S. (1995), *Phantasmic radio*, Durham, NC: Duke University Press.

Welfield, J. (2013), *An Empire in Eclipse: Japan in the Post-War American Alliance System*, London: Bloomsbury Academic.

Weller, G. (2006), *First into Nagasaki: the censored eyewitness dispatches on post-atomic Japan and its prisoners of war*, New York: Crown Publishers.

Wessel, J. and M. Hantman (1983), *Trading the future: farm exports and the concentration of economic power in our food economy*, San Francisco: Institute for Food and Development Policy.

West, C. (2004), *Democracy matters: winning the fight against imperialism*, New York: The Penguin Press.

West, C. (2007), 'Niggerization', *The Atlantic Monthly*, November, http://www.theatlantic.com/magazine/archive/2007/11/niggerization/6285/, accessed 23 January.

Westfall, J. (2007), *The Kierkegaardian author, authorship and performance in Kierkegaard's literary and dramatic criticism*, New York: Walter De Gruyter.

Wetherall, W. (1987), 'Nakasone Promotes Pride and Prejudice', *Far Eastern Economic Review*, 135(8): 86–87.

Wetzeling, K. (2001), *Ballet tanz*, October, 49.

White, E. (1993), *Genet: a biography*, New York: Alfred A. Knopf.

White, H. V. (1999), *Figural realism: studies in the mimesis effect*, Baltimore: Johns Hopkins University Press.

Whiting, R. (1977), *The chrysanthemum and the bat: baseball samurai style*, New York: Dodd, Mead.

Whiting, R. (2004), *The meaning of Ichiro: the new wave from Japan and the transformation of our national pastime*, New York: Warner Books.

Wigglesworth, A. (2013), 'The Growth of Civil Society in Timor-Leste: Three Moments of Activism', *Journal of Contemporary Asia*, 43 (1): 51–74, http://www.tandfonline.com/doi/abs/10.1080/00472336.2012.735545, accessed March 2014.

Wildes, H. (1954), *Typhoon in Tokyo: the occupation and its aftermath*, New York: Macmillan.

Williams, D. (2006), 'After Abu Ghraib: American empire, the left-wing intellectual and Japan Studies', in Kersten, R. and D. Williams (eds.): 126–45.

Williams, D. (2004), *Defending Japan's Pacific war: the Kyoto School Philosophers and post-white power*, New York: RoutledgeCurzon.

Wilson, E. (2009), 'Speed/pure war/power Crime: Paul Virilio on the Criminogenic Accident and the Virtual Disappearance of the Suicidal State', *Crime, Law and Social Change*, 51(3–4): 413–34.

Wilson, E. (2012), 'Criminogenic Cyber-Capitalism: Paul Virilio, Simulation, and the Global Financial Crisis', *Critical Criminology*, 20(3): 249–74.

Winnubst, S. (2007), *Reading Bataille now*, Bloomington: Indiana University Press.

Wittner, L. (1971), 'MacArthur and the Missionaries: God and Man in Occupied Japan', *Pacific Historical Review*, 40(1): 77–98.

Wolffe, M. (2001), 'Within the body ruins', *taz Hamburg*, September, 3.

Woodard, W. (1972), *The allied occupation of Japan 1945–1952 & Japanese religions*, Leiden: Brill Archive.

Wright, R. (1954), *Black Power*, New York: Harper.

Wynne-Jones, J. (2009), 'Tony Blair believed God wanted him to go to war to fight evil, claims his mentor', *The Telegraph*, 23 May, www.telegraph.co.uk/news/ religion/5373525/Tony-Blair-believed-God-wanted-him-to-go-to-war-to-fight-evil -claims-his-mentor.html, accessed July 2010.

Yamamoto, K. (2014), 'Nagasaki marks 69th anniversary of its atomic bombing', *Asahi Shimbun*, 9 August, http://ajw.asahi.com/article/behind_news/social_affairs/ AJ201408090034, accessed 9 August.

Yamamoto, Y. (1972), *Nihon kaizō-ron no gensō*, Tokyo: Japan.

Yamashita, Y., S. Terayama, and S. Aburai (1986), 'Ware-ware ni totte jyazu to wa nani ka', *Ongaku Geijutsu*, 8.

Yanagi, S. (ed.) (1981), 'Okinawa No Hanashi', *Yanagi Sōetsu Zenshū*, Tokyo: Chikuma shobō.

Yancy, G. (2005), 'Whiteness and the Return of the Black Body', *The Journal of Speculative Philosophy*, 19(4): 215–41.

Yayoi, S. (2009), 'The Creation of a Myth through the Destruction of Another: Hosoe Eikoh's Photographs of Mishima Yukio in Barakei', *Modern Art Asia*, 1 November.

Yellin, R. (2013), 'Crawling through the mud in style', *The Japan Times*, 24 July.

Yi, Lin (1992 [1938]), *The importance of living: a lyrical philosophy*, Singapore: Heinemann.

Yomota, I. and G. Hirasawa (2007), *Kankin to tōsō*, Tokyo: Sakushinsha.

Yoneyama, L. (1999), *Hiroshima traces: time, space, and the dialectics of memory*, Berkeley: University of California Press.

Yoshibumi, W. (2010), 'What was left unsaid about the atomic bombings: silence and the politics of commemoration', *Japan Focus: The Asia-Pacific Journal*, http://japanfocus .org/-Wakamiya-Yoshibumi/3402, accessed 23 August 2010.

Yoshida, Y. (1971), *Miru koto no anakizumu*, Tokyo: Kamensha, 1971.

Yoshimoto, T. (1968a), *Yōshimoto Takaaki zenchosakushū*, v. 15, Tokyo: Keiso shobō.

Yoshimoto, T. (1968b), *Kaitei Shinpan: Kyōdō gensō ron*, Tokyo: Kadokawa bunkō.

Yoshimoto, T. and K. Miyazawa (1989), *Miyazawa Kenji*, Tōkyō: Chikuma Shobō.

Yoshioka, Y. (2009), 'Body Resonance Based on Butoh and Organic Movement', *Herbst Tanzimpulse*, www.tanzimpulse.at/cms/index.php?did=herbst_tanz_09 ... pdf, accessed 29 January 2010.

Young, M. (2010), 'Bombing Civilians: An American Tradition', *The Asia-Pacific Journal: Japan Focus*, April, 19, http://www.japanfocus.org/-Marilyn-Young/3125, accessed January 2010.

Žižek, S. (1997), *The plague of fantasies*, London; New York: Verso.

Žižek, S. (2006), *The parallax view*, Cambridge, MA: MIT Press.

Žižek, S. and G. Daly (2004), *Conversations with Zizek*, Cambridge; Malden: Polity.

Zuckerman, E. (1984), *The day after World War III*, New York: Viking Press.

Zwigenburg, R. (2012), 'The Coming of a Second Sun: The 1956 Atoms for Peace Exhibit and Japan's Embrace of Nuclear Power', *The Asia-Pacific Journal: Japan Focus*, 10(6): 1, http://japanfocus.org/-ran-zwigenberg/3685/article.html, accessed 7 July 2012.

Index

Note: Locators followed by the letter 'n' refer to notes.

Asian orientalism 77
Asia-Pacific War 45, 123
'asiatic' 17–8, 75, 172
Asiatic despotism 54
As Long as I live 45
Astro Boy 11
atavism 5, 18
Atcheson, George 28
ATG (Avant-Garde Theatre Guild) 12, 72
Atomic Bomb Casualty Commission
    (ABCC) 9, 48
atomic bombs
    'ancillary effects' 38
    anti-nuclear movement 39, 50–1, 61
    classification of 6
    criminalization of 48
    development, use and effects 6–10,
        23–5, 26–7, 47–8
    geostrategic significance of 6, 9–10,
        26–7, 34, 185
    international ban on 'aggressive' use
        of 34
    representations of 11, 30–1, 45–7, 49–52
    ruins from 46–7, 51
    suppression of information of 27, 30,
        45, 48–9
    symbolic/religious appeal of 26–7,
        37–8
    tests 7, 26, 34, 38–9, 50–186
    threats 37
    weapons 38, 65
Atomic Energy Basic Law 40
atomic gaze 8–10, 14
    dynamics of 26–7, 53
Atomic Kid, The 50
atomic representations
    American and Japanese popular 49–54
'Atoms for Peace' programme 38, 40
Atsugi airforce base 24, 32, 38
Attlee, Clement 23
authoritarianism/anti-authoritarianism 4,
    57, 62, 64, 122
autonomy 3, 5, 23, 68, 92, 104, 128, 188,
    200 n.14
avant-garde/après-garde movements 4, 12,
    71–2, 74, 78, 99–104, 148, 191,
    196 n.4
Axis powers 20, 25, 193 n.6
Ayler, Albert 87
Azuma, Hiroki 124–5

Babe Ruth Story, The 59
'backward economies' 165
Baker, Josephine 78
Bakker, Reverend Jim 173
Baldwin, James 89
'Bali-dance' 103
Ballantine, Joseph 29
balloons 22, 179, 181, 183
Bandung Conference 40
bankruptcy 12, 173
'Banzai Onna' 78
Bara iro dansu (Rose Coloured Dance)
    81, 83
Baraka, Amiri 87, 182
Barakei (Ordeal by Roses, or *Killed by*
    Roses) 67
Barefoot Gen 11
Baruch Plan 7, 34
baseball 38, 58–9, 61, 80
Baseball Period, The 59
Bataan 20
Bataille, George 72, 113
Bateson, Gregory 28–9, 85
Battle of Iwojima 22
Battle of the Coral Sea 20
Baudrillard, Jean 147
Beginning or the End, The 49
Beheiren (Peace to Vietnam! People's
    Committee) 64, 67
Benedict, Ruth 28–9, 49, 51
Benjamin, Walter 8
Bentaga, Abdullah 79
Bergan, Edgar 30
Bergson, Henri 2, 75, 149, 200 n.1
Bernays, Edward 43
Between War and Peace 45
'Beyond Vietnam: Time to Break the
    Silence', speech 90
Bibi Bulak theatre company 158
Bibles 30
Bicycle Thief, The 45
Big Lie, The 45
Bikini Atoll 7, 34, 38–9
bio-chemical weapons and disasters 6,
    48, 115
biological determinism 18, 77, 84
biological indexing system 3, 148
biological weapons 6, 35
biopolitical management, biopower 3–4,
    148–9

UNIVERSITY OF WINCHESTER
LIBRARY

Index